The Politics of Nordsploitation

Global Exploitation Cinemas

Series Editors
Johnny Walker, Northumbria University, UK
Austin Fisher, Bournemouth University, UK

Editorial Board
Tejaswini Ganti, New York University, USA
Joan Hawkins, Indiana University, USA
Kevin Heffernan, Southern Methodist University, USA
I. Q. Hunter, De Montfort University, UK
Peter Hutchings, Northumbria University, UK
Ernest Mathijs, University of British Columbia, Canada
Constance Penley, University of California, Santa Barbara, USA
Eric Schaefer, Emerson College, USA
Dolores Tierney, University of Sussex, UK
Valerie Wee, National University of Singapore, Singapore

Also in the Series:

Disposable Passions: Vintage Pornography and the Material Legacies of Adult Cinema, by David Church
Grindhouse: Cultural Exchange on 42nd Street, and Beyond, edited by Austin Fisher & Johnny Walker
Exploiting East Asian Cinemas: Genre, Circulation, Reception, edited by Ken Provencher and Mike Dillon

The Politics of Nordsploitation

History, Industry, Audiences

Tommy Gustafsson and Pietari Kääpä

BLOOMSBURY ACADEMIC
NEW YORK · LONDON · OXFORD · NEW DELHI · SYDNEY

BLOOMSBURY ACADEMIC
Bloomsbury Publishing Inc
1385 Broadway, New York, NY 10018, USA
50 Bedford Square, London, WC1B 3DP, UK
29 Earlsfort Terrace, Dublin 2, Ireland

BLOOMSBURY, BLOOMSBURY ACADEMIC and the Diana logo are trademarks of Bloomsbury Publishing Plc

First published in the United States of America 2021
This paperback edition published in 2022

Copyright © Tommy Gustafsson and Pietari Kääpä, 2021

For legal purposes the Acknowledgements on p. x constitute an extension of this copyright page.

Cover design: Eleanor Rose
Cover image © Dark Horse Entertainment and Charles Aspéria

All rights reserved. No part of this publication may be reproduced or transmitted in any form or by any means, electronic or mechanical, including photocopying, recording, or any information storage or retrieval system, without prior permission in writing from the publishers.

Bloomsbury Publishing Inc does not have any control over, or responsibility for, any third-party websites referred to or in this book. All internet addresses given in this book were correct at the time of going to press. The author and publisher regret any inconvenience caused if addresses have changed or sites have ceased to exist, but can accept no responsibility for any such changes.

A catalog record for this book is available from the Library of Congress.

ISBN: HB: 978-1-5013-2733-9
PB: 978-1-5013-7394-7
ePDF: 978-1-5013-2730-8
eBook: 978-1-5013-2731-5

Series: Global Exploitation Cinemas

Typeset by Deanta Global Publishing Services, Chennai, India

To find out more about our authors and books visit www.bloomsbury.com and sign up for our newsletters.

Contents

List of figures		viii
Acknowledgements		x
1	The politics of Nordsploitation	1
	Periodization: Exploitation and Nordic exploitation	7
	Defining Nordsploitation	10
	Theories of exploitation	13
	The complexity of Nordsploitation	17
	The structure of the book	22
2	A pre-1970s history of Nordic exploitation	31
	Exploitation as art/art as exploitation	34
	Documentary images with exploitative elements	40
	The absence of exploitation	45
	Conclusion	49
3	Exploitative violence and pornography in the 1970s	55
	Conclusion	71
4	Moral panic, VHS censorship and fan culture counterforces 1980–99	75
	The video violence moral panic in Sweden	79
	Moral panic within the hour	82
	A twenty-year-long aftermath	88
	VHS censorship in the bigger picture: Extremes and counterforces	95
	Conclusion	100
5	The local and the transnational in Nordic exploitation cinema of the 1980s	105
	The Viking trilogy: Exploiting cultural history through genre film	108
	Nordic emulations of blockbusters	116
	The Visitors	120
	Visa Mäkinen and exploitation cinema from the margins	123

	Exploitation cinema goes mainstream	129
	Global exploitation: *Arctic Heat* (aka *Born American*)	131
	Conclusion	136
6	The entertainment violence factory: Mats Helge Olsson's action films of the 1980s	141
	The beginnings: Working within the Swedish Film Industry as an outsider	142
	The entertainment violence factory: *The Ninja Mission* and the marketplace for Nordic exploitation	146
	At work: Production and exploitative themes	157
	Genre aspirations	159
	Olsson's stars	162
	Conclusion	167
7	The rise of transnational exploitation in the 1990s–2000s	173
	Nordic exploitation in the 1990s: Film genres in transition	174
	Going excessive: Nazi zombies from Norwegian mountains	178
	The 1990s to the 2010s: Film cultures in transition	181
	Artistic exploitation	192
	Conclusion	194
8	Nordic Nazisploitation in the digital media environment of the 2000s	201
	The Nazi on film	203
	Nordic Nazisploitation: *Dead Snow*	206
	Comic Nazis: *Iron Sky*	211
	Carving space for neo-Nazisploitation	214
	Social media and *Dead Snow*	217
	Balancing ideologies	218
	Ideology strikes back	220
	Conclusion: The franchise	223
9	Kung Fu cops and killer bunnies: Proximity and distance strategies in Nordic exploitation film, 2010–19	231
	Contemporary patterns	234
	Policy incentives: The Nordic genre support programmes	236
	Going lo-fi	241

	Flirting with the mainstream	247
	Killer bunnies on the loose	251
	Conclusion	256
10	Conclusion: Beyond the art house	261
Index		267

Figures

1.1	The original *Blood Tracks* 'big box' artwork for the US market with the sticker that reads: 'From the makers of "A NIGHTMARE ON ELM STREET"', 1985	3
2.1	Screen grab from Swedish *Göta-Elf katastrofen*. ('The Göta Elf Catastrophe', 1908)	33
2.2	Advertising poster for Danish film company Fotorama's original version of *Den hvide slavehandel* (*The White Slave Trade*, 1910)	37
2.3	Swedish advertisement for the German STD film *Falsche Scham* ('The Scourge of Humanity', 1926)	42
2.4	Screen grab from Swedish documentary film *Med prins Wilhelm på afrikanska jaktstigar* (*On Safari in Africa with Prince Wilhelm*, 1922)	44
2.5	Screen grab from Danish-American sci-fi monster film *Reptilicus* (1961)	47
3.1	The original 'big box' artwork for *Smutsiga fingrar* (*Dirty Fingers*, 1973)	57
3.2	Screen grab from Swedish *Skräcken har 1000 ögon* (*Fear Has 1000 Eyes*, 1973)	58
3.3	Screen grab from Danish *Dværgen* (*The Sinful Dwarf*, 1973)	60
3.4	Screen grab from Swedish *Thriller – en grym film* (*They Call Her One Eye*, 1974)	64
3.5	Screen grab from Swedish *Thriller – en grym film* (*They Call Her One Eye*, 1974)	68
3.6	Screen grab from Swedish *Breaking Point* (1975)	69
4.1	Screen grab from *Studio S*'s episode on 'Video violence'	83
4.2	Headlines the day after the *Studio S*'s episode on 'Video Violence: "WE HAVE BEATEN PEOPLE ON THE STREET" – and we have 45 videos at home'	90
5.1	Screen grab from the Icelandic *Hrafninn flýgur* (*When the Raven Flies*, 1984)	112

5.2	The original VHS artwork from the Finnish slasher film *Kuutamosonaatti* (*Moonlight Sonata*, 1988)	118
5.3	The original VHS artwork for *Yön saalistajat* (*Hunters of the Night*, 1984)	128
5.4	The international original poster artwork for *Arctic Heat* (*Born American*, 1985)	135
6.1	Mats Helge Olsson on the set of *The Ninja Mission* (1984)	148
6.2	The original UK 'big box' artwork for *The Ninja Mission* (1984), 1994	150
6.3	Krzysztof Kolberger, Hanna Bieniuszewicz and Bo F Munthe in their 'ninja outfits' on the set of *The Ninja Mission* (1984)	152
6.4	Screen grab from Swedish *The Ninja Mission* (1984)	153
6.5–6.6	The original 'big box' artwork for *Animal Protector* (1988) and *The Mad Bunch* (1989)	163
7.1	The original VHS artwork for *Evil Ed* (1995)	176
7.2	The original DVD cover artwork for *Flænset: Jalosiens Instinkter* ('Shredded', 2000)	186
8.1	An image from the premiere of *Iron Sky: The Coming Race* (2019)	202
8.2	Screen grab from *Død snø* (*Dead Snow* 2009)	209
8.3	The US release artwork for *Dead Snow: Red vs. Dead* (2014)	212
8.4	Screen grab from *Iron Sky* (2012)	214
9.1	Screen grab from the trailer for *Kung Fury* (2015)	232
9.2	Screen grab from *It Came from the Desert* (2018)	235
9.3	Screen grab from *Hora* (*The Whore*, 2009)	244
9.4	Screen grab from *Bunny the Killer Thing* (2015)	252
9.5	Screen grab from *Bunny the Killer Thing* (2015)	254

Acknowledgements

We would like to thank a range of individuals and organizations that played an essential role in the process of researching and writing this book. Charles Aspéria, Hilmar Gudlaugsson, Gunnar Iversen, Reinert Kiil, Joakim Lindhé, Heikki Sulander, Isak Thorsen and Mathias Pedersen Wagner provided their time for interviews and access to material. Film archives and institutes including Kansallinen Audiovisuaalinen Arkisto and the Archival Film Collections and Library at the Swedish Film Institute were essential in compiling historical material on the films covered in this book. We would also like to thank Kate Moffat for providing critical feedback on the chapters as well as the three reviewers whose thorough comments and suggestions were helpful in shaping the final form of the book. Finally, we would like to thank Austin Fisher and Johnny Walker for their editorial guidance throughout the project.

1

The politics of Nordsploitation

Nordic cinema holds a distinct international reputation as an austere, artistic, experimental and socially relevant body of enthusiastically *serious* film culture. This reputation can be traced back to the 1910s with highly acclaimed films like *Afgrunden* (*The Abyss*, 1910), *Berg-Ejvind och hans hustru* (*The Outlaw and His Wife*, 1918) and *Körkarlen* (*The Phantom Chariot*, 1920), which moved the boundaries for film art, and are still, 100 years later, called 'poetic masterpieces' (Tapper 2006: 41). For academic scholars, the tradition of Nordic art cinema, continued by filmmakers like Ingmar Bergman, 'often functioned as a counterbalance to the hegemony of Hollywood' (Soila, Söderbergh Widding, Iversen 1998: 1). As argued by the authors of the field-defining volume *Nordic National Cinemas*, Nordic film history has been understood as a national cinematic project, the rationale for which is built on three factors: (1) the films are not exportable to markets outside the region; (2) state influence coordinates the production of cinema as a national project based on closely guarded notions of artistic relevance; and (3) the films produced in these contexts exhibit a 'national quality' that is distinct from American film (Soila, Söderbergh Widding, Iversen 1998: 2–5). For us, this narrow nationalistic perspective is both misleading and unproductive, as it only tells one side of the (his)story. It imposes limitations on studying films that have found themselves on a collision course with these national perspectives, and invariably marginalizes them to the fringes of film history.

The Politics of Nordsploitation approaches Nordic cinema from a perspective that very literally turns these factors upside-down as we mainly study films that (1) are meant for export, (2) are produced without state support and outside of the national project of domestic film institutes and (3) have a transnational quality that mirrors American films in complex, and often unexpectedly subversive, ways. This approach is predicated not only on the choice of topic for this book, but by a realistic assessment of the histories of the five distinct

Nordic film cultures. By only focusing on films that meet prescribed top-down designations of 'quality', the act of compiling national cinema histories has effectively written out a huge range of films that, in one way or another, have contributed to shaping these national film cultures, whether by instigating new co-production strategies or by catering to audiences overlooked by prescriptions of 'relevant' art cinema. Counteracting such mechanisms of exclusion, we explore Nordic film history to uncover the ongoing complex entanglements of cultural taste, commercial profit, social relevance and ethical norms that, for us, comprise the *politics* of Nordsploitation. Interactions among institutes, filmmakers, critics and audiences comprise negotiations on the parameters of cultural worthiness and artistic relevance that shapes the dynamics of inclusion and exclusion, of 'belonging', in these film cultures, and thus sets expectations for what can be considered exploitative.

One striking example of the dynamics of inclusion and exclusion based on, first, perceptions of artistic taste and cultural value and, second, on unbalanced negotiations between the national and the transnational, is the Swedish slasher/stalker film *Blood Tracks* (1985). The ways these dynamics shape the writing of film history becomes explicit when we consider that this film is not mentioned even once in the annals of Swedish film history. Not only did it probably reach larger audiences than most other Nordic films during the 1980s, with distribution on VHS in multiple countries such as Sweden, UK, Japan, West Germany, Spain, Canada, Belgium, the United States, South Korea and the Netherlands, but it also benefited from distribution and promotional efforts in these markets that did not frame it as a Swedish curiosity.

For example, a sticker was attached to *Blood Tracks*' 'big box' artwork distributed by Vista Home Video on the US market reading: 'From the makers of "A NIGHTMARE ON ELM STREET"'. The fact that the obscure Swedish filmmakers' previous film, *The Ninja Mission* (1984), had been distributed in the United States by New Line Cinema with some success led to this unique association of a no budget Swedish slasher with Freddy Krueger, one of the icons of horror cinema. This rather far-fetched connection is typical of marketing in the video era but in our case, it underlines the peculiar circumstances in which *Blood Tracks* signifies much more than its to-date marginalized status in Sweden. Instead, it is a film that had sufficient commercial viability – a distinctly unusual quality at the time – to be marketed in tandem with the highly successful *A Nightmare on Elm Street* (1984) and which thus had the capacity to reach international audiences whom paid, watched and enjoyed the film – despite having been written out of 'official' domestic film history. *Blood Tracks* ticks all the boxes for the upside-down perspective on Nordic film history as it unquestionably was meant for export; it was produced without state support and thus excluded from the national project; and it unabashedly mimicked American genre film, in this case the slasher.

Blood Tracks was directed by Swedish maverick film director Mats Helge Olsson under one of his Americanized aliases, in this case, Mike Jackson, a pseudonym suspiciously similar to megastar Michael Jackson. In many senses a run-of-the-mill slasher, the film is noteworthy for featuring plenty of examples of commercial audience diversification that helped it to stand out among contemporary American competitors such as *The House on Sorority Row* (1983) and *The Mutilator* (1984). First, *Blood Tracks* can be placed in the slim subgenre of Heavy Metal Horror as the equally slim narrative features Swedish glam rock band Easy Action travelling to the Colorado Mountains (in reality Swedish Funäsdalen near the Norwegian border) to shoot a music video. Second, it takes place during winter in the mountains, and thus includes snowy landscapes

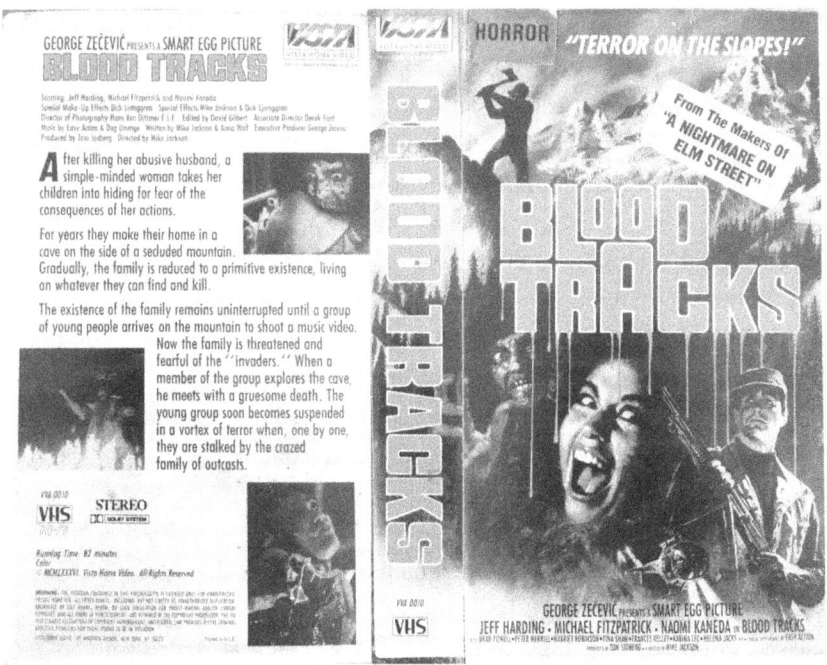

Figure 1.1 The original *Blood Tracks* 'big box' artwork for the US market with the sticker that reads: 'From the makers of "A NIGHTMARE ON ELM STREET"', 1985. Courtesy of Vista Home Video.

and a narrative that interacts with the cold weather as the band members and their groupies are killed off in one gruesome way after another. Snow-covered mountains were also featured on most of the international VHS covers, and in all the English-speaking markets, the imagery was coupled with the tagline: 'Terror on the slopes!'

Although the Heavy Metal Horror genre included films like *KISS Meets the Phantom of the Park* (1978), *Rocktober Blood* (1984) and *Trick or Treat* (1986), the latter featuring Ozzy Osbourne and Gene Simmons, 1980s feature films, more than ever, used real-life rock and pop stars and music to promote both the films and the bands. In an interview with two of the members of Easy Action, Peo Thyrén and Bo Stagman, they readily admit that the main purpose for their participation in *Blood Tracks* was publicity. Then again, they contextualize this decision by stating that Prince 'did the same thing' with the film *Purple Rain* (1984), although they are clearly aware that Easy Action, and the film they took part in, did not remotely play in the same league (*Blood Tracks*: 'Blodspår – Easy Action sopar igen spåren', 2012).

The commercial and international calculations made by the members of Easy Action, their label Warner Music, and Mats Helge Olsson, are especially intriguing in their cultural–political implications. When Peo Thyrén first contacted Mats Helge Olsson, the latter was in prison where he was serving time for debts that he had obtained as producer of *Sverige åt svenskarna* ('Sweden for the Swedes', 1980). Olsson immediately realized the commercial possibilities of the project and included music by Easy Action in an already ongoing film project and ensured that filming on their collaborative production started a few weeks later (*Blood Tracks*: 'Blodspår – Easy Action sopar igen spåren', 2012). To ensure that the film would not be forced to try to claw back profit from the insubstantial Swedish audiences, *Blood Tracks* was produced by Smart Egg Pictures, a London-based company that, among other films, co-produced *A Nightmare on Elm Street* (1984) – thus certifying the 'associated' connection on the VHS sticker – but also several instalments of the extremely successful Swedish franchise *Sällskapsresan* (The Charter Trip).

International connections were emphasized from the inception as the language of the film was English and most of the actors, besides the five members of Easy Action, were British and consisted of female photo models with no prior experience and male actors, of whom Jeff Harding was the only one to carve out a career in the film industry with supporting roles in films like *Spies Like Us* (1985) and *Alfie* (2004). While the snowy surroundings for the killings in *Blood Tracks* could be seen as locally 'exotic' for the slasher genre, underneath this superficial internationalism, its Colorado locations are, for example, undermined by the fact that all car license plates are clearly Swedish. Unlike the contemporary wave of Nordic Noir film and television series that use 'the more or less stereotypical distinctiveness of the Nordic countries in terms of national characteristics and temper, landscape and climate, and various cultural associations or markers' (Åberg 2015: 95), *Blood Tracks*, decades before, could – and would – only draw attention to the one distinctively 'international' Swedish feature, snow, while concealing as many of the location's other domestic characteristics as possible.

Clearly, no one involved in this project wanted to contain it to Sweden, where *Blood Tracks* was not even released theatrically and thus not rated by the Swedish Board of Film Censorship. The facts that this film received its main distribution internationally and was only released domestically on VHS are both contributing factors to its rejection from national film history. These circumstances are not necessarily that unique as in analysing marginalized underground or exploitation films in Europe, Ernest Mathijs and Xavier Mendik identify what they call the two corners of underground and exploitation film. The former includes artistic films that aspire to be alternative but are regardless ultimately included in national canons, whereas the latter comprise films 'that do not belong to the recognized repertoire, mostly because they are not deemed worthy enough. This latter category of films wants to become popular, but is often prevented of becoming part of the cinema establishment because the films are continuously dismissed as cheap or irrelevant rubbish' (Mathijs and Mendik 2004: 3–4).

It is not difficult to identify how *Blood Tracks* could be positioned in these arguments. Despite all of its international achievements, it was obviously considered as 'irrelevant rubbish' by Swedish authorities, but does this mean that films like these are not worthy of research or of inclusion into writing film history? Undeniably, the content of *Blood Tracks*, in this case a slasher with plentiful conventional nudity and gore for its genre, would have had an impact on both contemporary and historical assessments of the constitution of Swedish cinema, despite and thus perhaps because of, its often active marginalization from these confines. Trash does not imply only inherent low-budget characteristics, such as bad acting, poor editing and a weak screenplay, but also subjects and themes that typically include violence, disturbing images of distress and the seemingly senseless objectification of the female body. The act of labelling a film such as this as trash would have thus constituted a means of drawing boundaries between the acceptable and the impermissible in film culture, an act which in itself is heavily politicized, and which consequently reveals much about the dynamics of the so-called national project.

Mathijs and Mendik confront, and at the same time legitimize, this somewhat sensitive subject by discussing recurring issues in European underground and exploitation cinema. On the one hand, many films 'address issues of guilt, confession and testimony' in relation to 'the massive traumas of World War Two, the rise and collapse of communism, and decolonisation'. On the other hand, there is also a persistent characteristic of 'resistance, rebellion and liberation', where European underground and exploitation cinema positions itself against a mainstream culture, but also against hegemonic ways of reasoning, politically and ideologically. 'Arguably, alternative European cinema [. . .] does not always campaign for politically correct perspectives. But at the very least it seems to be championing, almost anarchically, a call for liberty' (Mathijs and Mendik 2004: 4–5).

To readdress this unbalance of power in writing national film histories, *The Politics of Nordsploitation* is primarily interested in 'forgotten' films that are typically categorized as cheap and irrelevant by cultural authorities, and if they happen to attract attention internationally, their domestic roots are conveniently forgotten. However, unsurprisingly, the (his)story of these films is by and large defined by resistance and rebellion against the national project, against a mainstream film culture and against censorship. In the interview with the two members of Easy Action, Mats Helge Olsson's film production practice was tellingly equated with the punk scene of the late 1970s, that is, as rebellious and defiant cultural production aimed against the norms of Nordic societies (*Blood Tracks*: Blodspår – Easy Action sopar igen spåren', 2012). These anti-establishment views, primarily consisting of nonconformist and anti-authoritarian ideological perspectives, and a do-it-yourself ethos, are attitudes that permeate the primary source material of this study. The big difference being, of course, that exploitation cinema has never been anti-commercial but instead has tried its best to be as commercial as possible.

Hence, the rationale of *The Politics of Nordsploitation* is to rewrite Nordic film history by focusing on exploitative tendencies and alternative ways of producing films outside of the national projects that constitute the aims of the Nordic film industries. Consequently, the films we discuss in this study are not made up of 'poetic masterpieces' or of challenging art cinema, and we do not intend to artificially transform films like *Blood Tracks* into socially or artistically valuable pieces of alternative or underground art. Objectively, there is no point in denying that the majority of the films studied here are artistically and stylistically inferior to mainstream film production. For instance, the following perspective from an online review of *Blood Tracks* summarizes its contribution accurately: 'Blood Tracks is very cheesy, cheap and silly, but finally it lives up to its promise as a real, bloody and nasty slasher. I'm not saying it's a masterpiece, because it's not – Mats Helge was for most of his career a very incompetent storyteller – but this ranks as his best together with The Ninja Mission' (Ninja Dixon 2011).

Nevertheless, to study these films in a historical cultural–political framework is vital as these missing or ignored moments of history in their different contexts can tell us a lot about alternative ways of film production and distribution, the development of genre filmmaking, the impact of changing social norms that these films and filmmakers faced, and not least the effects of film censorship. In fact, it would not be out of place to claim that the history of film censorship is intertwined with the history of exploitation and, therefore, it features as a key theme throughout the present study. This multi-layered and transnational history is also a political history where we outline many of the cultural strategies and financial models of an ignored film production type, which, crucially, eventually developed (or was integrated) into accepted mainstream practices, especially in the Nordic context of the twenty-first century. Change is therefore, for us, a key ingredient in the politics of Nordsploitation.

Periodization: Exploitation and Nordic exploitation

But what is exploitation, and what comprises exploitation in a Nordic context? In a conventional sense, it would be difficult to position *Blood Tracks* as normative exploitation cinema. After all, it is a relatively conventional slasher, produced in English, targeted at youth consumers and peppered throughout with contemporaneously popular music. However, understood from a specifically Nordic perspective, *Blood Tracks* does not play with normative cultural or economic rules, nor does it sit easy with censorship norms in 1980s Sweden where slasher films and gore, in particular, were often heavily censored. The fact that it refuses to consider these as obstacles and instead takes them on as opportunities qualifies it as exploitation for us. The ability of Olsson et al. to productively identify gaps in the domestic market as well as international opportunities to be exploited even with the minimal resources available for genre production at the time aligns these efforts with the opportunistic, but also culturally challenging forms of production that characterizes exploitation cinema. Thus, exploitation in a Nordic context both resembles and closely associates with transnational patterns of exploitation cinema even as it operates on unique registers that have to be addressed in their particular social and historical contexts as well as in reference to particular film cultural and industrial politics that change over time.

If the case of *Blood Tracks* gestures to the difficulties of identifying and addressing the constitution of Nordic exploitation, it does so in light of a research field dominated by American scholars and thus by American film examples. For instance, when American film scholar David Roche proclaims that 'Exploitation cinema is not a genre; it is an industry with a specific mode of production. Exploitation films are made cheap for easy profit' (Roche 2015: 1), it is an example of how foremost American film scholars tend to associate exploitation cinema with a specific period that stretches from the late 1950s to the 1970s (see, for example, Cook 2005: 52–64 and Doherty 2002: 1–13). At the same time, film historian Eric Schaefer traces the origins of American exploitation cinema to circa 1919, claiming that the classical era of exploitation in fact ended by the late 1950s (Schaefer 1999: 325–7). Accordingly, there are two forms of 'classic' exploitation. First, the period that Schafer examines in his original work on American exploitation before 1959 includes the sex hygiene film, the exotic documentary, the drug film and nudist film (Schaefer 1999: passim). Second, we have the era of 'new' exploitation circa 1960–80 that includes the sexploitation film but also genre films produced by American independent film companies such as Allied Artists, Howco and AIP (American International Pictures) (Roche 2015: 4). But what about the 1980s and beyond?

Film scholars Ernest Mathijs and Jamie Sexton argue that the market for exploitation films became 'murkier' in the 1980s as 'traditional outlets, such as drive-ins and grindhouse theatres, began to disappear'. Although the VCR created a new market for 'cheap films', they claim that straight-to-video films 'rarely became cult hits' (Mathijs and Sexton 2011: 152). Yet again, here the implied meanings are integrated into an explicitly American context, even as the dismissal of the video era also indicates the underlying formation of a hierarchization between the periods, between ways of distribution and between the geographical origins of the product. Put together, these processes of qualifying cult or exploitation cinema, in many ways, reveal a complex process of canonization of films that have largely been valourized for being 'uncanonizable'.

Despite these scholarly attempts at tracing and highlighting patterns of marginalized cinema, European film industries have seen their fair share of film production of exploitation films, even if the main market for such product was the United States with its huge drive-in circuit and local theatres in the inner-city areas. The main period for these endeavours coincided with the most prolific era of the European art film circa 1960–80 where 'quality' or 'valuable' European art cinema constituted the basis for the emergence of serious film criticism and Film Studies as a university subject. While the art as exploitation/exploitation as art crossover would often blur distinctions between respectable art and shady European exploitation, the latter, consisting of 'unworthy' genres like Nazisploitation or zombie splatter films, would have been predominantly kept in the scholarly closet at the time.

Not only is the periodization of European exploitation film different from their American counterparts, but film scholarship on clearly exploitative topics such as European sex hygiene films or exotic documentaries has been sparse. When research has been conducted on, for example, the exotic documentary these films have been analysed as valuable contributions to the national project and as forerunners of the documentary genre, not as exploitative films *per se* (see, for example, Brinch and Iversen 2006: 46). And while the 'classic' period between 1960 and 1980 has, in recent years, been the subject of academic research, such studies continue to be infrequent and not in any way comparable in scope to studies on European art cinema (or, for that matter, the American exploitation film). Furthermore, much of this research is often characterized by a defensive position and uncertainty as to whether the subject is worthy of study. In order to handle this tenuous situation, studies on classic European exploitation cinema tend to, roughly divided, either frame them through nostalgia or otherwise justify these 'lowbrow' films as culturally valuable in the same way and even on the same level as European art cinema.

The pioneer anthology, *Alternative Europe: Eurotrash and Exploitation Cinema Since 1945*, is a case in point of the latter where a majority of the individual chapters seek to legitimize their seedy research subjects in two ways. They either make claims that the films are socially viable reflections of a given society, as is done in Christopher Barry's chapter on Italian Cop films (Barry 2004: 77–89) or, alternatively, they argue that exploitation films 'share the artistic and ideological concerns more usually associated with the canonic auteurs of the Young German Cinema and the New German Cinema' as is done in Linnie Blake's chapter on Jörg Buttgereit's *Nekromantik* (1987) (Blake 2004: 192).

On the other hand, nostalgic approaches can be deemed as anti-academic in tone as they are often associated with fan behaviour and a wish 'to share in spreading the fun' as media scholar Danny Shipka remarks of his own research on Italian, Spanish and French exploitation films in the 'classic' period (Shipka 2011: 15). Although fan-scholarly work on exploitation cinema can be traced back to the 1960s (Ferrer 1963; Hitchens 1964), exploitation cinema has emerged as a viable 'field' since the 1990s with Jeffery Sconce's seminal article 'Trashing the Academy' (1995), for example, making an explicit case for the inclusion of exploitation films into academic scholarship on cultural, political, societal and economic grounds. However, as Ernest Mathjis points out, the debate over theorizing exploitation film continues, and many of the existing overviews are light on theory and more interested in writing the history of the exploitation film (Mathjis 2011). Intriguingly, two of the most prominent existing studies of Nordic exploitation cinema fall into the nostalgic and uncritical category: Jack Stevenson's study of the erotic cinema of Sweden and Denmark in the 1960s and 1970s (Stevenson 2010) and Daniel Ekeroth's compilation of Swedish exploitation films (Ekeroth 2011), both of which are clearly aimed at fans rather than students and scholars. Furthermore, a nostalgic approach hovers over an academic study such as David Church's *Grindhouse Nostalgia* (2015), where the author displays a relatively sympathetic appreciation of the analysed exploitation films and the audiences who consume them.

Defining Nordsploitation

Nordic exploitation cinema is, of course, European, and has to be placed in this context. At the same time, all five Nordic countries differ in three main ways from the type of film culture being produced in, for example, Italy, Spain, France, Germany and the UK. First, the periodization for different types of exploitation cinema does not work in relation to the Nordic countries. For example, the era of 'classic' European exploitation between 1960 and 1980 does not apply here since Denmark and Sweden were virtually exploitation free until circa 1970 when a number of sexploitation films from these countries flooded the international market. Meanwhile, films produced in Finland, Norway and Iceland were, with a few singular exceptions, lacking in any normatively exploitative qualities well into the 1980s. At this disjuncture, it is necessary to make it clear that we do not cover Nordic sexploitation films in this book as the Danish and Swedish variations of sexploitation have been extensively analysed elsewhere (see, for example, Stevenson 2010, Björklund and Larsson (ed.) 2016, and Larsson 2017), including the contribution of films like *Jag är nyfiken – gul* (*I am Curious – Yellow*, 1967) or the challenging work of auteurs like Ingmar Bergman to the emergence of New Hollywood (see Mathjis 2011; Stevenson 2010; Heffernan 2015). Instead, our focus will be on aspects of Nordic cinema that were considered to be truly problematic and even transgressive, and thus either written out of domestic film histories or included in ways that attempted to rewrite them into said histories – often at a cost of minimizing their transgressive tendencies. Although sexploitation was a debatable subject in the Nordic countries, it was never perceived as a problem on the scale of cinematic violence, gore and other seemingly immoral behaviour, a notion heavily reflected in censorship debates and decisions.

Consequently, the second way that Nordic exploitation cinema deviates from other international patterns is to do with its almost clinical lack of explicit violence, particularly during the 'classic' era of 1960–80. In comparison, the Italian Giallo, horror and Mondo films, for example, stand out as extreme in their use of violence and gore, as do the Spanish exploitation films of the era with their updated versions of Universal's classic monster tales, and horror films with religious symbolism (Shipka 2011: 14–15). The inclusion of cinematic violence and gore in Nordic films was a much more complicated process filled with huge challenges such as strict state censorship and a consistent and constant critical drumbeat that equated such elements with an undesirable form of cultural (namely American) imperialism. These challenges contribute to the creation of an alternative timeline compared to other European film cultures but also in relation to the ways the history of exploitation film has been written.

The third principal way that Nordic exploitation cinema differs from its European counterparts is the fact that Denmark, Finland, Iceland, Norway and Sweden are all what Mette Hjort and Duncan Petrie define as 'cinemas of small nations'. That is, these small nations have relatively small film industries, small populations and minor languages that limit the wider distribution of Nordic cinema, even between the Nordic countries themselves. In addition, the usual strategies to deal with this smallness – government subsidies and the use of national subject matters and picturesque local landscapes (Hjort and Petrie 2007: 1–3) – would often be out of reach for Nordic exploitation film as we saw with the example of *Blood Tracks*. For a long time, the smallness of Nordic cinemas translated to circumstances where the opportunities for exploitation film producers were minimized even further, as they had to operate on the outskirts of a national film industry and film culture operating on already minimal resources, generally managing to produce only one or two films.

On the other hand, the international outlook for Danish and Swedish sexploitation, and eventually violent direct-to-video exploitation films, reveals that Nordic exploitation producers took advantage of transnational production and distribution arrangements long before Hjort and Petrie's assertion of a shift from a cultural to an economic imperative in the international film industry, fuelled by a global neoliberal turn: 'Small nations by definition have very limited domestic markets for all locally produced goods and services – including culture – and so have been forced by the neo-liberal economic and political pressures of globalisation into a greater dependency on external markets' (Hjort and Petrie 2007: 15). This economic reality would ultimately evolve even more in the twenty-first century with the introduction of crowd funding and fan participation cultivation.

As a consequence of these cultural and political developments, Nordic exploitation functions on a different timeline compared to American and European exploitation cinema. For that reason we have chosen to work with a longer historical perspective that includes an early period (1910–20s), the two 'classical' periods, but also, due to the delay that Nordic genre and exploitation film experienced, a heavy focus on post-1980s film production with violent and gory content, especially in the new millennia. The purpose for adapting such a long historical timeline is twofold. First, a long historical overview is necessary to be able to explain the similarities and differences in the periodization of Nordic exploitation cinema within these five distinct film cultures. Second, it provides recourse to explain the specific development of Nordic exploitation film in relation to its international and contemporary competitors, especially as the conventions and cultural status of genre and exploitation film are often blurred in Nordsploitation.

The complex historical timeline and the blurring of genre and exploitation cinema in institutional discourse suggest that the Nordic form of exploitation is not simply about film texts that contain sex or violence, packaged in the cheapest possible frame and exhibited in slimy dives designed more for illicit activities than film spectatorship. We agree with Mathijs and Sexton when they suggest that exploitation cinema is a contextual, diverse practice and that it needs to be analysed as such (Mathijs and Sexton 2011: 2). Even more significantly, if contextuality plays such a huge role in defining exploitation, it is not sufficient to transplant theories written in what is largely an American context to the cultural and political contexts of these countries and industries.

Our analysis will focus on the transformations and relevance of the concept of exploitation cinema in the Nordic context, one that will be both eerily familiar and unavoidably strange to international readers. Transnational flows and crosscurrents are central and relevant in these contexts, but the ways they are dealt with and incorporated into the cinematic and cultural context is fundamentally different in the Nordic countries. The maverick production history of Swedish *Blood Tracks* can for instance be compared with the cottage industry that surrounded the Italian Giallo film, which was connected to a 'rising wave of [cinematic] violence' that the Mondo film had created and that resulted in more than 250 Giallo films produced in the 'classic' period. And although *Blood Tracks* was obviously inspired by the wave of American slashers that was produced around 1980, the Giallo film is said to be 'the forefather' for North American slasher films like *Friday the 13th* (1980) and *Prom Night* (1981) (Shipka 2011: 71). Yet, although both the Giallo and the North American slashers were predominantly targeted at domestic audiences and had important economic repercussions for their respective film industries (see Nowell 2011), Nordic films of a similar type – that is, largely conventional genre fare – were marginalized or entirely ignored not so much due to an excess of violence or other transgressive material, but because they dared to exploit these international genre conventions.

Theories of exploitation

As a consequence, the history of exploitation cinema, as written to date, will be challenged by some of these Nordic developments. Exploitation film has been theorized from a variety of conceptual and political angles, including from the perspective of gender politics (Cook 1985) and auteurist readings (Modleski 2007). These general patterns show that academic studies, as has been explained above, tend to prioritize films from the United States and large European film markets such as Italy and the UK, though other regional locations like Asia (Weisser 1997) and Latin America (Greene 2005; Ruetalo and Tierney 2011) have resulted in substantial scholarly interest and discussion. As we will show, the Nordic variation of exploitation is fundamentally different from many of these well-known examples as Nordic exploitation developed much slower and consisted for a long time only of maverick outsider directors operating in very precarious conditions, even when they were producing relatively standard genre fare. We therefore suggest that a lot more attention has to be paid to areas like film policy and industry practice as the connotations of 'exploitation' can take on various forms when considered alongside the smallness of the Nordic film industries and their audiences. Although Mathijs and Mendik's (2004: 1–2) suggestion that European exploitation cinema comprise an 'alternative cinema' to mainstream film production makes some sense in a Nordic context, the strict duality between mainstream films and underground productions is not entirely satisfactory when considering the particularities of the five Nordic film cultures. Thus, a somewhat conventional ninja film may not appear particularly exploitative in Hollywood, but transplanted to the film cultural context of 1980s Sweden – where 'ninja films' were more or less banned by default – they suddenly take on much more complex connotations, precisely as they do not fit into the confines of respectable domestic film cultures.

The expansive and diverse field of exploitation cinema studies provides the methodological basis for understanding Nordic exploitation film culture. Here, distinguishing between production, distribution, exhibition and reception contexts is particularly significant as it is important to consider exploitation films both as historically grounded texts that need to be understood in their context of production and as free-floating cult texts whose meanings are reinterpreted and reconstituted through time and cultural context. Although our focus is on historical patterns, we are also interested in the heritage and the impact that these films have had on Nordic filmmakers and, especially, the development of Nordic genre film. With that said, we have no intention to refurbish the films analysed in this study as 'cult films' or to redefine them as 'valuable' in the same category as European art film. We are especially mindful of activating nostalgic or retrospective readings. Although fan-based practices can lead to productive modes of understanding the complexity of the 'users' of these texts, Mark Shiel warns us against 'a historical relativism' that prioritizes the reading practices of contemporary consumers, including academics working on these films. Using Mark Jancovich' championing of the act of positioning and repositioning of films through time, he suggests these practices often tend to depoliticize the original implications of such controversial texts (Shiel 2003: 3).

Although this perspective tends to emphasize the importance of interpreting these films within their historical context of production, we need to be mindful of the ways retrospective reading practices influence the significance and impact of such films. For us, the intentions of the filmmakers at the time – did they identify themselves as part of 'exploitation' or were they in fact, exploiting the general cultural zeitgeist and the political economy of their respective national film industries at the time (as well as being mindful of global flows of cinematic influences) – are certainly of paramount importance. Such a historical perspective is necessary as Eric Schaefer, for example, reminds us that exploitation cycles are born and die out based on wider industrial transformations. For one, he suggests that the classical American exploitation was extinguished due to studios incorporating more exploitative material into mainstream productions, partly as a response to competition from television and the subsequent conscious strategy to try to stay up-to-date with changing consumer standards (Schaefer 1999: 325–6). This perspective applies to Nordic exploitation as well as the economic opportunities – and indeed, the *raison d'etre* – of most instances of exploitative production would invariably be predicated on wider industrial and policy circumstances.

Accordingly, we will be closer to Schaefer's methodology with regard to creating a contemporary – rather than a nostalgic or cultist – understanding of these films and filmmakers based on economic, moral, legal and stylistic imperatives. Yet, viewing practices and cult or fan affiliations continue to play a part in exploitation film cultures, arguably more so in the 2000s than before. Much of the contemporary resurgence of exploitation cinema can be attributed to Quentin Tarantino and Robert Rodriquez's retrosploitation film *Grindhouse* (2007), which drew inspiration from classic 1970s exploitation cinema. This has led to an explosion in distribution of forgotten 'classics' on bespoke DVD labels as well as cycles of resurgent retrosploitation production capitalizing on exploitation tactics. Similarly, scholarship has sought to reinterpret these practices of the heyday of American exploitation film cultures through publications such as *Grindhouse Nostalgia* (Church 2015) and *Selling the Splat Pack* (Bernard 2015). Both provide contemporaneous evaluations of the recent cycle of grindhouse films as self-conscious plays on/to the political economy of Hollywood cinema, with Church, in particular, suggesting that these 'transgressive' films are anything but marginal products and they in fact largely prop up the contemporary status quo by catering to emerging consumer segments. Similarly, Bernard's work suggests that technology plays a fundamental role in these practices as the advent of VHS and DVD has transformed modes of fan behaviour. Applying this to digital is vital as the form and materiality of both the products themselves and the viewing context/experience have invariably played a substantial role in the field. At the same time, digital technologies facilitate an easy replication of not only the films but also the visual signifiers of exploitation cinema (such as the missing reels, scratch marks, cigarette burns and general grit applied digitally to *Grindhouse*), leading to a complex cultural and intertextual politics where exploitation itself is exploited.

These concerns are very relevant to Nordic films as the 2000s have seen increased interest to produce films that reference not only the classics of exploitation cinema but also the retrosploitation of Tarantino, Rodriquez, Rob Zombie, Eli Roth and so on. Accordingly, digital technology fundamentally challenged the material conditions that made exploitation cinema and the exhibition context so specialist and so marginal in past times, but it has altered the referential and intertextual basis on which these films work. Although we do address these concerns over distribution practices, we do not prioritize them as exhibition spaces were not of paramount concern in the Nordic context. There were no specialist circuits dedicated to violent or pornographic films as Nordic theatres had to abide by regulations governing exhibition and censorship practices, which were some of the strictest in the world. However, the introduction of the VCR technique to general audiences in the Nordic countries around 1980 created a viewing platform that that was not easily controlled. And with the inauguration of a digital media environment uncoordinated by state regulations since the early 2000s, it is not surprising that notions of control have evaporated, and with them, the implication of exploitation as a concept has shifted as the political dynamics of marginalized/censored films with seemingly little social or cultural value have slowly entered the mainstream and canons of critical respect.

Finally, some words about film violence in the Nordic context. Film violence is a problematic term, and as other historical phenomena, it tends to change over the course of time. When all Nordic countries introduced film censorship in the early 1910s, the different governmental censorship boards had the common goal of protecting its citizens (foremost children, women and the 'uneducated') from harmful displays of sex, violence, immoralities and, not least of all, 'bad taste' (Solum 2013: 13; Gustafsson and Larsson 2018: 216). Over time, though, and due to political, economic and artistic fluctuations and liberalizations, sex, nudity and what were perceived as immoralities tended to be accepted and even celebrated within these film cultures. However, violence, and particularly 'entertainment violence', that is, violence not grounded in any form of social realism or critique of society, continued to be understood as a source of social and moral anxiety and controversy well into the new millennia. As James Kendrick points out, '[t]he fact that violence, like pornography, is something that is both difficult to define and can bring together the extreme political right and the extreme political left in mutual condemnation is testament to its polysemous nature and cultural salience' (Kendrick 2009: 3). The violent and transgressive Nordic films discussed in this book are thus central to understanding the societal and historical role of cinema in the Nordic countries, and ultimately how this role has changed and developed, not least in relation to domestic industrial practices and a global film culture.

For us, then, exploitation films and genre films that have exploited violence over the decades act as a prism to investigate films and production practices that have constantly existed in the margins of Nordic film history, but that have nevertheless made an impact over time on funding, filmmaking and film censorship. Consequently, this is not a study that in any depth aims to either analyse violence and gore aesthetically or understand the social effects of film violence on its audiences. We agree with scholars like Martin Barker and Stephen Prince that film or media violence is not a 'thing', and that 'there is no category of "media violence" which can be researched' (Barker 1997: 27–8; Prince 2000). Instead, we understand film violence according to Swedish media scholar Ulf Dalquist's definition, as a social construction, that is, an idea or phenomenon that we can discuss and relate to, but which does not necessarily exist as a concrete phenomenon in reality. The 'violent film', thanks to its social construction, thus figures as something negative when seen through a cultural perspective with a variety of synonyms such as entertainment violence, violence porn, torture porn and extreme violence. Based on this approach, the 'violent film' does not constitute a separate genre but consists of all kinds of violence that occurs in the film medium, lumped together by the societal antagonists of film violence into the social construction 'violent film', a concept that can thus house everything from Donald Duck cartoons to sadomasochistic pornographic films. 'The violent film' and 'extreme violence' are thus not a 'genre' but a concept that is equated with 'evil' (Dalquist 1998: 23–6). Hence, our focus will be on exploitation cinema featuring violence and other arguably degenerate modes of behaviour often deemed too transgressive for audiences by the Nordic cultural authorities and censors.

The complexity of Nordsploitation

In defining the essence of Nordsploitation, we are faced with a corpus of films and a diversity of policies and practices that in many ways defy homogenization under a singular label. Here, the two parts of this term – the Nordic and exploitation – suggest both a novel geocultural variation on exploitation cinema, and an exploitation of Nordicness, whereby these signifiers are the cultural capital sold to consumers. In part, this is both correct and misleading. For one, the concept of the Nordic appears misleading in its implication as we are talking about five distinct national cinemas. If we take the example of Nordic sexploitation as an example, it is not surprising that this conceptualization persists – it has a corpus of films and a demonstrable impact on film cultures worldwide and has resulted in significant media discussions and moral panic concerning their influence on audiences (see, for example, Björk 2016). Yet, not only does this production history largely apply to 'Scandinavia', but the peculiar circumstances that saw many of the liberal attitudes in Sweden and Denmark translated to boundary-pushing art films did not apply regionally. Although violence was consistently problematized as a potential societal problem, sexuality continued to be frowned upon, for example, in Finland with Teuvo Tulio's *Sensuela* (1973), a notorious case of Finnish sexploitation, facing extensive problems with censors and ultimately effectively destroying the career of its director.

If the very constitution of Nordicness requires interrogation, other qualifiers of an exploitation film culture were non-existent in these markets. While it is not surprising that sexploitation has received international interest, the circumstances for exhibiting or viewing Scandinavian exploitation in a New York theatre would have been very different in the domestic theatrical context. Crucially, theatres would have been the main means of consumption of films in the Nordic countries in the 1960s and the 1970s, but this was a space where the illegitimate or transgressive potential of exploitative content was heavily regulated due to the top-down censorship systems in place especially in Norway or Finland. Yet, this pales in comparison to the onslaught of home video censorship in the late 1980s, which resulted in notoriously excessive bans on violent films. The institutionalization of strict censorship in Norway, Sweden and Finland (see Higraff 2011; Skoglund 1971; Sedergren 1998) led to a different cultural–political balance from, for example, American exploitation cinema and resulted in a fundamentally different context for Nordic producers and audiences of genre cinema. Thus, definitions of transgressiveness – and exploitation by extension – are reliant on these contextual factors.

Furthermore, it has been incredibly difficult to produce 'authentic' exploitation films in the Nordic context due to the particularities – small markets, difficulties of financing, strict censorship and an officially sanctioned aversion against these types of film – of these small nation film cultures, and the fact that genre film would often tend to be categorized under exploitative content. As these film cultures were led by policies established by national film institutes that run on a mandate of public responsibility – being as they are, premised on funds from taxes – popular cinema, especially genre film, was perceived as something unbecoming of appropriate national film culture (see Gustafsson and Kääpä 2015: 1–2). Thus, up until at least the 1990s, genre film was actually perceived to be exploitative in that it did not meet domestic norms for the sociocultural role of film art. Consequently, even what would have in other contexts been relatively mainstream films, such as the Icelandic revenge saga *Hrafninn flýgur* (*When the Raven Flies*, 1984), or the Finnish slasher film *Kuutamosonaatti* (*Moonlight Sonata*, 1988), can here be considered exploitative. This applies even more to independent productions such as *The Ninja Mission* or *Arctic Heat* (1985), both films that run afoul of domestic censors but led to profitable international releases.

These distinctions provide a means to distinguish Nordic variations of exploitation cinema from other international trends or patterns. Here, the cultural–economic circumstances of Nordic film production, and not so much the transgressive thematic or aesthetic material, provides a way to see how and why they would be classified as exploitation. While sexploitation is covered in existing scholarship, Nordic films focusing on violence and other transgressive modes of representation have seldom produced sustainable or even identifiable patterns that would comprise a comprehensive 'culture' to be analysed. Because of these complex infrastructural challenges and the often-fragmented genre production cultures of these film industries, we need to posit a two-way distinction between a more localized form of exploitation and one that aspires to wider global film cultural standards. On one hand, we find cases of films that specifically exploit infrastructural elements, such as the lack of institutional support for domestic genre films, as a means to carve out a niche position in the marketplace and use this as publicity material. Here, examples such as *Moonlight Sonata* and *Besökarna* (*The Visitors*, 1988) were marketed as Finnish and Swedish horror films, respectively, and capitalized on genres such as the slasher and the supernatural horror comedy. While censorship continued to target imported film productions such as the *Halloween* and *Friday the 13th* franchises, Nordic producers were able to launch domestic variations, often explicitly using the notion of being a Nordic version of an established genre, to position themselves within the thematic and infrastructural trappings of a national cinema. For us, these films comprise the *localized exploitation film* that use genre formats but are predominantly aimed at domestic markets.

At the same time, an increased proliferation of films that aspired to international standards of film production, especially as relates to the action or slasher film, started gaining more foothold at the margins of these Nordic industries. These productions were predominantly produced independently and hence had to use visible and obvious commercial signifiers to capitalize on international trends. They would often exploit moral or ethical standards to make a name for themselves and would feature such gimmicks as dubbing in English or casting American 'stars' to masquerade their origins and to minimize any potential cultural discount that the impression of too much cultural specificity would generate. These are what we call *the global exploitation film* based on the fact that they were largely aimed at international markets with films such as *Arctic Heat* – a Cold War POW film starring Mike Norris, Chuck Norris' son – and those of Mats Helge Olsson – a Swedish maverick producing cheap genre films between 1983 and 1992. However, this is not only about language or aesthetic standards but also about the ways these producers navigated the complex media and cultural environments of their respective industries. In comparison to the localized exploitation productions, these films work outside of official norms and subsidy systems and, crucially, explicitly capitalize on the very fact of their outsiderness in domestic settings, even as they were the offspring of, as well as dependent on, the international video boom of the 1980s.

The economic realities of the Nordic film cultural context made productions challenging censorship or moral norms a huge personal risk for their producers, especially if the films were banned. Thus, the more localized exploitation tends to be more voluminous but, as we will see, heavily controversial in terms of whether these, in fact, should even be included under this categorization. However, the extensive timeline of this study will provide equal weight to both paradigms by writing two parallel, and at the same time intertwined, histories about Nordic exploitation that, eventually, come together as the marginalized exploitation films, and the new generation of filmmakers inspired by them were welcomed into the cultural canon and the 'real film business' in the early years of the 2000s. This allows us to draw a line between artistic horror films such as *Valkoinen peura* (*The White Reindeer*, 1954) and *Vargtimmen* (*Hour of the Wolf*, 1968) and 'real' exploitation like the seminal *Thriller – en grym film* (*They Call Her One Eye*, 1974). Although a film like *The White Reindeer* does appear as exploitative for some and has been read as a case of international exploitation cinema, we must remember that in Finland in 1954, this was a prestige production, winning several key awards and huge box office. Even more, it is acknowledged even to this day as a bona-fide classic of Finnish cinema. Thus, it does not qualify as exploitation cinema for this book, especially as its themes and cultural relevance have been extensively analysed in line with the development of Studio Era Finnish cinema.

Yet, genre and art films do form a crucial part of our analysis due to the nature of such productions within the political economy of Nordic film cultures. This especially applies to the 1970s and the 1980s when commercial genre production occupied a similarly marginalized status in these media environments as some of the exploitation films. While a film like *Arctic Heat* was certainly much more expensive than many of the factory-line productions from Italy or the United States, its reviled cultural–political status in Finland and its economic repercussions for its producers reflect similar circumstances where personal risk through contemporaneous eye-catching material would lead to domestic notoriety but also international success, providing a tangible illustration of the operations of global exploitation cinema. Meanwhile, more artistic, respectable productions like the Icelandic heritage epic *When the Raven Flies* would merge exploitative elements with national historical cultural traditions, performed significantly in Icelandic in contrast to the former's emphasis on English-speaking American protagonists, and thus provides a case study for localized exploitation. Although neither are clear examples of normative exploitation cinema, they do not fit in with traditional domestic cine-historical trajectories either, and comprise, for us, examples of the two types of film production that characterize Nordsploitation.

Finally, in order to cover these five in large parts ignored and forgotten exploitation film cultures over such a long period, we have been pushed to be innovative in the approach to different source materials. Although we have been able to rely on some previous research, most of the content in this book is new. Consequently, the traditional focus on the film text, the analysis, has been of minor importance in this study. Instead, we have searched the archives and used a wide variety of both traditional and unconventional source materials, such as reviews from five countries and in five languages (both by professional critics and amateur fans), articles, debates, official censorship material, official governmental reports, business material from filmmakers and film institutes, posters, VHS covers and other marketing materials, behind-the-scenes documentaries, regular documentaries, DVD commentary tracks, different televisions programmes, interviews, fan sites and social media materials to trace the complex cultural dialogue surrounding these productions.

It is also worth noting here that, for us, the threshold of inclusion of films into this book centres largely on them having secured a theatrical release. Thus, we do not include the wide range of short films only meant for distribution amongst peer networks or on sites like YouTube or even feature films from *Blödaren* (*Bleeder*, 1983) and *The Resurrection of Michael Myers Part 2* (1989) to *Hydra* (2003) and *Die Zombiejäger* (2005), which were released predominantly on VHS and DVD, respectively. Such productions do have their place, but as our focus is on the industrial and policy implications of exploitative productions, theatrical releases provide a better understanding of their significance. Although this study covers more lo-fi forms of exploitation, such as the films of Swedish indie maverick Mats Helge Olsson or Norwegian excessive exploitation filmmaker Reinert Kiil, even these very low-budget films are characterized by clear aspirations at more prestigious commercial theatrical exhibition contexts and to professionalized means of production and distribution practice, instead of the anything-goes Wild West of films designated for distribution through streaming sites.

The structure of the book

To explore this complex and contested history in the confines of a singular academic study is a methodological challenge. As we have suggested, the concept of Nordsploitation should not be taken for granted as retrospective or nostalgic readings can impose a homogenizing framework on over a hundred years of diverse film history. Yet, when considered as part of a historical continuum of artistic practices, production choices, cultural influences and policy decisions, Nordic film history operates on a dynamic of power where film political strategies and cultural–political debates operate in constant dialogue that shapes both patterns of development and opportunities in the sector. Although Nordic exploitation cinema may consist of disparate strands and intermittent efforts (at least until the early 2000s), many of the films we cover in this book are in many ways direct provocations and/or commercial tactics in response to these wider cultural–political developments.

To understand the particular conditions of individual films and their place in this historical continuum, we have adopted a chronological approach to charting the development of Nordsploitation. As each chapter either covers a specific time period or a thematic development, we have had to adopt diverse methodological tools to address them. The first four chapters of the study thus focus on the historical background to draw a picture of the moral boundaries and complex power dynamics in the societal debates between cultural authorities and filmmakers seeking to challenge (and commercially exploit) these discords. Subsequent chapters take a more focused look on specific films and filmmaking practices.

To start this analysis, Chapter 2 provides a historiography of early Nordic exploitation up until the 1970s. The key imperatives of this chapter are to establish the origins of Nordic exploitation as well as make the case for a different set of qualifiers to distinguish Nordic exploitation from other forms of transnational exploitation film culture. The focus is on addressing differential exhibition contexts and production modes that were a result of the smallness of these cultures. Unsurprisingly, there are substantial transnational similarities in the early patterns of global exploitation film genres such as the *Aufklärungsfilme* (educational film) and the exotic documentary, especially as these genres seem to have enjoyed more pronounced respectability in the Nordic and European context than in the Unites States, as Schaefer so vividly outlines (1999). The Nordic exotic documentary, for instance, greatly resembled its international counterparts in contents such as nudity, shock effects and racist perspectives towards the indigenous populations depicted. Yet, where its American counterparts were often received as low-budget exploitation, Swedish and Norwegian exotic documentaries were highlighted as examples of high-quality national film culture, which the hard-pressed film companies exploited to gain respectability. More surprising is the fact that two of the major and historically most important Nordic film companies, Nordisk Film Kompagni and Svensk Filmindustri, had their first great economic successes with pure exploitation films that, in fact, laid the foundation for their international consolidation during the 1910s.

Outside of such early cases, Nordic film history up to the 1970s was characterized by a noticeable absence of exploitation and exploitative material in all the Nordic countries, partly due to strict censorship and partly due to the lack of a market where exploitation films could be exhibited for profit. However, in the 1960s, Denmark and Sweden were at the forefront of an international liberalization movement that broke through the 'sex wall', eventually leading to the decriminalization of pornography in the two countries, and the (over) production of soft-core and hard-core sexploitation films that were aimed primarily at international markets. Nonetheless, the production of violent and transgressive films did not take off in the same way. On the contrary, violent films continued to be perceived as anomalies in the Nordic countries, even in Denmark that abolished film censorship for adults in 1969. Chapter 3 deals with the handful of very transgressive films that were produced for both a domestic and an international market, leading to an unusual wave of banned films in the 1970s, such as *They Call Her One Eye*.

Following from these challenges to filmmakers aiming to economically exploit international fads, and to also shake up the system, Chapter 4 focuses on the ways that transgressive content – especially violence – emerged as a considerable societal problem point during the 1970s, ending up in full-blown outbursts of moral panic in 1980 and 1981. The irony of the liberal permissive Norden is laid bare here as we find that, in fact, these countries had some of the strictest forms of censorship imaginable outside of explicitly politically repressive regimes. Although liberal ideas took hold, in film censorship, a sustained form of conservatism resulted in a massive public and political outcry against violence in films and led to a substantial witch-hunt against, especially, home video consumption in Finland, Norway and Sweden. Films were blamed for societal problems and youth transgression in ways that resemble and preceded the Video Nasties panic in the UK by two years. In 1980 and 1981, the national television services in Sweden, Norway and Denmark, respectively, broadcasted current affairs shows that identified the new VCR technique as 'foreign' and as a seducer and destroyer of children. Sweden was first to initiate this discussion and we illustrate the origins and development of this national example of a moral panic, leading to actual regulations and harsher censorship for the next 15 years. Yet, the chapter concludes on a more optimistic note with an examination of the counterdynamics available to bypass censorship, such as collectives and magazines set up to appreciate prohibited forms of film culture, black markets and a booming import of films from abroad by mail order, and film swapping.

Chapter 5 addresses a range of localized and global exploitation films in the 1980s. By conducting both close readings of individual films and production trends, this chapter explains how directors identified gaps in the domestic markets largely dominated by American films. By capitalizing on the notoriety of violent genre film, they were able to produce indigenous versions that sold both domestically and internationally. The decade saw an increased integration of Nordic film markets into the global mainstream, even as the Film Institute system continued to dominate production. Perhaps more than before, the action and slasher genres emerged as lucrative commercial enterprises, ones that could be, crucially, produced on the cheap and with little production expertise. These genres were also the ones most heavily targeted by the domestic censors, but film producers like Visa Mäkinen and Renny Harlin saw these objections not as an obstacle but an opportunity. The chapter adopts an analytical approach that reads these films as symptomatic of wider national film politics in similar terms to Blake's (2008) analysis of the German *Nekromantic* series, but we also highlight their dynamic roles in their industrial contexts where they both challenge and push the domestic film cultures in new directions – something not often discussed in studies of exploitation cinema.

Chapter 6 consists of a case study of the aggressively globalized form of Nordic exploitation film practised by maverick Swedish filmmaker Mats Helge Olsson. Olsson ran an 'entertainment violence factory' throughout the 1980s in the woods outside of the rural town of Lidköping, far from the establishment in Stockholm. Olsson made his directorial debut with a Lingonberry Western in 1975, and then went on to produce one of the most expensive films in Swedish film history, *Sverige åt svenskarna*, which also became one of its biggest financial failures and resulted in imprisonment for its aspiring producer. Yet, this did not quell Helge Olsson and he would start up anew, and with a group of enthusiasts, he created what was virtually a factory for the production of low-budget exploitation films aimed at the expanding international VHS-market. Starting with *The Ninja Mission* – a Cold War spectacle that cashed in on the ongoing Ninja craze and went on to top the US video rental chart – this underground assembly line factory produced a large number of exploitation films never meant for the domestic cinema circuit, but which were instead distributed internationally with varying success. The chapter focuses on the very conscious exploitation strategies used by Mats Helge Olsson to carve out a market for his productions but also on textual analysis of a sample of the films produced in this film factory, thus exploiting concretely the negative associations of the term 'entertainment violence', used as a repellent for more 'serious' filmmakers and Swedish society.

Chapter 7 investigates the thorough transformations that the Nordic film industries underwent throughout the 1990s and 2000s. After the explicitly oppressive 1980s, Nordic film industries went into a recalibration process in the 1990s, largely driven by society-wide economic depression and a significant decrease in the profitability of domestic film. This led to a fundamental shift in the film policies of all five nations. Exemplary cases are Denmark and Norway's 50/50 policy where a film would be able to get official support if it managed to ascertain half its budget from commercial sources. This meant a shift in the priorities for content as commercialism was no longer shunned but was instead considered a desirable aspect of a film production. These changes in perception led to a very different approach to genre cinema, which we characterize by a politics of proximity and distance where not only the films themselves but the cultural policies, funding decisions, critical commentaries, technological developments and professionalization of film production practices operate on a spectrum of sometimes seemingly paradoxical, but often complex registers. These registers may appear contradictory, at once highlighting explicit commercialism while referencing traditions of experimental art cinema. Yet, it is often this liminality that makes them function as exploitation cinema as they are able to challenge the policy infrastructures and taste cultures of their respective nations in multiple ways.

The 1990s was a time of recalibration when the occasional glimpses of innovation of the 1980s were curtailed by the film industrial circumstances that were largely unfavourable to popular genre production. As the digitalization of film production and distribution fundamentally altered the industry, they also made access to internationally competitive production standards much more feasible. And as more explicit commercial film policies were institutionalized as a direct response to the explicit disinterest in domestic cinema from audiences, Nordic film industries became increasingly integrated into a global film market. Emerging filmmakers who had grown up on a diet of genre product and heavily cut films on VHS seized the opportunities made available by new technologies and produced a wide variety of films that would not have been possible in the past. Now, cycles of particular variations of international genres emerged, such as the Norwegian slasher cycle; a true form of Nordsploitation with films mimicking international formulas but set in enthusiastically Nordic contexts, and crucially, marketed as such.

Chapter 8 provides another case study of a distinct pattern in Nordic exploitation cultures: Nazisploitation. This is a particularly productive case as it comprises an international exploitation genre that delves into some of the most notorious periods in human history but uses these historical developments for visceral thrills. The genre found its peak in the United States and Italy in the 1970s with the 'sadiconazista' variation consisting of explicit exploitation films set at concentration camps and focusing on exploiting nudity and gore. The Nordic variety emerges, on the other hand, as part of a much different context: the networked and innovative film cultures of the 2000s making use of professional advances in creative practices and digital technologies. Films like *Død snø* (*Dead Snow*, 2009) and *Iron Sky* (2012) use the Nazis as both villains and protagonists in comic tales where they both gesture to the Nordic countries' complex history with the Nazis during the Second World War but use them in ways that separates them from this real history. By using the Nazis as pure entertainment simulacra, these films exploit the national past and the contemporary film cultural present. But such flippant uses of history find an uneasy echo point in the present with the rise of real Nazis on the streets and on internet platforms.

Chapter 9 takes up some of the key transformations engendered by digital technologies and increased transnational integration to focus on significant patterns in Nordsploitation in the 2010s. Here, examples range from authentic exploitation like the hard-core rape–revenge film *Hora* (*The Whore*, 2009) to spoof films like *It Came from the Desert* (2017), to innovative 'new' media products like *Kung Fury* (2015). If in the 1980s, the limitations of technological and professional prowess indicated 'rebelliousness' as well as a sought after outsider status, now professional competence was a must-have in relation to industry standards and fan intertextuality. These developments wrap up much of the debate around our two-part concept of exploitation as the distinctions between a more globalized and a locally oriented form of film culture now combine in ways that make any such distinctions difficult to decipher. If Nordic exploitation had in the previous decades struggled with marginalization and legitimacy, by the 2010s Nordsploitation had both become institutionalized into national film policy and consolidated as an identifiable competition strategy.

To reinforce the sense that Nordic exploitation cinema has to be considered distinct from the global 'norms' of transnational exploitation film culture, both in terms of its cultural politics, but also in what kinds of empirical research materials must be included in the analysis, we finish this book with a concluding exploration of Lars von Trier, the enfant terrible of Nordic film, and a discussion of his *The House that Jack Built* (2018). This ending example is a typical case of 'exploitation as art' that tries very hard to become transgressive and upsetting 'exploitation'. However, *The House that Jack Built* is never able to fulfil this aspiration due to the fact that the filmmaker is part of a Nordic auteur tradition and thus, at the same time, part of a national project, where designations of exploitation are to do with not only excessive content but the ways films and filmmakers interact and, literally, exploit policies and funding infrastructures to their benefit. Unpacking these complex and invariably conscious balancing acts between proximity and distance comprises, for us, the essence of film cultural politics defining Nordsploitation.

References

Åberg, Anders Wilhelm (2015), 'Bridges and Tunnels: Negotiating the National in Transnational Television Drama', in Tommy Gustafsson and Pietari Kääpä (eds), *Nordic Genre Film: Small Nation Film Cultures in the Global Marketplace*, Edinburgh: Edinburgh University Press, pp. 91–103.

Barker, Martin (1997), 'The Newsom Report: A Case Study in "Common Sense"', in Martin Barker and Judith Petley (eds), *Ill Effects: The Media/Violence Debate*, London: Routledge, pp. 12–31.

Barry, Christopher (2004), 'Violent Justice: Italian Crime/Cop Films of the 1970s', in Ernest Mathijs and Xavier Mendik (eds), *Alternative Europe: Eurotrash and Exploitation Cinema Since 1945*, London: Wallflower, pp. 77–89.

Bernard, Mark (2015), *Selling the Splat Pack: The DVD Revolution and the American Horror Film*, Edinburgh: Edinburgh University Press.

Björk, Ulf Jonas (2016), 'A Modicum of Social Value? The Critical and Legal Discussion of *I Am Curious (Yellow)* in America', in Elisabet Björklund and Mariah Larsson (eds), *Swedish Cinema and the Sexual Revolution: Critical Essays*, Jefferson, NC: McFarland, pp 201–15.

Björklund, Elisabet and Mariah Larsson (eds) (2016), *Swedish Cinema and the Sexual Revolution: Critical Essays*, Jefferson, NC: McFarland.

Blake, Linnie (2004), 'Jorg Buttgereit's Nekromantiks: Things to Do in Germany with the Dead', in Ernest Mathijs and Xavier Mendik (eds), *Alternative Europe: Eurotrash and Exploitation Cinema Since 1945*, London: Wallflower, pp. 191–202.

Blood Tracks: 'Blodspår – Easy Action sopar igen spåren' (2012), Documentary Featurette, DVD, Studio S Entertainment: Stockholm.

Brinch, Sara and Gunnar Iversen (2006), *Virkelighetsbilder: Norsk dokumentarfilm gjennom hundre år*, Oslo: Universitetsforlaget.

Church, David (2015), *Grindhouse Nostalgia: Memory, Home Video and Exploitation Film Fandom*, Edinburgh: Edinburgh University Press.

Cook, Pam (1985), 'The Art of Exploitation, or How to Get into the Movies', *Monthly Film Bulletin*, 52, December.

Cook, Pam (2005), *Screening the Past: Memory and Nostalgia in Cinema*, London and New York: Routledge.

Dalquist, Ulf (1998), *Större våld än nöden kräver?: Videovåldsdebatten i Sverige 1980–1995*, Umeå: Boréa.

Doherty, Thomas (2002), *Teenagers and Teenpics: The Juvenilization of American Movies in the 1950s*, Philadelphia: Temple University Press.

Ekeroth, Daniel (2011), *Swedish Sensation Films: A Clandestine History of Sex, Thrillers, and Kicker Cinema*, New York: Bazillion Points.

Ferrer, Frank (1963), 'Exploitation Films', *Film Comment*, 2.6, 31–3.

Greene, Doyle (2005), *Mexploitation Cinema: A Critical History of Mexican Vampire, Wrestler, Ape-Man and Similar Films*, Jefferson, NC: McFarland.

Gustafsson, Tommy and Mariah Larsson (2018), 'Sexual Violence, Good Taste and the Education of the Cinema Audience: Gender and Censorship in 1920s Sweden', *Journal of Scandinavian Cinema*, 8 (3), 216–31.

Gustafsson, Tommy and Pietari Kääpä (2015), 'Introduction: Nordic Genre Film and Institutional History', in Tommy Gustafsson and Pietari Kääpä (eds), *Nordic Genre Film: Small Nation Film Cultures in the Global Marketplace*, Edinburgh: Edinburgh University Press, pp. 1–17.

Heffernan, Nick (2015), 'No Parents, No Church, No Authorities in Our Films: Exploitation Movies, the Youth Audience, and Roger Corman's Counterculture Trilogy', *Journal of Film and Video*, 67 (2), 3–20

Higraff, Vegard (2011), *Sensurert: Historien on statents filmkontroll*, Oslo: Kolofon Forlag.

Hitchens, Gordon (1964), 'The Truth, the Whole Truth, and Nothing but the Truth About Exploitation Films', *Film Comment*, 3.2, 1–13.

Hjort, Mette and Duncan Petrie (2007), 'Introduction', in Mette Hjort and Duncan Petrie (eds), *The Cinema of Small Nations*, Edinburgh: Edinburgh University Press.

Kendrick, James (2009), *Film Violence: History, Ideology, Genre*, London and New York: Wallflower Press.

Larsson, Mariah (2017), *The Swedish Porn Scene: Exhibition Contexts, 8mm Pornography and the Sex Film*, Bristol: Intellect.

Mathjis, Ernest (2011), 'Exploitation Film', *Oxford Bibliographies*, https://www.oxfordbibliographies.com/view/document/obo-9780199791286/obo-9780199791286-0096.xml?rskey=T5EL0O&result=1&q=exploitation#obo-9780199791286-0096-div1-0005 (Accessed 16 December 2019).

Mathijs, Ernest and Jamie Sexton (2011), *Cult Cinema: An Introduction*, Malden, MA: Wiley-Blackwell.

Mathijs, Ernest and Xavier Mendik (2004) 'Introduction: Making Sense of Extreme Confusion: European Exploitation and Underground Cinema', in Ernest Mathijs and Xavier Mendik (eds), *Alternative Europe: Eurotrash and Exploitation Cinema Since 1945*, London: Wallflower, pp. 1–18.

Modleski, Tania (2007), 'Women's Cinema as Counterphobic Cinema: Doris Wishman as the Last Auteur', in Jeffrey Sconce (ed.), *Sleaze Artists: At the Margins of Taste, Style, and Politics*, Durham, NC: Duke University Press, pp. 47–70.

Ninja Dixon (2011), 'Blood Tracks (1985)', Ninja Dixon, 15 November, http://ninjadixon.blogspot.com/2011/11/blood-tracks-1985.html (Accessed 7 December 2019).

Nowell, Richard (2011), *Blood Money: A History of the First Teen Slasher Film Cycle*, New York: Continuum.

Prince, Stephen (2000), 'Graphic Violence in the Cinema: Origins, Aesthetic Design, and Social Effects', in Stephen Prince (ed.), *Screening Violence*, New Brunswick, NJ: Rutgers University Press, pp. 1–44.

Roche, David (2015), 'Exploiting Exploitation Cinema: An Introduction', *Transatlantica: Revue d'etudes/American Studies Journal*, 2, 1–19.

Ruetalo, Victoria and Dolores Tierney (eds) (2011), *Latsploitation, Exploitation Cinemas, and Latin America*, New York and London: Routledge.

Schaefer, Eric (1999), *'Bold!, Daring!, Shocking! True!': A History of Exploitation Films, 1919–1959*, Durham and London: Duke University Press.

Sconce, Jeffery (1995), 'Trashing the Academy: Taste, Politics, and an Emerging Politics of Cinematic Style', *Screen*, 3 (4), 371–93.

Sedergren, Jari (1998), *Filmi poikki… Poliittinen elokuvasensuuri Suomessa 1939–1947*, Helsinki: SKS.

Shiel, Mark (2003), 'Why Call Them Trash Movies?', *Scope*, https://www.nottingham.ac.uk/scope/documents/2003/may-2003/shiel.pdf (Accessed 4 July 2019).

Shipka, Danny (2011), *Perverse Titillation: The Exploitation Cinema of Italy, Spain and France, 1960–1980*, Jefferson, NC: McFarland.

Skoglund, Erik (1971), *Filmcensuren*, Stockholm: Pan/Norstedts.

Soila, Tytti, Astrid Söderbergh Widding, and Gunnar Iversen (1998), *Nordic National Cinemas*, London and New York: Routledge.

Solum, Ove (2013), 'Kinolov i hundre år – en introduktion', in Ove Solum (ed.), *Film til folket: Sensur og kinopolitikk i 100 år*, Oslo: Fagbokforlaget, pp. 9–21.

Stevenson, Jack (2010), *Scandinavian Blue: The Erotic Cinema of Sweden and Denmark in the 1960s and 1970s*, Jefferson, NC: McFarland.

Tapper, Michael (2006), 'Körkarlen', in Steven Jay Schneider (ed.), 1001 *filmer du måste se innan du dör*, Stockholm: Wahlström & Widstrand.

Weisser, Thomas (1997), *Asian Cult Cinema*, New York: Boulevard Books.

2

A pre-1970s history of Nordic exploitation

Nordic cinema has a reputation for artistic taste and experimental content, that is, difficult and often non-commercial cinema reliant on state financial support. Yet, alongside and underneath this level of public respectability, several more controversial practices have formed among the film cultures of the region. In contrast to the persistent writing of Nordic film culture as a set of high art and experimental practices (see Soila, Söderbergh Widding and Iversen 1998), this chapter uncovers a prehistory of films and strategies inherent in Nordic cinema that is much more productively addressed in relation to the international literature on exploitation cinema. As with many practices of global exploitation cinema, analysis of these strategies indicates a much more complicated film culture than conventional film history has accepted. This chapter lays out the context for the emergence and existence of these films and strategies and considers domestic societal and moralistic notions that contributed to their formation. We outline a pre-1970s history of content that could be considered exploitative – defined by an interest in violence, sexuality, depictions of transgressive psychological conditions, genre forms, narrative challenges to conventions and authority – in order to trace these key patterns in Nordic film cultures and to outline what constitutes Nordic exploitation cinema beyond the already well-documented Danish and Swedish sexploitation of the 1970s.

To start with, there is no well-established tradition of Nordic exploitation films before the explosion of Danish and Swedish sexploitation in the 1970s. This absence is even more visible concerning exploitation of violence and gore, which is the focus of this study. There are several reasons for this – censorship, state intervention, the politics of the local film industries – which we will untangle along the way. Nonetheless, exploitative elements did exist and pure exploitation films were made. One of the earliest examples is the Swedish documentary short *Göta Elf-katastrofen* ('The Göta Elf Catastrophe', 1908), photographed, edited and directed by Charles Magnusson. Magnusson started his film career as an opportunistic cinematographer and local cinema owner in 1904, filming actualities such as travelogues, royalty and military exercises when, on 15 April 1908, the small canal boat Göta Elf capsized in the harbour of Gothenburg, drowning almost thirty passengers. Magnusson rushed down to the accident site and managed to film the salvage activities, including the macabre recovery of the corpses. The film then had its premiere at Magnusson's two cinemas in Gothenburg the same evening. *Göta Elf-katastrofen* was, subsequently, printed in a large number of copies and shown all over Sweden. In fact, some signs indicate that the film may have been completed with further material from the salvaging of dead bodies – the exploitative element – and distributed for another round. Two days after its Jönköping premiere, Jönköping's Cinema Theater announced: 'To the previously recorded images of the Göta Älf accident are today added images of the salvation of the bodies' (Åhlander 1986: 108). In 1936, projectionist Anders Carlsson was interviewed: 'The salvation was difficult and took a long time. There were divers, people, and boats, and for each "corpse" that was raised, Magnusson was there and took pictures. It was one of the ghastliest films I have ever seen, with corpse after corpse – but the film did great'. Seventy copies were sold across Europe, and the order telegrams flowed in: 'Send me another 40 m of corpses,' one requested (Idestam-Almquist and Allberg 1936: 79; agoraspeaks 2013).

Göta Elf-katastrofen caught the attention of the owners of the up-and-coming cinema company AB Svenska Biografteatern, whose owners considered expanding its operations to include production and therefore asked Magnusson to become the company's CEO. Svenska Biografteatern would, under the direction of Magnusson, change its name to Svensk Filmindustri and develop into Sweden's biggest film company in the following decades (Furhammar 2003: 28). The exploitative business mind of Magnusson would result in outright banned films such as *Trädgårdsmästaren* (*The Broken Springrose*, 1912) – the first Swedish film to be banned by governmental censorship – as well as films that would be considered high art, but always with profit in mind.

Another notable example of early exploitation production is the Danish short film *Løvejagten* (*The Lion Hunt*, 1907), directed by Viggo Larsen, featuring two big game hunters on safari in Africa (in reality, the Danish island of Elleore) where they observe animals and shoot two lions that are gutted and skinned. The exploitative ingredient here was that producer Ole Olsen had bought two old lions from a German zoo that were shot, killed and gutted in front of the camera. The film was first banned in Denmark, but Danes travelled in droves

Figure 2.1 Screen grab from Swedish *Göta-Elf katastrofen*. ('The Göta Elf Catastrophe', 1908). Directed by Charles Magnusson.

over the strait to Malmö in Sweden to see the film (Lorentz 1948: 96). Eventually 259 prints of *The Lion Hunt* were sold all over the world, which earned Nordisk Film Kompagni huge revenues, and marshalled in the 'golden age' of Danish cinema, enabling Nordisk Film to become the most prolific film company in Europe under the direction of Ole Olsen (Thorsen 2017: 24). Olsen and Nordisk Film Kompagi even produced an unofficial sequel, titled *Bjørne jagt i Rusland* ('Bearhunt in Russia', 1908), where five bears were purchased and hunted down in front of the camera (Thorsen 2017: 51).

Göta Elf-katastrofen and *The Lion Hunt*, as well as its producers Magnusson and Olsen, are examples of the unscrupulous climate that governed early cinema culture. In fact, early cinema culture shows similarities with the situation in the United States during the 1950s and 1960s where small distributor–producers dabbled in both exploitative low-budget fair as well as imported highbrow European art films, which were marketed for their sexual content. However, the factor that above all binds these periods together is the absence of actual censorship and the sense of anything goes in these circles. Without a doubt, exploitative films like *Göta Elf-katastrofen* and *The Lion*

Hunt constituted strong reasons that contributed to all the Nordic countries introducing film censorship during the 1910s. Censorship was instituted after lengthy discussions concentrating foremost on indignation over the activities of commercial speculators that profited from children, who were believed to learn criminal activities from these films, and whose moral values were thought to be obliterated by the mere existence of cinemas and flickering films showing, among other unscrupulous things, dead bodies and gutted lions (Klevjer Ros 2013: 89 and Gustafsson and Arnberg 2013: 56–66). Actually, both *Göta Elf-katastrofen* and *The Lion Hunt* were eventually cut and banned when Sweden introduced state film censorship in 1911 as the first country in the world to do so (Åhlander1986: 108).

What is especially noticeable here is the fact that the exploitative element is, and has always been, an inevitable part of the film medium, even in Nordic countries that have prided themselves for their reliance on 'traditional culture' and protection of their citizens by means of censorship. The introduction of state film censorship did not quell this exploitative element. Instead, it would find other ways and outlets, and two internationally established tactics that were applied in the Nordic context concerned the blending of art with exploitation, and the blending of documentary images with exploitative elements.

Exploitation as art/art as exploitation

In the seminal Danish Encyclopedia, *Gyldendal*, 'exploitation film' is defined as follows:

> film type, often cheaply produced, which is promoted based on a sensational topic like sex or violence. Exploitation film has roots far back in film history and Denmark, for example, had great international success with a series of films about prostitution in the early 1900s, among them August Blom's *Den hvide slavehandel* (['The White Slave Trade'] 1910), made possible by the contemporaneously soft Danish censorship laws. (*Gyldendal* 2018)

The encyclopaedia definition of *Den hvide slavehandel* as a low-budget exploitation film is telling from today's viewpoint, but the writing of history, including film history, is a process that almost unavoidably changes and redefines its subject. *Den hvide slavehandel* and *Afgrunden* (*The Abyss*, 1910) were two influential Danish films that clearly played with exploitative issues and that caused, in equal amounts, sensation and indignation when originally released (Engberg 1993: 67). Nonetheless, these films have later been redefined as innovative early examples of film art, and especially as films that spearheaded longer and more artistic films (see, for example, Olsson 1989a: 314 and Thorsen 2017: 86). Another example of this redefinition process is to prescribe these types of films as ones with social importance, which is what Danish film historian Marguerite Engberg does when she provides a political interpretation of these films as 'erotic melodramas' connected to 'the lengthy struggle for [female] equality' around the turn of the century 1900 (Engberg 1993: 63). However, these revisions of history tend to downplay the fact that these films' commercial success was foremost unconnected to any social importance or artistic value but, instead, to their sensational subject matters focusing on white slavery and sex. As film historian Ron Mottram notes, 'Nordisk declared there was a growing tendency toward films of 600 to 900 meters in Europe that exploited sensational subjects – exciting action combined with murder, poisoning, and prostitution' (Mottram 1988: 81). Consequently, these films were regularly either cut or banned all around Europe and in the United States, and by such activities, deemed as immoral and lascivious. Nevertheless, at the same time this scandalous reputation often promoted the sale of Danish films and especially films produced by the Danish Nordisk Film Kompagni, whose sales rocketed over the decade (Thorsen 2017: 94, 177).

The strategy to move into the production of longer films with sensational subjects enabled the parallel manifestations of exploitation as art/art as exploitation in Nordic film culture. These two cinematic paths have seldom been connected to one another in Nordic film studies despite their quite apparent generic and stylistic closeness, as these films have been traditionally received as either art *or* exploitation, as the film-historical examples above showed. Film historian Eric Schaefer has observed that this art/exploitation paradox is as old as the commercial film medium, and that what are often perceived as exploitation films did, indeed, emerge from the mainstream film industry, where 'their origins can be traced to respectable films made with the alleged "good intentions" of decreasing human suffering' (Schaefer 1999: 17).

We will approach *Den hvide slavehandel* and *The Abyss* from this dual perspective to discuss their exploitative elements and their cultural–political position during a turbulent period when film language developed, a cinema culture emerged, and societal authorities would eventually castigate the new film medium through censorship with the desperate intent to curtail its rising popularity. *Den hvide slavehandel* and *The Abyss* have many exploitative traits in addition to their titillating subjects. They could be considered low-budget productions despite their length as three-reelers, since these films were made before their film companies, Nordisk Film Kompagni and Kosmorama, respectively, became producers of serious and more artful films according to the film d'art tradition of the 1910s. Thus, both these films represented very successful ways to commercialize vice under the guise of social messages (Schaefer 1999: 18). What is more, *Den hvide slavehandel* was also a scene-for-scene remake of Danish film company Fotorama's film *Den hvide slavehandel* (*The White Slave Trade*, 1910) that had an extremely successful run at Løvebiografen (The Lion Cinema) in Copenhagen during the spring of 1910. Ole Olsen sent director August Blom to the cinema with the intent to write down every scene, and less than four months later Nordisk released their own version. Comparisons between the two versions reveal 'that not only the plot but also camera angles and the composition of images are remarkably alike' (Thorsen 2017: 77). No attempt was made to hide this blatant plagiarism. On the contrary, Nordisk Film promoted their version as an improvement over Fotorama's original. Fotorama, in turn, answered with ads in the daily press where they warned audiences of the inferior quality of its competitor but also stated that they were not able to take legal action since motion pictures were not protected by copyrights laws ('Advarsel til Publikum' 1910).

Such practices may appear as unscrupulous and as examples of the early film business's dubious morality, but they also testify to the fact that the commercial aspects of the film industry have always been tightly connected to an exploitative streak. Schaefer, for example, highlights the cycle of white slave films as precursors of the exploitation film, pointing out 'their promise of titillation, their professional educational mission, their topicality, and their construction of a social Other' (Schaefer 1999: 18). Danish film scholar Casper Tybjerg points out that the white slave topic – the supposed trafficking of white women for the purpose of prostitution – was prolific with countless variations in novels, dramas and films of the time. Nordisk Film Kompagni had, for example, released a film titled *Den hvide slavinde* ('The White Slave Woman') already in 1907 (Tybjerg 1996: 59–73). And of course, Nordisk Film took the opportunity to cash in on the rush and produced sequels such as *Den hvide slavehandels sidste offer* ('The White Slave Trade II', 1910). Therefore, the question could be not so much who plagiarized whom, but how each of these films fits within the wider popular discourse of the time.

Figure 2.2 Advertising poster for Danish film company Fotorama's original version of *Den hvide slavehandel* (*The White Slave Trade*, 1910).

In any case, *Den hvide slavehandel* is foremost a good example of how contemporary actualities and intertextuality are turned into commercially viable activities within the emerging film industry. These patterns are clearly visible components of the narrative of the film, which focuses on Anna (Ellen Diedrich), a young girl from a poor but honest home. She is offered a well-paid job in London. Her fiancée, Georg (Lauritz Olsen), is somewhat sceptical of the good offer, but Anna rejects his distrust and leaves for London. To Anna's horror, the job turns out to be in a luxurious brothel where Anna is immediately put to work. She is able to protect herself from a viscous rape attempt, almost strangling her attacker, but is not able to escape. Anna manages to smuggle a letter to her parents, who seek the assistance from the Association for Fight against White Slave Trade. Georg travels to London and hires a detective. Together they track down the brothel and liberate Anna, but they are followed by the assailants who, after a wild car chase, violently overwhelm them and steal Anna back. She is now transported to the port to be sold to another country. However, Scotland Yard has been notified. They enter the ship, and after an exciting brawl, Anne is rescued once more and reunited with her family.

As can be observed, the longer format enabled the filmmakers to create a mix of several popular genres of the time, including the chase film, the sensational serials films, and the melodrama (Singer 2001: 189–92). The rape attempt and the two quite violent rescue attempts stand out in this otherwise run-of-the-mill tableau melodrama so common for early North-European film production (See, for example, Forslund 1980; Olsson 1989b; Florin 1997; Thorsen 2017), both due to the explicit and raw violence as well as for the dynamic swiftness with which these scenes were executed. The exploitation elements in these kinds of films were otherwise mostly implemented through the story, and more importantly, via marketing in cinema programmes and advertising where the sensational content would often be heavily exaggerated (Gustafsson 2014: 26).

The inspiration for the white slave films is rather complicated and can be traced to phenomena such as emigration and prostitution, as well as to societal questions of decency. Swedish historian Ann Hallner has studied the real model for the fictive Association for Fight against White Slave Trade in *Den hvide slavehandel*, namely The National Vigilance Association (NVA), which had different national committees in Europe around the turn of the twentieth century. The Swedish committee of the NVA had been very active in their work against regimented prostitution and promoting higher decency among men, trying to educate them about venereal diseases, prostitution and other sex-related subjects in ways that were considered too explicit, even pornographic, thus, consequently losing (male) members in droves. The concentration of the alleged slave trade with white women was, according to Hallner, a policy change implemented to halt this reduction in membership (Hallner 2009: 433–4).

Furthermore, this concern was connected to the great emigration where around 2.5 million people left the Nordic countries for the United States between 1850 and 1920, that is, almost one third of the entire population. At the outset, emigration was seen as of little concern, but as more and more people left the Nordic countries, campaigns in all these countries were instigated in order to stop the drainage of the populations. Moreover, when, especially in the beginning of the twentieth century, single women started to leave Norden in search of prosperity in the United States, these concerns were transformed into warnings of what could happen 'over-there' (Runblom and Norman (eds) 1976: passim: Hallner 2009: 433). In other words, the white slave stories that flooded the market around 1910 were part of a bigger story where nationalistic cries for 'blood and soil' were used as political expressions to elevate race to be the crucial legitimizing factor of a nation. Svenska Biografteatern, headed by Charles Magnusson, produced two films in this vein, *Emigranten* (1910) and *Emigrant* (1910), which were veritable horror stories about the hardships that awaited Swedes in North America, particularly accentuated in *Emigrant* as it includes a notorious anti-Semitic caricature of a Jewish pawnbroker that cheats the main character of his last belongings before he dies alone. Notably, *Emigrant* was part of a series of films called 'Swedish Cinematographic Art' that was meant to launch Svenska Biografteatern as Sweden's most prolific production company, thus providing another instance of blending art with exploitation.

The Abyss, which instantly made Danish actress Asta Nielsen into an international film star, is another example of how the lack of governmental censorship allowed film companies to push the limits of moral decency in order to make even greater profits. The narrative focuses on an actress who betrays her beloved, the son of a priest, to elope with a gypsy circus artist. He, however, soon tires of her and she in turn kills him – the end. As Swedish scholars Bertil Wredlund and Rolf Lindfors comment: 'As you can figure out from the plotline, this is not a film with any literary qualities whatsoever' (Wredlund and Lindfors 1991: 18). Nevertheless, *The Abyss* did have long drawn-out kisses and included two scenes where Asta Nielsen danced, foremost in the 'Gaucho Dance', which evoked strong sexual tensions at the time and became a worldwide sensation. In Norway, the dance scenes were cut (Engberg 1993: 67) but in Sweden, the film was screened with great success when released in October 1910. However, when the Swedish state film censorship came into place in 1911, *The Abyss* was severely cut, including both the dance scenes and the murder scene towards the end (Statens biografbyrå 1911).

State film censorship was introduced in 1911 in Finland and Sweden, followed by Denmark and Norway in 1913. In practice, this meant that Nordic film companies had to negotiate, literately and figuratively, with the film censorship bodies over exactly what the norms for decency, sex, violence and even taste were and how the law should be interpreted. The film production and distribution companies had to face a harsh reality where, during the first decade, one in ten films was banned and one in four films was cut (Gustafsson and Larsson 2018: 227–9; SOU 2009: 46; Furhammar 1986: 22). Danish and Swedish film companies soon adapted their production strategies to these circumstances since an outright banned film could lead to severe financial losses. As part of this process, the explicit exploitative elements that had characterized the early film production diminished in volume (Thorsen 2017: 106). Nevertheless, cinema's negative reputation was prolonged, despite the censorship boards' relentless work, mostly by the circumstances whereby film producers, distributors and cinema owners continued to use alluring and suggestive film titles, by exaggerated descriptions in cinema programmes, and not least of all by the fact that fan magazines, which were not censored, continued to publish nude and semi-nude pictures of stars and even visual material from censored films (Gustafsson 2014: 37–40).

Documentary images with exploitative elements

In addition to these sensationalist fictional narratives, explicit exploitative elements would continue to manifest in the *Aufklärungsfilme* (educational film), most notably in the sex hygiene film and the exotic documentary. Eric Schaefer suggests that the sex hygiene film constituted the true origin for the exploitation film, and that this film type 'moved from being relatively common and accepted to the scourge of the young movie industry' in just a few years. Consequently, a separate industry consolidated around these types of films in America (Schaefer 1999: 18). In Europe, the time span featuring a general acceptance of these type of films seems to have been much longer, however, and they continued to be part of the regular film industry into the sound era, especially as sex hygiene films and exotic documentaries were screened and censored on the same basis as regular films.

A large number of *Aufklärungsfilme* were imported to the Nordic countries, mainly from Germany in the 1910s and then from the United States and the Soviet Union in the 1920s and 1930s. These instructional films used the melodramatic format, with documentary elements, to handle and discuss problems such as pacifism, alcoholism, venereal diseases, prostitution and homosexuality (Björklund 2012: 56–92). One common feature of the films was that they attributed a social status to individual and sexual problems – a social status that was later linked to several different moral declarations (Dyer 2003: 23–9). The way in which these social problems were given shape often bordered on the downright sensational. But owing to the fact that the films were shown under the guise of enlightened pedagogy they were able to make their way through the censorship process surprisingly often. Many educational films were also highly successful features in, for example, the Swedish cinema repertoire.

For instance, the very explicit German STD film *Falsche Scham* ('The Scourge of Humanity', 1926), marketed simultaneously as a pedagogical warning and an audience sensation, managed to squeeze through the censorship board based on the ruling that the film could only be shown separately for men and women, a decision that, of course, only heightened the sense of sensation (Statens biografbyrå 1926). Another example was the Russian *Prostitutka* ('Prostitute', 1926), which was marketed with drawings of nude women and as 'A box-office magnet like few others!' in the cinema owner's journal ('En ny rysk film i stil med "Den gula biljetten"' 1929). Of the latter film, the reviewer in *Stockholms Dagblad* wrote: 'A genuine film with a purpose, ruthless and clearly produced with the best intention to be informative regarding venereal diseases, which are depicted by means of, among other things, tables and gruesome living examples', while the reviewer in *Aftonbladet* noted that the 'alluring title had attracted a full house' (both reviews quoted in 'Prostituerad' 1929).

The fact that these educational films were shown at regular cinemas in competition with regular feature films tended to magnify the sensationalism of their marketing, which in turn led to their credibility being undermined. These critical perspectives thus opened the films to unintentional readings that perceived them as pornographic or otherwise morally dubious, although the truly sensational content often consisted of (perhaps not so sexy) horror images of things like far-gone syphilis wounds. However, the Nordic countries did not produce any sensational *Aufklärungsfilme* during the interwar period. On the contrary, their dubious reputation, especially surrounding their credibility, meant that only one known sex education film was produced in Sweden before the war, namely the animated *Från cell till människa* ('From Cell to Human Being', 1936). During and after the Second World War a number of sex education films were produced, and while these feature films dealt with controversial topics such as abortion and STDs, they were produced by reputable film companies and they included or collaborated with real-world experts, unlike, for example, the American exploitation films produced by small companies outside the mainstream with pretend experts. In addition, the content of the Swedish films was in line with the officially pursued sexuality policy, which means that they could be placed more clearly in the sexual education genre (Björklund 2012: 95–152).

A genre where the explicit visual exploitative element lived on was in the Norwegian and Swedish ethnographic documentary of the late 1910s and 1920s, which shared many characteristics with what Schaefer discusses in relation to the

Figure 2.3 Swedish advertisement for the German STD film *Falsche Scham* ('The Scourge of Humanity', 1926), marketed simultaneously as a pedagogical warning and an audience sensation. *Biografägaren* No. 11, 1926.

American exotic documentary of the 1930s, that is, nudity and the aim to shock and amaze its audiences in different ways (Schaefer 1999: 267–8). In the same way as with the lenient attitude towards the educational film, the censorship boards usually ignored bare breasts and buttocks, and even full-frontal female as well as male nudity, in films that portrayed 'primitive' and thus exotic populations in Africa, Asia and Oceania with eloquent titles such as *In Borneo – The Land of the Head-Hunters* (1920), *Blandt Syd-Amerikas Urskovsindianere* ('Among Amazon Indian's in South American', 1922), *Bland vildar och vilda djur* (*Among Savages and Wild Animals*, 1920) and *Med prins Wilhelm på afrikanska jaktstigar* (*On Safari in Africa with Prince Wilhelm*, 1922) (Brinch and Iversen 2006: 45–50; Gustafsson 2014: 160–6). In Swedish film history, these exotic documentary films are classified as 'the first great period for Swedish documentary film' (Furhammar 2003: 70) and in Norwegian film history, these 'travel films' are seen as the lever for the development of the feature length documentary film (Brinch and Iversen 2006: 46).

Modern wildlife documentaries usually treat one species of animal and seldom look at a whole habitat in order to avoid the risk of comparing humans to animals. Another difference is that modern wildlife documentaries attempt to convey a measure of ecological understanding and knowledge of the animals' manner of living (Chris 2006: 30, 60, 77). The exotic Nordic documentary of the 1920 is completely different. These films dealt with the whole habitat, primarily aiming to 'discover' and display rather than to portray and create understanding. This was evident from the ways the films would include depictions of Nordic men in constant engagement with big-game hunting – a phenomenon that would never be included in a modern wildlife documentary. In this way, people, animals and nature were reduced to commercial attractions and sensations, all under the guise of documentary science that verged on the exploitative (Gustafsson 2014: 160–1).

These full-length documentary films contain sensational elements such as comparisons between Africans and dead gorillas, staged footage showing the cowardice of 'natives' as compared to the 'courageous' Nordic white hunters, endless hunt scenes where animals are killed in front of the camera, and last but not least, 'humorous' dance scenes where the camera is cranked too fast in order to make the indigenous dancers look foolish. It should be emphasized that these constructions of non-white ethnicities had commercial motives that drew from the cultural mores of the time. For instance, the Swedish government did not support the film industry until the 1960s. This meant that Swedish production companies' investment in wildlife documentaries had to pay off in the cinema repertoire before these 'anthropological' films were loaned out, free of charge, to schools for educational purposes. Making the films 'amusing' was, thus, a highly conscious narrative device used to entice family audiences to the cinema, because wildlife films had a reputation for being deadly dull in comparison with the latest Swedish comedy or American melodramas (See, for example, Berg 1924; O S 1925; Anon. 1927).

Schaefer remarks that the Great Depression of the 1930s was a decisive factor for the emergence and consolidation of exploitative elements in the American educational film and the exotic documentary as it 'offered images of a way of life unconstrained by pressures of the modern consumer economy under capitalism' (Schaefer 1999: 271). That is, the exploitative elements were framed as pure entertainment in these low-budget films produced outside the Hollywood

Figure 2.4 Screen grab from Swedish documentary film *Med prins Wilhelm på afrikanska jaktstigar* (*On Safari in Africa with Prince Wilhelm*, 1922), displaying the 'humorous' comparison between the backs of a black man and a dead mountain gorilla. Courtesy of Svensk Filmindustri.

system. Nordic films in the same genre were, in contrast, expensive productions with two essential purposes: to elevate the film industry's tarnished reputation through the cultural value of education, and to promote the nation-state through nationalist ideologies and the concept of national cinemas. The latter approach was especially evident in the rave reviews that these documentaries received at the time of their premieres (see, for example, Anon. 1921; Anon. 1922; -bis 1922). The Nordic exotic documentary was, in other words, a kind of colonial endeavour without the actual colonizing process during a time when white adventures and explorers mapped the so-called dark corners of the world.

The resemblance of these films to the Italian Mondo tradition, starting with the critically praised *Mondo Cane* (1962), is explicit, not least in the mix of the exploitative and educational elements. However, in suggesting this comparison, the commercial reasons for Mondo films should be highlighted here as they contrast with the often 'idealistic' aims of the documentary genre but that, in fact, affect the claims to reality and 'truth' by documentary filmmakers of such exploitative anthropological films. Humour, explicit nudity and shock are all ingredients that are put into play in both the Nordic and Mondo films. Yet, the crucial difference between the two is that the early Mondo films had at their core a sensational presentation of the world, whereas the Nordic exotic documentary of the 1920s and 1930s was presented and received as the truth, regardless of staged sequences and unethical and aesthetically angled presentations of their subject matter, all, crucially, framed in the guise of a nationalist project. This last element is significant in that it sets these productions apart from, for example, the Mondo features and establishes an important precursor for future directions in Nordic exploitation cinema, where Nordic production strategies and international trends would exist in complex modes of dialogue, especially in the ways international trends would be incorporated into the specific film cultural and industrial contexts of these five countries.

The absence of exploitation

The 1940s through to the 1960s was a period that saw an absence of the type of exploitative explicit sex and violence that had distinguished the pre-war film. The most significant reason for this absence was the fact that all the Nordic countries had by now strict film censorship laws that were rigorously enforced, combined with the fact that these industries operated in the restricted confines of small nations. They did not have room or market scope for independent filmmaking with alternative distribution routes as was the case in the United States where the production code was undermined by a range of low-budget film companies that catered to young audiences at drive-ins and grindhouse cinemas in the 1950s and 1960s, creating the era of 'classic exploitation' (Sanders and Sanders 2003: 92–115). Accordingly, Nordic film companies had to learn how to navigate the censorship policies, and, as a consequence, the process of outright banning Nordic film productions thus became very rare. For instance, only one Norwegian film was banned during this period, *To mistenkeliga personer* ('Two suspicious people', 1950). Yet, this film, regarded as one of the best Norwegian films of the period, was not banned for violence or nudity but because it depicted real persons who sued the filmmakers (Iversen 2011: 185–7). One notable Swedish example was *Det händer i natt* ('It Happens Tonight', 1956) that was banned no less than two times by the censors, despite it being a parody of the American gangster film (Statens biografbyrå 1956 and 1958). In 1964, the Swedish film *491* was banned for its depiction of sexualized violence, but after a fierce public debate on film, art and censorship, *491* was released with four cuts (Statens biografbyrå 1964), thus paving the way for a more lenient attitude towards depictions of sexuality. These debates in Sweden led to the commissioning of two public inquiries, one on censorship and one on the limits of freedom of speech that both proposed the abolishment of film censorship and the removal of the obscenity clause in the Swedish penal code (Björklund 2016: 126). As a result, pornography was legalized in 1971 but censorship of film violence remained in place until 2011.

The same debates took place in the other Nordic countries, but with rather different outcomes. Denmark abolished film censorship for adults in 1969, thus paving the way for sex comedies and outright explicit pornographic film production. In Norway, this shift did not occur, mostly due to stricter censorship and the fact that Norwegian cinemas were run by municipalities (Henriksen 2016: 9). In Finland, an even stricter film censorship met cinematic depictions of sex and violence, with a range of notorious instances of domestic films receiving cuts of several minutes or being laden with high taxation designated for morally dubious productions (Pantti 1998: 118; Sedergren 2006: 320–4). Films such as *Jengi* (*The Gang*, previously titled *Take Me When Young*, 1963) was hit by a 10 per cent tax rate and over five minutes of cuts (as well as a mandated name change) while *Sensuela* (1973), by the revered Golden Age director Teuvo Tulio, was the first domestic film to receive an 18 rating and a 30 per cent tax rate (later reduced to 10 per cent after over four minutes of cuts). Both films featured storylines about young adults being corrupted by the vices of the big city, leading to their producers, rather predictably, to claim that their depiction of youthful promiscuity and aggression was socially motivated.

Obviously, violence was depicted in Nordic films but in moderate amounts that were carefully curtailed via both legal censorship and the self-censorship that followed. One could suggest that Nordic filmmakers tried to exploit subjects, such as youth crime, but they had to do this without explicitly exploitative elements such as raw violence and gore for fear of having their profit margins restricted by censorship. This also affected the import of films, where all those films that Schaefer discusses in his seminal study on the American exploitation film (1999) never reached the Nordic countries and their national censorship boards, where they most likely would have been banned or so heavily cut that it would have been unprofitable to screen them.

However, two films that explicitly connected with the transnational flow of American exploitation cinema should be mentioned as they clearly fall in line with the exploitative low-budget American science fiction film of the late

Figure 2.5 Screen grab from Danish-American sci-fi monster film *Reptilicus* (1961), taking place at Raadhuspladsen in central Copenhagen. Courtesy of Studio S Entertainment.

1950s: the American-Swedish co-production *Rymdinvasion i Lappland* ('Space Invasion in Lapland', 1959) and Danish-American co-production *Reptilicus* (1961). The fact that both films have become cult items and were co-productions with American film companies means that they can be addressed as part of the general trend where American studios sought cooperation with European producers to get access to cheaper studios, locations and tax relief as well as due to the growing importance of overseas markets. In fact, *Rymdinvasion i Lappland* was heavily recut with new scenes and actors and released as *Invasion of the Animal People* (1962) in the United States. This was a low-budget film directed by Virgil W Vogel, who had previously worked as an editor, most notably on Orson Welles' *Touch of Evil* (1955), but who went on to direct television series such as *Bonanza* (1959–73), *Centennial* (1978–9), *Magnum, P.I.* (1980–8) and *Miami Vice* (1984–90). The 'Animal People' in the film consisted of a six-metres-tall alien that lands in the most-northern and snowy part of Sweden and is then hunted down by scientists. The violence is moderate, but the Swedish Board of Film Censorship deemed it as R-rated (Statens biografbyrå 1959).

The second film *Reptilicus* (1961) saw none other than American International Pictures (AIP) contribute the American component to this Danish-American co-production. The film was made in Denmark with Danish actors, but in two versions, one in Danish directed by the Dane Poul Bang, and one in English for the American market, directed by Sidney W Pink. *Reptilicus* was part of the Godzilla craze that followed after the original Japanese *Gojira* (*Godzilla*, 1954) became an international success, and it was in fact the second collaboration between Pink and Danish-born but neutralized American screenplay writer Ib Melchior after their success with *The Angry Red Planet* (1959), also an AIP release. Curiously, this film also starts up North, as a mining engineer finds the frozen tail of a prehistoric lizard. The tail is brought back to Denmark's Aquarium, where it defrosts and regenerates, ending up growing into a giant lizard known as Reptilicus. The beast breaks free and spreads horror in Denmark, and the Danish army eventually confronts it at Copenhagen City Hall Square with a bazooka full of anaesthetics.

Both these science fiction/monster films were anomalies in Nordic film production at the time. Swedish reviewers, for example, dismissed *Rymdinvasion i Lappland* as 'unnecessary' (Enra 1959) and a 'lifeless space fantasy' (e.g. 1959). Still, both productions gesture forward to state-funded genre films like the Norwegian *Trolljegeren* (*Trollhunter*, 2010) and *Gåten Ragnarok* (*Ragnarok: The Viking Apocalypse*, 2013), but now built around Nordic mythologies instead of international exploitation/monster connotations (Gustafsson 2015: 199–200), as well as wilder self-conscious (retro-)exploitation films like *It Came from the Desert* (2017) and *Bunny the Killer Thing* (2015), which would in the 2010s return back to these more internationalized dynamics.

In addition to these international genre emulations, further developments in the Nordic film cultures took place from the 1950s to the 1970s with regard to how the limits for depictions of violence were met and eventually pushed to more extreme margins. American studio productions, which dominated Nordic cinema screens, were routinely cut (but more seldomly banned) for violence and on moral grounds for exhibiting 'bad taste'. That is, films could be banned or cut for being 'worthless' by the censorship bodies, although 'quality' was not a legal ground that the law covered (Bengtsson 1998: 307). That left Hollywood productions already hampered by the Production Code as harmless, or as Swedish censor Hans Haste put it in 1957: 'The fist fights in American films are a kind of folklore, a form of ballet and should not be taken seriously' (quoted in Bengtsson 1998: 330). However, this moral stance against violence came to be challenged by the European film, by both genre films verging on the exploitative and art films that pushed the boundaries for what the film medium would be allowed to depict for general audiences. And as Nordic genre films often tried to bypass censorship laws with the uses of comedy, satire and dream sequences, the art film used the shield of social realism to push the boundaries. For example, Ingmar Bergman's *Jungfrukällan* (*The Virgin Spring*, 1960) – later remade as the exploitation horror film *The Last House on the Left* (1972) – caused heated debates when the censorship board released it without any cuts based on its 'artistic qualities' (Statens biografbyrå 1960; Åhlander 1977: 66). The release of the violent scenes in *The Vigin Spring* was an extreme exception to the rule. At its Stockholm world premiere, fifteen audience members walked out during the screening, and several left weeping due to the intense rape scene (Balio 2010: 139). The editor-in-chief for Sweden's largest daily *Dagens Nyheter*, Olof Lagercrantz, accused Bergman for exploitation, saying, '[w]here spirit and soul should have been we only hear the rattling of dead mechanics. I have nothing against a theatrical jesting game but call it what it is – buffoonery' (Lagercrantz 1960).

The European art film, of course, affected the Hollywood film industry, thus contributing to a large degree to the New Hollywood renaissance that, among other things, presented explicit and stylized violence in the guise of art in significant films such as *Bonnie and Clyde* (1967), *The Dirty Dozen* (1967), *Easy Rider* (1969) and *The Wild Bunch* (1969), all of which passed through the Swedish censorship without a single cut. This leniency towards exploitation as art/art as exploitation did not apply to the exploitation of violence by domestic filmmakers in the Nordic countries, regardless if these efforts were stylistically addressed as art, as can be seen from the critical furore that greeted Bergman's film or the censorship impositions with *The Gang*, for one. Consequently, similar developments as witnessed with New Hollywood in the United States or with respected filmmakers like Pier Paolo Pasolini in Italy cannot be detected in the Nordic countries when it comes to violence, not even in Denmark, the most permissive of the Nordic countries when it came to sexuality.

Conclusion

Although largely an anomaly in Nordic film culture, exploitation cinema in its many disguises has continually existed on the fringes of these small national film industries. Censorship, state intervention and the politics of these local film industries kept much of the explicit exploitative elements at bay as film production faced a constant struggle with cultural authorities and commentators that tried their best to be respectable. Nonetheless, early Danish and Swedish film producers unscrupulously exploited sex, violence and sensations in order to make a profit. In fact, two of the biggest and most important film companies, Nordisk Film Kompagni and Svenska Biografteatern/Svensk Filmindustri, benefitted from such practices, which created a financial base for the expansion into larger and more reputable productions, as well as the opportunity to expand internationally. When state censorship quelled these exploitative trends, exploitative elements moved on to the imported *Aufklärungsfilme* as well as to the locally produced and prestigious high-budget exotic documentary film, with its images of nudity, shock and animal violence.

The 1940s and 1950s saw an extended period of absence of exploitation, mostly due to the extremely harsh film censorship in all five Nordic countries, but also because Nordic film cultures did not have the numerical population for a specialized teenage market that corresponded to the circumstances that Schaefer describes in the classical period of exploitation in the United States (Schaefer 1999). However, the 1960s saw heated debates about liberalization, including about the freedom of speech and film censorship, where many insisted that film was art and that this should allow them the liberty to depict sex and nudity as well as realistic violence on the cinema screen for adult audiences. Although Denmark and Sweden decriminalized pornography, and Denmark even abolished film censorship for adults in 1969, Finland, Norway and Iceland did not follow suit and insisted on their hard censorship policies towards the film medium in place. And although Denmark and Sweden were flooded by soft and hard-core pornography films in the late 1960s and throughout the 1970s, cinematic violence and gore were still, as we will see in Chapter 3, an abnormal part of the practices of film producers, film critics and film censorship authorities.

References

'Advarel til Publikum' (1910), Advertisement in *Politiken*, 5 August.
Agoraspeaks [pseudonym] (2013), '1908', *Göteborgs biografer*, https://kinnegbg.wor dpress.com/2013/06/23/1908/ (Accessed 7 June 2019).
Åhlander, Lars (ed.) (1977), *Svensk filmografi 6 1960–1969*, Stockholm: Svenska filminstitutet.

Åhlander, Lars (ed.) (1986), *Svensk filmografi 1 1897–1919*, Stockholm: Svenska filminstitutet.
Anon. (1921),'Bland vildar och vilda djur', Review, *Stockholms Dagblad*, 29 November.
Anon. (1922), 'Med prins Wilhelm på afrikanska jaktstigar', Review, *Göteborgs-Posten*, 2 March.
Anon. (1927), 'Negerdans på film sprider glädje både på bio och i skolsal', *Filmnyheter* No. 6.
Balio, Tino (2010), *The Foreign Film Renaissance on American Screens, 1946–1973*, Madison, WI: University of Wisconsin Press.
Bengtsson, Bengt (1998), *Ungdom i fara: Ungdomsproblem i svensk spelfilm 1942-62*, Uppsala: Stockholm University.
Berg, Bengt (1924), 'Bengt Berg om sin elefantfilm samt om bildningsfilmen, publiken, staten, operan m.m.', *Tidskrift för svensk skolfilm och bildningsfilm*, No. 4.
-bis [pseudonym] (1922), 'Filmpremiärer', *Stockholms-Tidningen*, 14 March.
Björklund, Elisabet (2012), *The Most Delicate Subject: A History of Sex Education Films in Sweden*, Lund: Critica Litterarum Lundensis.
Björklund, Elisabet (2016), 'The Limits of Sexual Depictions in the Late 1960s', in Elisabet Björklund and Mariah Larsson (eds), *Swedish Cinema and the Sexual Revolution: Critical Essays*, Jefferson, NC: McFarland, pp. 126–38.
Brinch, Sara and Gunnar Iversen (2006), *Virkelighetsbilder: Norsk dokumentarfilm gjennom hundre år*, Oslo: Universitetsforlaget.
Chris, Cynthia (2006), *Watching Wildlife*, Minneapolis and London: University of Minnesota Press.
Dyer, Richard (2003), *Now You See It: Studies in Lesbian and Gay Film*, London and New York: Routledge.
-eg [pseudonym] (1959), 'Rymdinvasion i Lappland', Review, *Östergötlands Folkblad*, 20 August.
Engberg, Marguerite (1993), 'The Erotic Melodrama in Danish Silent Films 1910–1918', *Film History*, 5, 63–7.
'En ny rysk film i stil med "Den gula biljetten"' (1929), Advertisement, *Biografägaren* No. 11.
Enra [pseudonym] (1959), 'Rymdinvasion i Lappland', Review, *Norrköpings Tidningar*, 20 Augusti.
Florin, Bo (1997), *Den nationella stilen: studier i den svenska filmens guldålder*, Stockholm: Stockholm's University.
Forslund, Bengt (1980), *Victor Sjöström: hans liv och verk*, Stockholm: Bonniers.
Furhammar, Leif (1986), 'Från pionjärår till storhetstid. Kap 1: Svensk film 1897–1911', in Lars Åhlander (ed.), *Svensk filmografi 1 1897–1919*, Stockholm: Svenska filminstitutet, pp. 9–23.
Furhammar, Leif (2003), *Filmen i Sverige: En historia i tio kapitel och en fortsättning*, Stockholm: Svenska filminstitutet and Dialogos.

Gustafsson, Tommy and Klara Arnberg (2013), *Moralpanik och lågkultur: genus- och mediehistoriska analyser 1900-2012*, Stockholm: Atlas bokförlag.

Gustafsson, Tommy (2014), *Masculinity in the Golden Age of Swedish Cinema: A Cultural Analysis of 1920s Films*, Jefferson, NC: McFarland.

Gustafsson, Tommy (2015), 'Slasher in the Snow: The Rise of the Low-Budget Nordic Horror Film', in Tommy Gustafsson and Pietari Kääpä (eds), *Nordic Genre Film: Small Nation Film Cultures in the Global Marketplace*, Edinburgh: Edinburgh University Press, pp. 189-202.

Gustafsson, Tommy and Mariah Larsson (2018), 'Sexual Violence, Good Taste and the Education of the Cinema Audience: Gender and Censorship in 1920s Sweden', *Journal of Scandinavian Cinema*, 8 (3), 217-33.

Gyldendal (2018), 'Exploitation-Film', Available Online: http://denstoredanske.dk/Kunst_og_kultur/Film/Filmgenrer_og_-perioder/exploitation-film (Accessed 26 November 2018).

Hallner, Ann (2009), 'Från vit slavhandel till trafficking: En studio om föreställningar kring människohandel och dess offer', *Historisk Tidskrift*, 129 (3), 429-43.

Henriksen, Marius (2016), 'Norsk og dansk filmhistorie: En komparativ studie om hvordan filmpolitikk påvirker produksjon av film mellom Norge og Danmark i perioden 1960-2000', unpublished Master dissertation, Institutt for arkeologi, konservering og historie, Oslo: Oslo University.

Idestam-Almquist, Bengt and Ragnar Allberg (1936), *Vid den svenska filmens vagga*, Stockholm: Albert Bonniers förlag.

Iversen, Gunnar (2011), *Norsk filmhistorie: Spillefilmen 1911-2011*, Oslo: Universitetsforlaget.

Klevjer Ros, Nils (2013), 'Veien till kinoloven 1907-1913', in Ove Solum (ed.), *Film till Folket: Sensur og kinopolitik i 100 år*, Bergen: Fagbokforlaget.

Lagercrantz, Olof (1960), 'Jungfrukällan', Review, *Dagens Nyheter*, 12 February.

Lorentz, Gunnar (1948), 'Från Lejonjakten i Obsis' park till björnscenen i Dalby hage', *Biografbladet*, 2, 95-6.

Mottram, Ron (1988), '"The Great Northen Film Company": Nordisk Film in the American Motion Picture Market', *Film History*, 2, 71-86.

Olsson, Jan (1989a), 'Liebe Macht Blind and Frans Lundberg: Some Observations on National Cinema with International Ambitions', *Film History*, 3, 307-16.

Olsson, Jan (1989b), *Sensationer från en bakgård: Frans Lundberg som biografägare och filmproducent i Malmö och Köpenhamn*, Stockholm: Symposion.

O. S. (pseudonym) (1925), 'Abu Markúb och hundra elefanter. Bengt Bergs film och föredrag om resan uppför Nilen', *Tidskrift för svensk skolfilm och bildningsfilm*, No. 8.

Pantti, Mervi (1998), *Kaikki muuttuu...: elokuvakulttuurin jälleenrakentaminen Suomessa 1950-luvulta 1970-luvulle*, Turku: Suomen elokuvatutkimuksen seura.

'Prostituerad' (1929), Advertisement, Biografägaren No. 13.

Runblom, Harald and Hans Norman (eds) (1976), *From Sweden to America: A History of the Migration*, Uppsala: Acta University Upsaliensis.

Sanders, Don and Susan Sanders (2003), *The American Drive-In Movie Theater*, St Paul, NM: Motorbooks International.

Schaefer, Erik (1999), *Bold! Daring! Shocking! True!: A History of Exploitation Films, 1919–1959*, Durham and London: Duke University Press.

Sedergren, Jari (2006),*Taistelu elokuvasensuurista: valtiollisen elokuvatarkastuksen historia*, Helsinki: SKS.

Singer, Ben (2001), *Melodrama and Modernity: Early Sensational Cinema and Its Contexts*, New York: Columbia University Press.

Soila, Tytti, Astrid Söderbergh Widding, and Gunnar Iversen (1998), *Nordic National Cinemas*, London and New York: Routledge.

SOU (2009), *Avskaffande av filmcensuren för vuxna: men förstärkt skydd för barn och unga mot skadlig mediepåverkan: betänkande 2009: 51*, Stockholm: Fritze.

Statens biografbyrå (1911), Censorship Card for *The Abyss*, Stockholm: Riksarkivet, Statens biografbyrås arkiv, 1.998.

Statens biografbyrå (1926), Censorship Card for *Falsche Scham*, Stockholm: Riksarkivet, Statens biografbyrås arkiv, 37.426.

Statens biografbyrå (1956), Censorship Card for *Det händer i natt*, Stockholm: Riksarkivet, Statens biografbyrås arkiv, 88.933.

Statens biografbyrå (1958), Censorship Card for *Det händer i natt*, Stockholm: Riksarkivet, Statens biografbyrås arkiv, 91.567.

Statens biografbyrå (1959), Censorship Card for *Rymdinvasion i Lappland*, Stockholm: Riksarkivet, Statens biografbyrås arkiv, 93.850.

Statens biografbyrå (1960), Censorship Card for *Jungfrukällan*, Stockholm: Riksarkivet, Statens biografbyrås arkiv, 95.321.

Statens biografbyrå (1964), Censorship Card for *491*, Stockholm: Riksarkivet, Statens biografbyrås arkiv, 101.516.

Thorsen, Isak (2017), *Nordisk Films Kompagni 1906-1924: The Rise and Fall of the Polar Bear*, Herts and Bloomington, IN: John Libbey Publishing.

Tybjerg, Casper (1996), *An Art of Silence and Light*, unpublished PhD-dissertation, Copenhagen: Københavns Universitet.

Wredlund, Bertil and Rolf Lindfors (1991), *Långfilm i Sverige 1910–1919*, Stockholm: Proprius.

3

Exploitative violence and pornography in the 1970s

After the abolishment of the so-called porn paragraphs in Denmark (1969) and Sweden (1971), both countries dived headlong into the sexploitation wave where, for example, almost 20 per cent of all Swedish feature films of the 1970s would exploit sex in some way (Furhammar 2003: 328–9). The Danes, on their side, scored a number of huge commercial successes with two series of soft-core and hard-core porn films, respectively, the Bedside films series (seven films, 1970–6) and the Zodiac films series (six films, 1973–8), disguised as sex comedies and erotic comedies (Nissen 1997: 91). However, the exploitation of violence and gore continued to be an anomaly in these film cultures. An exception could be made with the two Danish Kartoffelwesterns (Potato Westerns), *Præriens skrappe drenge* (*Tough Guys of the Prairie*, 1970) and *Guld til præriens skrappe drenge* (*Gold for the Tough Guys of the Prairie*, 1971), which included some violence but foremost these films were parodies of the Italian Spaghetti Western with elements of soft-core pornography. In addition to these Danish takes on the Western film, the Swedish variant, the Lingonberry Western, resulted in three instalments, the parody *Wild West Story* (1964) – starring, among others, American Gerald Mohr, the lead actor in *The Angry Red Planet* – as well as the intense and hence R-rated films *I död mans spår* ('Dead Man's Trail', 1975) and *The Frozen Star* (1977). In *I död man spår*, for example, a rape attempt and drowning scene were cut before its release (Statens biografbyrå 1975c).

Nevertheless, in this heap of nudity and pornography, a handful of filmmakers and films tried their best to go all the way with the literally forbidden portrayal of violence and gore for the sake of entertainment and commercial shock value. Here we will discuss six films produced in Denmark and Sweden in the early 1970s that, by all accounts, stand out in the Nordic context of sex films as they combined hard-core sex with twisted violent stories that even surpassed their American counterparts. The six films took highly dissimilar approaches to genre conventions, dabbling with crime, horror and psychological drama, but the three common denominators across all of them were sex scenes combined with violence and gore, extremely harsh treatment by the censors and an utterly abhorrent reception from the critics. Curiously enough, all but one of these films were released, or were at least planned to have been released, in 1973, but due to censorship troubles, some of the films were delayed for several years.

First out was *Smutiga fingrar* ('Dirty Fingers', 1973), a hardboiled crime story directed by Arne Mattsson, forever iconized as the director of *Hon dansade en sommar* (*One Summer of Happiness*, 1951) that greatly contributed to the creation of the image of the 'The Swedish Sin' around the world. *Smutsiga fingrar* was, according to Mattsson, based on authentic police reports and told the story of how a female drug addict commits suicide after a bad trip. Her brother and his friend then try to track down the dealers, leading them into the unforgiving underworld of Stockholm. The film was initially banned by the censorship board but the Swedish Film Review Council, an advisory governmental body, decided to release it after four cuts (Åhlander1988: 184; Statens biografbyrå 1972).

The sheer commercialism and capitalization on violence was definitely considered as a novel attribute of the film, and although it was marketed as an 'International thriller in color' on the posters, it was still made in Swedish and, to our knowledge, only exported to Norway, although it would have an afterlife on VHS on the Nordic video market. *Smutsiga fingrar* could thus be categorized in the localized form of exploitation. Nonetheless, *Smutsiga fingrar* originally included exploitative scenes like never seen before in a Nordic feature film, for example, explicit torture scenes, a scene where a man's face is torn to pieces by a razor-covered glove and a scene where a drugged-out girl is sexually abused. Unsurprisingly, the critics loathed *Smutsiga fingrar* and called it a 'violent pornographic bread roll party' (Bergström 1973). In a more elaborate analysis, another critic wrote, 'A speculation such as this may possibly make the cash register ping somewhere, but for Mattsson's artistic reputation, this gold fever is catastrophic' (Nordberg 1973). *Smutsiga fingrar* was made towards the end of Mattsson's very long directing career, and his films had gotten bad reviews for quite some time by then, something that contributed to the fact that he left Sweden and continued to make films in Yugoslavia, where he had already directed the Swedish-Yugoslavian sexploitation film *Ann och Eve – de erotiska* (*Ann and Eve*, 1970). However, he returned to Sweden for his final directional effort in collaboration with Mats Helge Olsson in *The Mad Bunch* (1989).

Exploitative Violence and Pornography in the 1970s   57

Figure 3.1 The original 'big box' artwork for *Smutsiga fingrar* (*Dirty Fingers*, 1973). Circa 1980. Courtesy of Frekvensia GeTe AB.

Smutsiga fingrar was made outside of the system – produced by the notorious film producer Inge Ivarson, most famous for the educational sexploitation film *Ur kärlekens språk* (*Language of Love*, 1969) – and only managed to stay for three weeks in Stockholm's cinemas. Inge Ivarson wrote the screenplay and produced our second example of a film that drew from this pool of porn and violence, *Skräcken har 1000 ögon* (*Fear Has 1000 Eyes*, 1973). This film was directed by Torgny Wickman, who also directed a string of sexploitation films, among those *Language of Love*. *Fear Has 1000 Eyes* is noteworthy because it is one of the earliest Nordic films that ventured into the horror genre. Released in 1973, the film had actually been completed already in the spring of 1970 with a limited release in ten countryside towns during the same autumn. The release pattern for the film is unusual as the first version that passed censors without cuts had been ninety-nine minutes long, but then, two years later, the distributor handed in a shortened version of eighty-one minutes, which was shown in Stockholm cinemas around Christmas 1973. The censorship card reads 'Still yellow' for this second round with the censors, meaning that the film was still unfit for children under the age of fifteen (Statens biografbyrå 1970). It is unknown why the distributors shelved the film for more than three years, before re-releasing it. Reviews in the rural papers for the first version were generally bad, with reviewers constantly complaining about the seemingly unnecessary attempts to 'mix in pornography at all costs to attract audiences' (Neglin 1970).

In an interview with Inge Ivarson on the DVD-release of *Fear Has 1000 Eyes*, he states that 'We sold all our films on the fact that we had a little sex tinge' and claims that this film made up its costs in Sweden and then did well abroad (*Skräcken har 1000 ögon*: 'Bolmört i mitt öra' 2005). Unlike *Smutsiga fingrar*, *Fear Has 1000 Eyes* got international distribution in countries like France (*Les envoutées*), Finland (*Natten har tusen ögon*), UK (*Fear Has 1000 Eyes*), United States (*Sensuous Sorceress*) and Italy (*Giochi erotici di una giovane assassina*), the latter country probably for the reason that the film's female star, Anita Sanders, had a minor career as a blond bombshell in Italy, where she made topless appearances in, among other films, Federico Fellini's *Giulietta degli spiriti* (*Juliet of the Spirits*, 1965) and Pier Paolo Pasolini's *I racconti di Canterbury* (*Canterbury Tales*, 1972).

Fear Has 1000 Eyes is set in an isolated Swedish manor house. It is winter, which gives an exotic Nordic spice to funfair horror ingredients such as 'voodoo' and devil worship, not often associated with the cold and snow. A young priest lives in the manor house with his pregnant wife (played by Anita Sanders), and in order for her to have some company, the man arranges for her friend Hedvig

Figure 3.2 Screen grab from Swedish *Skräcken har 1000 ögon* (*Fear Has 1000 Eyes*, 1973). Courtesy of Klubb Super 8 Video.

to visit. Hedvig, however, has unbeknownst to the others given herself to the Devil and now she uses her powers to bring about one horror after another, often with sexual overtones and several times with fatal outcome. Beyond the generous doses of nudity and soft-core sex, we get comparatively moderate amounts of violence, but this includes a chopped-off head (three years before *The Exorcist*, 1973) and the ritual cutting of an upside-down cross into a bare breast as part of the action-filled ending.

The second batch of reviews agreed with each other and complained about the editing, the 'story's complete lack of comprehensibility and logic' (Schiller 1973), and 'that it seems as if the order of the scenes has been drawn in a lottery' (Brossner 1973). Something is surely missing in the eighteen minutes that the distributor had shortened from the film, perhaps more hard-core scenes, according to the first batch of reviews, but most likely the climaxes of the scenes since all of them end abruptly and we are quickly transported to the next unfulfilled scene.

In Denmark, two violent sexploitation films were produced in 1973. *Englene* ('Angels', 1973), of which only fragments have survived, is a biker film and according to Danish film scholar Isak Thorsen, the film included a scene where 'young candidates for confirmation and their parents sit in a church when the bikers enter and begin harassing them, the parents flee and the priest tries to protect the candidates but is crucified while the young female candidates either have sex or are raped in front of the altar' (Thorsen 2015). The director, Jørgen Hallum, had hoped to 'scratch the bourgeoisie in the eyes' with this film (Hall 1973) and although the film only sold 10.218 tickets, it made headlines in Denmark when a cinema owner who screened the film, in typical exploitation fashion, 'warned against the film on national television, which he found "horrible and disgusting"' and then singlehandedly raised the age of allowance from the legal sixteen to eighteen years of age. The cinema received a bomb threat saying that if *Englene* was not cancelled, a hand grenade would be thrown at the cinema (Thorsen 2015).

The other Danish film, *Dværgen* (*The Sinful Dwarf*, 1973), is considered one of the more twisted and violent Nordic sexploitation films produced during the 1970s. It was a Danish–US co-production where, according to Jack Stevenson, the American one-time producer Nicolas Poole, 'lodged himself in the penthouse suite of Copenhagen's exclusive Hotel Sheraton and led a festive existence there until the bill came due, at which point he skipped town' (Stevenson 2010: 204). This ultra-low-budget film was directed by Vidal Raski (a pseudonym for Spanish-American director Eduardo Fuller) and advertised as a 'porn-thriller'. The film tells the story of a poor writer, who with his young wife moves into a creepy guesthouse run by a former renowned actress and her son Olaf (Torben Bille) who is, as the film enthusiastically claims, a dwarf. The writer's wife discovers that the guesthouse proprietors keep young girls trapped on the top floor as Olaf has got them addicted to drugs and lets perverted men entertain themselves with his prisoners for a fee while he himself watches.

Unlike previously discussed films, this film was produced in broken English, meaning that it was aimed at an international market, rather than at domestic audiences. Accordingly, *The Sinful Dwarf* was first released in a shortened version in the United States in December 1973, and then uncut one month later in Denmark, but different versions were also released in Japan, West Germany and Austria in 1974 and 1975. In Sweden, the abridged version of *The Sinful Dwarf* was outright banned as 'sadistic' (Statens biografbyrå 1974d). This is not entirely surprising as *The Sinful Dwarf* contains hard-core scenes and some scenes with torture and humiliation, for example, a scene where a woman is whipped bloody, and a scene, often shortened in export versions, where Olaf rapes a woman with his walking stick, although the end of the stick is off-screen. Perhaps due to the low budget, the brutality is often lacking explicit details and often reduced to kitschy over-the-top hysterics. But such a comfortable distance is challenged by the film's formative composition, where the spectator is often

Figure 3.3 Screen grab from Danish *Dværgen* (*The Sinful Dwarf*, 1973), featuring Torben Bille as the malicious dwarf Olaf. Courtesy of Njuta Films.

put in a voyeuristic position equal to that of the sadistic dwarf. Even so, *The Sinful Dwarf* has a John Waters-esque quality to the dialogue and the absurdities. For instance, the film's, and Olaf's, bizarre obsession with children's toys, and the fact that Olaf and his depraved mother keep four women locked up in the attic and sell them to men, is a parallel to the scenario in *Pink Flamingos* (1972) where the Marbles kidnap young women, have them impregnated and then sell the babies to lesbian couples. The mother, played by one-time actor Clara Keller (under the pseudonym Anne Sheldon Williams), and her drinking partner Winne, played by long-time Danish actress Gerda Madsen, consume enormous quantities of gin and deliver dialogue and perform out-of-key song numbers as Nordic counterparts to Divine and Mink Stole, that is, in a black comedy manner that strongly deviated from the popular light-hearted Nordic film comedy of the time. Meanwhile, the dwarf was played by Torben Bille, who was the only name headlined on the Danish posters. Bille worked as a 'professional dwarf' at circuses and did minor acting parts in ten Danish films between 1970 and 1986 (Danskefilm.dk), among them parts in two of the hard-core Zodiac films, *Skorpionens tegn* (*Agent 69 in the Sign of Scorpio*, 1977) and *Skyttens tegn* (*Agent 69 Jensen in the Sign of Sagittarius*, 1978). Danish film critics were disgusted 'that Bille would exploit his handicap in such a manner' (quoted in Stevenson 2010: 204), yet all of these components provide a distinct camp quality to this Nordic schlockier.

The film that has probably gotten the most attention abroad is Swedish *Thriller – en grym film* (*They Call Her One Eye*, 1974), directed by Bo Arne Vibenius. Vibenius started out as a line producer for several of Ingmar Bergman's films, such as *Persona* (1966) and *Vargtimmen* (*The Hour of the Wolf*, 1968), but also gained success as a director for commercials, such as the commercial for SAAB, *7 km/tim* (1972), showing car crashes in ultra-slow motion, which earned him a Golden Lion at Cannes Lions International Festival of Creativity in 1973. In 1969, he made his directorial debut with the children's film *Hur Marie träffade Fredrik, åsnan Rebus, kängurun Ploj och . . .* ('How Marie met Fredrik, the donkey Rebus, the kangaroo Ploj and . . .'). Vibenius had sought financial support from the Swedish Film Institute for this production, but the application was rejected. Instead, he borrowed money from friends and relatives as well as from investors, though in the end, the film would become a personal financial disaster for Vibenius (Åhlander 1977: 501). *They Call Her One Eye* was thus conceptualized as a pure commercial enterprise by Vibenius to recuperate the losses from what he considered an innovative children's film, but which the reviewers keelhauled for its eye-catching product placement, added into several scenes in order to raise the necessary funds (see, for example, Sima 1969 and Holm 1969). This sort of unrestricted commercialism was frowned upon in the leftist-leaning Nordic countries during the late 1960s and all through the 1970s, and when Vibenius provocatively declared that he intended to shoot a 'super commercial shit movie' in 1970 the reviewers would be sure to remember to push this statement down his throat four years later (Säverman 1974).

For *They Call Her One Eye*, Vibenius once again used his own production company, BAV Film AB, without any support from the Swedish Film Institute. In fact, they were not even contacted, and rightly so, since an application for financial support would most definitely have been turned down. The production of this low-budget film, budgeted at 1 million SEK according to Vibenius, started during autumn 1972 and the filming took place in Stockholm and on the island of Öland (Anon. 1973a: 3). *They Call Her One Eye* tells the story of a young girl, Frigga (Christina Lindberg), who is raped by an elderly man and ends up mute as a result of this traumatic event. As a teenager, she is tricked into a brothel, where she is drugged and forced to have sex with unknown men by her pimp. Her parents kill themselves in grief over her situation. To take revenge, Frigga practices to become an expert on weapons and martial art techniques and then takes bloody revenge on all her enemies. While the content focusing on female revenge, as well as elements of more formal experimentation may appear novel for its time, the narrative of the film also unmistakably mimics the sensational elements – and some of the problematic gender politics – of the Nordic white slavery films of the 1910s that shamelessly mixed art with exploitation. At the same time, *The Sinful Dwarf* could also be included in this mini-revival of artistic exploitation but now the sensational components of the film consisted solely of explicit depictions of nudity and violence rather than capitalizing on the sociopolitical implications of white slavery that no longer was considered a tangible issue as it had been during the period of great emigration.

In order to exploit the sensational premise and promote *They Call Her One Eye*, the actors were, by contract, forbidden to reveal who was hiding behind the director pseudonym Alex Fridolinski, something that was, unsurprisingly, revealed almost immediately in the popular press (Åhlander 1988: 247), especially as Vibenius was listed in the opening credits as both the screenwriter and the producer of the film, revealing his heavy involvement. Another significant part of the promotion focused on the revelation that Swedish nude model, actress and innocent-looking starlet Christina Lindberg would play the lead role in this rape–revenge story. Lindberg rose to stardom through nude photographs in a range of Swedish men's magazines, which landed her a role in the hugely successful black comedy *Rötmånad* (*What Are You Doing after the Orgy*, 1970). This was followed up by a number of Swedish and international soft-core sexploitation films such as *Exponerad* (*Exposed*, 1971), *Made in Sweden* (1971), *Furyô anego den: Inoshika Ochô* (*Sex and Fury*, 1973) and *Anita – ur en tonårsflickas dagbok* (*Anita – Swedish Nymphet*, 1974). Yet, *They Call Her One Eye* was, to say the least, a huge step away from the sexploitation field for Lindberg, as instead, she ended up in a hard-core film with explicit violence on a level that had never before been seen in Sweden.

Most notoriously, the film includes a scene where Lindberg's character has her eye punctured, in close-up, by a scalpel, and rumours that a real corpse was used during filming have circulated as an increasingly detailed story ever since (See, for example, Stevenson 2010 212; Ekeroth 2011; Lumholdt 2012). In interviews with Lindberg, for instance, she tends to change her story about this episode from being quite uncertain about it to recalling more and more details, although her recollections are still based solely on hearsay (Bengtsson 2011: 13; Lumholdt 2012). Similarly, film scholar Alexandra Heller-Nicholas questions this rumour by claiming that 'for those familiar with eyeball-heavy film violence [. . .] the scene is not particularly exceptional' (Heller-Nicholas 2011:40). Even so, the gore quality of this eye-gouging scene is high, especially considering it being pre-digital and made in Sweden in the 1970s, a country without a tradition of gory special effects and makeup. In order to put an end to the rumour, we showed the clip to and conducted an interview with a Danish MD who stated that he could not confirm the realness of the scene, and that he leaned towards it being fake, since 'the eye environment behaves wrong at the moment of puncture' (Gustafsson 2019).

Since Lindberg did not do hard-core scenes, these were performed by a 'live couple' from one of Stockholm's sex clubs and then inserted into the film by Vibenius (Bengtsson 2011: 13). According to an interview with Lindberg, Vibenius persuaded her to allow the insertion of these hard-core scenes, which was written into the contract. Lindberg was also poorly paid but was promised, in typical exploitation fashion, a percentage of the film's income. But eventually, Vibenius backed out of this commitment when Lindberg refused to take part in a staged fight on the beach in Cannes to promote the film (Lumholdt 2012).

In many ways, the exploitative shenanigans behind the scenes are played out, though in much more moderate form, in the film. The narrative of *They Call*

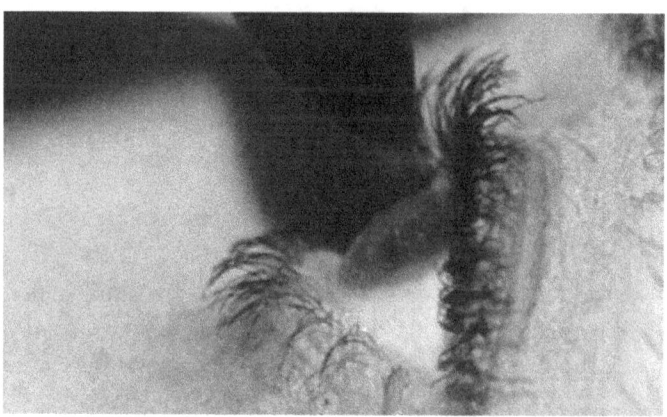

Figure 3.4 Screen grab from Swedish *Thriller – en grym film* (*They Call Her One Eye*, 1974), where Christina Lindberg's character has her eye punctured, in close-up, by a scalpel. Courtesy of Synapse Films.

Her One Eye follows the general three-act structure for rape and revenge films where the female character is first raped and violated, then rehabilitates herself, followed by an act where the character exacts revenge and/or kills their rapist(s). Often compared to precursor films in this subgenre like *The Virgin Spring* and *The Last House on the Left*, *They Call Her One Eye* nevertheless differs in a crucial way since the former films staged a scenario where the female character is killed in the first act and the vengeance is carried out by substitutes, usually family and friends. In *They Call Her One Eye* the female lead instead carries out the vengeance herself, thus anticipating films like *I Spit on Your Grave* (1978) and *Ms.45* (1981), but also Nordic exploitation films such as *Hora* (*The Whore*, 2009). The films that were inspired most by *They Call Her One Eye* are, undeniably, *Kill Bill Vol.1* and *Vol. 2* (2003 and 2004). In an interview, Quentin Tarantino admitted that the character of Elle Driver, with her distinctive eyepatch, is based on Lindberg's character in *They Call Her One Eye*. Tarantino also claimed that of 'all revenge movies I've seen, that is definitely the roughest. There's never been anything as tough' (Mashiyama 2013: 120). Nonetheless, the eyepatch is not the only thing that inspired Tarantino. The whole female revenge scenario, and especially the training sequences that Uma Thurman's character, The Bride, are put through, is directly copied from the Swedish original, of which Tarantino owned a videotape in Swedish without subtitles (Mashiyama 2013: 120).

Vibenius, a fierce advocate for realism, put Lindberg through two months of weapons and martial arts training with a Swedish karate champion before the filming began (Lumholdt 2012). This champion was New Zealand born Marshall McDonagh, who was actually the coach for the Swedish national team at the time of filming (Oyama Karate Kai 2019). McDonagh also played a small role in the film, as the karate instructor who trains Frigga. This practice of using real martial arts instructors to train the actors, and then for the instructors to play 'themselves' in the film, was something that would be frequently exploited by, for example, Mats Helge Olsson's entertainment violence factory in the 1980s.

The emphasis on realism was also enhanced by the fact that the film was produced entirely in Swedish. In contrast to *The Sinful Dwarf* and its use of accented English, this suggests that Vibenius aimed *They Call Her One Eye* primarily at the domestic market. As rumours of the violent content started to spread, Vibenius let himself be interviewed, once again in typical exploitation fashion, in one of Sweden's biggest men's magazines just days before the censors would review *They Call Her One Eye*. He even provided the magazine with stills of the most likely scenes to be cut, boldly proclaiming: 'I think that the film will be released. Film censorship is a sensitive subject during an election year', thus drawing attention to the Swedish Board of Film Censorship as a governmental body whose decisions were shaped by political motives (Anon.1973b: 25). However, on 4 April 1973, the Swedish Board of Film Censorship decided to ban *They Call Her One Eye* with the motivation: 'taking into account the repeated elements of violence and sadism occurring in "Thriller – en grym film" – and after hearing recommendations from the State's Film Review Council – [the board have] decided, with support of §3 of the Cinema ordinance, the film to be coarsening and harmfully exciting and not allow it for public screening' (Statens biografbyrå 1973).

This was the first time a Swedish film had been banned since *491* was deemed illicit due to its depictions of sexualized violence in 1964. However, unlike the fierce debate that followed the banning of *491*, the debate surrounding the banning of *The Call Her One Eye* was short and unapologetic. Slightly dispirited, Vibenius first tried to defend his film as art: 'I wanted to show how violence changes and destroys people. The film certainly does not contain such entertainment violence that you see in cheap Wild West films' (Anon. 1973b: 25). The condescending nod to cheap Western films could have meant either American Westerns or Italian Spaghetti Westerns, as both were considered as detested representatives of violent American low culture. The Swedish Board of Film Censorship decided, for example, to make five severe cuts to Sergio Leone's *Per un Pugno Di Dollari* (*A Fistful of Dollars*, 1964), and then, when it was censored a second time prior to its video release in 1980, to make yet another cut (Statens biografbyrå 1966 and 1980). Nonetheless, already the next day, a cocky Vibenius, trying to take back the initiative, claimed that 'he was not yet broken. This is great publicity for me. If the film is banned in Sweden, then Japan will surely buy it. There, Christina Lindberg is a big name. I will also sell it at the Cannes Film Festival. There you have a greater interest in this type of film' (Anon. 1973c: 32). This wishful thinking was brutally shot down, first by poet and film critic Hanserik Hjertén:

> [Vibenius] claims to portray violence as a deterrent but says in the next moment that he wants to meet people's demand for brutal eye candy, a duality that indicates a crack in his soul. He firmly denies that 'Thriller' serves as entertainment violence. But when he began production a couple of years ago, he called it a 'super commercial shit movie' that would make money. If that is the case, then, I think Vibenius should not try to serve us any fairy tales. Wanting open mindedness for pure speculation, that is one thing, and can at least be respected as cynicism. But banging the drum and hiding this speculation behind attaining the role of a socially well-meaning freedom fighter, that is just sad. (Hjertén 1973: 18)

A year later, on 6 May 1974, the Swedish Board of Film Censorship decided to ban *They Call Her Eye One* a second time, regardless of the massive cut of 510 metres that Vibenius himself had done before handing in the film for re-examination. The board stated that, despite the cuts, 'the abbreviated version has not changed character' (Statens biografbyrå 1974a). Despite this, a third version, now shortened beforehand by another 95 metres, was examined by the board a few days later and managed to squeeze through with an additional four censorship cuts totalling 98 metres (Statens biografbyrå 1974b). Altogether, *They Call Her One Eye* was shortened by a baffling twenty-six minutes before its Swedish release.

The third version that was examined and cut by the board was in fact identical with the recut and dubbed-into-English version that had minor success in the US drive-in and grindhouse cinema circuits. After the debacle with the first ban Vibenius had, as promised, travelled down to the Cannes Film Festival in 1973, where he marketed the film with the tagline, 'Banned in Sweden'. He eventually sold the distribution rights for the North American market to American International Pictures who removed the hard-core frames, dubbed, and renamed the film to *They Call Her One Eye* (Åhlander 1988: 247; Stevenson 2010: 212). It was this severely hampered and English dubbed version that hit

Stockholm cinemas in November 1974, although under its original Swedish title, *Thriller – en grym film*, where it was advertised with the white lie, 'The first Swedish film ever to be totally banned by Swedish film censorship. Now in its American version' ('Thriller – en grym film' 1974).

The reviewers were, undeniably, predetermined to loathe *They Call Her One Eye*, but in the absolute trashing that followed, it should be remembered that the critics only had access to the truncated American version of the film. To illustrate, one reviewer complained about the film's incomprehensibility, noting that the main crook manages to survive a 'rain of bullets where everybody dies. Suddenly he sits at a desk and speaks on the phone. This is how it is in films of this kind' (Säverman 1974). The main reason that the villain survived was because the censors saved him by cutting out the ending revenge scene, totalling two minutes and fifty-one seconds, where Frigga first shoots him in both kneecaps, then buries him under rocks, tying a rope around his neck, which is tied to a horse. Frigga places a bucket of oats in front of the horse, and then sits and waits for the horse to pull the rope in order to get to the food (Statens biografbyrå 1974b).

Film critic and documentary filmmaker Jonas Sima graded *They Call Her One Eye* zero (on a scale of one to five) and wrote, 'Out of compassion no participant shall be accused. Except Bo A Vibenius, who tries to hide his shoddiness behind the pseudonym Alex Fridolinski. Take him to the pillory!' (Sima 1974). Another critic called the film 'embarrassing', noting that this 'white slavery' story was 'utterly mad and also so clumsily staged that the audience laughs more at the clumsiness than suffers from the harmful excitement the censors were afraid of' (Schiller 1974). Finally, 'the grand old man' among Swedish film critics, Jurgen Schildt, ended his review in typical, for the period, anti-American fashion: 'At the Festival cinema at Sturegatan, it smells more devilish than McDonald's multinational deep fat fryers around the corner on Kungsgatan' (Schildt 1974). McDonald's had, in fact, opened its first restaurant in Sweden in October 1973, located at Kungsgatan in Stockholm.

They Call Her One Eye stayed only one week at the Festival cinema – once one of Stockholm's central premiere cinemas with 700 seats, owned by Europa Film, who also distributed the film in Sweden – before it was replaced by Italian-Spanish Euro Crime *Il Consigliore* (*Counselor at Crime*, 1973) with Martin Balsam in the lead role, another violent film that the Swedish Board of Film Censorship made seven cuts to (Statens biografbyrå 1974c).

Vibenius would stake out a final try as an outlaw director, this time under the pseudonym Ron Silberman Jr., writing, directing and producing the exploitation

Figure 3.5 Screen grab from Swedish *Thriller – en grym film* (*They Call Her One Eye*, 1974), where Christina Lindberg's character takes revenge on her kidnapper/pimp, played by Heinz Hopf. This scene was cut in its entirety in its original Swedish cinema release. Courtesy of Synapse Films.

film *Breaking Point* (1975), advertised as a 'Pornographic Thriller'. In fact, in this film everybody, with the exception of Ralph Lundsten, who wrote the original score, worked under colourful pseudonyms like Robert Taylor, Urban Hitler, Adolf Deutch and Oscar Wilde. Vibenius himself used no less than three pseudonyms: beside the directorial one, he named himself Stan Kowalski as the producer, and Nat Sharp as the writer. Only a few of the actors have been identified, foremost amongst them Greek–Swede Andreas Bellis who played the lead role, and who had previously worked as a cinematographer on *They Call Her One Eye* but also as a second unit cameraman on films such as *Jag är nyfiken – gul* (*I Am Curious (Yellow)*, 1967) and *Jag är nyfiken – blå* (*I Am Curious (Blue)*, 1968).

Breaking Point was produced in twelve days in December 1974, that is, a mere month after *They Call Her One Eye* was brutally shot down at the Swedish box office. This was a low-budget project, apparently financed by a small surplus from the international export of *They Call Her One Eye*. This time the production was, already from the start, clearly aimed at an international market as it was made in English. Furthermore, the English sounding pseudonyms support this goal, although to our knowledge, the film was only exported to France (Åhlander 1988: 291–2; Trampe 2011).

Breaking Point is Kafkaesque and disturbing, underscored by the use of sound effects such as children's screams and atonal electronic music. A middle-aged white-collar worker (Bellis) at the Wennergren Center in Stockholm complements his routine existence with compulsive erotic approaches on a number of women. Some he brutally murders and some he rapes after repeatedly having heard a television news statement claiming that 89 per cent of all women want to be raped according to a governmental report. This means that most of the rapes are portrayed, with hard-core scenes, as voluntary. In his imagination, he becomes involved in a bank robbery, where he obliterates the perpetrators with a special type of ammunition that blow them to pieces. By the end of the film, his wife and daughter return from a trip and everything goes back to 'normal'.

Breaking Point is often scorned as the 'most bizarre' and 'insane' film ever produced in Sweden (Ekeroth 2011: 42). Jack Stevenson declares it to be 'tasteless, violent, pornographic and some would certainly say misogynist – all meant no doubt to reflect the sickness endemic in society at large' (Stevenson 2010: 212–13). The Swedish Board of Film Censorship made a similar assessment and banned the film for being 'violent/sadistic' (Statens biografbyrå 1975a). Even so, just two weeks later Vibenius handed in a shorter version with four cuts totalling three minutes that passed the censors. This included cut scenes where an

Figure 3.6 Screen grab from Swedish *Breaking Point* (1975), with Gree–Swede Andreas Bellis in the lead role. Courtesy of Liberty Video.

unconscious woman is forced to conduct fellatio, and where a woman is brutally beaten to death with an ashtray (Statens biografbyrå 1975b). What was released was thus a film without the explicit and illegal violence but with the legal hardcore sex scenes still intact since these where portrayed as voluntary. One could argue for that these alternations changed the meaning of the film, making it even more bizarre, but in fact, the censor just followed the letter of the law.

The decriminalization of porn in Sweden in 1971 was part of a wider debate on sexual liberalization that had started in the 1960s, and as film scholar Mariah Larsson has established, this liberalization effected the output and sales of pornographic material well before the actual decriminalization, including film production, which is why we, for example, saw complaints about there being too much porn in a Swedish film such as *Fear Has 1000 Eyes* made in 1970 (Larsson 2017: 28–9). However, liberalization included debates about sexual freedom that concerned activities such as incest and child pornography, of which the latter in reality was legal in Sweden between 1971 and 1980. In this era of sexual liberalization, a committee of seven men and one woman was appointed by the government to give suggestions for new sex crime legislation in 1971. By the end of 1975, some of these suggestions began to seep out, and when the full report was released in 1976, they proposed, among other things: legalization of incest between adults, lowering the age of consent to 14, and reducing the punishment for rape, taking into account in the assessment of rape cases whether the victim had made sexual invitations beforehand (SOU 1976: 17–19).

The report was severely criticized by the women's movement, and eventually scrapped (see, for example, Boëthius 1976) but it is not hard to draw parallels between it and Vibenius's fantasies and/or criticisms of rape and/or consent in *Breaking Point*. Another more problematic feature in Vibenius's oeuvre that is not discussed is the deceptions of rape and rape fantasies of children, especially considering his debut as a children's film director. *They Call Her One Eye* starts with the brutal and drawn-out rape of Frigga when she is seven years old, and *Breaking Point* includes two disturbing scenes where the main character first visits a schoolyard and, in the context of him being a rapist and murderer, it is implied that he is about to lure one of the children away, and it is a relief when he does not. However, later he returns to the school and does lure a child away, taking them for a ride in his car out into the woods. There the camera sneaks around the snowy landscape as the audience is not allowed to see what is going on inside the red Volvo which can be glimpsed between the trees. Finally, the film cuts to inside the car where the man feeds the child candy. After a while, the child requests to go home and the man answers, 'Sure', and drives the child home. Although 'nothing happens', this flirtation with the forbidden is never discussed by censors or reviewers, but most definitely, it became part of the negative assessment that these films, especially *Breaking Point*, received.

Typically, Vibenius used these censorship decisions in the film's marketing, proclaiming, 'Forbidden by the censorship – now released!' and 'This year's sensation at the Cannes Film Festival'. However, after the debacle with *They Call Her One Eye* and no doubt due to the controversial content in *Breaking Point*, he had lost the distribution deal with the heavy weight industry player Europa Film. *Breaking Point* was instead distributed by Elit-Film AB, a small distribution company that specialized in sexploitation and who had previously distributed successes such as *Language of Love* and *Exposed*, but now turned out imported low-budget porn films like *Positions danoises* (1977) and *Ferdinand, der Pussyschreck* (1977). Consequently, *Breaking Point* was never screened in Stockholm's cinemas, and had only a limited release in small towns such as Borås across Sweden. The film would eventually have a continued life when it was released on VHS in 1980.

Conclusion

Although Denmark and Sweden were flooded by soft- and hard-core pornography films in the late 1960s and throughout the 1970s, cinematic violence and gore were still considered an abnormality by film producers, critics and censorship. The duality with art as exploitation/exploitation as art, so present in the 1910s, worked for a while and especially in relation to some European art films and New Hollywood films, but when a filmmaker like Bo Arne Vibenius tried to defend his violent creation *The Call Her One Eye* as art, he got slammed and ridiculed. That particular sort of commercial violence was not considered free speech and definitely belonged in the realm of the scorned global patterns in exploitation cinema.

As Isak Thorsen claims in connection to the two Danish violent sexploitation films *Englene* and *The Dwarf*, '[t]hese exploitation titles [that] challenged taboos by combining sex and Christianity or sex and violence emerged after the Danish porn wave had ebbed. The novelty of sex and pornography had worn off, and these exploitative and provocative films can be understood as an attempt to revitalize the subcultural, transgressive potential of sex and pornography within a more liberal climate' (Thorsen 2015). The circumstances under which the Scandinavian porn wave had ebbed out by this time can be connected to the fact that almost all of the six transgressive films containing sex and violence produced in Denmark and Sweden during the 1970s were completed in, or meant to be released, in 1973. *The Sinful Dwarf* and *They Call Her One Eye* can thus be interpreted as commercial exploitation films that broke both moral and legal laws – in the disguise of art and freedom of speech – just for the sake of making some money in a period when plain pornography did not cut it anymore. Vibenius' problematic flirts with paedophilia can likewise be interpreted as a way to challenge taboos just for the sake of breaking taboos (and making some money off the side). Hence, commercial or entertainment violence was obviously not an accepted aspect of Nordic film cultures as the 1970s turned into the more conservative 1980s. And while a rape–revenge classic such as *I Spit on Your Grave* can be discussed as a film 'in which Hollywood has attempted to make sense of feminism' (Heller-Nicolas 2011: 10), *The Sinful Dwarf* and *They Call Her One Eye* are, conceivably, prime examples of what a Swedish film censor meant when he compared American and European film violence, claiming that '[t]his perverted European rawness is much worse' (quoted in Bengtsson 1998: 330).

References

Åhlander, Lars (ed.) (1977), *Svensk filmografi 6 1960–1969*, Stockholm: Svenska filminstitutet.
Åhlander, Lars (ed.) (1988), *Svensk filmografi 7 1970–1979*, Stockholm: Svenska filminstitutet.
Anon. (1973a), '"Thriller – en Grym Film" totalförbjuds', *Aftonbladet*, 29 March, 3.
Anon. (1973b), 'De svenska filmbilderna som ni kanske aldrig får se: Filmen som ska sälja på våld', *FiB Aktuellt*, 13, 24–5.
Anon. (1973c), '"Censurstoppet är fin reklam"', *Aftonbladet*, 30 March, 32.
Bengtsson, Bengt (1998), *Ungdom i fara: Ungdomsproblem i svensk spelfilm 1942-62*, Uppsala: Stockholm University.
Bengtsson, Ronny (2011), 'Christina Lindberg, Exposed', in Daniel Ekroth, *Swedish Sensation Films: A Clandestine History of Sex, Thrillers, and Kicker Cinema*, New York: Bazillion Points.
Bergström, Lasse (1973), 'Smutsiga fingrar', Review, *Expressen*, 3 January.
Boëthius, Maria-Pia (1976), *Skylla sig själv: En bok om våldtäkt*, Stockholm: Liber förlag.

Brossner, Karl-Erik (1973), 'Skräcken har 1000 ögon', Review, *Sydsvenska Dagbladet*, 13 October.
Danskefilm.dk, 'Torben Bille', https://danskefilm.dk/skuespiller.php?id=1195 (Accessed 21 May 2019).
Ekeroth, Daniel (2011), *Swedish Sensation Films: A Clandestine History of Sex, Thrillers, and Kicker Cinema*, New York: Bazillion Points.
Furhammar, Leif (2003), *Filmen i Sverige: En historia i tio kapitel och en fortsättning*, Stockholm: Svenska filminstitutet and Dialogos.
Gustafsson, Tommy (2019), Interview with medical doctor Mathias Pedersen Wagner, Copenhagen, 29 May.
Hall, E. (1973), 'Vi vil kradse borgerskabet i øjnene', *Ugens Rapport*, 23 July.
Heller-Nicholas, Alexandra (2011), *Rape-Revenge Films: A Critical Study*, Jefferson, NC: McFarland.
Hjertén, Hanserik (1973), 'Regissör Vibenius siktar på censuren?', *Dagens Nyheter*, 11 April, 18.
Holm, Annika (1969), 'Hur Marie träffade Fredrik, åsnan Rebus, kängurun Ploj och...', Review, *Dagens Nyheter*, 16 December.
Larsson, Mariah (2017), *The Swedish Porn Scene: Exhibition Contexts, 8mm Pornography and the Sex Film*, Bristol: Intellect.
Lumholdt, Jan (2012), 'Interview with the Swedish Sin Queen: Christina Lindberg', DB Cult Film Institute, 21 January, https://web.archive.org/web/20120216003737/http://www.dbcult.com/printed-media/christina-lindberg-interview/ (Accessed 2 May 2019).
Machiyama, Tomohiro (2013), 'Quentin Tarantino Reveals Almost Everything That Inspired *Kill Bill*', in Gerald Peary (ed.), *Quentin Tarantino: Interviews, Revised and Updated*, Jackson, MI: University Press of Mississippi, pp. 118–26.
Neglin, Yngve (1970), 'Skräcken har 1000 ögon', Review, *Helsingborgs Dagblad*, 29 September.
Nissen, Dan (1997), 'Den populære kunst: Genrefilmen som social seismograf', in Ib Bondebjerg, Jesper Anderson and Peter Schepelern (eds), *Dansk film 1972–1997*, Copenhagen: Munksgaard-Rosinante.
Nordberg, Carl-Eric (1973), 'Recension: "Smutsiga fingrar"', Review, *Tidningen Vi*, 3 January.
Oyama KarateKai (2019), 'Sensi Marshall McDonagh', http://oyama.se/historia/sensei-marshall-mcdonagh/ (Accessed 3 May 2019).
Säverman, Ove (1974), 'Thriller – en grym film', Review, *Dagens Nyheter*, 29 November.
Schiller, Hans (1973), 'Skräcken har 1000 ögon', Review, *Svenska Dagbladet*, 17 December.
Schiller, Hans (1974), 'Erbarmlig Thriller', Review, *Svenska Dagbladet*, 29 November, 13.
Schildt, Jurgen (1974), 'Thriller', Review, *Aftonbladet*, 28 November, 38.
Sima, Jonas (1969), 'Jonas Sima filmsynar barnens julbiokul', Review, *Expressen*, 14 December.

Sima, Jonas (1974), 'Thriller', Review, *Expressen*, 28 November, 40.

Skräcken har 1000 ögon: 'Bolmört i mitt öra' (2005), Documentary Featurette, DVD, Klubb Super 8: Stockholm.

SOU (1976), *Sexuella övergrepp: förslag till ny lydelse av brottsbalkens bestämmelser om sedlighetsbrott: betänkande 1976:9*, Stockholm: Liber förlag.

Statens biografbyrå (1966), Censorship Card for *Per un Pugno Di Dollari*, Stockholm: Riksarkivet, Statens biografbyrås arkiv, 104.613.

Statens biografbyrå (1970), Censorship Card for *Skräcken har 1000 ögon*, Stockholm: Riksarkivet, Statens biografbyrås arkiv, 109.400.

Statens biografbyrå (1972), Censorship Card for *Smutsiga fingrar*, Stockholm: Riksarkivet, Statens biografbyrås arkiv, 111.550.

Statens biografbyrå (1973), Censorship Card for *Thriller – en grym film*, Stockholm: Riksarkivet, Statens biografbyrås arkiv, 111.887.

Statens biografbyrå (1974a), Censorship Card for *Thriller – en grym film*, Stockholm: Riksarkivet, Statens biografbyrås arkiv, 113.323.

Statens biografbyrå (1974b), Censorship Card for *Thriller – a cruel picture*, Stockholm: Riksarkivet, Statens biografbyrås arkiv, 113.336.

Statens biografbyrå (1974c), Censorship Card for *El Consigliore*, Stockholm: Riksarkivet, Statens biografbyrås arkiv, 113.339.

Statens biografbyrå (1974d), Censorship Card for *The Sinful Dwarf*, Stockholm: Riksarkivet, Statens biografbyrås arkiv, 113.272.

Statens biografbyrå (1975a), Censorship Card for *Breaking Point*, Stockholm: Riksarkivet, Statens biografbyrås arkiv, 114.584.

Statens biografbyrå (1975b), Censorship Card for *Breaking Point*, Stockholm: Riksarkivet, Statens biografbyrås arkiv, 114.631.

Statens biografbyrå (1975c), Censorship Card for *I död mans spår*, Stockholm: Riksarkivet, Statens biografbyrås arkiv, 114.581.

Statens biografbyrå (1980), Censorship Card for *Per un Pugno Di Dollari*, Stockholm: Riksarkivet, Statens biografbyrås arkiv, 121.173.

Stevenson, Jack (2010), *Scandinavian Blue: The Erotic Cinema of Sweden and Denmark in the 1960s and 1970s*, Jefferson, NC: McFarland.

Thorsen, Isak (2015), 'Incorporation of the Transgressive: Sex and Pornography in Danish Feature Films of the 1970s', *Cine-Excess*, http://www.cine-excess.co.uk/incorporation-of-the-transgressive-sex-and-pornography-in-danish-feature-films-of-the-1970s.html (Accessed 20 May 2019).

'Thriller – en grym film' (1974), Cinema ad, *Aftonbladet*, 27 November, 35.

Trampe, Fredrik af (2011), 'Bo Arne Vibenius filmer', *Sunkit*, https://www.sunkit.com/bo-arne-vibenius-filmer/ (Accessed 12 May 2019).

4

Moral panic, VHS censorship and fan culture counterforces 1980–99

After a wave of liberalization in the Nordic countries, the tide started to turn during the 1970s. As we saw in Chapter 3, Nordic forays into global trends in exploitation film featuring cinematic violence and gore were publicly reviled by film institutes, film critics and film censorship alike. Furthermore, this public outcry was about to get even worse with the introduction of the new media technology of home video. For a while, the VCR circumvented film censorship laws and glimpses of previously outlawed global exploitation films slipped into the homes of the Nordic welfare state before the door was slammed shut with unforgiving VHS censorship during the 1980s and 1990s. Nevertheless, these glimpses of media freedom inspired and consolidated a persistent exploitation fan culture community in all the Nordic countries. It is to these developments we now turn as the discussion in this chapter lays the groundwork for the upcoming chapters focusing on the 1980s and 1990s.

The public outcry over the 'video nasties' in the UK in 1982 and 1983 is internationally well documented (see, for example, Martin 2007; Mathijs and Sexton 2011; Pearce 2013; Brown 2014), but similar outbreaks connected to the production and dissemination of popular culture occurred throughout the 1980s and during early 1990s worldwide. One notable example is Tipper Gore's crusade against the 'filthy fifteen', as the future Second Lady co-founded Parents Music Resource Center (PMRC) in 1985, which was to raise parental and consumer awareness of music that contained explicit content through labelling of albums. This was done in collaboration with influential organizations such as the National PTA and the American Academy of Paediatrics, and the effort met with success since the campaign resulted in the practice of institutionalizing 'voluntary' warning labels for violent or sexually explicit lyrics (Gore 1987: passim; Shrieve 1999). In the Nordic countries several similar and simultaneous outbursts happened, especially concerning heavy metal music as when, for example, television show host Siewert Öholm, a Baptist in secular Sweden, bashed American heavy metal band W.A.S.P. on Swedish public television, accusing them of Satanism, after a concert in Stockholm in 1984.

These outbursts have often been claimed to be part of a worldwide wave of conservative neo-moralism aimed against provocative displays of violence and sex in media such as films, video games and popular music. However, this is foremost a Western phenomenon and it can be connected to a number of interrelated issues emanating from the societal turmoil created by, amongst other things, the liberalization of the 1960s, 'the protest of 68', the oil crisis, the feminist and gay liberations movements and the rise of the evangelical right in the United States. Conservative neo-moralism is only one force that achieved political success in alignment with neoliberalist politics and economics, often exemplified by the elections of British prime minister Margaret Thatcher in 1979 and American president Roland Reagan in 1980. Being part of an ever more globalized world, the Nordic countries were certainly affected by these political and cultural fluctuations but at the same time, they responded differently towards these challenges.

In all the Nordic countries, lengthy and sometimes heated discussions over film and television violence (yet not so much over nudity and sex) took place during the entire 1970s. In Swedish equivalents to PTA's magazine *Our Children*, *Lärartidningen/Svenskskoltidning* ('The Teacher's Magazine/Swedish School Newspaper') and *Barn i hem, skola, samhälle* ('Children at Home, in School, and in Society') a recurring subject was 'television violence'. The continuous discussion about television violence was usually accentuated by a new alarmist report that demonstrated a link between fictional violence and real-life violence, or it could be prompted by the airing of a television series or a film by public television that caused upset. An example of the latter was when Swedish public television occasionally broadcasted Universal's classic horror films from the 1930s, such as *Frankenstein* (1931), *Dracula* (1931), *The Mummy* (1932) and *The Invisible Man* (1933). Other programming that led to harsh criticism were the broadcasting of popular American television series such as *Baretta* (1975-8), *Kojak* (1973-8), *Canon* (1971-6) and *The Rockford Files* (1974-80), which were said to be examples of 'a human vision [that] reflects a society from which we should distance our self. Television violence creates contempt for humans' (quoted in Gustafsson 2014: 78-9). Similar discussions roared in Denmark and Norway in the late 1960s and throughout the 1970s, often framed through the perspective of how children could be harmed by this foreign-produced entertainment violence (Strandgaard Jensen 2013: 228, 246; Smith-Isaksen 2013: 197–201).

The above-mentioned media products would probably not stir up much public emotions on their violent content today, and the main reason that campy horror films from the 1930s were able to raise any form of attention could be explained by one single phenomenon: film censorship. All Nordic countries have had forceful governmental film censorship since the silent age, banning and cutting tens of thousands of films and, in that way, keeping Nordic audiences away from explicit (and most implicit) depictions of violence and pornography. Denmark abolished film censorship for adults in 1969 but kept it for children until 1997. However, the abolition of censorship was only institutionalized across the Nordic countries much later, starting with Finland in 2001, Norway in 2004, Iceland in 2006 and finally Sweden in 2011 (*Avskaffande av filmcensuren för vuxna* 2009: 38–9). Nordic audiences were thus unprepared to confront what was perceived to be overtly and sadistically (that is, elongated) violent scenes that only had the purpose to scare, arouse or create suspense for their audiences.

This sentiment towards the film medium was a cultural thing too, as film for a long time was at the bottom of a cultural hierarchy that was topped by great literature and the theatre. The auteur movement, which started in France with André Bazin's *Cahiers du cinéma* and the subsequent new waves of cinema in Europe, and eventually New Hollywood, elevated the film medium, or at least parts of it, to a new cultural level where censorship could be and was challenged. In Sweden two governmental investigations, one on free speech and one on the future of film censorship were launched in 1964 and completed in 1969. The investigation on free speech suggested that the section on 'moral obscenity' should be removed from the law. It would be replaced by a clause that regulated public display of pornographic material, but in practice, this proposal meant that pornography in written and visual form was free to be distributed. Hence, this legislation was in line with the liberal development of the late 1960s, where soft-core cinemas and the establishment of sex clubs had already taken place in both Sweden and Denmark. Interestingly, the investigation of film censorship also concluded that censorship should be abolished since adult audiences with normal mental abilities were unlikely to be hurt by either sexual or violent depictions. However, after the usual referral procedure, the investigation resulted in no action and film censorship continued for another forty-two years, the exception being depictions of sex and nudity, which were now permitted (Gustafsson and Larsson 2009: 446–7). In Norway, the same debate raged during the 1960s, and when home video arrived as a new consumer media product, there were even proposals for a new type of film regulation with the intention of abolishing film censorship for adults in 1982. However, by then, the debates about 'video violence' had become pervasive and the proposal was scrapped in favour of an even harsher law that forced video store owners to register all their titles (Smith-Isaksen 2013: 196–201).

The act of promoting the film medium as art, and thus exploiting (and provoking) moral and audiovisual boundaries through subjects such as sex, nudity and violence, literally placed the film industry and its products in the social spotlight in all Nordic countries. To explain the relevance of these developments further, it is worth noting some of the political discrepancies between these countries to outline how such norms fed into film politics. In 1964, Norwegian film workers boycotted the influential governmental-municipal film company Norsk Film A/S in order to generate discussion on cultural policy and the film medium's (low) position in Norway (Iversen 2011: 203–8). In Sweden, films like Vilgot Sjöman's *491* (1964) and Ingmar Bergman's *Tystnaden* (*The Silence*, 1963) caused lengthy debates and commotion that stretched through all layers of society, all the way up to the Swedish government. Although *491* was first banned by the Swedish Board of Film Censorship, *The Silence* was released without cuts, and reached record audiences in Sweden and abroad due to its sexual subjects and nudity. In the United States, *The Silence* was distributed by Janus Films that marketed it as a pure exploitation film, ignoring its heavy philosophical and artistic qualities. Later on, *491* was released with a few cuts, after intervention from the Swedish government and, very literally, became the motive for the inauguration of a new political party based on moral imperatives, Kristen demokratisk samling (Christian Democratic Assembly), in 1964 (Lennerhed 2016: 116–25).

Despite such moments of resistance, the legalization of pornography opened the floodgates, especially in Denmark and Sweden where, for instance, hard-core magazines could be found on display in supermarkets for everyone to see, including children. These liberal perspectives put forward on a political level were, however, not always in sync with what ordinary people believed. The 1970s became a decade of debates where liberalization was pushed forward on all fronts, at the same time as its obvious drawbacks became apparent. Between 1971 and 1980, for example, child pornography was legal in Sweden. In 1976 a governmental investigation of sexual crimes was presented, which suggested measures such as the reclassification of the crime of rape as well as reduced penalties. Causing an uproar, the investigation was eventually scrapped (*Sexuella övergrepp* 1976). Rather than being an expression of conservative neo-moralism, the fight against unconcealed manifestations of sexual liberation gone overboard were led by second-wave feminists on the left of the political spectrum in the Nordic countries (see, for example, Boëthius 1976), with arguments suggesting that pornography was often linked to domestic violence and sexual harassment (Carlsson 2005).

In the beginning of the 1980s, when the VCR was introduced as a household product in the Nordic countries, the seemingly disparate discourses on liberalization, censorship, television violence, pornography and nationalism came together in a fusion that literally exploded in public outcries and moral panic. Calls for stringent regulation and censorship became part of the societal and political agenda for the next twenty years. In 1980 and 1981 the national television services in Sweden, Norway and Denmark, respectively, broadcasted three current affairs shows that drew public attention to predicted problems connected to VCR as a new, unknown and foreign media for moving images. Hence, the Nordic debates actually preceded the debate about video nasties in the UK by two years. Since Sweden was first out of the gate, we will concentrate on this national example of moral panic to highlight some of the particularities of these Nordic debates. We will also turn to Finland's excessive censorship regime and subsequently conclude this chapter with a discussion about the implications these censorship practices had for consolidating a persistent exploitation fan culture community in Finland and Sweden.

The video violence moral panic in Sweden

We will use the concept of moral panic to investigate the links between video violence and low culture. The concept of moral panic was coined by Marshall McLuhan in 1964, but it was not until Stanley Cohen's influential sociological study, *Folk Devils and Moral Panics* (1972) that moral panic became a theoretical concept (McLuhan 1964; Cohen 2007). Moral panics have since then been used in a number of sociologically oriented studies to examine the reactions against different phenomena such as street crime, HIV/AIDS, Satanism, child pornography and drug use (Hall, Stuart et al 1978; Weeks 1989; Jenkins & Maier-Katkin 1992; Ost 2002; Meylakhs 2006). In this chapter, however, moral panic will be used historically in relation to mass media, foremost audiovisual media such as film and video. Unlike the sociological orientation, which focuses on social and power-related structures in the functioning of moral panics, we will emphasize a contextual perspective to understand moral panics and the media studied. For that reason, we understand the term moral panic as very strong responses to certain people, groups or phenomena (here the consumption of new media) that is perceived as a threat to the values and interests of society. The concept of *moral* clarifies that the social unrest stirred concerns a perceived demoralization, that is, a threat to society's fundamental values, whereas the concept of *panic* gives an indication of the strength of these reactions.

The Swedish, and eventually Nordic moral panic about the video violence phenomenon was instigated with the airing of an episode called 'Who Needs Video?' of the long running current affairs show *Studio S* (1975–84) on 2 December 1980. Literally overnight, this resulted in the historically largest level of complaints aimed at Swedish public television and police raids against video shops in Stockholm the following day. Furthermore, the minister of education, Jan-Erik Wikström appointed an on-the-spot investigation on the possibility of censoring video films, or alternatively prohibiting sales and rentals to minors. This investigation was completed within three weeks, ignoring an ongoing investigation into video distribution that had been ongoing for four years (Höjdestrand 1997: 97).

The *Studio S* episode about video violence was produced with the intention to create sensation around a new and relatively unknown media technique that the VCR was at the time. Only 3.5 per cent of Swedish households owned a VCR in 1980, and the rental of videos was still a very modest business – in the Nordic countries it was often an extra income for radio and camera stores or petrol stations with somewhere around 500–1,000 titles available on the market (Höjdestrand 1997: 48, 97; Jacobsson 1980; Smith-Isaksen 2013: 195). At this time, all major Hollywood studios were still reluctant to make their films available via the video technology and refused to release their films on the market. Instead, a multitude of international small producers dominated the world market with B or even C films of varying quality (Grainge, Jancovich and Monteith 2008: 457–8). It was also quite expensive to rent a video for a day, in Sweden about 40 SEK (approximately 4 GBP in 1980), which the current consumer price index shows to correspond to approximately 16 GBP. To buy and own a video cassette was almost unheard of, since a single film could cost up to 1,000 SEK or 300 GBP in today's monetary value (Historia.se; Pound Sterling Live; Wasko 2008: 472–4).

All major newspapers published full-page reportages on the evening's spectacular broadcast, which had been moved back from 8.00 pm to 9.35 pm to 'spare the young ones' as Erik Eriksson, producer for *Studio S*, emphasized (Wennerholm 1980). One evening newspaper illustrated their article with two images from *The Texas Chainsaw Massacre* (1974) under the headline: 'Tonight public television will show them – on an R-rated slot' (Jacobsson 1980), whereas another newspaper blasted on with: 'VIDEO SHOCK' and announced that the episode would contain 'the most violent images that have ever been shown on Swedish television' (Westlind 1980).

These articles were based on the information that the producers of *Studio S* had mailed out before the broadcast. It is thus possible to identify the first governing components that would develop into a full-blown moral panic about video violence. In particular, two components were highlighted. First, the claim that children aged eleven to twelve years were the most frequent customers who rented these violent films without their parents' knowledge. Second, the allegation that the video market almost exclusively consisted of violence and porn (Kaplan 1980). Consequently, the new technology came to be associated in an excessive way with violence and sex, and with its uncanny ability to spread these evil things to defenceless children without any control or regulation. The other Nordic countries had, as well, focused on children's wellbeing in relation to the VCR early on (Strandgaard-Jensen 2013: 234; Smith-Isaksen 2013: 199–201). In comparison, the connection between children and violence was made much later in the UK panic on video nasties, in fact, not until 1983 when 'The Video Violence and Children Report', infamously based on forty-seven respondents, claimed that 45 per cent of all seven- to sixteen-year-old children were watching these films (Brown 2014: 19–20).

In the publicity material, one of *Studio S*' studio anchors, Pelle Bergendahl, argued that 'these are films where the story is merely a pretext for showing violence, and where violence and misogyny often are ends in themselves' (Westlind 1980). This feminist perspective on the VCR and video violence was linked to the second wave of the women's movement in the 1960s and the 1970s, where the struggle for women's social and economic freedom had been in focus, parallel to the liberalization of female sexuality via the pill, the right to abortion and the struggle to change the general perception of women's sexual lives (Rydström and Tjeder 2009: 173–9, 196–202). In connection to this, the images of women in popular culture, and women's subordinate position within the same culture, were severely criticized by the women's movement. Such responses were evident, not least because the pornographic market had grown rapidly in the late 1960s and the 1970s. However, this public openness towards pornography also meant that a new kind of criticism could be formulated that connected explicitly to contemporary gender politics (Mulvey 1975/1995: 30–43; Gustafsson and Larsson 2009: 445–7, 462–64; Arnberg 2010).

Moral panic within the hour

The *Studio S* episode was structured by four interrelated items: (1) pre-edited reportages where children were interviewed and segments where children rented videos in order to show how easy-to-access these films were, (2) pre-edited reportages where representatives of the video distributors were confronted, (3) studio debate between ten parents and two politicians, where the two studio anchors, in a very tangible way, allied with the parents against the politicians and (4) nine clips from seven exploitation films that were put on display as typical examples of the video market.

The episode started with a picture of a girl. With video technology, still images were projected on the child's forehead from various horror film VHS covers, whereas a voice-over posed the rhetorical question: 'Should 11-year-olds be allowed to watch sadistic violent films on video?' Studio anchor Göran Elwin then welcomed the audience, standing in front of a couple of television sets, a top-fed VCR, and some video cassettes. He warned the audience of the violent elements in the episode and then turned directly to watching children and parents: 'You who have children, don't let them stay up and watch this, I think that would be unnecessary. And this, of course, goes for any children who may sit alone in front of the television set. Go to bed now and sleep well.'

As Swedish sociologist Erik Höjdestrand has noted, the children in the *Studio S* episode became 'strangely freed from subjectivity. [. . .] Their consumption of films is not an active act: the films are subjects and they are objects' (Höjdestrand 1997: 36). This is not surprising since the participating children were made passive, thus vulnerable for the suggestive power that the new video technology was considered to possess. This is a very conscious strategy since it becomes difficult to argue against someone who only claims to have the children's interests in mind (Dalquist 1998: 120). This also differs from many sociological studies of moral panic where the subject usually consisted of human agents, mainly boys and young men, who are portrayed as Folk Devils, that is, individuals or groups

Figure 4.1 Screen grab from *Studio S*'s episode on 'Video violence', with studio anchor Göran Elwin, originally broadcasted by Swedish Public Television on 2 December 1980. Courtesy of Studio S Entertainment.

that are stereotyped and designated as social enemies (Goode and Ben-Yehudea 2009: 27–8. See also Cohen 2007).

Consequently, here the commercial video technology is identified as the Folk Devil when Elwin continued with a demonstration: 'It's a market, a market with video cassettes, and it's quite easy to rent a cassette in a store. You have a VCR, you insert the tape into the VCR like this, and then press this button. Then you can watch films like this one,' whereupon a nineteen-second clip from *The Boogeyman* (1980) was shown where a boy climbs up a wooden trellis on a house, followed by a short scene where a woman stabs herself with scissors in the throat.

> As you could see, this started out quite cute, but then it became scary and nasty, and this is something that quite well illustrates the video market today. It has become nastier and nastier. On the table here, we have some cassettes that are marked as such: 'The film is about a murder gang, insane, who in terrible ways mutilates their victims. A story so macabre that you wonder how the screenplay writer's psyche works. A speculation in blood. A horrendous blood-dripping thriller, where no effort is made to protect you from horror experiences, corpses, or buckets of blood.'

Two of moral panic's most distinctive features are the fact that self-appointed experts on the criticized media are not themselves users, which is often combined with strong rhetorical exaggerations where the most deviant examples are hand-picked as representative for the scorned media in question (Goode and Ben-Yehuda 2009: 233). However, *Studio S* could illustrate its critique of the VCR on live television in a very distinct way with clips from seven low-budget exploitation films: *The Boogeyman* (1980), *The Texas Chainsaw Massacre* (1974), *A Taste of Hell* (1973), *Death Trap* (1977), *Terror* (1978), *Tool Box Murders* (1978) and *Tourist Trap* (1979). Only two of these films were on the UK Director of Public Prosecutions' list released in June 1983, *Death Trap* and *The Toolbox Murders*, whereas *The Texas Chainsaw Massacre* figured as the ultimate example of video violence both in Denmark and Norway (Brown 2014: 19; Strandgaard-Jensen 2013: 226).

Even though most of the film clips that were shown appear quite outdated today, one has to keep in mind that these types of images had never been shown publicly on Nordic (or most European) television before. Seventy years of film and television censorship had effectively built a cocoon around this sort of extreme film violence, which was now broadcast on prime time in every living room in Sweden. Moreover, as the violence was connected to children's consumption of videos, the results could not have been more shocking. Accordingly, the shock had immediate effect in the television studio when unprepared parents and politicians reacted strongly to what they saw, as stand-ins for the equally unprepared television audiences. This happened on several occasions in the episode, for instance when giggling fifth grade pupils loosely described events from *The Texas Chainsaw Massacre*, which then was crosscut with a clip from the film where a screaming woman is hung on a meat hook.

However, the explicit connection made in *Studio S* between children and video can be questioned for three reasons. First, this connection was achieved through creative editing. In two pre-recorded reportages, viewers are led to believe that underage children were allowed to rent violent videos, but they are only filmed as they go into the store, and then afterwards as they are interviewed outside the respective video stores. It may as well have been somebody from the television team who rented the videos, a suspicion that is underbuilt by the fact that none of the children seemed to have a clue as to what they had rented. This was then edited together in a 'revealing' way with one of the owners of a video store who firmly denies that they rented violent films to anyone under the age of fifteen.

Second, the practice of not renting to minors was confirmed by the police raids that were conducted against Stockholm's video stores the day after the broadcast, where the police seized all leases they came across. Of these leases, only 3 per cent had been made with minors, and in almost all cases, the children in question had rented children's films with their parents' permission (Höjdestrand 1997: 68).

Third, another inconvenient circumstance emerged in a reportage on video violence from a retrospective historical perspective in the television show *Filmkrönikan* (1956–2008) in 2002. Here, children who participated in the original *Studio S* episode in 1980 were interviewed. It thus turned out that *Studio S* had picked up these children from school without the parents' knowledge, shown them selected parts of *The Texas Chainsaw Massacre*, before the studio anchor Elwin carefully and strictly instructed them what to answer, and in what way. Afterwards they had received 200 SEK and had been treated to McDonalds.

As in the UK, the use of unfounded statistics was an important part of the panic, which had tremendous impact due to the fact that they were presented on public broadcasting television. On one occasion, television audiences were informed that in the 'so-called serious market' there was 'a lot of violence and porn films'. A sign of statistics was then displayed showing the following numbers: 'Violence and sex: Video stores 51 percent; Radio and television stores 40 percent' – 'statistics' that were uncritically referred to for years to come, despite the fact that the market changed completely over the course of a couple of years.

These statistics were based on the film descriptions in five distributor catalogues, one of which Elwin quoted from at the beginning of the episode, and not on an actual inventory of the video market. The statistics do not reveal what types of violence were considered under the 'violent' category, and more importantly, the statistics do not separate between depictions of violence and depictions of sex. In this way, sex and violence are linked together in a manner that equated them as evil. The statistics about porn films may seem irrelevant in a current affairs show concerned with the threat of video violence, but the effect of adding seemingly factual significance in such a pointed but also vague way was that these 'evil forces' seemed to reinforce each other. In the long-lasting public debates that followed *Studio S*, not least in the debates in the Swedish Parliament, video violence was thus likened to a series of other phenomena, such as violent porn, drugs, devil worship and even to the Third World War (Höjdestrand 1997: 123–4). For what could be worse than a threatening nuclear war in the middle of one of the coldest periods of the Cold War?

In the episode, no pornography was shown, but *Studio S* had already made a program about the spread of pornography in Sweden in 1976 in which still images of animal and child pornography had been shown. The great attention stirred by that episode contributed to a turnaround from the 1960s liberal approach to pornography towards a more powerful and public feminist problematization of pornography, where women's groups and female politicians gradually rolled back parts of the total freedom that had been afforded to pornographic content in the 1970s (Arnberg 2010: 247–54). The motive to rhetorically include porn films in the episode about video violence was therefore mainly based on moral and political reasons in order to influence the public and politicians. In addition, graphic depictions of violence in film were still illegal in the Nordic counties outside of Denmark. Thus, this formed another area open to attack, not least, as was suggested by *Studio S*, if these films managed to bypass censorship, they would reach innocent and vulnerable children.

During the live broadcasting of the episode, eight men and six women were present in the studio. As mentioned, the studio anchors and the politicians were all men who were there in their official roles, whereas the parents were there as parents. The two studio anchors soon steered, with the help of suggestive questions and violent film clips, the debate onto an emotional path. The parents were addressed by their first names and with questions about how it felt to see these clips, implicitly: how did it feel that their children watched these films? All women made at least one comment during the evening. Of them a woman named Kerstin was the one who took most space – she was also the only woman introduced by her occupation, paediatrician. Of the men, one sat quietly all night, whereas the other three took as much space as Kerstin in the debate. The three dads thus took up as much studio time as the six mothers together. Only one of the men was introduced with his profession, medical doctor.

Two patterns could thus be distinguished. The first was that the men took more space, and the second was that the medical profession was given greater presence in the debate, suggestively connecting with the psychological implications of the harmfulness of video violence for children. Nonetheless, the MD title only had a superficial function. The male MD turned out to be a practicing pathologist but commented on child abuse and child psychiatry, whereas the female paediatrician did not refer to her profession but instead turned out to be the most emotionally behaved parent – thus stereotypically confirming the idea of women as irrational and emotional (See, for example, Höjdestrand 1997: 52). At one point she started sobbing as she said: 'you have to do something!', in response to the minister of education's refusal to immediately revise the Swedish constitution in order to stop the video violence.

Overall, the women in the studio behaved more emotionally, reacting like 'sensitive mothers' in short emotional outbursts to one horrible film clip after another, whereas the men in turn mostly reacted to the women's outbursts with longer expositions. Only in one case, a man responded emotionally as a dad, which occurred after being shown a second clip from *The Texas Chainsaw Massacre*. Elwin chose to introduce the clip after a first round of discussion where children, as if it were a fact, were identified as the main consumers of video violence, and where seven out of ten parents had turned over the responsibility to the politicians, believing themselves to be powerless in face of this development.

> We don't want to torment those in the studio or the viewers more than necessary, but there is a very common theme in these films, which I think we'll have to watch for a moment – and that's the theme of misogyny and sadism against women. There are rape scenes and there are sadistic scenes, such as in the clip that we would like to show to, among others, Jan-Erik Wikström. It's a short excerpt from a scene where a woman is tortured for a total of eleven minutes.

What followed was the episode's longest film clip, ninety-four seconds, where three male 'hillbillies' from a crazy family are trying to persuade their grandfather to kill a young captured woman with a hammer. The woman is brutally held down over a bucket, while she makes violent resistance and screams throughout the scene. However, the old man is far too physically weak and drops the hammer repeatedly, so the painful scene goes on and on for what seems to be forever – however, not for eleven minutes as Elwin claimed. Finally, the woman turns herself loose, the clip ends and the discussion returns to the studio.

Höjdestrand suggests that this clip was the dramatic highlight of the *Studio S* episode and it is easy to understand why (Höjdestrand 1997: 47). It was at this precise moment that *The Texas Chainsaw Massacre* achieved cult status and was canonized as the ultimate evil of the commercial video market in the Nordic countries. It was also with this clip that the VCR's 'inherent' misogyny was confirmed more effectively than before. In addition, this heart-pumping clip shifted the focus from children to a more abstract evil connected to video violence, which became something that threatened everything and everyone. As a result, the dramatic curve of the episode actually reached its highest point immediately after the clip was shown, and it took the form of a strong emotional attack on the politicians in the studio.

The indignant father turned directly to the minister of education Wikström: 'You are a politician. You are the minister of education with a responsibility for culture. But you are also a human being, and it would be very interesting if you, as a human being, could give us a review of these film clips that we have just seen.' Noticeably upset, Wikström replied that the whole situation was terrible, partly because these violent images existed, partly because he thought it was most unfortunate that these film clips had been broadcast on public television at all, since this contributed to the proliferation of violence. The evangelical minister concluded with a powerful Bible quote directed at the video dealers: 'Things that cause people to stumble are bound to come, but woe to anyone through whom they come. It would be better for them to be thrown into the sea with a millstone tied around their neck' (Luke 17.1–2). This did not, however, seem to please the upset parents. The female paediatrician, Kerstin, shouted: 'Our children are watching this without our knowledge [. . .] you have to change the law!' A moment later, another mother repeated the claim: 'There must be a temporary ban you can use tomorrow or whenever. We cannot wait for a change of the constitution!' Then an elderly man broke into the discussion and equalled video violence with child pornography, whereby he implied that neither one had any justification in relation to the Freedom of the Press Act since they were both perversions. The two politicians, nevertheless, maintained that the Freedom of the Press Act and the Swedish Constitution could not be changed overnight. 'We are working with slow-moving tools.'

In the distraught but excited situation, orchestrated by the studio anchors, a woman finally said, 'They aren't going to do anything. And it's not about freedom of speech, it's about speculation. They want to make a quick buck on innocent children!' One of the studio anchors then put out the question whether video technology should be banned altogether, and only one of the ten parents objected to that proposal, which illustrates the degree of incitement that had been stirred up within the episode's hour-long broadcast.

A twenty-year-long aftermath

The day after the broadcast of *Studio S*, the hard-pressed minister of education appointed an on-the-spot investigation, whereas the newspapers swarmed with reportages and debate articles about video violence. Thirty sex newspapers immediately commented on video violence on their editorial pages, and all but four connected it to children (Höjdestrand 1997: 57, 67). The Social Democratic newspaper *Arbetet* reported that children had been so shaken when they came to school on Wednesday morning that they 'trembled and barely could hold their pens when they were writing' (Anon. 1980a). However, adolescents were included in these media reports, but crucially, they were not portrayed as objects in the same manner as children but, instead, as active and masculine coded subjects traditionally linked to media violence. For example, the front page of *Aftonbladet* was covered by the bold wartime headline: 'WE HAVE BEATEN PEOPLE ON THE STREET – and we have 45 videos at home' (*Aftonbladet* 1980). This was accompanied by an article where two teenage boys confessed that they used to beat people because they had nothing else to do. This 'terror gang', called Fonziegänget (The Fonzie Gang, named after the character played by Henry Winkler in *Happy Days* (1974-1984)), had terrorized inner-city Stockholm throughout the autumn and had therefore been part of the newsfeed several times. But now, readers were finally offered an explanation to their deviant behaviour – the consumption of films on video. 'When you saw the first scary murder, you definitely reacted, but now you don't care,' they told the interviewer. What is more, they not only watched videos but owned these films and could watch them repeatedly. The boys said that the gang owned between 5,000 and 6,000 video films, of which the majority were violent films (Willborg 1980). This statement was accepted without question by the journalist, which was a common journalistic omission in the debate that followed. It should be repeated that the entire Swedish video market consisted of 500–1,000 titles at this time, and that one single video film could cost up to 100 GBP to buy in 1980 (PoundSterlingLive 2017) – which would have meant that Fonziegänget would have owned videos to a value of approximately half a million pounds!

Similar proof of this video addiction, or 'videoholicism', and its horrible consequences, were repeatedly front-page news in the UK during the video nasties scare. In the summer of 1983 headlines like, 'Fury Over the Video Rapist' and 'A Video Nasty Killer' fuelled the imagination of readers and government officials alike as perpetrators suddenly used films like *I Spit On Your Grave* (aka *Day of the Woman*, 1978) and *Zombie Flesh Eaters* (*Zombie 2*, 1980) as scapegoats for their crimes (Brown 2014: 25–6). Nevertheless, no research was seemingly needed during this initial phase because the harmful effects of video violence were perceived to be self-evident. Swedish sociologist Ulf Dalquist believes that media violence could be used 'both as an excuse and an explanation to violent behavior' (Dalquist 1998: 44), in other words, newspapers and perpetrators

Figure 4.2 Headlines the day after the *Studio S*'s episode on 'Video Violence: "WE HAVE BEATEN PEOPLE ON THE STREET" – and we have 45 videos at home'. *Aftonbladet*, 3 December 1980.

such as Fonziegänget found a common point of reference in their use of video violence to justify their immoral behaviour.

In another article published the same day, the connection between adolescent boys and media violence was further scrutinized and strengthened. Here, a pedagogue argued, '[w]hat a young boy admires most in film is the aggressive and cold male ideals'. The pedagogue led a project in five Stockholm schools where he screened 'violent films' such as *Bonnie and Clyde* (1967), *Bullitt* (1968) and *Cabaret* (1972) for junior high school students. The intention was to teach them to perceive the 'toughness ideal' as a 'sick' male ideology that permeated film culture, and that was 'created by adults for purely commercial reasons'. In establishing such actions, this pedagogue can be regarded as a 'moral entrepreneur', a self-appointed expert who took advantage of the situation in order to promote himself or herself or a moral agenda (Goode and

Ben-Yehuda 2009: 26–7, 53–4, 67). In other words, the criticism was aimed against Hollywood's image of manhood, which 'unfortunately spreads across the world at light speed' (Melin 1980). A couple of days later, Sweden's largest morning paper, *Dagens Nyheter* wrote about the project, highlighting the risk that young boys (and specifically, not girls) would be inspired by film violence and their 'sick heroic ideals' (Olson 1980).

While this 'sick ideal' was linked to video violence and teenage boys, with American mainstream film culture receiving much of the blame, the international video market mainly consisted of European-produced B and C films. Accordingly, a century old dichotomy between Europe and the United States was activated, driven by the perception that American culture was, by definition, superficial and commercial, which made it possible to equate it with the depravation of the video market (Gustafsson and Arnberg 2013: 28). Hence, the discussion about the VCR and videos came to include the perceived danger of low culture and bad taste entertainment and the threat that this would be spread to young Nordic citizens. This nationalistic-protective approach can be observed in the other Nordic countries (Strandgaard-Jensen 2013: 244) as well as in the UK, where the video technique and these films were perceived as 'foreign invaders with bad dubbing and titles that talked about cannibalism' (Brown 2014: 27).

The outburst of concern over video violence is linked to the discussion of misogyny, not least via the explicit connection made in the *Studio S* episode using *The Texas Chainsaw Massacre*, but also implicitly by the fact that film violence in general was brought together with porn films to comprise a singular immoral phenomenon. Even though *Studio S* did not show any porn and despite the fact that the violent films used in the episode did not contain any sex scenes – with the exception of an unfinished rape scene in one of the clips – the newspaper commentaries steamed with allegations that video violence was the same as sexualized violence. According to *Arbetet*, the video market consisted 'almost exclusively [of] violence and pornography' (Anon. 1980b). In another article in the same newspaper, the managing editor sharply distanced himself 'from the contempt for human beings, the cruelties, the violent porn, the anal fascist philosophy, and all capitalization of perversities', which, for him, equated to the normal state of the video industry (Ekblom 1980). In the editorial for the Christian newspaper *Dagen* 'violent pornography', 'sexual seduction' and 'child pornography' were brought together and equated with the video releases supposedly hitting the shelves uncontrolled (Anon. 1980c). At the same time, the evening newspaper *Expressen* wrote about 'violent pornography of the cruellest sort' (Wennerholm 1980), whereas *Göteborgs-Tidningen* wrote about 'violent pornographic perversions' (Sundahl and Lisell 1980). The list of examples where violence and pornography/sex were brought together goes on and if no one was to act, according to child psychiatrist Olle Elthammar, the market would soon be flooded by 'sadistic sex films' (Anon. 1980d).

As noted, the women's movement's focus on pornography had been an important part of the public debate during the second half of the 1970s. However, the emphasis on violence in relation to pornography has a prehistory that dates back a few years. American and Israeli sociologists Erich Goode and Nachman Ben-Yehuda, respectively, have studied the debate about the film *Snuff* (1976), a film in which a woman is raped, tortured and murdered – all under the pretence that this was a snuff film, that is, that everything had happened for real in front of the camera. The belief that *Snuff* was authentic had contributed to the formation of the organization Women against Violence against Women (WAVAW) in 1976. In 1977, WAVAW joined an older organization, Women against Pornography (WAP), which in turn formulated the link between pornography and violence based on three arguments: (1) pornography *is* violence against women, (2) pornography is *caused* by violence against women and (3) pornography *causes* violence against women. The two leading women in this campaign, which was to be firmly established during the 1980s, were the controversial radical-feminists Andrea Dworkin and Catharine MacKinnon (Goode and Ben-Yehuda 2009: 223–8). This debate became part of the so-called Sex Wars conducted by feminists in the 1970s and the 1980s (Duggan and Hunter 1995).

The debate about the authenticity of *Snuff* and snuff films reached Sweden in the fall of 1982 when the lingering moral panic was ignited due to the question of whether the banned film *Cannibal Holocaust* (1980) was a snuff film (Höjdestrand 1997: 133–7). This rumour had started already after its Italian premiere, when director Ruggero Deodato was arrested on obscenity charges, and on the suspicion that he had made a snuff film. This then turned into a worldwide phenomenon as country after country banned the film. According to Christopher Brown, the VHS distributor of *Cannibal Holocaust* in the UK used this fear and sent 'an anonymous complaint tipping off Mary Whitehouse of the National Viewers' and Listeners' Association' (Brown 2014: 16, 70). From there it spiralled on to public outcries, to legislation, and on to Sweden, where it was picked up to reignite the debate, in the process demonstrating the transnational qualities of the international video market.

The films that *Studio S* placed in the undefined 'video violence genre' belonged, in six out of the seven cases in the historically and culturally disregarded genre of the horror film. The horror film has a number of subgenres, but in this case, most of the films can be placed into the slasher/stalker subgenre where, usually, a psychotic male monster kills a number of youngsters of both sexes in different brutal ways. There is no doubt that there exists a sexual undertone in many slasher films, something that, using psychoanalysis, is often interpreted as sexual fear or sexual frustration in particular with the masculine coded monster. Nudity and sexual activities among the young victims are also a key part of these genre conventions. However, explicit sexual violence such as rape does not exist in this genre (Clover 1993: 23-9). The film in which a rape was about to be committed, *A Taste of Hell*, is not a horror film but could instead be placed in the more culturally appreciated war film genre. Hence, that film was part of the mainstream film culture, where extremely problematic rape scenes have been *legio* throughout film history, for instance in films such as *The Son of the Sheik* (1926), *Gone with the Wind* (1939) and *Straw Dogs* (1971) (Projansky 2001: passim).

Nonetheless, as the social construction of gender and gender relations are constantly evolving, it may be worthwhile to point out that many films that were part of the 'video violence' scare in the Nordic countries as well as in the UK, that is, low-budget horror films produced between 1974 and 1986, have been culturally re-evaluated. American Scandinavist and film scholar Carol J Clover has researched this period and found, in opposition to the general belief, that female roles are far more progressive in these despised films than in the more conservative mainstream film. For example, young women appear as strong and independent, that is, as self-evident heroes and often as the only survivor who singlehandedly vanquish the masculine monster. Clover specifically highlights the role of Sally (Marilyn Burns), the woman who was beaten in the infamous clip from *The Texas Chainsaw Massacre* in *Studio S*, as the first significant example of this new female activity. 'For nearly thirty minutes of screen time – a third of the film – we watch her shriek, run, flinch, jump or fall through windows, sustain injury and mutilation. Her will to survive is astonishing; in the end, bloody and staggering, she finds the highway' (Clover 1993: 36).

Furthermore, Clover argues for the increased popularity of these low-budget horror films – *Halloween* (1978) famously took in 75 million USD at the US box office – which contributed to the fact that progressive elements, such as strong roles for women, found their way into mainstream film culture. This meant a normalization and increased competition for hero roles previously monopolized by men. For instance, these developments can be seen as inspiration for praised female roles such as Clarice Starling (Jodie Foster) in *Silence of the Lambs* (1991) and Beatrix Kiddo (Uma Thurman) in *Kill Bill Vol 1* and *2* (2003–4) (Clover 1993: 3–20). Another example is the cultural re-evaluation of an exploitation film such as *The Texas Chainsaw Massacre*. Today, it is featured at the top in a number of lists that rank the world's most influential horror films, as well as included in Museum of Modern Art's permanent collections in New York as a valuable and unconventional artwork (Rockoff 2002: 42).

Yet, despite these eventual economic and cultural re-evaluations of exploitation cinema, the Nordic countries, and especially Sweden and Finland, were at the forefront in restricting their influence through censorship. The on-the-spot investigation into video violence proposed in the wake of *Studio S* presented two proposals. First, a ban on marketing of video violence to minors. Second, a ban on video violence for all ages. The Swedish government chose the less extensive proposal focusing on marketing, but after considerable criticism and debate, by the summer of 1981, the government introduced a law that imposed a total ban on so-called extreme violence, whereby video distributors and video store owners could be prosecuted in retrospect for renting videos with rough and sadistic violence. However, due to the opposition of the right-wing party, Moderata samlingspartiet, in the Swedish Parliament, the new law was not set in action until 1 August 1982 (Höjdestrand 1997: 98, 139).

Immediately, a number of video store owners were reported to the police, and the shortcomings of the new law soon became apparent. The application of the law was at the municipal level of jurisdiction, resulting in circumstances where films that were found to contain unlawful extreme violence in one district court could be freed in a neighbouring district court. Between 1982 and 1985, a total of forty-seven video titles were tried, but only twenty-five of these were found to contain illegal violence by all district courts, whereas the rest of the films were judged differently from district court to district court. Furthermore, the law stated that the violence must have 'human origin', which is why, for example, ghost and demon films such as *The Boogeyman* – from which *Studio S* had taken their first film clip – were freed by several district courts (Höjdestrand 1997: 163–9).

These figures can be compared to the statistics used by *Studio S* in the original episode, which often figured in the debates on video violence, and that claimed that between 40 and 51 per cent of the video market consisted of 'very serious violence and porn films'. However, by 1985 many Nordic households owned a VCR at the same time as the video market had changed dramatically and grown to 15,000 titles, porn films not included. By this time, all Hollywood studios had started to release their films on the video market, which in turn meant that the presence of speculative B and C films decreased markedly. In comparison, this meant that Swedish district courts agreed that a measly 0.0016 per cent of all video films violated the new law when it came to depictions of extreme violence.

In order to compensate for the legal uncertainty that the new law had resulted in, a change in the cinema ordinance was introduced from 1 January 1986. The change meant that video distributors were allowed to submit their films, on a voluntarily basis, to the Swedish Board of Film Censorship where the films were examined and often censored despite the fact that these films were not primarily for public consumption, which was the area in which the cinema ordinance was to be applied. To avoid what amounted to a lottery on legality, many distributors submitted their videos because a film that passed the Board of Film Censorship could not be prosecuted in retrospect for containing illegal extreme violence (Dalquist 1998: 107).

VHS censorship in the bigger picture: Extremes and counterforces

In 1982, Norway followed Sweden and introduced a law that extended film censorship to include videos, and in Denmark an appropriateness-label for videos was introduced in 1984 (Smith-Isaksen 2013: 198; Strandgaard-Jensen 2013: 234). In the UK, the Video Recording Act of 1984 became law on 1 September 1985. The act gave the British Board of Film Classification the power to rate videos like cinematic releases, resulting in heavy cuts, prosecution and convictions for distributors, and banning and censoring of films to this day (Brown 2014: 18–21). In Finland, a set of similar debates raged about the impact of violence with *The Texas Chainsaw Massacre*, again (despite the fact that the film was completely prohibited since its first attempted theatrical release in 1974), as the key catalyst for what became one of the most extensive home video laws in Europe, the 1987 Video Act that prohibited all films rated 18 from home video release. Before the institution of the 1987 Video Act (Ääni- ja kuvatallennetuottajat ry, Audiovisual Content Producers Ltd.), film importers had practised self-censorship for home video releases. The justification for these self-censorship practices was that VET (Valtion elokuvatarkastamo, The Finnish Board of Film Classification) would have to approve theatrical and home video releases by pre-screening the film and order cuts before permits were received. This resulted in many of the importing companies cutting out what they deemed as excessive or egregious content to anticipate potential time and cost delays with VET. These edits would prove to be most contentious for film producers and viewers as they were often done without much finesse in order to avoid having to resubmit the same film multiple times. One particularly notorious instance features future Hollywood director Renny Harlin cutting over eleven minutes of material out of *The Evil Dead* (1981) so it would not befall misfortunes with the censors. The film did receive a release on home video in its cut form but was eventually prohibited in 1987 under the K-18 label. Even more surprisingly, Harlin would counter the censors himself a few years later with his film *Arctic Heat* (1985), leading to one of the most notorious cases of a domestic production meeting the scrutiny of VET.

The debates leading up to constituting the act largely followed the same trajectories as in the UK and Sweden. Both political and cultural debates predominantly focused on whipping up a sense of moral panic about protecting young children from violent influences. At the same time, some expressed concern over the negative influences of hegemonic cultural industries, namely Hollywood, on identity and culture in a marginal region. For example, YLE, the national broadcaster, took part in these debates with several broadcast specials focusing on different stakeholders. In one particulate programme, *Videolaki valmisteilla*, aired on 12 December 1985, two twelve-year-olds were interviewed in a video store. They profess to having seen everything already available, though rather eloquently, they also suggest that they do not consider these films a problem as their parents have educated them to view them as fairy tales. The section cuts to Gustav Björkstrand, the minister for culture, who leans back in his chair to state, while smirking, that he has seen very few of the films and that the cultural minister should in principle know more about what is out there in the field, yet he has not had the time to do so. But, he adds, 'knowing what kind of product is out there', it does not exactly appeal to him either. Björkstrand acknowledges that the use of censorship is problematic, but he does not believe the markets can be left to be self-regulating as, according to him, there are huge economic pressures on the sector – the implication is that without regulation, the industry would run rampant with immoral content. Despite some of the critical questions raised by the programme, its framing of the debates as involving impressionable children with the ability to have access to all these tapes would have only reinforced the urgency for top-down legislation as was the case with the *Studio S* episode in Sweden.

Finnish film and television historian Jari Sedergren (1999) has categorized Finnish censorship to three paradigms: impropriety, violence and political connotations. The political dominated up to the 1980s due to the strained relations and diplomatic influence of the neighbouring USSR. Although pornographic material continued to be an issue into the 1990s, it was violence that proved to be the most inflammatory and far-reaching of these areas – resonating, as we will see, into the contemporary era as it influenced many of the key consumption habits of future generations of film producers and directors. Thus, with the establishment of the 1987 Video Act, video stores were allowed a one-year transition period in which all these films – often already heavily cut – would be outright banned from being available on VHS, with police raids starting in 1988. The 1987 Act resulted in some fundamental conceptual problems as different media platforms were now governed by different means of regulation and oversight (Sironen 2006: 20–47). The act, and the banning of 18-rated films, only applied to VHS. Yet, domestic broadcast and cable television, for example, were outside of the act's remit, resulting in the screening of a film like *Die Hard* (1988) uncut on television, but missing about four minutes forty seconds on VHS, and the availability of uncut versions of the *Friday the 13th* series (which were under a blanket ban in both cinemas and VHS) with Finnish subtitles on cable provider Filmnet. Simultaneously, theatrical releases continued to be available with 18 ratings, which resulted in some distributors capitalizing on the commercial value of supposedly transgressive material unavailable on VHS, including theatrical releases for the somewhat tame *Prom Night II: Hello Mary Lou* (1987) in 1991, but now with an advertising campaign that highlighted that this was 'the original uncensored version' more prominently than any of its actual content. It is also intriguing to note that the category of K-20 was sometimes prominently highlighted on the VHS covers of films like *The Exterminator* (1980), despite the fact that such a category did not officially exist.

Thus, other film platforms were exempt from the excesses of video censorship, but VHS releases were hit with the hardest levels of oversight (see Samola 1989 for more on these debates). This resulted in some egregious cuts to content with the relatively exploitation-like *The Exterminator*, *Bloodsport* (1988), but also the very mainstream *Rambo III* (1988) and *Robocop* (1987), victims of some of the most excessive cuts. Each of these films was censored by more than ten minutes. These censorship customs resulted in some peculiar self-censorship practices on behalf of the video distribution companies fearing to have to go through the re-submission process with VET, but also now being increasingly aware that some of their films were now struggling to meet the feature length standard. Two memorable instances include re-editing some of the martials arts battles in *Bloodsport* (as the film was cut by seventeen minutes and ten seconds, largely by its distributor Showtime), so it seems Jean-Claude Van Damme's character appears simultaneously both in the audience and the fight court, or the infamous head explosion scene from *Maniac* (1980), with the film pausing at the moment the head of the character played by Tom Savini explodes, resulting in a lengthy still image of blood splatter that some found more disturbing than the uncut scene. The tendency of the distributors not only to edit out particularly prodigious moments of violence but to cut out the majority of the scene, or re-edit them to boost the running time of the film, resulted in often incomprehensible films that fundamentally changed some of the intentions of the producers. Some argue that it also consolidated the concentration of VHS distribution networks to a handful of distributors who would be able to continue to operate in such a tightly policed environment as well as in the reduction of companies taking 'risks' with importing quality films, such as those of John Woo, with potentially problematic content, especially as these existed outside of the Hollywood mainstream and would have had to appeal to niche audiences.

To provide a counterbalance to the undeniable cultural and economic impact the harsh censorship had on films on VHS, all Nordic countries saw counter-dynamic moves such as fanzines, film swapping, illegal import of violent films, black markets, amateur video production and film festivals. Sweden had several action and horror fanzines such as *Black, Violent Vision, Shock, Broken Minds, Röd Snö* (Red Snow) and *Magasin Defekt*, whereas Norway had *Rage* and Denmark produced, despite its lack of grown-up film censorship, fanzines such as *Trauma* and *Inferno*. The illegality to publicly screen or privately distribute films with 'extreme violence' in most Nordic countries was a prerequisite for the development of the film swapper, and this also explains why some of them had extensive international contacts in order to get hold of uncensored video films. Fanzines often took in ads, where foreign distributors with postal order services informed readers of their catalogues and prices (Bolin 2000: 58–62).

Within this 'underground' sphere, there also circulated amateur video films, produced by aspirant filmmakers who were encouraged by the films they had seen as well as by the underground credibility these censorship norms, largely unintentionally, generated. Sweden, for instance, is a country with a long tradition of organized social movements, and this has meant that the state has sponsored cultural activities on reading, popular music, and amateur filmmaking. These aspiring filmmakers could thus apply for state subsidies (a symbolic sum) for their activities, but when they applied for funding for full-length feature films from the Swedish Film Institute, they were always rejected (Bolin 2000: 68). Instead, they produced short films and music videos that were screened in so-called zero budget film festivals, where amateur film and video producers can present their works. These kinds of festivals are often arranged as club meetings for members in order to circumvent the legislation on censorship. Festivals of this kind are arranged at several levels: locally, nationally and on a Nordic level. It is also a common phenomenon elsewhere in Europe and the United States, where festivals of this kind can gather hundreds of participants (Bolin 2000: 64).

The initiators behind *Magasin Defekt* were also the organizers for Fantastisk Film Festival in Lund in Sweden that came on to the scene as a small alternative horror and fantasy film festival for students in 1995, but that developed into a comprehensive film festival over the years, eventually being accepted in 2001 to be a part of the European Fantastic Film Festivals Federation and receiving subsidies from the Swedish Film Institute.

In Finland, organizations like Gore Hound and Dark Fantasy were set up as collectives addressing the now prohibited forms of film culture. They published magazines and organized screenings of films, even organizing a petition to repeal the Video Act in 1998 that generated 22,000 signatures. Simultaneously, these restrictions led to a booming industry in the import of films from abroad through mail order and other means, which at one point was estimated to be up to 20 per cent of the VHS industry (Carlson 1992). The fan black market in copies of cut or censored films was big business, and several more or less legitimate fan community 'organizations' like Rhinoceros emerged to capitalize on the availability of uncut versions from Holland or Denmark, from where these could be imported and copied onwards to Finnish consumers through closely-knit networks. Though some of the most extensive offenders were shut down by the authorities, the grassroots distribution of tapes, as well as the means to gain legal access to these very same films through domestic television, only emphasized the improbable foundations of the act.

These operations were significant in increasing the availability of content and many of the excesses of the censors only increased fan affinity with these films. Even though the act was repealed in 2001, resulting in the abolishment of most forms of censorship, its 'positive' influences are still felt. These have led to intriguing fan cult phenomena, including connoisseurship of cut VHS tapes, which sell for several hundred euros on the second-hand market. Sellers would also provide an additional digital copy of the VHS print but with the missing censored material included amongst the 'original' content. Undoubtedly, nostalgia plays a key role in individuals patronizing an inferior technological format such as VHS, but these developments also emphasize the ways fan activities operate on the basis of affinity instead of rational economic logic (Hills 2002: 4–5). As scholars of fan studies have suggested (Jenkins 2013:1–8), fans use texts (which these cut VHS tapes certainly are) in unexpected ways that often expand or challenge their original constitution. Here, a particularly intriguing practice is the act of not only re-editing scenes cut by the censors back into an otherwise VHS-based format but also of prioritizing the censored versions in themselves. Consequently, we have seen Facebook communities like the 'video butchery' site emerge where connoisseurs have posted comparisons of uncut and cut versions of films compiled into a single clip, which would summarize all edits made to the Finnish VHS of the film by showing the cut scene with text overlays elaborating on the minutes and seconds of the cuts. These would then be distributed to a range of message boards where users would comment on them and share their memories of viewing the films on video.

Most importantly, these activities would feed into production arrangements as the 'fanboys' of the 1980s and the 1990s graduated into film production and would use many of the sentiments and tactics learned from these outlawed texts to produce their own variations of exploitation film. Such modes show that any understanding of exploitation cinema is about production, but it is also very much concerned with the reception context where fans make complex uses of these texts, often in ways that challenge original meanings.

Conclusion

Emanating some two years before the video nasties scare in the UK, the very public moral panics concerning video violence in all the Nordic countries demonstrate a cultural closeness as well as a common derogatory perspective on commercial exploitation, not least the shared solution that consisted of simply banning these films. Being small nations, the ability to act fast and decisively to stop this 'foreign invasion' of commercialism in the form of entertainment violence was harshly used, but as the Finnish and Swedish fan examples reveal, the new media context of home video could not be hindered, just delayed. As we saw, under-the-counter markets developed for banned and uncut films.

The circumstances where film and video violence continued to be illegal to screen publicly and to rent privately contributed to the fact that these films continued to be produced outside of the ordinary Nordic film industries, and of course without the support of the national film institutes. Cut, scorned and ridiculed, the low-budget exploitation films that did get produced by Nordic filmmakers became the pariah of the Nordic film industries, which still in the 1980s continued to profile themselves on the European art cinema circuit. Often these films were not even recognized as Nordic productions, which suited filmmakers such as Mats Helge Olsson and Renny Harlin well, since the 'Nordic', 'Swedish', 'Scandinavian' or 'Finnish' trademark did not sell violent films but instead stood for sex and nudity both domestically and internationally. Nevertheless, the VCR and the VHS-tape made it possible for filmmakers to produce commercially viable, if not successful, films directly to the international video market, where bad taste, violence and transnational qualities, such as bad dubbing, became assets, as well as led to continued reappreciation of these films in the decades to come.

References

Aftonbladet (1980), 3 December, front page.
Anon. (1980a), 'Barnen darrade då de kom till skolan', *Arbetet*, 3 December.
Anon. (1980b), 'Videogrammen: Vems frihet?', *Arbetet*, 3 December.
Anon. (1980c), 'Video – på ont och gott', *Dagen*, 3 December.
Anon. (1980d), 'Barnpsykiaterna [sic]: Stoppa videovåldet', *Svenska Dagbladet*, 4 December.
Arnberg, Klara (2010), *Motsättningarnas marknad: Den pornografiska pressens kommersiella genombrott och regleringen av pornografi i Sverige 1950–1980*, Lund: Sekelbokförlag.
Avskaffande av filmcensuren för vuxna: men förstärkt skydd för barn och unga mot skadlig mediepåverkan (2009), SOU 2009:51, Stockholm: Regeringen, http://www.regeringen.se/49bb97/contentassets/6d410698d3d3489c925851a01745b16a/avskaffande-av-filmcensuren-for-vuxna---men-forstarkt-skydd-for-barn-och-unga-mot-skadlig-mediepaverkan-sou-200951 (Accessed 12 October 2017).

Boëthius, Maria-Pia (1976), *Skylla sig själv: en bok om våldtäkt*, Stockholm: Liber.
Bolin, Göran (2000), 'Film Swapping in the Public Sphere: Youth Audiences and Alternative Cultural Publicities', *Javnost – The Public: Journal of the European Institute for Communication and Culture*, 7 (2), 57–73.
Brown, Christopher A. (2014), *The Video Nasties Moment: Examining the Films Behind the Scare*, London: lulu.com.
Carlson, Kristina (1992), 'Kieltolaki, jota ei valvota', *Suomen Kuvalehti* 1/1992.
Carlsson, Ulla (2005), *Våld och pornografi i medierna: åsikter om medievåldets och pornografins påverkan på unga människor*, Göteborg: Nordicom/Medierådet.
Clover, Carol J.(1993), *Men, Women and Chainsaws. Gender in the Modern Horror Film*, London: BFI.
Cohen, Stanley (2007), *Folk Devils and Moral Panics. The Creation of the Mods and Rockers*, 3rd edn, London and New York: Routledge.
Dalquist, Ulf (1998), *Större våld än vad nöden kräver? Medievåldsdebatten i Sverige 1980–1995*, Umeå: Borea.
Duggan, Lisa and Nan D. Hunter (1995), *Sex Wars: Sexual Dissent and Political Culture*, New York: Routledge.
Ekblom, Harry (1980), 'Råheterna inget nytt . . .', *Arbetet*, 3 December.
Goode, Erich and Nachman Ben-Yehudea (2009), *Moral Panics. The Social Construction of Deviance*, Malden, MA and Oxford: Wiley-Blackwell.
Gore, Tipper (1987), *Raising PG Kids in an X-Rated Society*, Nashville, TN: Abingdon Press.
Grainge, Paul, Mark Jancovich and Sharon Monteith (2008), *Film Histories. An Introduction and Reader*, Edinburgh: University of Toronto Press.
Gustafsson, Tommy (2014), *Det var en gång: Historia för barn i svensk television under det långa 1970-talet*, Malmö: Universus/Roos&Tegnér.
Gustafsson, Tommy and Klara Arnberg (2013), *Moralpanik och lågkultur: Genus- och mediehistoriska analyser 1900–2012*, Stockholm: Atlas Akademi.
Gustafsson, Tommy and Mariah Larsson (2009), 'Porren inför lagen: Två fallstudier angående den officiella attityden till offentligt visad pornografisk film 1921 och 1971', *Historisk tidskrift 129*, 3, 445–65.
Hall, Stuart, Brian Roberts, John Clarke, Tony Jefferson and Chas Critcher (1978), *Policing the Crisis: Mugging, the State and Law and Order*, London and Basingstoke: Palgrave Macmillan.
Hills, Matthew (2002), *Fan Cultures*, New York: Sage.
Historia.se – Portalen för historisk statistik, http://www.historia.se/ (Accessed 26 October 2017).
Höjdestrand, Erik (1997), *Det vedervärdiga videovåldet. Att upprätta moralisk ordning*, Uppsala: Acta Universitatis Upsaliensis.
Iversen, Gunnar (2011), *Norsk filmhistorie*, Oslo: Universitetsforlaget.

Jacobsson, Pelle (1980), 'Skräckfilmerna som barnen lånar hem', *Aftonbladet*, 2 December.
Jenkins, Philip and Daniel Maier-Katkin (1992), 'Satanism: Myth and Reality in a Contemporary Moral Panic', *Crime, Law and Social Change*, 17 (1): 53–75.
Jenkins, Henry (2013), *Textual Poachers: Television Fans and Participatory Culture*, New York: Sage.
Kaplan, Tony (1980), 'Studio S i kväll: Videovåld', *Arbetet*, 2 December 1980.
Lennerhed, Lena (2016), '*491* and the Censorship Controversy', in Elisabet Björklund and Mariah Larsson (eds), *Swedish Cinema and the Sexual Revolution: Critical Essays*, Jefferson, NC: McFarland, pp. 116–25.
Martin, John (2007), *Seduction of the Gullible: The Truth Behind the Video Nasty Scandal*, Plymouth: Stray Cat Publishing Ltd.
Mathijs, Ernest and Jamie Sexton (2011), *Cult Cinema: An Introduction*, Malden, MA: Wiley-Blackwell.
McLuhan, Marshall (1964), *Understanding Media: The Extensions of Man*, New York: McGraw-Hill.
Melin, Lena (1980), 'Lär ungdomarna genomskåda tuffhetsidealet', *Aftonbladet*, 3 December.
Meylakhs, Peter (2006), 'The Discourse of the Press and the Press of Discourse: Constructing the drug Problem in the Russian Media', in Chas Critcher (ed.), *Critical Readings: Moral Panic and the Media*, Maidenhead: Open University Press.
Mulvey, Laura (1975/1995), 'Spelfilmen och lusten att se', in Lars Gustaf Anderssonoch Erik Hedling (eds), *Modern filmteori 2*, Lund: Studentlitteratur.
Olson, Björn Anders (1980), 'De ser våldsfilm på skoltid', *Dagens Nyheter*, 6 December.
Ost, Suzanne (2002), 'Children at Risk: Legal and Societal Perceptions of the Potential Threat that the Possession of Child Pornography Poses to Society', *Journal of Law and Society*, 29 (3): 436–60.
Pearce, Harry (2013), *Video Nasties: A True Story of Court Cases, Cock Ups and Collateral Damage*, Seattle: WA: CreateSpace Independent Publishing Platform.
Pound Sterling Live (2017), https://www.poundsterlinglive.com/bank-of-england-spot/historical-spot-exchange-rates/gbp/GBP-to-SEK-1980 (Accessed 26 October 2017).
Projansky, Sarah (2001), *Watching Rape: Film and Television in Postfeminist Culture*, New York: New York University Press.
Rockoff, Adam (2002), *Going to Pieces. The Rise and Fall of the Slasher Film, 1978–1986*, Jefferson, NC: McFarland & Co.
Rydström, Jens and David Tjeder (2009), *Kvinnor, män och alla andra. En svensk genushistoria*, Lund: Studentlitteratur.
Samola, Juha (1989), 'Erään lain vaiheita', in Tilda Maria Forselius ja Seppo Luoma-Keturi (eds), *Uhka silmälle – 7 esseetä kauhun katsomisesta ja videohysteriasta*, Like, Helsinki.

Sedergren, Jari (1999), *Filmi poikki . . . Poliittinen elokuvasensuuri Suomessa 1939-1947*, Suomen Historiallinen Seura, Helsinki

Sexuella övergrepp: förslag till ny lydelse av brottsbalkens bestämmelser om sedlighetsbrott (1976), SOU 1976:9, Regeringen: Stockholm.

Shrieve, Krystn (1999), 'Ventura County Seeks Help; Tipper Gore May Be Enlisted In Health Services Row', *Los Angeles Daily News*, 19 May, http://www.nytimes.com/20 00/05/19/us/2000-campaign-vice-president-s-wife-tipper-gore-seeks-privacy-under-public.html?pagewanted=all&src=pm (Accessed 9 October 2017).

Sironen, Jiri (2006), *Videolaista elokuvien aikuisensuurin poistumiseen: Sensuuripuhunnat ja kuvaohjelmien kulttuurinen sääntely 1980-luvulta nykypäivään*, Pro-Gradu, Jyväskylän yliopisto.

Smith-Isaksen, Marte (2013), '"Så videovold – villedrepe"', in Ove Solum (ed.), *Film til folket: Sensur og kinopolitikk i 100 år*, Olso: Fagbokforlaget.

Strandgaard Jensen, Helle (2013), *Defining the (In)appropriate: Scandinavian Debates About the Role of Media in Children's Lives, 1950–1985*, Florence: European University Institute.

Sundahl, Sune and Jens Lisell (1980), 'Offensiv mot videovåldet', *Göteborgs-Tidningen*, 4 December.

Wasko, Janet (2008), 'Talkin' 'Bout a Revolution: Home Video', in Paul Grainge, Mark Jancovich and Sharon Monteith, *Film Histories: An Introduction and Reader*, Edinburgh: University of Toronto Press.

Wennerholm, Mats (1980), 'Bilden som alla föräldrar borde se', *Expressen*, 2 December 1980.

Weeks, Jeffrey (1989), 'AIDS, the Intellectual Agenda', in Peter Aggleton, Graham Hart and Peter Davies (eds), *AIDS: Social Representations, Social Practices*, London and New York: Routledge.

Westlind, Thomas (1980), 'Videochock i TV i kväll', *Göteborgs-Tidningen*, 2 December 1980.

Willborg, Bert (1980), 'Vi brukar slå ned folk på gatan', *Aftonbladet*, 3 December 1980

5

The local and the transnational in Nordic exploitation cinema of the 1980s

Exploitation cinema is a contested notion. Not only does it have different cultural political roles in diverse national and regional contexts, but its meanings vary over time. These concerns are especially pertinent in Nordic cinema, where the very existence of exploitation cinema culture – in the normative sense – is debatable. While the 1970s produced plenty of Nordic sexploitation titles, a few noteworthy examples of more transgressive content, such as *Dværgen* (*The Sinful Dwarf*, 1973) and *Thriller – en grym film* (*They Call Her One Eye*, 1974), were produced entirely independently of official funding sources. Yet, to talk of an exploitation film culture outside of the sexploitation trends that pervaded the industry would be overstating the case. This, however, does not invalidate exploring continuations in these patterns, especially as they pertain to a sustained underground practice that slowly emerges into an ever more significant role in domestic and regional film policy.

The story of Nordic exploitation offers a narrative of intensifying production activities that made use of transgressive and eye-catching content. As we outlined in Chapter 4, the 1980s saw popular outcry over video violence, which generated headlines and, undoubtedly, public interest in precisely these themes. This chapter will explore a range of significant case studies from the 1980s that offer a new type of balance between transgressive material and officially sanctioned forms of film culture. Key to understanding these transformations is to explore the infrastructure of film funding and distribution. The 1970s had seen Nordic producers challenged by dwindling audience figures and structural challenges in funding, leading to a decline in the number of films produced in Finland and Sweden, for example. At the same time, the policy circumstances for films with explicitly commercial aims encouraged producers to bypass the film institutes on two significant levels. First, Nordic sexploitation films had generated an international reputation, allowing them to claw back costs from being sold abroad. This provided a feasible financial model for packaging content in ways that would sell to international audiences on the back of this reputation. Second, comedies with low production values (such as those of Finnish producer Spede Pasanen) would certainly not be able to reclaim money through the use of quality stipends, for example, but they were successful enough at the domestic box office to allow producers like Pasanen to continue steady operations. Yet, in terms of the bigger picture for these national film cultures, films like *They Call Her One Eye* and the independently produced comedy *Uuno Turhapuro* ('Numbskull Emptybrook', 1973) have to be considered anomalies as, in general, film institutes and the larger film studios, such as Svensk Filmindustri and Nordisk Film, had control on overall production strategies and trends.

Yet, in the 1980s new policies on the types of content that could be supported under institutional funding emerged (see Pantti 2000; Soila, Söderbergh Widding and Iversen 1998). Genre was one target of these key strategies as its commercial potential was slowly acknowledged by the film institutes, no doubt motivated by the dominant position imported Hollywood genre productions maintained at the domestic box office (see Ahonen et al. 2004; Gustafsson and Kääpä 2015). Yet, the production of genre films in the Nordic film industries has consistently had different implications than in most other film industrial contexts. In this context, highlighting links to popular genres, such as the horror and action film, has often been a means to distinguish these products from the domestic mainstream (which tend to be prestige literature adaptations and historical epics), at least up to the end of the 1980s. Paradoxically, these circumstances led to a situation where (nominally commercial) genre productions were not considered direct competition for mainstream domestic films, but were, instead, expected to carve out a slice of the domestic market share of imported genre products with which they were often directly competing. A key challenge was that they would have to do so from the basis of a severely restricted resource base, especially as the professional and technical infrastructure was very limited at least up until the digital reinvigoration of the 2000s. As Hjort and Petrie (2007: 2–5) have outlined, these are small nation cinemas, which are severely limited by the fact that their populations are small and that the majority of the films produced do not travel, not even to their Nordic neighbouring countries. Thus, for an independent film to make money from a theatrical screening is a hugely problematic proposition, especially if the production is budgeted at internationally competitive standards. Consequently, not only did commercial genre films evolve in opposition to normative film policies, but they were often considered marginal or 'exploitative' due to the fact that they were explicitly commercial in nature.

For Nordic exploitation films, the 1980s were a particularly difficult time due to the double-bind of the financing system and the strict censorship codes. These productions would be required to consciously navigate a complex environment where they would have to appeal to a range of audiences and cultural political standards. Simultaneously, they would have to ensure they would not be castigated for including too much excessive content, as we saw with films like *They Call Her One Eye* receiving prolonged bans, which inevitably impacted the producers' ability to generate return on investment. At the same time, due to the exact same strict censorship norms that befell imported genre films like *The Terminator* (1984), *A Nightmare on Elm Street* (1984) and *Robocop* (1987), the latter shortened with thirteen cuts by the Swedish censors (Statensbiografbyrå 1987), domestic genre films were afforded space to manoeuvre as they would at times, though not consistently, be treated with more leniency than imported films.

The chapter will be organized according to what we identify as two distinct forms of Nordsploitation, modes that distinguish these production cultures from other international variations of national or regional exploitation cinema. The first of these forms focuses on localized productions that use exploitative genre conventions in the framework of national film cultures. For us, these films comprise the *domestic or localized exploitation film* that use international genre formats but are predominantly aimed at domestic markets. Our initial case study focuses on Hrafn Gudlauggson's Icelandic Viking Trilogy (1984–91) to evaluate the integration of national heritage traditions with exploitative content. The negotiation between the genres of heritage and action film allows these productions to carve out a mutually beneficial space of exploitation where the challenges and advantages of each respective genre of film balances each other out. From here on, we move to explicitly competitive genre cinema that seeks to emulate and exploit international genre conventions in domestic contexts. Case studies for this section – the Finnish slasher film *Kuutamosonaatti* (*Moonlight Sonata*, 1988) and the Swedish supernatural thriller *Besökarna* (*The Visitors*, 1988) – comprise two distinct approaches for evaluating the balance between exploitative tendencies and officially sanctioned film culture as they both use imported genre formulas, but only the former received financial support from a domestic cultural institute, the Finnish Film Foundation.

Simultaneously, much more 'traditional' types of exploitation production, aligned much more closely with global patterns and trends in exploitative film content, continued during the decade, often produced independently and with little concern for official designations of film culture. For these productions, being sanctioned by official gatekeepers was a potential marketing gimmick on which to generate notoriety and interest, especially as the films would often aim to be distributed at international markets. The films of Finnish director Visa Mäkinen provide an initial starting point here as they integrate a range of exploitative tendencies into the frameworks of both farcical domestic comedies and imported genre formulas which allow them to tap into contemporary popular cultural currents. But crucially, they have no allusions to critical or institutional respectability like our other two examples of localized exploitation cinema, *Moonlight Sonata* and *The Visitors*.

Yet, these insulated examples of exploitation cinema do not paint a comprehensive picture of film cultural dynamics during the era. The final case study of this chapter expands on these discussions by focusing on Renny Harlin's action film *Arctic Heat* (aka *Born American*, 1985), which directly engaged international audiences by reducing the cultural specificity of its Finnish roots. By aligning with US counterparts like *Missing in Action* (1984) and *Rambo: First Blood Part II* (1985), the type of cinema exemplified by *Arctic Heat* constitutes what we call *the global exploitation film*. Such productions were largely aimed at international markets (in comparison to localized exploitation whose main audiences would have been domestic) exemplified by their use of international actors and English as their main language. For this chapter, then, the focus is largely on domestic films aimed at theatrical distribution and concretely engaging in commercial competition on a level that would affect general film cultural politics in each respective media ecosystem.

The Viking trilogy: Exploiting cultural history through genre film

To start this discussion, we turn to Icelandic cinema, which has not been covered much here as the country's film production infrastructure was only finding its feet in the 1980s (see Söderbergh Widding 1998: 96–101). The establishment of the Icelandic Film Foundation in 1979 enabled regular film production that unsurprisingly drew heavily from the nation's cultural history. A key film in this sense was what the critics called the 'Icelandic Classic' or 'a small masterpiece from Iceland' (see Gudmundsson 2010: 47), *Land og synir* (*Land and Sons*,

1980) by Ágúst Guðmundsson. Focusing on the travails of a family torn between traditional rural lifestyles and the lures of the city, the film is a heritage epic that captures debates over the modernization of the country through cinematic language emphasizing closeness between hardship and landscape. Guðmundsson's next film, an adaptation of the traditional saga of Gisli, *Útlaginn* (*Outlaw: The Saga of Gisli*, 1981), combines these heritage themes with material often associated with exploitative content, especially the use of violence. The story – about a local clansman who runs afoul of a competing tribe – is captured in a striking visual style that emphasizes misty landscapes and atonal wordless vocal score music, which gives the film an otherworldly quality. The saga's dream sequences are especially heightened by the aural and visual world of the film, harkening more to the style of John Boorman in films like *Zardos* (1973) than contemporary Icelandic cinema, even as the original saga provides the film with a driving revenge narrative. At the same time, it was advertised upon release as a 'strong adaptation of an Icelandic classic' (Anon. 1981) and it was put forward for an Academy Award nomination that did not materialize.

What makes this film a significant indicator for the 1980s as a whole was how it engaged the Icelandic saga traditions and the country's natural scenery in a cinematic framework emphasizing visual and narrative conventions from the fantasy genre. Such references do not make it 'conventional' exploitation by any means, but the combination of tradition and commercial genre establishes a pattern that would be replicated in a set of key texts combining heritage with the violent tropes of imported genre production. In particular, *Hrafninn flýgur* (*When the Raven Flies*, 1984), the first of the three very loosely connected films in director Hrafn Gunnlaugsson's Viking trilogy, provides an appropriate illustration of how these dynamics operate. In *When the Raven Flies*, the film's protagonist Gest comes to Iceland to avenge the death of his parents at the hands of marauding Vikings, playing off two local groups against one another. Through the use a range of intertextual genre references from *Yojimbo* (1954) to *Per un pugno Di dollari* (*A Fistful of Dollars*, 1964), the film provides a concrete challenge to the heritage and historical prestige of Icelandic cinema. The violence is plentiful and especially the throwing knife Gest uses to kill his victims provides a frequent reminder of the genre aspirations of the production. Indeed, *The New York Times* suggests that as '[g]ory as the film is, Mr. Gunnlaugsson imbues it with a slow, determined grace' (Maslin 1985), indicating that for the international critics the film reached quality standards beyond its genre roots. For *The New York Times* critic, it was the ways the film contextualized the violence that mattered: 'Watching it I was struck by the horrible contrast with American films that too often trashily cater to the markets of pornographic sex, bloody violence, sci-fi fantasy and nightmare horror that gives kids the creeps' (Maslin 1985).

Yet, Icelandic critics had a somewhat different perspective on these dynamics. Earlier media reports focus on the authenticity of the shoots, including costumes and locations that harken back to historical veracity and a sense of national culture that provides 'a faithful picture' (Sverrison 1984). They describe the ways the narrative does not only dryly appropriate conventions from the traditional sagas but provides a setting for an entertaining story that can be enjoyed by all audiences. By outlining the more appealing qualities of the film, the article establishes an intriguing opposition between popular and traditional culture, which it then continues to address by exploring the ways *When the Raven Flies* meets both heritage and popular culture demands. Concluding with quotations from a letter from the Berlinale Film Festival focusing on the film's outstanding efforts in combining historical veracity with gritty cinematography, the article suggests the film holds a distinctly important position in promoting the Icelandic film industry (Sverrison 1984).

Domestic reviews continued this largely positive assessment as critics commended the film for both its narrative qualities and its use of impressive production values that stand out in the Icelandic context. In comparison to foreign critics, they make few references to transgressive content or even to the films' more violent qualities. Instead, the film is perceived as an impressive national epic that can advance Icelandic cinema in competing internationally, especially through the professionalization of Icelandic film production. Several critics would reinforce this perception by commenting on the quality of the acting and the professional standards of costumes and sets, or how the epic visuals make use of Iceland's natural scenery (see, for example, Indrigason 1984).

However, being an Icelandic–Swedish co-production, the often-contradictory reviews *When the Raven Flies* received in Swedish newspapers demonstrate the film's transgressive qualities, especially in relation to its, for the era, stylized violence. Prominent critic Hans Schiller wrote: 'The most surprising thing about *When the Raven Flies* is that it is very well acted and also technically driven in a way that is rare in Nordic film. These two factors, plus its principle concerns that reach beyond pure financial profit, make *When the Raven Flies* into a film that reaches beyond silly violence pornography' (Schiller 1984). In leftist newspaper *Arbetet*, the reviewer focused on its moral ambiguity: '[The film] has obvious production value but also contradictory traits. Its final point is that violence breeds violence, but the staging of mass murder testifies to a rather yummy delight in the physical details of death. The protagonist is a hallmark slasher, but is enshrined with Christ's attributes such as crucifixion, stigmatization, and the opening of the tomb connected to his character' (Olsson 1984). Both Swedish critics suggest the film exceeds the professional standards of most Nordic films but does so in a way that includes morally ambiguous and thematically transgressive elements unbefitting the moral standards of Nordic cinema. It is especially intriguing to note how both focus on exploitative vocabulary to highlight the film's merits while they are very careful in distinguishing it from violence porn or the slasher film, both which, presumably, rank low in cultural merit for these commentators.

To emphasize this curious balancing between respectable cultural heritage and exploitative genre film, a more contemporary perspective from The Icelandic Film Centre (2017) suggests *When the Raven Flies* destroys the stereotypical Hollywood image of the Viking age by providing a more grounded perspective on such cultural imaginaries. For them, the 'earthly' qualities of the costumes, weaponry and other material elements in the mise-en-scene of the film ensure it a unique place in national film culture. For us, these elements can be labelled 'ethno-symbolic', following the work of Anthony Smith (2009: 22–41), in that they draw on associations and 'feelings' constructed through long-term historical use of such conventions across the arts and literature as well as in film and media. This correlation between ethno-symbolic and transgressive forms of culture is essential to understanding how these more localized forms of Nordic exploitation cinema facilitate their careful balancing between adhering to domestic standards for cultural and censorship norms while conveniently challenging them through moderated transgressions from these norms.

While *Outlaw* had already been considered a substantial contribution to the development of Icelandic film culture, *When the Raven Flies* was much more successful in terms of its domestic reception and international distribution, with the film even winning a best director Guldbagge (the Swedish film awards). As it moved away from the more fantastical qualities of the sagas and focused on a grittier framework, it was perceived largely as a case of respectable heritage cinema. While this description makes it difficult to place *When the Raven Flies* in the continuum of exploitation cinema, its violent content (concurrently a huge problem in most of the Nordic countries) and adherence to genres such as the Spaghetti Western (at the time still censored and considered transgressive) distinguishes it from the normative confines of the heritage genre. Accordingly, films such as these are consistently difficult to place as they balance between dynamics that require them to closely connect to respectable forms of national culture – being as they were partially financed by domestic cultural subsidies – and appear different from them to generate audience interest domestically and internationally.

To illustrate the uniqueness of this intervention in Icelandic cinema, *When the Raven Flies* was soon followed by a sequel, *Í skugga hrafnsins* (*In Shadow of the Raven*, 1988). The film continues the complex proximity and distance politics of its predecessor and combines elements from the sagas with a narrative drive derived from historical epics and Westerns. The film takes up the themes of *When the Raven Flies* without being a continuation of its narrative as it focuses on a new protagonist, Trausti, who returns from Norway back to Iceland to reclaim his place as one of the leaders of the local clans. The clans are engaged in warfare and Trausti attempts to make peace amongst them. Yet, they soon betray him and kill his wife and most of his kin. The second half of the film focuses on revenge as Trausti forces some of the traitors to join him in battle where, eventually, all but him perish in a bloodbath.

Again, the focus is very much on that unique balance of national heritage conventions and genre cinema that allowed the first film to stand out both domestically and internationally. At the same time, *In Shadow of the Raven* provides nods to the contemporaneously prominent sword and sorcery genre

Figure 5.1 Screen grab from the Icelandic *Hrafninn flýgur* (*When the Raven Flies*, 1984), depicting one of the many violent scenes from the film that clashes with its heritage origins. Courtesy of Viking Film.

as it dips in the same pool of influence as major blockbusters like *Excalibur* (1981) or *Conan the Barbarian* (1982), especially as these two examples contain sparse fantastical elements. Furthermore, it would not be difficult to connect the Viking trilogy with J. R. R. Tolkien who, in writing *The Lord of the Rings*, took inspiration from the Icelandic sagas. What makes *When the Raven Flies* and *In Shadow of the Raven* stand out in comparison is the way they emphasize bleak landscapes and a grimy sense of reality that the contemporary critics seem to have identified as authenticity – a strategy that allowed them to be perceived as part of Icelandic film history and not only as easily dismissed genre fodder. Accordingly, *In Shadow of the Raven* received enthusiastic reviews with the Icelandic *Morgunbladid* newspaper calling it a 'great film' that everyone must see (Anon. 1988). The comments are part of an article explaining the critical success of its international distribution and include coverage of four-star reviews by the Swedish national broadcaster SVT and a positive evaluation by *Variety*. Such strategies frame the film as a domestic event and a substantial advance for the domestic film industry.

At the same time, many elements deter from this heritage impression. A considerable role in both films is played by their music score, which mixes contemporary ethno-synth pop with a dirge that sounds very similar to Ennio Morricone's music for the Spaghetti Westerns the films' narratives emulate (via Kurosawa, of course). Although the soundtrack provides the films with an accessible transnational core, it also distances the films from a clear sense of traditionalism in the Icelandic context. A further distancing device comes from the ways the films stage their lurid violence. For example, the use of the throwing knife provides impressive 'kill scenes' for the first film, but the same violence would clash with censors in many parts of the world. *In Shadow of the Raven* makes use of other innovative kills such as death by sauna where the villain entices the heads of the clans to a sauna meeting, which he subsequently floods with boiling steam. These elements allow the films to tap genre norms while providing unique localized twists on them – clever intrigue was one of the distinguishing qualities of Eastwood's character The Man With No Name – whereas their commitment to finding new and brutal means of destroying flesh are more akin to a Jason Vorhees. These homages/borrowings from international genre film were also noted, in a negative sense, by Swedish reviewers, as 'Gunnlaugsson occasionally borrows effects from other films (a severed head from "Soldier Blue" [1970], a female wielding a knife from "Throne of Blood" [*Kumonosu-jō*, 1957]). Admittedly, he keeps the action pace of a Western as he has shortened the Icelandic story too, but the effects overtake the grimy style' (Grut 1988).

When the Raven Flies and *In the Shadow of the Raven* establish an often-paradoxical relationship between international genre forms and Icelandic film culture that embodies the necessity to identify them as exploitation cinema. These comprise what we call the Nordic exploitation cinema's proximity and distance dynamics. To explain, they exploit the circumstances of small nation film cultures where domestic aspirations require them to be 'authentically' Icelandic and, at the same time, sufficiently different from domestic norms to stand out alongside imported films. Their genre roots distinguish them from other domestic productions (i.e. they distance them from the normative conventions of Icelandic film) as they highlight film vocabulary that communicates to the tastes and sensibilities of audiences inundated with international genre programming (proximity to Icelandic audience tastes). Simultaneously, the sagas give the films transferable cultural capital (proximity to domestic norms) that makes them appeal to international audiences (distance from international genre norms). Iversen's (1998: 137–8) description of these films as 'Cod Westerns' encapsulates why these films need to be seen as exploitation cinema and not only as genre or heritage films. They operate as commercial forms of film production that make conscious use of cultural and generic heritage where exploitation is not just about exploiting taboos or moral boundaries, but also about the politics of specific national film cultures and the careful, conscious positioning of individual films into these structures.

If the first two parts of the Viking trilogy exploit a range of cultural and generic frameworks to navigate cultural obstacles for small nation cinemas, the third film in the series, *Hvíti víkingurinn* (*The White Viking*, 1991), emphasizes the advantages to be gained by working with these registers. The theatrical cut explores the attempts of protagonist Asgur to free his beloved Embla from the Norwegian king who has sent Asgur on a mission to convert Iceland to the Christian religion. Yet, *The White Viking* was originally shot as a five-hour epic focusing on Embla – and released as *Embla* in its director's cut on DVD in 2007 – and seems to be modelled on the contemporaneously popular Nordic heritage film such as Danish *Babettes gæstebud* (*Babette's Feast*, 1987). The producers cut the film to two hours and focused on the male character whose narrative goes through a similar revenge trajectory as the other films in the trilogy. The five-hour cut is a much more immersive experience that avoids many of the problems of the theatrical version. This is especially the case with the conclusion of the shorter cut that features a very brief, and thus somewhat abstract glimpse of the spirit world of the sagas, an element that is not directly addressed in any concrete way in the other films. As part of the full cut, the inclusion of such elements makes sense and emphasizes how this instalment differs from its predecessors, but here it only contributes to the unfocused impression the film generates.

Whereas the earlier two films focused on localized revenge narratives, the scope of *The White Viking* extends outside of local political intrigue. The collision of old and emerging forms of religious belief had been an underlying factor in the previous films, whereas here, the sprawling scope of the film focuses on the role of religion in imperial conquest. Consequently, the ambitions of *The White Viking* are more in line with large-scale historical epics than the violent genre/heritage hybrids that had made the previous installments so successful. Indeed, it was not surprising that the critical reaction to the film veered from the earlier parts of the trilogy as some called it uninvolving (Anon. 1991), whereas others suggested the film was a narrative mess (Björnsson 1991).

The Viking trilogy in total can hardly qualify as exploitation in any conventional sense, even with an excessive film like *When the Raven Flies*. Clearly, they were not perceived as exploitative productions by the majority of domestic critics but, instead, as significant contributions to a small national film culture that could be used to project Icelandic cinema to international audiences. While the violent content of the first two instalments made some Nordic reviewers react in a negative way, the failure of the theatrical version of *The White Viking* emphasizes the dynamics involved in balancing between heritage and genre expectations. Here, heritage provides a means to tick boxes for publicly funded filmmaking, but simultaneously, it is increasingly important that boxes verifying commercial aspirations are also ticked. Genre references act as a convenient shorthand to achieve this as showcased by *The White Viking*'s ambiguous positioning where its short version is too abstract and too culturally specific, while the full cut is appropriately epic in its running time but only suitable for television release. Such appeals to very different cultural registers situate it in a problematic liminal space different from its predecessors which had met both commercial and heritage demands even as they were transgressive enough to seem to challenge them. In comparison to the explicit Nordic exploitation films of the 1970s, the Viking trilogy emphasizes that exploitative elements are invariably dictated by dominant directions in domestic film politics. What seemed exploitative for some critics, as was especially the case with *When the Raven Flies*, may, in fact, consist of a judicious combination of ethno-symbolic and imported conventions. That these would be difficult to place alongside contemporaneous exploitation films from Italy, for example, is not the point. What matters is that they touch on many similar strategies as 'authentic' exploitation films but do so in a context where these strategies have to be contextualized in very different ways, such as by using innovative slaughter mechanisms that draw on particular cultural and environmental contexts.

Nordic emulations of blockbusters

The Viking trilogy provides an example of the ways the 1980s Nordic film cultures incorporated genre material into their confines. At the same time, Hollywood film production continued to dominate these film cultures as was the case in most other global contexts. This cultural domination takes place not only through uneven competition at the box office but also by setting standards for popular entertainment. Crucially, in many instances, it is precisely such attempts by domestic producers to meet 'international standards' that resulted in a film being labelled exploitative by critics and cultural authorities. To uncover some of these patterns, we focus on two horror films, the Finnish survivalist slasher *Moonlight Sonata* and the Swedish haunted house tale *The Visitors*. These films provide an important point of critique to evaluate the role of genre in Nordic film politics, as they showcase how exploitation takes place not only at the margins but also at the centre of these small nation film industries. Both films are clearly based on Hollywood predecessors, especially *Friday the 13th* (1980) and *Poltergeist* (1982), respectively, but these influences are frequently contextualized with ethno-symbolic references to national customs and environmental factors.

The decision to commence production on a Finnish slasher film in the late 1980s was certainly unusual at the time. Not only were domestic horror films scarce but undertaking a project adhering to the standards of banned or heavily cut productions like *Halloween*, *Friday the 13th* and *A Nightmare on Elm Street* (1984) seemed to challenge all the mantras of the Finnish Film Foundation on 'worthwhile' cultural production. Although all instalments of the *Friday the 13th* franchise, for example, were under a strict ban in Finland, these films made their ways to consumers through various other channels. The outlawing of what were, at best, formulaic slashers, made them into notorious grails, resulting in clear demand for domestic variations of the genre, though for them to be economically and politically feasible, they would have to meet both the cultural and moral standards of the era.

Moonlight Sonata is best described as a fusion of imported and domestic influences, especially in its frequent emphasis on the rural periphery of northern Lapland. Much as Tobe Hooper's work on *The Texas Chainsaw Massacre* (1974) did to Texan landscapes, or Walter Hill's *Southern Comfort* (1981) to the Louisiana swampland, *Moonlight Sonata* emphasizes stalk and slash conventions by painting the northern landscapes in hues of dread and despair. It makes pointed use of the natural landscape and snow to set these well-known generic tropes in the Finnish cultural imaginary, a factor that must have been essential in securing the funds required for the production. These elements are key parts of the plot, which follows a burnt-out model, Sanna, recuperating in a cabin in the countryside where she is harassed by local handyman Arvo. The plot facilitates the use of many well-worn genre conventions including the use of the first person POV shots to peep on the undressing Sanna in the sauna and chases through the snow that firmly plant the film in its generic imaginary.

This combination of transgressive genre tropes and indigenous cultural heritage emphasizes the double standards that were in place in Finnish film politics at the time as not only is the film unpleasant in its depiction of masculinity but it is also surprisingly gory. The climax with Arvo pursuing the protagonist through the snow in a tractor culminates with him burning to death on top of the exploding machine. The shots of Arvo's charred skinless face feature imagery that was heavily cut by censors at the time in exploitation films like *The Exterminator 2* (1984), but also in mainstream entertainment like *Predator* (1987). All in all, *Moonlight Sonata* is by no means excessive in its violence, but the fact that it was given a K-14 rating indicates that it was conceived as popular mainstream entertainment, which clearly puts it in a different category from its genre brethren, which had by 1988 been more or less totally banned.

Such developments are essential in testifying to the shifting roles of transgressive material in contemporary film politics. The 1980s saw new strategic policy developments in Nordic film cultures, which were struggling to maintain audience interest and resulted in the Finnish Film Foundation, for example, allocating money to comedies that had been perceived to be, if not outright exploitative, at least unworthy of inclusion into the often narrowly and abstractly defined prestige of national film culture. As part of this strategic shift, *Moonlight Sonata* was provided with financial support by the Finnish Film Foundation and the film was produced on the sizeable budget

Figure 5.2 The original VHS artwork from the Finnish slasher film *Kuutamosonaatti* (*Moonlight Sonata*, 1988), featuring a superimposed scene of nudity absent from its theatrical and subsequent DVD release. Courtesy of Showtime Oy.

of 4.4 million FIM (approximately 400,000 GBP), which makes it not only a major production in Finland but also a novelty in comparison to international benchmarks as the budget qualified it as a large-scale mainstream film in its indigenous film industry context. In comparison, authentic slashers such as *A Nightmare on Elm Street* had a budget of 1.8 million USD, which in comparison to mainstream Hollywood fare, equated to a small independent production in the 1980s American cinema. The fact that *Moonlight Sonata* received 2 million FIM in production support from the Finnish Film Institute and a post-release 'quality' grant of 300,000 FIM indicates that its profile was clearly much more respectable than that of a mere genre film. Furthermore, director Olli Soinio was provided a 10,000 FIM state grant for artistic achievements and Kari Sorvali, who played the villain of the film, won the best actor Jussi (the Finnish Film Award) of the year.

These acknowledgements suggest a considerable transformation in the Foundation's stance on not only genre material but also the definition of transgressiveness. To emphasize how significant such a shift aligning domestic film policy with the competitive standards of the marketplace was, the film's profile on the Finnish Film Archive portal includes the following key words to describe it: violence, sexual behaviour, voyeurism, nudity and murder. Such definitions are not particularly outlandish when describing international genre cinema, but for 1980s Finnish cinema, especially for a production that gained substantial financial and creative support, they are very unusual. These seeming contradictions also emerged in critics' reactions to the film, which were for the most part favourable. They would often compare the film to *Psycho* (1960) instead of the more obvious slasher comparisons, potentially due to the cultural capital such associations would create. Lumirae (1988), for example, outlines how *Moonlight Sonata* works best in its 'authentic Finnishness'. Although he acknowledges its genre roots, he argues that the film is uniquely built on the domestic mythology and milieu. Other critics saw the film as an example of the opposition between the city and the countryside, which has been a key theme in Nordic film culture since its inception. Such associations are integral to enhancing the film's reputation by lifting it from the dubious swamps of genre cinema. At the same time, more critical perspectives emerged with Tapani Maskula (1988) describing *Moonlight Sonata*'s approach to genre as clumsy while Mikko Piela (1988) did not hold much enthusiasm for the film, describing it as a functional domestic horror tale. Yet, largely, critics perceived its genre roots positively with Asko Alanen (1988) arguing that it is a successful genre variation of *The Texas Chainsaw Massacre* and praising the director for his use of horror conventions, and even comparing the score to John Carpenter's work.

The critical discussion and the positioning of the film as an award-winning domestic production as well as an exemplary case of popular genre cinema exemplifies the ongoing debates on the role of genre in Nordic film cultures. As was the case with Gunnlauggson's Viking trilogy, the integration of potentially transgressive genre formulas into domestic film culture was by the 1980s perceived favourably. A large part of this acceptance was to do with the competence of the director as well as the ways the key creatives were able to play the media in their favour. We already saw this with some of the positive publicity *When the Raven Flies* generated through set visits and interviews, linking the production to heritage cinema as well as evoking innovation through its genre content. In many of his interviews, Soinio (1988) was very conscious in positioning his work both in proximity to notions of traditional national film culture as well as to simultaneously distance it from these norms. He did this by highlighting the film's combination of horror and comedy and by concretely mobilizing both discourses of national authenticity and popular commercialism to indicate the multilevelled appeals of the film. Both *When the Raven Flies* and *Moonlight Sonata* give rise to arguing that genre production provides a productive strategy when its connotations are exploited in carefully managed ways by domestic cultural producers to generate attention through notoriety (but invariably with adjacent gestures to cultural respectability). They provide malleable material that allows these producers to access the established parameters for both acceptable and transgressive film culture. What becomes especially clear is that genre content is not seen as a problem as such and, instead, the key is how these potentially exploitative modes are managed, especially if exploitative elements merge with ethno-symbolic signifiers.

The Visitors

If *Moonlight Sonata* exploited its role as a domestic genre film to great success, the Swedish production *The Visitors* provides a necessary counter-perspective. As with *Moonlight Sonata*'s use of the slasher format, *The Visitors* mobilizes conventions of the haunted house film, especially from mainstream American successes like *Poltergeist* and *House* (1985). Produced independently without the support of the Swedish Film Institute, the production organization of *The Visitors* was premised on a limited company funding model that allowed individuals and companies to buy shares in the production (Åhlander 1997: 544–5). Such financial organization facilitated the gathering of funds to produce genre films and distribute them in domestic theatres despite lacking the official stamp of 'quality'. Relying on independent capital was invariably risky in these small nation contexts as the audience size and any subsequent return on investment would be inevitably restricted. Simultaneously, genre material would facilitate a quick potential shortcut to international markets. *The Visitors* was budgeted at 9.5 million SEK, and in order for the film to make money, 975,000 admissions were required in the Nordic countries. Also, by using fully synchronized dubbing into English, the plan was to make it readily accessible on the international video market, which it succeeded in doing, as *The Visitors* was sold to the United States and many other markets (Åhlander 1997: 545).

In the film a family moves into a haunted house in the Swedish countryside and, immediately, problems start to surface with wallpaper peeling off and kitchen furniture taking on a life of its own. These instances fragment the harmony of this ideal yuppie family unit as a ghostly presence in the attic drives them apart. Thus, the plot of the film follows an established pattern that could be easily marketed to domestic audiences as a Swedish variation of the haunted house genre, whereas the genre content would provide transferable capital for international markets, especially when those markers of cultural discount, such as the Swedish language, would be subsequently erased. *The Visitors* is technically proficient, especially in its use of suspense, and although the original version is in Swedish and depicts contemporaneous neoliberal yuppie lifestyles, it contains few instances of exploitation of ethno-symbolic elements on the scale of *Moonlight Sonata* or *When the Raven Flies*. It would not qualify as traditional exploitation cinema either, as there are few truly transgressive elements of gore or deviant sexuality. But what makes it relevant here is its proximity to domestic film culture – its pronounced use of Swedish language in its domestic version and the domestic audiences' inevitable association of the film with Swedish cinema – and its distance from these same registers including the extensive genre references and ability to mimic international aesthetic and formative conventions.

As with the reception of *Moonlight Sonata* or *When the Raven Flies*, the Swedish critical reception sheds light on the film's balancing between domestic and international elements. In Sweden, the critics largely approached *The Visitors* as a positive example of a Swedish genre film, with its debt to its genre roots perceived as particularly successful: 'I was scared and impressed. The fact that the young brothers Ersgård were able to produce such a successful copy of this particular genre is both very surprising and very fun' (Olsson 1988). Here, the film's relevance comes from its ability to emulate its genre predecessors, which for this critic was both impressive and surprising. Others addressed its lack of explicitly ethno-symbolic content in more detail. However, this absence was not perceived as a negative aspect but as something that allowed the film to contribute a professional sheen to its domestic production culture:

> The action in *The Visitors* is reasonably simple. The resolution of the movie verges on the banal. What nevertheless gives the film such an incredibly strong effect on its audience is what, in the absence of better words, can be called its 'form'. Shape and content should go hand in hand, but in this case, you can talk about form that has managed to go beyond its content. The movements of the camera, the lighting, the editing, the music and the story's own rhythm are harmoniously interacting elements, which suggest that even a hardened observer will forget to study how it has been achieved. This is a very promising example of film craft. (Olsson 1988)

In the ethno-symbolic exploitation cases covered so far, the use of genre formats emerged as a pragmatic means to introduce some of the formative and aesthetic standards of international genre film into domestic production cultures. As we will see, much of the Nordic genre resurgence in the 1990s is based on the notion of professionalization of film production, but the debates around *The Visitors* suggests that the seeds for this argument were clearly planted a decade earlier. The fact that films such as *Moonlight Sonata* and *When the Raven Flies* managed to exploit international narrative and visual conventions while tapping into a range of domestic cultural reserves allowed them to gain prominence in the domestic markets. *The Visitors* continues this formula as well, however, the fact that it did so outside of the officially sanctioned film institute-dominated film culture gives it a radical potency where its significance was not so much about instituting change in domestic film policy but utilizing the domestic audience's inevitable media literacy on genre film. Film critic Björn Fremer, for example, saw the film as the best Swedish cinema had to offer in the 1980s. Comparing it to the style of filmmakers such as Brian De Palma, he argues the film may be able to connect with young audiences, especially as it compares favourably with its American counterparts (Fremer 1988). Others, such as Hans Schiller from *Svenska Dagbladet* were far less impressed and suggested the film meets general technical requirements but fails badly in comparison to the counterparts it tries to imitate (Schiller 1988).

The Visitors was not the only production trying out this strategy as the US–Swedish co-production *Scorched Heat* (1987) – an ultra-low budget horror comedy which was filmed in South Dallas and in Southern Sweden and shot in heavily accented English – was aimed straight for the direct-to-video market. But whereas *The Visitors* generated some critical and commercial interest in Sweden and internationally, *Scorched Heat* quickly evaporated into obscurity. Regardless, the fact that most positive perspectives focused on *The Visitors*' technical proficiency – which featured heavily in critical evaluations of the 1980s genre films – suggests that the Nordic institutional cultural context translates to different understandings of exploitation cinema. In this restrictive and puritan context still prioritizing notions of art and cultural merit, the very idea of commercial genre cinema can become exploitative. This balanced contradiction operates as a signifier of market competency (another disputed term in the policy environment of the Nordic film cultures of the 1980s) that allows projects to appear as either innovative expansions of domestic policy environments – such as with *Moonlight Sonata* – or as unwarranted commercial provocations undeserving of financial public support – as was the case with *The Visitors*' lack of official support. Consequently, instead of highlighting morally or ethically transgressive content, the challenge these films pose in their respective film cultures is much more to do with rethinking the political economy of these film cultures.

Visa Mäkinen and exploitation cinema from the margins

The development of films like *Moonlight Sonata* and the Viking trilogy has seen genre material incorporated into officially sanctioned film production, with the generally positive critical reception and award recognition indicating that these are not typical transgressive or marginalized exploitation films. Yet, not all Nordic genre production would aspire to this fine balance between commercial and ethno-symbolic forms of exploitation. Some, such as the films of maverick filmmakers Visa Mäkinen, Renny Harlin and Mats Helge Olsson would fit much more clearly with traditional definitions of exploitation cinema. These films were produced independently off the system and feature explicit violence or sexuality in ways that would often clash with the parameters established by the cultural authorities. These authorities would in response make use of similar mechanisms to shun these films as they did with imported genre films they considered problematic: through censorship and critical castigation. Harlin and Mäkinen's films illustrate some of these complexities in Finland and will be covered in this chapter whereas Chapter 6 will be devoted to Olsson due to the scope of his operations in VHS-based exploitation.

First venturing into film production in the 1970s with comedies produced on minimal budgets and operating independently from the small southwestern town of Pori in Finland, Mäkinen produced twelve films between 1979 and 1991. The productions were completed without assistance from the Finnish Film Institute and in conditions best described as a cottage industry. His forte initially was to do with low-brow farces based on crude humour and folk characteristics, which were consciously modelled after the financial success of Finnish comedian director Spede Pasanen's films that had provided a model for economically successful film production in the crisis years of the early 1970s (see Toiviainen 1975: 7–22; Autio 2002: 25–58). Pasanen had been able to release one film per year theatrically with domestic box office figures sometimes exceeding 700,000 spectators for comedies such as *Uuno Turhapuro*. Following this production model, Mäkinen's films were often produced with television technology and featured an identikit troupe of performers and production technicians to ensure efficient and low-cost production.

Mäkinen's first film *Oi juku - mikä lauantai* ('Gosh What A Saturday!', 1980), advertised as a 'fun contribution' to the Finnish New Wave (see Kääpä 2015 for more on the New Wave), was a light farce produced on a minimal budget of 200,000 FIM with no official backing from the Finnish Film Institute. The film's loosely connected narrative of a group of youth eloping to a party met, predictably, with critical scorn upon its release. The marketing of the film emphasized its credentials as a – to quote – 'certifiably commercial' production, which positioned this explicit capitalization on contemporaneously popular youth films like *Saturday Night Fever* (1977) as distinctly different from the socio-realist production dominating Finnish cinema at the time. Although a small disappointment at the box office with only 31,473 spectators, the budget was justifiably low to compensate for these audience figures and allowed Mäkinen to continue production with more financial investment and professional actors. Yet, the quality of the films did not improve, at least in the eyes of the Finnish critics who called his next film *Mitäs me sankarit* ('We Heroes', 1981) a farcical and largely plotless compendium of 'childish' and 'rudimentary' sketches (Toiviainen 1981). The one positive comment for the film suggested that the plot of the film was 'affectionate', though the critic would also go on to undermine this by suggesting, somewhat sarcastically, that the director is finally taking film production 'seriously' (Wettenhovi 1981). Despite the critical pummelling, *Mitäs me sankarit* was a huge success with 142,328 spectators, and established a pattern whereby critical condemnation clashed with the films' popular appeal, a pattern that would continue to follow Mäkinen's films throughout the early 1980s.

These films were not conventional exploitation, but low-brow entertainment that used farcical elements and silly gags to entice audiences. They also made use of local resources, including product placement for local businesses, to cut down on essential production costs like catering. Meanwhile, Mäkinen's productions would mobilize army reserves from a nearby military base, which allowed the films to tap into the military farce genre. By operating outside of the normative film institute structure and securing capital from private sources, the locality of these productions, allowing small time vendors like sausage shacks to sponsor them, makes the films prime instances of Nordsploitation. However, Mäkinen did delve into more traditional exploitation thematics when, under the pseudonym Frank Siponen, he produced *Pi pi pil. . . Pilleri* (*The P . . . p . . . pill*, 1982) at a cost of a much more substantial 1 million FIM. This sex farce, focusing on a professor who develops a pill to increase his sexual potency was critically dismissed (one reviewer suggested that the only positive quality of the film is that the sound is audible). Such dismissals did not deter Mäkinen and instead he, in typical exploitation manner, confronted critics directly with a statement preceding the opening credits of his next film *Likainen puolitusina* ('The Dirty Half Dozen', 1982): 'now all the film critics who have used a complementary ticket can leave. This film has no appropriate material for you.'

In making such statements, Mäkinen seems to be emphasizing that he is producing films with different standards of entertainment from the conventional norms. Yet, such attempts at confrontation and the critics' continued positioning of the films in lower cultural registers reveals as much about the stakes in some of these 'culture wars' as they do about the films themselves. Tapani Maskula (1981) suggested that the more conventional farce *Kaikenlaisia karkulaisia* (*Fugitives of All Kinds*, 1981) shows that 'Pori-based imitation of slick American entertainment is as stupid and pointless as reaching out to the moon', thereby placing the film in the category of both 'pointless' pop culture entertainment and domestic exploitation of international standards with little cultural value, especially as, and largely because, it has been produced on limited resources. Similar concerns apply to *Likainen puolitusina* where Tuuli (1982) found four problems with its construction: 'It is crudely written, weakly directed, smuttily shot, and cut without rhythm.' And while the critics generally acknowledged their attempts to target generic narrative formulas, some suggested films like the spy parody *Agentti 000 ja kuoleman kurvit* ('Agent 000 and the Curves of Death', 1983) are akin to 'buying an automatic washing machine that has to be cranked with a handle' (Huida 1983).

These comments provide a snapshot of the general level of discussion that greeted Mäkinen's films. The criticism focused mostly on their inept production standards as well as their dishevelled handling of national traditions such as the military farce genre. But foremost, the debate came down to the fact that cultural authorities – both critics and the Finnish Film Institute – would not accept them as appropriate contributions to national film culture. The idea of a filmmaker simply bypassing national cultural authorities without permission was not anything new as these sorts of accusations had also met Pasanen's films, and Finland has a long history of crude 'folk comedies'. Yet, the ways in which filmmakers like Mäkinen actively flaunted their opposition to cultural norms can be considered exploitative as he used gaps in the infrastructure – unstable industrial conditions, transformations in audience taste – to consolidate profitable if critically derided forms of film business. Yet, Mäkinen's success rate came crashing down with *Vapaaduunari Ville-Kalle* ('Free lancer Ville-Kalle', 1984) bombing massively at domestic theatres with only 551 viewers. New approaches had to be adopted, resulting in a change of genre with *Yön saalistajat* (*Hunters of the Night*, 1984), an attempt to produce a Finnish version of the contemporaneously popular cop action film. For us, this is arguably Mäkinen's most exploitative film as it sees him adopt international genre standards to very (in this case, literally) localized conditions, trying to capture a part of the commercial zeitgeist as well as make use of the type of still-outlawed violent content guaranteed to generate lucrative controversy.

The protagonist of *Hunters of the Night*, Pete, is an undercover cop who infiltrates a criminal gang. In best 'Poliziottesco' fashion, he disobeys his superiors, gets romantically involved with the gang leader's mistress and antagonizes their main henchman Reuna, a psychopathic drug addict with a penchant for killing his enemies with ninja throwing stars. The plot of the film provides a barebones excuse to string together clichés from undercover narratives. Yet, where the film does make an impact is on setting these conventions in the context of Finnish cinema of the 1980s. While there had been emulations of gangster films in the studio era and a few cases in the new wave period (see Kääpä 2017: 145–52), the explicit use of these conventions was unusual and resulted in some valuable advance publicity for the film (as well as consolidating its eventual cult reputation). Yet, the film was a huge bomb upon its domestic theatrical release, attracting only 1,670 viewers. As it had cost over a million Finnish marks, it constituted a huge personal risk for its enterprising director-producer, a notion perhaps exemplified best by the fact that it was released with no end credits as the film had run over budget and the credits had been too expensive to complete). Its reputation has arguably been sustained by its first domestic television broadcast reaching 1.5 million viewers, but this would not have helped Mäkinen with his finances. Combined with the lack of support from the Film Foundation, the film's performance was a considerable personal disappointment for Mäkinen, and considering the risk involved in these productions, it was not surprising that commercial action thrillers in this vein would be absent from Finnish screens until the 1990s.

Most intriguingly for our purposes, *Hunters of the Night* initially received an 18 rating from the domestic censorship board, citing its violent content. This decision constitutes a true anomaly in Finland as while there had been censorship problems in the past with domestic films such as *Sensuela* (1973) receiving the same rating and an increased tax rate, the case with *Hunters of the Night* was more complex. While *Sensuela*'s transgressive content was specifically to do with sexually explicit material, reflecting its attempt to capitalize on the contemporaneously still popular sexploitation content being pumped out of Sweden and Denmark, *Hunters of the Night* met resistance due to its violence. This resulted, perhaps ironically, in a situation where the film was treated on an equal level with imported genre films such as *Revenge of the Ninja* (1983) that were heavily cut or banned outright for excessive violence. Similarly, the use of the ninja throwing star in *Hunters of the Night* proved unpalatable for the censors who demanded cuts to the film. Yet, Mäkinen's work was not intended as marginal VHS-based exploitation along the lines of how a film like *Revenge of the Ninja* would have been perceived in Finland, but as a form of popular cinema intended for general audiences. For example, the spy spoof *Agentti 000 ja kuoleman kurvit* was cut by 74 metres in addition to early cuts by the producers to ensure it would be released in the K-12 category, indicating Mäkinen's willingness to play along to receive as low a rating as possible (Toiviainen 2019). In the case of *Hunters of the Night*, the idea must have been to capitalize on the reputation of these contentious and often outright banned films. Hence, the notorious 18 rating would have constituted considerable cultural capital for the film, and while the film was eventually cut to get a lower rating for the video market, most of the marketing focused on its sensationalist qualities and notoriety created by its censorship problems. The VHS cover, for example, prominently exclaimed: 'Now on VHS! Domestic crime film – sex – drugs – blackmail – death – they were desperate and ready to put all on the line.' This was a way to cater to an audience seeking domestic films exploiting the thrills of the Poliziottesco or American cop films but conducted with the novelty of a domestic film meeting these same transgressive standards – especially in a film market where such products were invariably scarce.

Intriguingly, many of the domestic critics anticipated these self-conscious attention grabbing tactics as some suggested that the film's producers were under the impression that popular success would be attained 'with nudity and burping' (Neumann 1984). Yet, Toiviainen (1984), for example, showcased a more finely attuned appreciation of the film: 'even though the plot is familiar from a thousand international examples, the picture, sound, and editing meet the standards of better circles.' The focus here was once more on its technical qualities, which is not surprising considering *Hunters of the Night* was explicitly positioned as domestic competition for imported cinema. Its reception reflects the ways that domestically produced commercial genre films were critiqued for their attempts to emulate international conventions, often characterized by domestic critics as revelling in ethical murkiness and low artistic quality. But for many, the technical qualities of international productions operated simultaneously as a yet-to-be-attained gold standard that *Hunters of the Night* came close to, at least in its depictions of violence. While critics were of two minds about its use value, the excessive violence and genre standards of *Hunters of the Night* played a significant role in generating its cult reputation. A gory death by a ninja throwing star in another context would not have meant much at all, but here, the brief scene of Reuna murdering a henchman takes on a whole new meaning as a truly transgressive element in Finnish cinema culture – a notion that was especially amplified by the scene being cut by the censors.

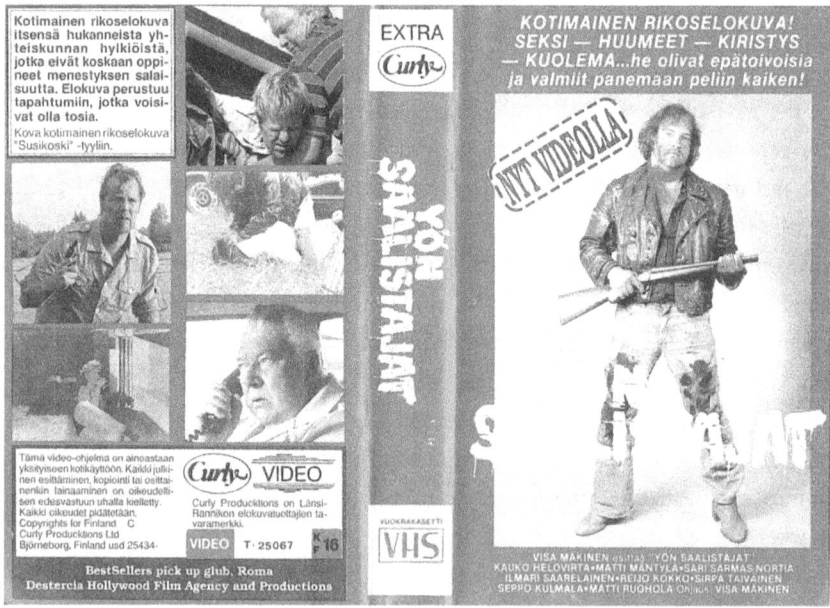

Figure 5.3 The original VHS artwork for *Yön saalistajat* (*Hunters of the Night*, 1984), with the caption translating to 'A domestic crime film – sex – drugs – extortion – death. They were ready desperate and ready to lay it all on the line.' Courtesy of Curly Produktions Ltd.

This type of violence as entertainment was still distinctly rare in Finnish cinema as well as in other Nordic countries, and its inclusion here must be viewed as a conscious commercial tactic. Again, the dynamics of proximity and distance characterize these tactics well, as the scene distances *Hunters of the Night* from most mainstream domestic cinema, whereas it also positions it in close proximity to audience preferences for similar imported genre films. While Mäkinen's film did not act a sustainable role model for domestic productions, it serves as a useful reminder of the ways Nordic producers in the 1980s were connected to transnational flows of genre and exploitation cinema even when producing films for local markets. At the same time, the economic and political realities of producing films in these small film cultures meant that such productions were invariably risky and, often inadvertently, marginalized as curiosities or failed experiments.

Exploitation cinema goes mainstream

The incorporation of transnational genre elements into these localized contexts, as we have seen, operated largely on the commercial logic of popular cinema. While domestic film policy slowly transformed to incorporate commercial genre elements, this was never a given as any consolidated patterns of genre production would only emerge in the latter half of the 1990s. Thus, the particular cultural–economic contexts of these countries made even attempts at relatively tame genre films such as what Steve Neale has defined as the 'action adventure' film seem exploitative. For him, the genre comprises the following distinctly non-controversial and non-transgressive elements: 'a propensity for spectacular physical action, a narrative structure involving fights, chases and explosions, and in addition to the deployment of state-of-the-art special effects, an emphasis in performance on athletic feats and stunts' (Neale 2000: 52). Such a description is far removed from any normative definitions of exploitation cinema, yet, in Nordic film productions of the 1980s, such elements were distinctly different and even transgressive, especially as they connoted an undesirable form of Americanization, perceived to be antithetical to much of the film policy of the 1970s and 1980s.

At the same time, Nordic film cultures have produced a fair share of films that fit this description. For example, a range of action films produced in Norway, such as *Orions belte* (*Orion's Belt*, 1985) and *Etter Rubicon* (*After Rubicon*, 1987), were often controversial due to the ways they merged genre formats with domestic infrastructure. Norwegian film historian Gunnar Iversen notes that *Orion's Belt* was a precursor to genre production in the region as it broke through the official funding barriers. The Norwegian Statens Filmproduksjonsutvalg refused to co-finance this 15 million NOK action spectacle no less than two times just because it was a genre film, before eventually giving in on the third attempt (Iversen 2011: 254–5). While critics took aim at its emulation of the conventions of US entertainment (Larssen 1985; Roed 1985), simultaneously, the development of such explicitly commercial productions was received enthusiastically by several commentators as a necessary strategy for Norwegian film production (Ellingsen 1985; Paulsen 1985). By mobilizing such discursive mechanisms, genre conventions were assimilated into the history of Norwegian national cinema and not the other way around. This was not, at least in hindsight, a case of genre conventions overtaking ethno-symbolic or heritage content.

While these 'helicopter films' (described as such because they feature a comparatively excessive use of helicopters on screen and as a vehicle to attain glamorous aerial shots) have been discussed extensively by Iversen (2005: 270–4), it is worth noting that much more traditional types of transnational exploitation, crucially with distinct global aspirations, were also produced during the 1980s. Swedish producers were especially prolific in producing excessively violent action films that hid their production origins. Often dubbed into English or spoken with extremely shaky accents and featuring protagonists pretending to be Americans, these films were aimed at international markets where the production standards of genre films were generally low and success could be attained with even limited resources. Björn Carlström and Daniel Hübenbecher's direct-to-video *War Dog* (1986) is a case in point, focusing on a Vietnam War vet (played by the American actor Timothy Earle) who goes after a general running an experiment to create super soldiers for the US military. The film is impressively violent as it features excessive and bloody shootouts, including the invariably shocking (and thus simultaneously lucrative) role played by the graphic murder of children, to such an extent that the UK DVD release continues to be cut by eighty-nine seconds to this day. While such productions are significant contributions to a more VHS-based exploitation subcurrent, this film, despite generating a small cult audience, would not have had any significant impact on wider policy or film cultural patterns. Thus, Chapter 6 expands on these concerns in relation to Swedish maverick Mats Helge Olsson's work (with whose company both Carlström and Earle worked) as his film factory transitioned from theatrical releases to VHS according to the laws of the market. Yet, to culminate this discussion of transnational exploitation cinema rejected by domestic cultural authorities which was largely successful with their intended international audiences, the Finnish–US co-production *Arctic Heat* (*Jäätävä polte*, 1985) provides an intriguing comparison to many of these small budget productions.

Global exploitation: *Arctic Heat* (aka *Born American*)

The films we have focused on so far have provided diverse perspectives on exploitative strategies amidst small nation film cultures dominated by film institute policy frameworks and challenged by overwhelming audience preference for imported productions. *Arctic Heat*, a collaboration between two young Finnish upstarts, the future film mogul Markus Selin and the soon-to-be Hollywood action meister Renny Harlin, provides another angle on these dynamics. An action film emulating imported counterparts like *First Blood* (1982) and various Chuck Norris films (for more on this see Kääpä, 2011: 55–70), *Arctic Heat* does away with most ethno-symbolic content (though it does prioritize snow – a future hallmark of many key Harlin films) in favour of directly targeting international appeal. By focusing on three American protagonists who accidentally venture into forbidden Soviet territory while on holiday in Finland, the film touches on many key Cold War-era political tensions. As the hapless Americans are subsequently arrested and locked up in a dystopian prison, they have to fight to survive as the Soviet and US politicians are more preoccupied with Cold War appeasement than the survival of their citizens.

The narrative is aimed at audiences familiar with productions featuring the Cold War and POWs – including obligatory torture and violent fight scenes – but Finland's geopolitical role as a liminal space between the American and Soviet powers holds crucial significance here. It functions as a means to rationalize the film's production context and gives it that necessary sense of distance from similar material hitting the VHS shelves worldwide. Yet, the production was financed independently as it did not receive any support from the Finnish Film Institute, a fact not entirely unsurprising considering the political climate in the early 1980s. Despite this lack of official support, it was the most expensive film ever produced in Finland at the time of production with a budget of 17 million Finnish marks.

Filming commenced in 1984 to produce a raw demo reel that was used to entice the financier Cinema Group to prop up the funding for an international production with Chuck Norris attached to star, a promise that seems outlandish in hindsight considering Harlin and Selin were two unknown producers with no real credentials. Norris pulled out eventually due to other contractual obligations though he was replaced shortly by his son Mike Norris. Star power – or rather big last names – was only one part of this operation as organizing a shoot with huge explosions and gun battles in the mould of Norris and Stallone films of the time was difficult to organize as professional knowledge and an appropriate level of technical expertise in pyrotechnics was largely non-existent in the Finnish film industry. Thus, the crew of the film consisted of professionals from Finland and elsewhere with key roles such as music score and editing allocated to Brits. In addition, Harlin hired Swedish maverick filmmaker Mats Helge Olsson as a special effects adviser, potentially due to the success of Olsson's Ninjasploitation film *The Ninja Mission* (1984), and Olsson was also cast as a malicious priest in the film.

The organization of the production reveals a lot about its cultural–political role. Whereas all the other examples discussed in this chapter were predominantly produced with indigenous forces, here the model is designed to ensure the production is global from its inception. With large parts of the financing, talent and creative input inspired by Hollywood, other strategies soon followed. Selin launched a franchising campaign for the film including a novel adaptation, as well as clothes and other paraphernalia displaying the logo of the film. This type of merchandizing was very unusual for Finnish cinema at the time even if the rationale, clearly, was to capitalize on Hollywoodized marketing campaigns for franchises. As this was done in a small film culture context, however, these campaigns would have appeared truly disruptive at the time. Unsurprisingly, these tactics met with plentiful scorn from journalists who found it difficult to amalgamate such explicit commercial aspirations with 1980s Finnish cinema culture.

These aspirations apply to the film's content as well, not only in terms of its unabashed adoration of the Hollywood genre format but also its role as potentially problematic political cinema. The narrative makes use of conservative US propaganda about the communist threat as well as capitalizes on right wing paranoia about the ways the state ignores the individual, as evident in the epilogue statement: 'The American government made an official complaint due to these events. The Soviets never responded and officially the event never took place.' These sorts of cynical anti-government narratives are a hallmark of the *Rambo* (1982-2019) and *Missing in Action* (1984-1988) franchises but replicating some of these political positions – instead of the carefully managed neutrality of much of Finnish cinema of the time – would allow the producers to exploit the free publicity that such controversy would inevitably bring.

Despite aligning its politics with some of the more overt Reaganite perspectives of the era, *Arctic Heat* occupies a distinctly controversial role in Finnish film politics of the mid-1980s. While a film with this particular content would have hardly proven controversial had it been an international genre film, *Arctic Heat* encountered problems with the Finnish authorities as it was still considered a domestic production. The film was effectively banned for the majority of 1985 but the reasons for this appear debatable as it was officially banned for its violence (which did not prove problematic for *Rambo: First Blood II* or *Missing in Action* – though both were cut) as well as its politically sensitive content. The producers complained about the decision and even the Undersecretary of the State, Klaus Törnudd, viewed the film at the Finnish Film Institute and recommended cuts and a higher level of taxation to allow it to be screened (see Sedergren 2008). The film board kept the decision in place in February 1985 but this time there was no mention of political factors. In March, the film was presented to evaluators in a version cut by over three and half minutes with cuts focusing on both torture and scenes of violence, yet even this was unsuccessful. An eventual case appeal at the High Court overturned these decisions to allow the film to be released in December 1985 with only minor further cuts. These battles with censors were consistently attributed to violence, but in retrospective it has been discovered that key factors for such heavy opposition was due to the Russian ambassador to Finland Vladimir Sobolev insisting that the film violated the two countries' Agreement on Friendship, Trust and Good Neighbourly Relations (Tikka 2008). Despite the potential of controversy to create free publicity, these complications had a huge impact on the finances of the film's producers as the delay in the film's release meant that their investment was effectively frozen in bureaucracy, indicating again the precarious position producers of genre cinema faced at the time.

Critics saw the whole scandal as 'more or less smoke without fire' (Peltonen 1986). For them, the film was 'a noisy and empty spectacle that would not have made the news had its producers not been Finnish, if it did not deal with the Soviet Union, and if these factors did not act as free advertising for the film'. In many ways for domestic critics, the unique role of the film as a Finnish production that meets internationally competitive standards seems to have been the most worrying facet of the film, not so much its politics or its violent content. It is worth noting that while many critics found the film to be technically proficient, it was often precisely this closeness to the oft-derided action genre that caused problems, especially, again, as the production standards were now on par with imported productions. Such critiques were not unusual, but more of a continued reflection of cultural norms that continued to view popular genre cinema as lacking in cultural merit.

Yet, the factors that made the film stand out in a negative sense domestically allowed it to succeed internationally, suggesting again the cultural variability of terms like exploitation and marginality. Interestingly, the industry magazine *Variety* (1987) reviewed the film in positive terms: although, for them,

> the plot borders on the incomprehensible, energy and flash of action staging is displayed throughout, and Mike Norris et al. put in a convincing natural performance that ought to soon make them familiar names and faces for casting directors to consider. There is plenty of violence spouting from the Rambo vein, but where it occurs, it makes sense. Henrik Paersch's cinematography has a no-nonsense steadiness that works hand-in-glove with director Renny Harlin's smooth handling of a large cast through the plot's minefields.

These comments are illuminating as they identify precisely the same areas as the Finnish critics but in largely opposite ways. Instead of considering violence and professional steadiness as obstacles, these elements, for them, provide the film with the required professional and commercial sheen that enabled it to penetrate the US markets. While *Arctic Heat* was eventually released on four prints in Finland in December 1985 and gained only 33,000 spectators, the film succeeded in its target markets – the United States – not only in terms of critical reception but also financially. Thus, the film facilitated Harlin's move to Hollywood to start his career on productions such as *A Nightmare on Elm Street 4* (1988) and *Die Hard 2* (1990). Selin emerged in the late 1990s as the key figure at Solar Films, arguably the most successful production company in Finland.

For us, *Arctic Heat* is most productive as a means to shed light on some of the key political cultural debates of the time. While Harlin's film is full of exploitative visuals and thematic content, it does not meet the qualifications of traditional exploitation due to its comparatively large production

The Local and the Transnational in Nordic Exploitation Cinema of the 1980s 135

Figure 5.4 The international original poster artwork for *Arctic Heat* (*Born American*, 1985), with Mike Norris in the leading role. Courtesy of DG Film.

infrastructure and the wide commercial distribution it received. Yet, domestically, it was received in similar terms to mainstream international genre productions, shunned critically and falling foul of the authorities. These mechanisms emphasize the power these gatekeepers of 'official' film culture continued to hold, effectively being able to determine the fate of film entrepreneurs with their decisions. The problematic fate of the film was not isolated to Finland, as in Sweden, for example, the censors first banned *Arctic Heat*. Then when the distribution company, Hem Films Scandinavia, handed in a seven-minute self-censored cut, it was released as R-rated (Statens biografbyrå 1986a and 1986b). However, in the American markets it performed well and was received as a genre pic on par with other similar productions. Thus, as had been the case with many of the other films covered here, the contested history of *Arctic Heat* underlines how exploitation needs to be seen as a contextual term that means very different things in such diverse contexts.

Conclusion

In comparison to the often radical and marginal exploitation films of the 1970s, the 1980s saw an increasing level of integration between exploitative material, mainstream genre film, commercially minded filmmakers, and domestic film production infrastructure. As part of an increasingly commercialized production culture, Nordic film institutes slowly started offering funding support for genre films. While these films would not normally meet the standards of exploitation cinema, many of these productions were effectively received in similar terms due to the ways they were positioned within these structures. While Church (2015: 5–14) has argued that a huge part of labelling films as exploitation comes from their distribution and exhibition practices, the Nordic situation is markedly different. Here, for example, the alternative space of the grindhouse did not exist, and being classified as exploitation is invariably much more premised on standards and guidelines established by film institute production policy than on exhibition practices. Independent productions outside of these confines, in particular, were invariably a huge risk for the producers who would have to compete financially on an equal level with imported productions. As the domestic failures of *Hunters of the Night*, *Arctic Heat* and *The Visitors*, and their inability to qualify for state subsidies, testifies, the consolidation of such genre patterns was hindered by these disappointments until the late 1990s when both new technologies and increased professionalization in film production management ushered in a new era.

This chapter has identified two exploitation narratives. First, localized genre productions exploited gaps in the markets by providing domestic appropriations of often controversial international narrative and aesthetic influences, but predominantly focused on communicating with domestic audiences. For example, the Viking trilogy provides an innovative approach to national cinema by combining ethno-symbolic content and exploitative tendencies. The use of violence and nudity consolidated Icelandic cinema as a potentially internationally competitive force (with intertextual references to respectable international films). This approach also applies to *Moonlight Sonata* where elements from the slasher genre were adapted to an explicitly domestic environment, resulting in the film winning critical accolades and various forms of financial support from the Finnish Film Institute. These films 'exploit' both commercial and critical frameworks as the adaptation and assimilation of international genre conventions functions as a pragmatic strategy – these films could use elements from outlawed genres like the slasher, but they would have to be localized in a way that makes sense domestically.

Second, productions with a clear aim to gain international distribution were much more explicit in using exploitation cinema trends, including excessive violence and transgressive iconography that would be more at home in American genre productions. This was a problematic proposition at the time as the film industry operated more as a form of publicly subsidized domestic culture rather than a business (which it invariably is). Producers would thus need to survive and in a lot of ways appease two very different masters – one for commercial survival and sustainability, the other for cultural respect and institutional backing. For us, this balancing is the essence of Nordic exploitation where transgression is not so much defined by exploiting cultural norms but making use of different discourses – here the often-opposed rhetoric of heritage and internationalized commercialism – to carve out a space amidst the difficult landscape. The problems faced by *Arctic Heat* and *Hunters of the Night* testify to the moral and political complications faced by such films where film politics operate as a dynamic play of inclusion and exclusion with directors using exploitative content to try to align with (and simultaneously disassociate from) different registers – including official guidelines and commercial audience preferences – in these challenging infrastructures.

The contested role of many of these Nordic case studies brings us to a wider question – what is at stake in labelling these films as exploitation? Are we forcing this label on films that were simply aspiring to commercial success? The concept of exploitation is often considered in negative terms as an illegitimate use of cultural resources or a transgressive means to exploit taste boundaries. While many of the films addressed in this chapter certainly contain politically problematic content, exploitation, at least in this context, is best considered as an innovative economic and cultural strategy to gain a foothold for entry into hostile markets. Here, 'exploitation' is inherently to do with the socioeconomic and political foundations of the Nordic welfare state model – which extends to its cultural industries – where to be exploitative would not have the same moral or political connotations as in other film cultures. As these film financing arrangements dominate the discussion, to be exploitative in the Nordic context is not only connected to transgressive content but the fact that some of these explicitly commercial genre films were effectively taking advantage of social services and public money. While most 'respectable' films would do the same, those few instances where commercial genre producers were able to gain public money for commercial productions resulted in contentious debates over the fact that film institutes were finally identifying commercialism as a means to expand their market share of the domestic box office. This makes relatively ordinary genre productions occupy a similar cultural space as much more problematic imported exploitation films, even as 'authentically' exploitative films such as *Arctic Heat* had to ascertain alternative financing models.

In some ways, Nordic exploitation cinema is a typical case of first-world problems. Bored with the respectability of their cultural confines and clearly motivated by business instincts, would-be auteurs observed the expansive market for slashers and other forbidden content – as well as the huge black market in uncut films networked throughout most of Northern Europe via important nodes like the Netherlands and Denmark. They identified an opportunity to produce sanctioned but still 'dangerous' domestic films that would allow audiences access to forbidden content, albeit now often sanitized and recontextualized for a domestic audience. However, despite these complicated film politics, the words 'not allowed' did not belong in Swedish filmmaker Mats Helge Olsson's vocabulary, as he exploited both the Swedish Film Institute and the fast-growing international home video market with his entertainment violence factory, which is explored in Chapter 6.

References

Åhlander, Lars (ed.) (1997), *Svensk filmografi 8 1980–1989*, Stockholm: Svenska filminstitutet.
Ahonen, Kimmo et al. (eds.) (2004), *Taju kankaalle*, Turku: Kirja-Aurora.
Alanen, Asko (1988), 'Kuutamosonaatti', Review, *La Strada*, 3/1988.
Anon. (1981), 'Útlaginn', Review, Morgunblaðið, 25 November.
Anon. (1987), 'Born American', Review, *Variety*, 20 January.
Anon. (1988), 'Í skugga hrafnsins', Review, Morgunbladid, 15 November.
Anon. (1991), 'Hvíti víkingurinn', Review, *Dagbladid Visir*, 30 October.
Autio, Tommi (2002), *Spede: Pertti Pasasen elämä*, Helsinki: Tammi.
Björnsson, Björn(1991), 'Hvíti víkingurinn', Review, *Morgunbladir*, 3 November.
Church, David (2015),*Grindhouse Nostalgia*, Edinburgh: Edinburgh University Press.
Ellingsen, Thor (1985), 'Den holder, den', Review, *Dagbladet*, 9 February.
Fremer, Björn (1988), 'Besökarna', Review, *Kvällsposten*, 29 April.
Grut, Mario (1988), 'Korpens skugga', Review, *Aftonbladet*, 29 October.

Gudmunsson, Agust (2010),'Land og Synir: An Interview with Agust Gudmundsson', *Scandinavian-Canadian Studies*, 19, 42-54.
Gustafsson, Tommy and Pietari Kääpä (eds.) (2015), *Nordic Genre Film*, Edinburgh: Edinburgh University Press.
Hjort, Mette and Duncan Petrie (eds.) (2007), *The Cinema of Small Nations*, Edinburgh: Edinburgh University Press.
Huida, Jarmo (1983), 'Agentti 000 ja kuoleman kurvit', Review, *Satakunnan kansa*, 18 September.
Icelandic Film Centre (2017), 'When the Raven Flies', available at: https://www.icelandicfilms.info/films/nr/75.
Indrigason, Fridkrik (1984), 'Hrafninn flygur hatt', Review, *Morgunbladir*, 7 February.
Iversen, Gunnar (2005), 'Learning from Genre: Genre Cycles in Modern Norwegian Cinema', in Andrew Nestingen and Trevor Elkington (eds), *Transnational Cinema in the Global North*, Detroit: Wayne State University Press, pp. 261–78.
Iversen, Gunnar (2011), *Norsk filmhistorie: Spillefilmen 1911-2011*, Olso: Universitetsforlaget.
Kääpä, Pietari (2011), '"Born American?" – Renny Harlin Meets the Dream Factory', *Film International*, issue 2, 55–70.
Kääpä, Pietari (2017), 'From Industry to Art: The New Wave as a Transnational Phenomenon', in Henry Bacon (ed.), *Finnish Cinema: A Transnational Enterprise*, Basingstoke: Palgrave, pp. 145–70.
Larssen, Bjørn H. (1985), 'Omkjærlighet og krig på Svalbard', *Nordlys*, 9 February.
Lumirae (1988), 'Kuutamosonaatti', Review, *Demari*, 4 November.
Maskula, Tapani (1981), 'Kaikenlaisia karkureita', Review, *Turun Sanomat*, 26 August.
Maskula, Tapani (1988), 'Kuutamosonaatti', Review, *Turun Sanomat*, 8 November.
Maslin, Janet (1985),'Raven from Iceland', Review, *The New York Times*, 25 April.
Neale, Steve (2000), *Genre and Hollywood*, New York: Routledge.
Neumann, Horst (1984), 'Yön saalistajat', Review, *Porin lehti*, 21 November.
Olsson, Hans E. (1984), 'Korpen flyger', Review, *Arbetet*, 25 August.
Olsson, Mats Olof (1988), 'Besökarna', Review, *Chaplin*, No. 3.
Pantti, Mervi (2000), *Kansallinen elokuva on pelastettava*, Helsinki: SKS.
Paulsen, Kaar (1985), 'Altfor god til å være norsk!', *Adresseavisen*, 9 February.
Piela, Mikko (1988), 'Kuutamosonaatti', Review, *Uusi Suomi*, 4 November.
Peltonen, Osmo (1986), 'Jäätävä polte', Review, *Kansan Uutiset*, 20 December.
Røed, Liv Nerstad (1985), 'Praktfullt – i Michelets ånd', *Verdens Gang*, 9 February.
Schiller, Hans (1984), 'Korpen flyger', Review, *Svenska Dagbladet*, 25 August.
Schiller, Hans (1988), 'Besökarna', Review, *Svenska Dagbladet*, 29 April.
Sedergren, Jari (2008), 'Jäätävä polte', available at: http://sedis.blogspot.com/2008/02/jtv-polte.html (Accessed 4 July 2019).
Smith, Anthony (2009), *Ethnosymbolism and Nationalism: A Cultural Approach*, New York: Routledge.

Söderbergh Widding, Astrid (1998), 'Iceland', in Tytti Soila, Astrid Söderbergh Widding and Gunnar Iversen, *Nordic National Cinemas*, London and New York: Routledge, pp. 96–101.

Soila, Tytti, Astrid Söderbergh Widding and Gunnar Iversen (1998), *Nordic National Cinemas*, London and New York: Routledge.

Soinio, Olli (1988), 'Kuutamosonaatti', Review, *Aamulehti*, 4 November.

Statens biografbyrå (1986a), Censorship Card for *BornAmerican*, Stockholm: Riksarkivet, Statens biografbyrås arkiv, 126.039.

Statens biografbyrå (1986b), Censorship Card for *BornAmerican*, Stockholm: Riksarkivet, Statens biografbyrås arkiv, 127.073.

Statens biografbyrå (1987), Censorship Card for *Robocop*, Stockholm: Riksarkivet, Statens biografbyrås arkiv, 127.136.

Sverrison, Asgrimur (1984), 'Hrafnnin flygur: efterminnilegt kvikmyndaverk', Review, *Myndmal*, 2 February.

Tikka, Juha-Pekka (2008), 'Jäätävä polte', *Ilta-sanomat*, 13 February.

Toiviainen, Sakari (1975), *Uusi suomalainen elokuva*, Helsinki: SKS.

Toiviainen, Sakari (1981), 'Mitäs me sankareita', Review, *Ilta-sanomat*, 21 August 1981.

Toiviainen, Sakari (1984), 'Yön saalistajat', Review, *Ilta-sanomat*, 5 October.

Toiviainen, Sakari (2019), 'Yön saalistajat', commentary available at elonet.fi: https://elonet.finna.fi/Record/kavi.elonet_elokuva_119843 (Accessed 17 January 2020).

Tuuli, Markku (1982), 'Likainen puolitusina', Review, *Katso*, 37.

Wettenhovi, Hannu-Pekka (1981), 'Mitäs me sankareita', Review, *Satakunnan Kansa*, 21 August.

6

The entertainment violence factory

Mats Helge Olsson's action films of the 1980s

I shoot mainly at night, because then you can't tell where you are.

Mats Helge Olsson

Swedish director, producer and cinematic factotum Mats Helge Olsson made his directorial debut with the Lingonberry Western – a Swedish variation of the Western genre – *I död mans spår* ('Dead Man's Trail') in 1975, and then went on to produce and direct a number of films of which a majority never saw the light of day. During the 1970s, he worked within the Swedish film funding system, but for most of the 1980s, he operated as an independent film director and producer, making exploitative action and horror films aimed at the fast-growing international direct-to-video market. As specified by Andy Willis and C. P. Lee, the categories of 'straight-to-video' or 'direct-to-video' were and are 'widely accepted to indicate low-budget, poor-quality products not worthy of theatrical distribution' (Willis and Lee 2009: 58). A consequence of this prejudice is that these types of films are seldom considered when national or international film history has been written, and thus continue to exist outside mainstream film cultures. In Swedish film history, Mats Helge Olsson has been dismissed and is, accordingly, not even mentioned in the latest historical overview of Swedish film (Furhammar 2003), or he has been used as a laughable example in order to ridicule his efforts (Ekeroth 2011: 40, 64, 81).

However, regardless of the quality of his films, Olsson constitutes a unique case of an individual who made Swedish transnational exploitation films for the international video market outside of a state-sanctioned system guarded by canonization, censorship and funding issues. Here, we will focus on the very conscious exploitation strategies used by Olsson to carve out a market for his productions. Olsson's practices, as we will explain, indeed constituted a factory for 'entertainment violence' where, on the one hand, global forms of exploitation, aimed squarely at the international markets, were manufactured. On the other hand, Olsson's factory also produced films that were local variations of exploitation cinema, that is, Nordic genre films with explicit violence that began to appear in the 1980s, produced with support from the film institutes and thus sanctioned by the state. Yet, Olsson's films consciously exceeded their contemporaries in most categories due to their low production values, with stories that enhanced the 'entertainment' factors of violence and gore, and not least, because their open contempt for state support and censorship allowed them to be successfully sold at the global market place.

Consequently, this chapter will pick up the thread from Chapter 5 where we left off with the one-off production of *Arctic Heat* (1985) and continue our exploration of global exploitation strategies. These alternative strategies within production and distribution included the creation of an elaborate system of financiers, the creation of an exploitation family, the use of explicit violence and gore, 'international' settings, actors and genres, the formation of a home-grown star system and an international distribution network for direct-to-video sales. We will also apply an auteur perspective on Olsson's films themselves, performing textual analysis on a sample of films produced in the factory in order to provide an opportunity to enhance the understanding of these films beyond the commercial and practical strategies that Olsson had to adapt to, by emphasizing and contextualizing themes such as the Cold War, and key elements such as genre aspirations and gender representations. First, however, we will demonstrate how Olsson, already from the beginning, perceived himself as an outsider who, in a distinctly exploitative way, managed to exploit the Swedish Film Institute and its so-called F-Fund.

The beginnings: Working within the Swedish Film Industry as an outsider

Mats Helge Olsson (born 1953) entered the film business by making two exploitative Lingonberry Westerns, the already mentioned *I död mans spår* and *The Frozen Star* (1977), both produced in 1974, when Olsson was only nineteen years old. These films were shot at and around High Chaparral, an ever-evolving Wild West theme park located in Småland in southern Sweden. The theme park was founded in 1966 by 'Big Bengt' Erlandsson, an entrepreneur and Americana enthusiast, who built the theme park as a copy of the Cartwright family's hometown from the highly popular television series *Bonanza* (1959–73). One of the conditions for getting the building permit for this humongous theme park was that the buildings were used as film and televisions sets (Ekeroth 2011: 95). Hence, 'Big Bengt' produced and also acted in *The Frozen Star*, a film that the evening newspaper *Aftonbladet* dubbed, 'The world's worst film' at its premiere in 1977, three years after it was made (Anon. 1977). Most likely, *The Frozen Star* was meant to be screened at the theme park High Chaparral but due to its amateurish qualities, it was shelved. Nonetheless, in 1977, it was screened on three occasions (Fröberg 1977: 63) and the only reason for this was that public screenings were a prerequisite for obtaining production support from the Swedish Film Institute's F-Fund (Åhlander 1989: 353). The F-Fund was a loss guarantee fund effective during the 1970s and the early 1980s, which stipulated that if the budget of a Swedish film production with cinema circulation was in the 'red', the F-Fund could reattribute the film producers with 20 per cent of the budget, though at the most 640,000 SEK. Apparently, Mats Helge Olsson found a backdoor into the Swedish film funding system, which he would exploit all-out, eventually, and singlehandedly, contributing to the termination of the F-Fund.

After the two Lingonberry Westerns, Olsson met and befriended esteemed Swedish actor Per Oscarsson, with whom he would collaborate on four films: *Heja Sverige!* ('Hurrah Sweden!', 1979), *Tvingad att leva* ('Forced to Live', 1980), *Sverige åt Svenskarna* ('Sweden for the Swedes', 1980) and *Attentatet* ('The Assault', 1980). Oscarsson acted in all four films, Olsson produced all four and directed two of them and Oscarsson directed and wrote the screenplay for *Sverige åt svenskarna*. With the exception of *Attentatet*, which had limited distribution, the other three films were distributed by Europa Film AB, at the time the second biggest film company in Sweden. The first of these films, *Heja Sverige!*, showcased Olsson's exploitative tendencies, as he shamelessly cashed in on the hidden camera craze that hit the Scandinavian countries after the huge success of South African film *Funny People* (1976, distributed in Sweden in 1978 and in Denmark in 1980).

Whereas *Tvingad att leva* and *Attentatet* were standard low-budget thrillers, *Sverige åt svenskarna* was something entirely different. It was the film that would make the still young, only twenty-seven at the time, Mats Helge Olsson infamous and an outcast in the Swedish film business. With an initial budget of 4 million SEK the film was supposed to be a historical slapstick epic á la *Monty Python and the Holy Grail* (1975), taking place in Sweden during the fifteenth century, but with historical accuracy when it came to clothes, localities and other parts of the mise-en-scene. This included an impressive number of the Swedish actor elite, and thousands upon thousands of extras. However, the film and the budget mushroomed to a still unknown number, but it is estimated that the final bill for *Sverige åt svenskarna* came in somewhere around 20 million SEK, making it one of the most expensive Swedish film productions to date (Åhlander 1997: 116).

This extravagant spending was partly due to Oscarsson's inexperience as director for this large-scale film (he only had a collective directorial effort on his merit list), and partly due to Olsson's voluminous producing style where he considered the Swedish Film Institute, the main funder of Swedish films, to be 'the film industry's public employment agency' where one could collect their unemployment benefits (Meiland 1980: 22–3). According to available data, Olsson received 1.46 million SEK from the Swedish Film Institute, and at least 2 million SEK from Europa Film AB, the distributor (Åhlander 1997: 116). However, during the lengthy pre- and post-production of *Sverige åt svenskarna*, Olsson launched another thirteen film projects, which he pitched to the Swedish Film Institute in Stockholm with titles such as *Tvingad att leva* (1980, 'Forced to Live'), *Attentatet* (1980, 'The Assault'), 'Filmens underbara värld' ('The Wonderful World of Film'), 'Läckan' ('The Leck'), 'Sverige åt svenskarna 2' ('Sweden to the Swedes 2'), 'Den stora matchen' ('The Great Game'), 'Slaget om Sverige' ('The Battle of Sweden'), 'Drömmar', ('Dreams'), 'Heja Sverige 2' ('Hurrah Sweden!, Part 2'), 'Pojken i dimman' ('The Boy in the Mist') and 'Somewhere Sometime' (Mats Helge Olsson's applications to the F-Fund, 1978–80).

As costs piled up on the production of *Sverige åt svenskarna*, Olsson did not try to tighten the budget but instead threw more money on the fire by ingeniously using an inconsistency in the Swedish Film Institute's F-Fund. After having discovered that the Swedish Film Institute paid a loss guarantee for all films with cinema distribution, Olsson found another loophole. In the regulations of the F-Fund there was a clause stating that the film producer could borrow, in advance, from this loss guarantee the tidy sum of 360,000 SEK by only presenting an idea, a budget and some raw material from the ongoing production. Within a year, Olsson had thus borrowed the sum of 5.5 million SEK for thirteen film projects, including the 1.46 million SEK for *Sverige åt svenskarna*, out of which he eventually completed only four finished films ('Bokföringsorder' 1980). In March 1980, as Olsson applied for the project 'Somewhere, Sometimes', the Swedish Film Institute, in a bliss of indecisiveness, decided to grant Olsson a final payment of 360,000 SEK, at the same time as they warned him that there would be no more money until Olsson's 'stock of unfinished films were no more than two' (Henricson 1980).

A contemporary interview with Bernard Claydon, employed in the implausible combination of carpenter and editor on the production of *Sverige åt svenskarna*, tells of the chaos that prevailed during the production, with everyday misunderstandings, amateurs hired on a whim for film crew and constantly bouncing salary checks. 'It was the same story every time you asked for the salary. There was no money. That is, if you were not there when Mats Helge came back from Stockholm in the Cadillac with funding from the Film Institute' (Windén 1981: 64).

Apparently, Olsson frequently went to the Swedish Film Institute in Stockholm in order to get more money, and one way that this transpired was through the so-called 'scrapfilm'.

> Mats Helge asked me to put some material together that he could present at the Film Institute. It was Sunday and he was going to Stockholm on Monday. I went through many reels with clips from *Heja Sverige!*, for which he had already received money. These were outtakes with technical flaws, scenes where the joke fell flat, or which were just too bad. Just shit. It did not matter, just as long as there was something to present. Finally, we had some reels. And the next day, MHO was able to borrow money on these scrapings. (Windén 1981: 64)

Even before Olsson was ousted from the Swedish film industry, he flaunted contempt for what he perceived as a highbrow culture that, somewhat paradoxically considering his own spending, wasted the taxpayers' money on films and television programmes that nobody wanted to see. 'I could build Hollywood for the now about 30 billion that they [SFI] have spent on film productions over the years. To make a lot of crap, that is' (Meiland 1980: 25). Hence, he embraced an anti-establishment stance and an aesthetic philosophy that distanced his filmmaking from the 'state approved' one, that is, of films supported by the Swedish Film Institute, which on a formal level functioned as a kind of guarantor for the quality of the finished films. As film scholars Ernest Mathijs and Jamie Sexton point out, the exploitation film context often entailed an anti-establishment attitude aimed primarily against an establishment that, paradoxically and especially in a European context, often involved some sort of financial state involvement that the filmmakers tried so hard to distance themselves from (Mathijs and Sexton 2011: 14, 28).

Olsson continued this 'grand' tradition, but with very inconsistent results as *Sverige åt svenskarna* finally premiered in August 1980 to devastating reviews. This is 'a misbegotten freak of a film that lacks a constructive central idea. Loose verbal and visual gags do not make a film and the whole production appears like a single huge ploy' (Lönroth 1980). Still, the film managed to lure 140,000 people to the cinemas, which is not a bad figure for Sweden. Nevertheless, the astronomical production costs made *Sverige åt svenskarna* into one of the biggest economic failures in Swedish film history. Moreover, it led to personal bankruptcy and an eight-month prison sentence for its aspiring producer, of which he was incarcerated for four months ('Beslut', Konkursansökan 1981; Lundberg 1987: 14).

This legal development would be used, and continuously exaggerated, by Olsson to construct his 'anti-establishment attitude' for years to come, where the debt that he had acquired in connection with *Sverige åt svenskarna* tended to rise with each interview given, from the original 400,000 SEK to 2 million SEK in 1981 (Windén 1981), 20 million SEK in 1986 (Anon. 1986: 20) and 30 million SEK in 1987 (Lundberg 1987: 14). Yet, the legal debacle and his literal ousting from the Swedish film industry did not quell Olsson. He would start up anew on a grand scale in his small hometown of Lidköping, located in the woods of the rural province of Västergötland, far from the traditional film centre in Stockholm, the capital city of Sweden. In Lidköping, he and a group of enthusiasts created what was virtually a factory for the production of low-budget exploitation films aimed at the expanding international VHS-market during the 1980s.

The entertainment violence factory: *The Ninja Mission* and the marketplace for Nordic exploitation

Starting with *The Ninja Mission* (1984) – a Cold War spectacle that cashed in on the ongoing ninja/Kung Fu craze and managed to reach fifteenth place at the US box office (Anon. 1984b: 9), as well as also figuring in the top ten of the US video rental chart – this underground assembly line factory produced a large number of exploitation films never meant for the domestic cinema circuit. Instead, these films were distributed internationally with varying degrees of success. Using original VHS covers and company credits information available on IMDb, sixteen countries and thirty-four distribution companies can be identified as being involved in their international distribution.¹ The productions included straightforward slasher films like *Blood Tracks* (1985), a trilogy of action films with eco-critical and Cold War narratives starring David Carradine, and even a children's film, *Spökligan* ('Ghostbusters', 1987), which, for obvious reasons, tried to cash in on the *Ghostbusters* (1984 and 1989) franchise. Just as in the preceding period, when Olsson milked the Swedish Film Institute for money for films that were never produced, there is no transparent information on the exact number of films that were made in this entertainment violence factory between 1984 and 1990.

Nevertheless, when Mats Helge Olsson started up anew in 1983, his financial circumstances had changed dramatically, and he now depended on the video boom that swept over Western Europe, United States and Japan. After a slow start in the late 1970s, home video entertainment became a household product during the 1980s, and by 1987, roughly 35 per cent of all Swedish, Norwegian and Finnish households owned a VCR, whereas the same number for American and British households were 43 and 42 per cent, respectively (Våldsskildringsutredningen 1988: 47). In the beginning of the 1980s, this fast-growing market was still in development, and Hollywood studios were more than reluctant to release their films on VHS. In fact, both Universal and Disney sued Sony in 1976, seeking to have the VCR impounded as a tool of piracy. This lawsuit was then dragged through several iterations, until the US Supreme Court

---

1 *The Ninja Mission* (1984): New Line Cinema (USA, theatrical), Distribuidora Internacional de Filmes (Brazil, VHS), Media Home Entertainment (USA, VHS), Missing in Action (UK, VHS), New Line Home Video (USA, VHS), Pan-Canadian Film Distributors (Canada, VHS), VPS Video (West Germany, VHS), Video for Pleasure (Netherlands, VHS), Novio (Norway, VHS), Transworld Video (Sweden, VHS).
Blood Tracks (1985): Succéfilm AB (Sweden, theatrical), Avatar Film Corporation Limited (UK, VHS), CIC Victor Video (Japan, VHS), Highlight Video (West Germany, VHS), Malo Video (Canada, VHS), R.C.V.2001 Video (Belgium, VHS), Vista Home Video (USA, VHS), Saekyong Video (South Korea, VHS), Virgin Home Video (Sweden, VHS). R.C.V.2001 Video (Netherlands, VHS), Cannon Video (USA, VHS).
Eagle Island (1986): Esselte CIC Video (Netherlands, VHS), Top Tape (Brazil, VHS), Medusa Video (Poland, VHS), Albatros Video (Spain, VHS).
Spökligan (1987): Alpha Pictures (Sweden, VHS), NS Video (Spain, VHS).
Fatal Secret (1988): Magic Video (West Germany, VHS), Video Rondo (Poland, VHS).
Animal Protector (1988): Eriga Video distribusjon (Norway, VHS), Nea Kinisi Video (Greece, VHS), Video Rondo (Poland, VHS), Vic Video Brazil, VHS), Acuarela Video (Argentina, VHS), Aros Video (?, VHS).
The Mad Bunch (1989): Atlas Video (USA, VHS), RCA/Columbia-Hoyts Home Video (Australia, VHS), HIT of Poland (Poland, VHS).
The Hired Gun (1989): Hellas Cosmos Video (Greece, VHS) CB Films Video (Spain, VHS).
Russian Terminator (1990): Arena Home Video (USA, VHS), VDM Video (Netherlands, VHS).

Figure 6.1 Mats Helge Olsson on the set of *The Ninja Mission* (1984). Photographer: Joakim Lindhé.

finally ruled that 'the home recording of television programs for later viewing constituted "fair use"' in 1984 (Castonguay 2006).

The big studios' unwillingness to release new and even older films on video, in turn, created a semi-vacuum where the ever-increasing consumer demand was in part supplied by a multitude of small independent and international companies that hijacked the video market by the beginning of the 1980s, and then held on to a share of this, by 1990, 14.9 billion dollar market, for a decade (Grainge, Jancovich and Monteith 2008: 457–8; Wasko 1994: 114). These companies could produce their own films, pre-buy the licensing rights to a film in production or simply buy the finished film, often with temporal limitations and for a given geographical area. Pre-sales thus became of utter importance for the direct-to-video market (Mathijs and Sexton 2011: 28). The producers of independent exploitation films had to, on the one hand, tie together an intricate network of financiers, but could, on the other hand, get by on a much more modest budget compared to the production of an average Hollywood film or a state-funded European art film.

Mats Helge Olsson had gained this precise experience during the production of *Sverige åt svenskarna*, working with a large number of small and local financial backers in order to plug the gaps in the ever-expanding budget. Olsson's old production company had gone bankrupt, though, and for the production of these direct-to-video films he, and his financial adviser, created a string of production companies in order to spread the economic risks: Smart Egg Picture, Zodiac Film Group, Alpha Pictures, Swedish Action Film Force, The Producers Corporation, The Investment Group and Profore Movie Productions.

The Ninja Mission was an exception to this tactic since it was 'a VTC production', produced by Charles Aspéria and Guy Collins. The budget for *The Ninja Mission* was, allegedly, 295,000 USD, roughly 210,000 GBP in 1984 (Lundberg 1987: 13), which corresponded to a low-budget film by Swedish standards in 1984, and a mere tenth in comparison to the budget for *Sverige åt svenskarna*. In a contemporary interview, Olsson claimed that the money came from an 'English video company, which commissioned him to make a row of action films' (Anon. 1984a). However, VTC, or Video Tape Center, was one of the leading distributors of films on VHS in Sweden at the time, part of the Gylling Group, a Swedish/Norwegian media mini-conglomerate that brought radio and other electronic technology from Sony, Samsung and Apple to Scandinavia. In addition, VTC had their own video rental store in Stockholm, one of the first of its kind in Sweden (Videogramutredningen 1981: 179).

Starting modestly with a catalogue consisting mostly of porn films, VTC soon moved into distributing cheap older B-films in the exploitation area, such as *The Man From Button Willow* (1965) and *A Taste Of Hell* (1973), but also newer euro trash films like *Zombie Flesheaters/Zombi 2* (1979) and *The Inglorious Bastards* (1978), as well as children's films like a collection of *Bugs Bunny*'s shorts and *Gulliver's Travels* (1939) ('Kosmokatten' 2005). Aspéria also acted as producer for several horror/exploitation films, including two directed by Ulli Lommel, *Brain Waves* (1982) and *The Devonsville Terror* (1983). Collins in turn, being at the start of his career, went on to produce B-films like *Highlander II* (1991) and *Space Truckers* (1996).

The production of *The Ninja Mission* did establish the foundations for Olsson's entertainment violence factory, as it was entirely filmed in and around

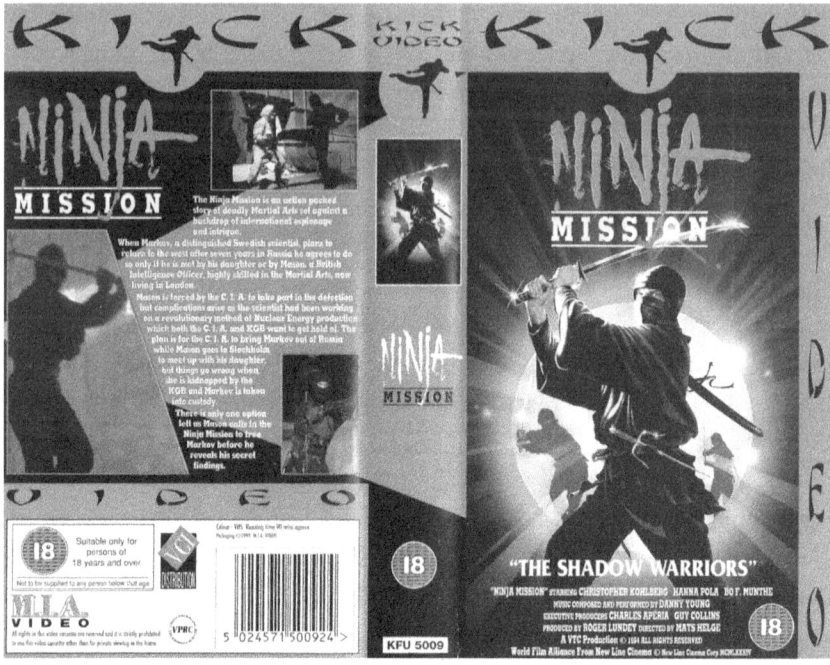

Figure 6.2 The original UK 'big box' artwork for *The Ninja Mission* (1984), 1994. Courtesy of M.I.A Video/VCI Distribution.

Lidköping, using the old and closed down Cementa factory as part of the mise-en-scène, the local hospital as the KGB's headquarters and portraying the stream Lidan as the river Neva (Åhlander1997: 306). The film crew consisted of a mix of international and local talent, whereof a number would stay on and be included in the future 'exploitation family' (Mathijs and Sexton 2011: 27). The screenplay was written by Matthew Jacob, a British actor who subsequently wrote several of the *Young Indiana Jones* television films (1992–6), but who in fact made his debut as a screenwriter with *The Ninja Mission*. Along with Aspéria and Collins, the film was produced by Roger Lundgren, who would produce the majority of the films made in the factory. Three other recurrent members of the family already in place for this first film was musician Dag Unenge, photographer Peter A. Svensson and future film director Anders Nilsson. Unenge would, under a number of Anglo-American aliases, write the synthesizer-based scores for all of Mats Helge Olsson's exploitation films. Svensson would shoot many reels of footage in the entertainment violent factory, and Nilsson, under the guise foremost of Andrew Nelson, appeared here in the dual roles of supervising sound editor and camera operator. Eventually, he would become Olsson's protégé, writing and directing films in the factory, and later on even receiving great success with a series of films about policeman Johan Falk, starting with *Noll tolerans* ('Zero Tolerance', 1999).

The cast included Germans, Swedes and Brits, but the two lead stars were picked from Poland. Krzysztof Kolberger and Hanna Bieniuszewicz, who appeared under the westernized names Christofer Kohlberg and Hanna Pola, did their only roles outside of the Polish film and television industry, where they had successful careers both before and after this appearance in *The Ninja Mission*. According to Polish factotum Jurek Kasprzyk, he convinced Mats Helge Olsson that 'Polish actors were half as expensive but twice as good', which was the main reason that they were hired. However, Poland, being a communist state at the time presented some obstacles, especially since *The Ninja Mission* was a Cold War narrative and because of the fact that the two Poles would play characters that were fighting against KGB agents. For that reason, Kasprzyk wrote a fake screenplay and presented it to the Polish authorities to evade political censorship (Kasprzyk 2013).

Other prominent roles were played by Swedish veteran actors Curt Broberg and Hans Råstam (under the pseudonym Hans Rosteen). Mats Helge Olsson himself played the main evil Russian enforcer, whereas Bo F Munthe – who introduced Ninjutsu to Europe and was the owner of and instructor at European Ninja Center in Stockholm (Bujinkan 2007) – doubled as 'special combat coordinator' as well as acted as the main ninja. In fact, most of the ninjas and stuntmen in the film came from his martial arts club. The whole credit list at the end of the film was filled with Americanized names, as would be the case for all films made in the entertainment violence factory, a usual practice at the time when name changes and dubbing went hand in hand on the international VHS film market (Hedling 2009).

As can be glimpsed, the film crew had a similar ad hoc composition as it had during the chaotic production of *Sverige åt svenskarna*, where talent was created out of nothing and participation was based on a sort of professional friendship where you might, or might not, get your pay check. Everybody, including Olsson, seemed to be doing two or three tasks at once, confirming the high degree of improvisation that characterized the work at the factory. While Unenge and Nilsson were young (both were born in 1963) and probably happy to get a shot at the alluring film business, older actors such as Broberg and Råstam found another surge of life at the end of their careers. Nonetheless, *The Ninja*

Figure 6.3 Krzysztof Kolberger, Hanna Bieniuszewicz and Bo F Munthe in their 'ninja outfits' on the set of *The Ninja Mission* (1984). Photographer: Joakim Lindhé.

Mission was also an exception to the rule for three reasons. First, Aspéria seems to have had a greater say in matters, being the main financier and providing the international contacts. Second, the presence of an actual screenplay seems to have straightened things up a bit. Third, *The Ninja Mission* was marketed towards popular audiences and shown at cinemas around the world, even in Sweden where the National Board of Film Censorship made ten cuts totalling nearly seven minutes of screen time (Statens biografbyrå 1984a).

The Ninja Mission was foremost intended to cash in on the ninja craze that had hit Western Europe and the United States in the late 1970s and the early 1980s. A large number of hastily made martial arts films were produced by companies like the US-based Cannon Films headed by Israeli cousins Menahem Golan and Yoram Globus who especially excelled in this film genre. Their catalogue included The Ninja Trilogy, a series that comprised *Enter the Ninja* (1981), *Revenge of the Ninja* (1983) and *Ninja III: The Domination* (1984), all starring Japanese martial arts star Shô Kosugi. Cannon also produced *American Ninja* (1985) and its sequels. All these Ninja films were outright banned in Sweden for their violent content (Statens biografbyrå 1981, 1984b, 1985). These films were also banned or heavily cut by the National Boards of Film Censorship in

Finland and Norway, but in Denmark, they were released to cinemas with some success. In addition, they stirred an extensive debate over the negative influence of 'Eastern' martial arts techniques on Nordic youngsters; and the ninja came to symbolize this unlawful foreignness. An illustrative example is the Swedish governmental investigation of Video Violence where all films available on VHS were divided into genres, rated from 1 to 16, and where 1 was considered to be the least harmful genre (Cartoons) and 16 constituted the most harmful genre (the fanciful construction Police Violence Films). On this list, the very tiny genre of ninja films ended up at the very respectable thirteenth place, that is, it was considered the fourth most harmful genre (Våldsskildringsutredningen 1988: 160).

Being a Cold War narrative and taking place in snowy Nordic environments, *The Ninja Mission* had an angle that made the film unique in relation to most other ninja and martial arts films. The story is straightforward. A Russian scientist and defector has invented a new energy source that will give the world safe and clean energy at no cost. The Russians kidnap him and his daughter (played by Hanna Pola) to ensure that the scientist follows orders. However, the Americans too, led by Mason (Krzysztof Kolberger), want to get their hands on this new energy source. In collaboration with a group of specially trained CIA ninjas, they infiltrate the Soviet Union in order to rescue the scientist and his daughter and bring them to safety in Sweden.

This film is characterized by fast paced editing, the use of darkish red and blue camera filters and a screenplay that puts total emphasis on the action scenes, which includes both car and helicopter chases, numerous shootouts and black-clad ninjas with an arsenal of classic weaponry such as katana swords, crossbows and ninja throwing stars. A spectacular extravagant gore scene crowned the film where a flying ninja slashes off the head of a Soviet soldier from the mouth up. This 'money shot' was filmed in slow motion, as were most of the action scenes which, quite unpredictably for a ninja film, did not excel in martial arts fighting scenes as the ninjas, instead, preferred to shoot their adversaries rather than to kick or punch them down.

The use of slow motion as a filmmaking effect has been seen as an artistic choice, and it was used as such to break down the production code in Hollywood, for example to portray extreme violence in *Bonnie and Clyde* (1967) and *The Dirty Dozen* (1967), two films that passed through the Swedish Board of Film Censorship without any cuts whatsoever (Statens biograbyrå 1967a and 1967b). However, with the video violence debates raging, the use of slow motion

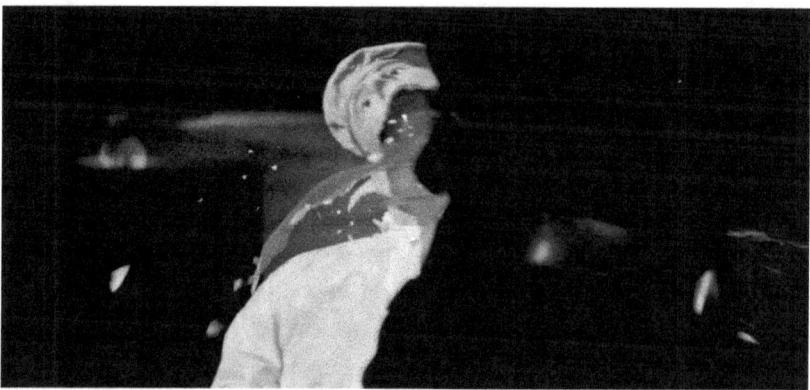

Figure 6.4 Screen grab from Swedish *The Ninja Mission* (1984), featuring the 'money shot' where a flying ninja slashes off the head of a Soviet soldier from the mouth up in slow motion. Courtesy of Horse Creek Entertainment.

to display violence of any kind was interpreted as a guideline to perpetrating violence as well as mentally harmful for its (underage) audiences. In a television interview in 1987, Mats Helge Olsson specified his view on slow motion and its connection to censorship in Sweden:

> Here are some slow motion sequences that are censored. If you have 'Bang Bang' you should not depict that slowly; look here, the camera goes slower so you can see how the cartridges leave the chamber, and that is counted as censorship, but if Peckinpah had done the same, then it would be shown because it is considered to be a high-budget film, a serious film. If you make a low-budget film, then there are other censor norms because it is regarded as pure entertainment, and then it is viewed as mere entertainment violence. On the other hand, if you have technical staff and a budget hundred times higher for the same thing, then it is considered serious, and then you cannot stop such a big film. [The interviewer:] And you are not a director with artistic status, are you? [Olsson:] No, no, no, I am squarely placed in the entertainment box as 'Bang Bang'. (Olsson 1987)

In order to fully capitalize on his self-confessed entertainment aspirations, Olsson was at pains to include as many commercial aspects into his films' palette as possible. Due to the international cast in *The Ninja Mission*, many of the actors were professionally dubbed, an extracurricular expense that was covered by the unusually generous budget. Such efforts were essential to allow the film to pass off as an American mainstream production. Subsequently, in Olsson's later work, this expense was gradually phased out in order to save money, with the result that the authenticity for settings and international action got lost in translation due to the fact that the local talent talked English with a heavy Swedish accent.

In addition to these strategies, as well as the commercial and historical connection to the ninja craze and the Cold War, *The Ninja Mission* highlighted modern stylistic features, such as personal computers integrated into the story, a distinct visual style with colour filters, and a music number where the scantily clad Hanna Pola sings in playback to the pre-recorded song 'Baby You Ran Away' by Swedish singer Susie Tapper. All these ingredients typify a distinct commercial philosophy that was unusual and even deemed odd in Nordic film industries of the time. In fact, this thinking constitutes an ultra-low-budget version of High Concept cinema, a term coined by Justin Wyatt to describe how Hollywood adjusted its production of films in the early 1980s to what would eventually become the era of blockbusters and superhero adventure films (Wyatt 1994). Within the confines of the entertainment violence factory, Mats Helge Olsson would continuously tap popular culture and contemporary events in order to seek commercial and youth-related relevance for his films. However, over the years these strong commercial instincts would stagnate and become less and less pertinent.

On 29 June, 1984, *The Ninja Mission* premiered in Sweden. The day after the papers crushed the film with devastating reviews:

> Mostly it looks like a graduation film shot after a brief intensive course for prospective filmmakers who wish to learn the art of shooting, or in other ways, rapidly destroying people on the silver screen. For the next semester, we will go on to learn how to capture the audience's interest by adding a so-called story. Successful students such as Mats Helge will then see that it is possible, although tricky, to combine shootouts with a story, and perhaps even some simple dialogue. (Sörenson 1984)

> If you try to ignore everything else and just concentrate on the action scenes, *The Ninja Mission* remains an almost indescribably poor film. The stuntmen stand motionless with their arms hanging forever, waiting for the hero to knock them down. During a battle in a ventilation system, the combatants seem to step in and out of the walls; Soviet soldiers leap out from behind shelters and virtually queue in front of the machine gun so the brave ninjas can shoot them down. And these are scenes where the filmmakers really have made an effort. Mats Helge – formerly Mats Helge Olsson – gives bad films a bad reputation. (Blomkvist 1984)

It should be mentioned that the reviewers, and Swedish cinema audiences, only saw the heavily censored version of *The Ninja Mission*, which undoubtedly contributed to these merciless perceptions and the fact that the film only survived a mere week in Swedish cinemas. In Denmark, the film fared better and the uncensored version managed to take in 575,342 DDK at the box office ('Film vist i danske biografer i perioded 1976–2011' 2012). However, the film was picked up by New Line Cinema for the US market and premiered in its uncut version on 31 August 1984 on sixty screens, eventually grossing 957,293 USD in its original run of sixteen weeks (Anon. 1984b: 9; Anon. 1985: 16, 8, 90). *Variety* was also much more positive in its review: 'it's all nice bloody fun for those craving action [---] Direction of the action scenes is well handled, as are the special effects. Overall good production values should make this item a suitable sell for action-oriented markets worldwide' (Besa 1984: 136). The film then continued its life as a top VHS rental in the United States in 1985 before eventually being marketed as a westernized ninja film on, above all, the Southeast-Asian cinema circuit.

Apparently, Aspéria and Collins sold the world rights for *The Ninja Mission* to New Line Cinema. However, the content of this contract is unknown and there have been some debates over how much money *The Ninja Mission* eventually grossed, and how that money was allocated between the distributor, New Line Cinema, the producers, Aspéria and Collins and the entertainment violence factory in Lidköping, led by Mats Helge Olsson. In contemporary interviews, Olsson mentioned a number of different figures, such as that *The Ninja Mission* had been screened in fifty-six different countries (Olsson 1987), that it had sold 10,000 VHS copies á 600 GBP in the UK (Anon. 1986: 20), that the film had made 33 million SEK (Hansson 1986: 19) and that it had been playing at ninety cinemas simultaneously, only in New York (Lundberg 1987: 13). In a somewhat speculative Swedish documentary about Mats Helge Olsson and the making of *The Ninja Mission*, *Regissören som försvann: historien om The Ninja Mission* (2013), the figure 250 million SEK (roughly 30 million USD) is mentioned as the film's total revenue. If there would be any merit to these sums, New Line Cinema would most probably have contracted Olsson after this. Ostensibly, Mats Helge Olsson received a measure of reimbursement for his work, but probably not nearly in proportion to the final revenues, which seemed to have ended up in the coffers of New Line Cinema.

At work: Production and exploitative themes

Although the financial outcome was meagre, the seemingly huge international success of *The Ninja Mission* formed the basis, and the aspirational inspiration, for Mats Helge Olsson's 'impossible' entertainment violence factory for the rest of the decade. The number of films produced is still elusive but at least twelve films were released, and in interviews and other reportages about the factory, another seven titles are mentioned ('Fear of Dawn', 'The Final Chase', 'Gun Crazy', 'A Matter of Honor?', 'The Night Guest', 'Road Pirates', 'Silent Chase'). That would give an average of two to three films produced per year, which would have been quite an impressive output speed for such a small production company. Yet, in interviews, Olsson often bragged about the fact that he had already made about forty films, and that he was making seven films at the same time (Lundberg 1987: 13). This is an unsustainable equation, but as with the exaggerated figures for *Sverige åt svenskarna* and *The Ninja Mission*, this is also an attitude that reflects Olsson's need to appear commercially assertive as well as rhetorically position him in opposition to 'elitist' Swedish film culture rather than being simple outright lies. This self-perception could be interpreted as inflated entitlement and pure arrogance but, at the same time, his attitude 'reflects the degree of commitment, dedicated labor (and long hours)' that actually went into the work of producing and directing films at a pace that was unheard of in a Nordic context (Mathijs and Sexton 2011: 26).

However, this self-confident anything-goes defiance became an internalized part of the film production at the factory, where the lack of money was compensated by a sturdy exploitation family spirit: working without (too much) payment, and a vigilante attitude towards the film work. In interviews and on-the-production-site reportages, the director often degraded his own productions as 'cliché or junk films' made for teenagers who did not care for dialogue or character development but instead wanted fast paced editing and action (Lundberg 1987: 13). 'I have no intention of making films for the critics. I am making fun junk that amuses and entertains. I would not in a million years try to get governmental funding to do a serious film about some housewife with sexual problems in the suburbs' (Anon. 1986: 6).

The actual film production situation in the entertainment violence factory seems to have been characterized by the same creative chaos as during the production of *Sverige åt svenskarna*. That is to say, everyday misunderstandings, amateurs hired on a whim for film work and/or acting, a 'family' that takes care of all aspects of the production, no retakes, and perhaps most significantly for the finished productions, the lack of a coherent screenplay, were par the course (Lundberg 1987: 12–15). In a reportage for the current affairs show *Rekordmagazinet*, aired on Swedish Public Television, the reporter compares the film production facilities with a pre-school, saying that 'Mats Helge appears to be no more than a bearded kindergarten teacher as he walks around with his visitor' (*Rekordmagazinet* 1987). In the same reportage, two young girls are hired for the production of a horror film, and when asked what they are supposed to do, they answer: 'We have no idea.' The reportage then continues in the same demeaning manner:

> REPORTER: In the only clean room sits the girl who ensures that Mats Helge's wild ideas are written down in screenplays. It is currently a lot of monsters and evil sudden death. Are you writing all the stories for this company?
> THE GIRL [Madeleine Bruzelius]: I usually do, yes.
> RE: How long does it take you to write a script?
> MB: Sincerely, in a best case scenario, one week, otherwise a couple of weeks.
> RE: What did you do before you came here and started writing scripts?
> MB: I'm a pre-school teacher.
> RE: Are you, really?

Even though Mats Helge Olsson has interchangeably been called Lidköping's Fassbinder and Lidköping's Spielberg, in the first case ironically, and in the second case commercially degradingly, the recurrent use of inept and haphazardly written screenplays paved the way for films with no room for character development, paper-thin stories, action scenes shot in near darkness and in the exact same locations around Lidköping – all accompanied by the similar sounding wall-to-wall soundtrack of synthesized music, written by Dag Unenge. Although these factors, perhaps, were of no importance for an international contemporary teenage consumer of VHS entertainment violence, these technical and stylistic flaws and idiosyncrasies are what binds these films together when analysed in hindsight.

Then again, these exploitation films were not made in a cultural vacuum. As became clear with *The Ninja Mission*, international film productions inspired the work at the entertainment film factory but, simultaneously, a defiant attitude aimed at Swedish societal values such as anti-commercialism and the protection of morals characterized these activities. For us, the addition of an auteur perspective into the critical analysis of these films, seldom used when analysing film culture outside art cinema, provides an opportunity to enhance and understand these films beyond the very conscious commercial and practical strategies that Olsson had to adapt to in order to carve out a market for his productions. Our analysis of key patterns in the entertainment violence factory's productions since *The Ninja Mission* will reveal that Olsson was both hopelessly out of step with youth culture, and yet, at the same time, strangely in alignment, almost prophetic, when it came to using contemporary and other relevant thematic and aesthetic markers for his films.

Genre aspirations

The entertainment violence factory produced films in four particular subgenres: the ninja film, the action film, the slasher film and the children's film. With the exception of children's films – a staple in Nordic film culture since the Second World War – the ninja, the slasher and even the action film were seen as 'American' abnormalities in Swedish film culture, routinely cut or banned by the Swedish Board of Film Censorship. As genre films were still understood as foreign intrusions into the Welfare home, Olsson's factory explorations of these largely Americanized genre conventions to locally produce genre films turned them into what we call global exploitation, partly due to their inherent 'foreignness', partly due to their explicit use of exploitations strategies outside of established norms in Swedish film culture.

Trying to repeat the success of *The Ninja Mission*, Mats Helge Olsson's exploitation family continued to produce several more ninja films that either displayed 'ninja' in the title or included characters that resembled ninjas with reference to their black costumes and hoods, but whose (non-existent) martial art skills were severely obscured by selective editing and narrative choices to cover up the otherwise obvious lack in trained martial arts professionals. The first of these ninja films was *Eagle Island* (1986), filmed under the working title 'The Ninja Mission 2' (Ekeroth 2011: 53).

Eagle Island was another Cold War vehicle that used a common trope in Swedish popular culture, namely the threat of Spetsnaz commando troops delivered covertly by Soviet submarines that were said to operate around the Swedish Baltic coastline. The Soviet threat had a historical background that went back to the sixteenth century and a series of wars fought between Sweden and Russia until 1808–9 (Burgman 2001: 16–51). However, on 27 October 1981, a Soviet nuclear-armed submarine was actually stranded 10 kilometres from the main Swedish naval base at Karlskrona after hitting an underwater rock. Throughout the 1980s, this incident was followed by at least ten reports of other submarine sightings as well as intense television imagery of Swedish Navy helicopters firing depth charges into coastal waters against suspected intruders.

Using this incident, internationally known as 'Whiskey on the rock', according to the class of the submarine, and Western suspicions of Soviet Union aggression, Olsson cashed in on the Cold War theme. This theme was prominent in Hollywood action films of the time with significant installations such as *Firefox* (1982), *Red Dawn* (1984) and *Rocky IV* (1985), painting a very negative picture of the potential military threat of the Soviet Union. Simultaneously, the Cold War thematic appeared in fellow Nordic exploitation genre films such as Norwegian *Orions Belte* (*Orion's Belt*, 1985) and Finnish *Arctic Heat*, but Olsson's contributions followed idiosyncratic stylistic and thematic pathways.

The film starts with a sequence where divers leave a submarine, all while the credits emerge and the title song 'Eagle Island' is performed on the soundtrack by singer Christer Jern. The text, 'Somewhere in Northern Europe . . .', is then displayed before the divers submerge from the sea and the action can begin. The island hosts an army base, and the Soviet Spetsnaz soldiers, aided by a spy collaborator, are after a secret code to spy satellites over Europe. However, this plan is thwarted by the commander (played by American actor Tom O'Rourke) who takes matters into his own hands, defeating the Russians. To complicate things further a couple of female birdwatchers secretly land on the island, constituting the sole 'female interest' in the film. The action comprises of endless shootouts between soldiers (in Swedish military uniforms) and the Spetsnaz troops (in their ninja outfits). But in a memorable over-the-top scene (though without too much gore), a Soviet ninja crudely tortures a Swedish officer, using an iron file to chip away at his teeth, with clear connotations of the infamous torture scene between Laurence Oliver and Dustin Hoffman in *The Marathon Man* (1976).

Eagle Island also develops a distinct narrative feature characteristic of the factory, namely the intercutting between characters who talk to each other on either a telephone or a walkie-talkie, a trope that would be used extensively in all of Mats Helge Olsson's later productions. This is a narrative technique that has been around since the silent age and has, for example, been aestheticized in the Italian White-Telephone Films of the 1930s (Bordwell and Thompson 2010: 255). Yet, the overuse of these telephone conversations would become conspicuous as they comprise excessively lengthy scenes only dedicated to conveying information designed to move the plot forward. They stand out here by becoming excessively clumsy due to their mechanistic and repetitive intercutting. Yet, the extensive telephone-related crosscutting between different sets and milieus does also work as a way to expand these films' spatial worlds: it provides a cost-efficient way of disguising them as international or American productions set in a range of countries, thus hiding their low production values and their local production realities.

A significant new recruit to the exploitation family for the production of *Eagle Island* was Timothy Earle, who would participate in altogether seven of Mats Helge Olsson's productions, mainly as an actor but who would also become important as a language coach, 'drilling the Swedish actors in American military jargon' (Lundberg 1987: 15). This would soon become an essential feature since the economic model for the films did not allow them to be properly dubbed, leaving the mainly Swedish cast to speak English with a heavy accent.

The ninja and Cold War thematic would return in *Russian Terminator* (1990, aka *Russian Ninja*), featuring a ninja with some feeble martial arts skills. Disappointingly, but also illustratively, the action consists of endless shootouts between Russians crooks and two James Bond-like agents, trying to solve yet another kidnapping. In comparison to the careful attention (by Olsson's standards) to genre pleasures in *The Ninja Mission*, the bloodless and nonsensical action is particularly aggravating as are the attempts to establish the Terminator/ninja antagonist as a threatening Schwarzenegger-like foe, who is made ludicrous by bad dubbing and even worse acting. But meanwhile, the entertainment violence factory ploughed on with two other action films, directed by some of the other 'family' members but continuing many of the themes established by Mats Helge Olsson. These consisted of *Silverhawk* (1987), directed by Olsson's protégé Anders Nilsson, and *The Hired Gun* (1989), co-directed by Arne Mattsson, who with this film would end a long career within the film industry. Mattsson directed more than sixty films but is probably best known internationally for *Hon dansade en sommar* (*One Summer of Happiness*, 1951), notorious for its nude scenes, which caused controversy at the time and, together with Ingmar Bergman's *Sommaren med Monika* (*Summer with Monika* aka *Monika, the Story of a Bad Girl*, 1953), spread the image of 'Swedish Sin' around the world (Lunde 2016: 11–12).

The Hired Gun is an action film in the vein of *The Wild Geese* (1978), a mercenary flick with Roger Moore and Richard Burton that became a huge success in Sweden, both in its original cinema run as well as when it was released on VHS in 1983 after seven cuts (Statens biografbyrå 1982). Once again, Mats Helge Olsson turned distinctly Swedish milieus into international locations. The film starts with a lengthy scene in 'Africa' with shootouts and numerous explosions on a beach. The story then turns into a Nazi film – a significant trope in Nordic exploitations films – as the former mercenary heroes are hired by a neo-Nazi organization to retrieve secret documents from the Second World War, hidden at an American military base, but conveniently located in Denmark. The narrative of the film provides little of interest and the largely gore-free battle scenes display the film's low-budget and hasty shooting schedule. However, the film contains a particular auteurist stamp by Mats Helge Olsson that appears here for the final time: since *The Ninja Mission*, he had maintained a Hitchcockesque habit of appearing as a bad guy that is violently massacred. His role as a soldier killed in the prologue of *The Hired Gun* marks the culmination of this trend (and in many ways, ironically, his career as producer). Nonetheless, resembling Hitchcock and many other film directors, Olsson maintained a preference to hold on to certain actors from one film production to the next, and these actors were, temporarily or permanently, included into the larger exploitation family.

Olsson's stars

The casting of the entertainment violence factory's films provides another chapter in their ongoing flirtations with commercialism and internationalism. Particularly, a trio of action films, *Animal Protector* (1988), *Fatal Secret* (1988) and *The Mad Bunch* (1989), are distinguishable by the fact that they all feature American actor David Carradine, perhaps most famous for his roles as Kwai Chang Caine in the television series *Kung Fu* (1972–5) and as Bill in Quentin Tarantino's *Kill Bill, Vol 1* and *2* (2003 and 2004). The hope was, needless to say, that Carradine would contribute a highly desirable international flair as well as provide some actual martial arts skills to these productions: the bonus of the benefits of having a professional actor on set must have also been a considerable appeal for the factory members.

According to an interview with Ingmar Andersson, camera operator for all three films, Carradine was hired to do one film but eventually, and unbeknownst to himself, headlined three. In other words, Mats Helge Olsson and the entertainment violence factory took advantage of the fact that Carradine, at the time, was in bad shape due to a heavy drug and alcohol addiction. Apparently, Carradine had no idea what the film(s) that he acted in were about and was just handed his dialogue on a piece of paper just prior to each take (Andersson 2013). Mats Helge Olsson then improvised the films around these takes, saving some takes for the additional two films beside the main one that was nominally being produced, *Animal Protector*. When exploring the films, this becomes quite obvious as Carradine's presence is very limited in both *Fatal Secret* and *The Mad Bunch*. In the former, he only appears in two scenes and in the latter, he appears in three scenes, of which one is a fight scene where he is killed off. Regardless of this, on all contemporary VHS editions, Carradine tops the bill or is the only actor mentioned on the cover.

The three films are all set in the United States, and have additional international settings, but are entirely shot in the usual places around the Lidköping area. The films use the Cold War as a narrative trope but now with a focus on American organizations such as CIA and FBI as the culprits. In *The Mad Bunch*, Carradine's character is an upstanding crisis negotiator, a professor

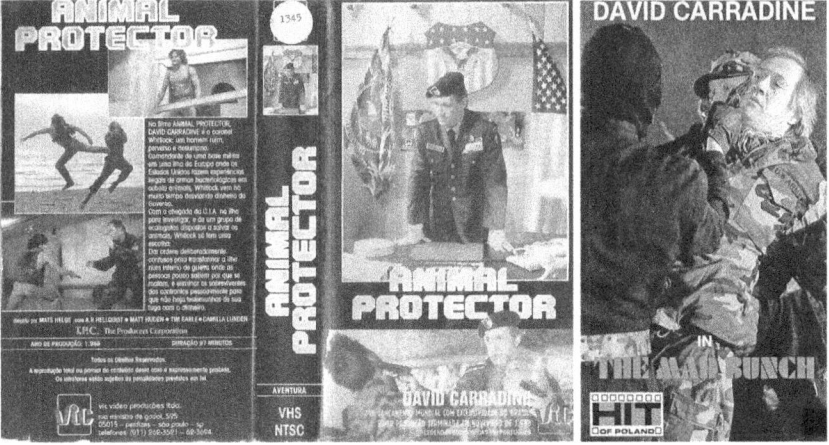

Figure 6.5 and 6.6 The original 'big box' artwork for *Animal Protector* (1988) and *The Mad Bunch* (1989), featuring American actor David Carradine on the covers. Courtesy of Vic Video (Brazil) and HIT of Poland (Poland), respectively.

of 'peace research', who is kidnapped by CIA and FBI because world peace is bad business for these organizations. The professor's daughter (played by Camilla Lundén) hires a nitwit mercenary group, called The Action Force Team, who wreaks havoc as they try and fail to rescue the professor who is killed during the operation. This Action Force Team have clear connotations to the American *The A-Team* (1983–7), the humorous action–adventure television series, and Mats Helge Olsson even tries to induce humour into the team's activities by including several straight slapstick scenes. He also introduces the entertainment violence factory's very own action hero, played by the bodybuilding aspiring actor Anders Roland Hellquist, in an effort to make his productions profitable in a way that action film icons such as Arnold Schwarzenegger, Chuck Norris and Jean-Claude van Damme had done in the 1980s.

Hellquist also played the action hero in *Fatal Secret*, another CIA gone rogue vehicle where Carradine briefly appears as the evil crook. The film continues a prevalent trend in Nordic producers bashing American politics as, at the beginning of the film, a high ranking CIA officer utters what can be read as a sarcastic comment on Reagan's War on Drugs, initiated by Nixon in 1971 and made into a CIA concern in 1982 (Scott and Marshall 1991: 2): 'I don't like CIA making deals with this kind of top draw scum that we got here. I especially hate drugs. Murderers, rapists, spies I can handle, but narcotics . . .'

In addition to its political alignment, *Fatal Secret* is interesting for two other reasons. It was the first time that actor Camilla Lundén appeared in a female lead role, Lundén being the only actor who actually became a name within the Swedish film industry after her stint at the entertainment violence factory, for example playing leads in praised films like *Glädjekällan* (*Spring of Joy*, 1993) and *Spring för livet* (*Run for Your Life*, 1997), the latter for which she was nominated as best actress in a lead role at the Swedish equivalent of the Academy Awards, Guldbaggegalan.

The second reason is that this is the first time that Mats Helge Olsson, even on a basic level, had considered levelling out the gender dynamics of an otherwise thoroughly masculine world of the 1980s action film. Granted, this is done in an unsophisticated way but these gestures were made previous to a seminal film like *Thelma & Louise* (1991) and in advance of gender dynamics being considered an issue in Nordic film culture, which eventually produced female action heroines like Lisbeth Salander in *Män som hatar kvinnor* (*The Girl with the Dragon Tattoo*, 2009) and Saga Norén in the television series *Bron/Broen* (*The Bridge*, 2011–18). Arguably, the single most important reason for this gender consideration is the involvement of Camilla Lundén. In *Fatal Secret* Lundén plays the defected CIA agent Kim Brown that takes off with a secret floppy disc and a large sum of money, ending up being hunted by both the corrupt CIA and a drug syndicate. To aid her, she has two tough female companions, Jane and Alex (played by Eva Anderson and Eva Öström), and together they form a sort of equivalent to the all-male Action Force Team in *The Mad Bunch*, but without any degrading slapstick moments. As they steal the money and the disc, Olsson deliberately plays with audiences' preconceived gender notions, as their identities are concealed by helmets and motorcycle attire, thus leading audiences and the characters in the film to believe that they are in fact male. However, during a lengthy shootout and chase, Brown is shot and wounded, whereas the other two are captured. During an interrogation, none of them shows any weakness, and instead, Jane draws a knife, stabbing a villain, but in the commotion, Alex is killed.

Meanwhile, Brown looks up John Mitchell (played by Hellquist), a former lover and spy, who reluctantly agrees to come out of retirement and help her. Mitchell cleans her wounds, which leads to a rare sex scene in Mats Helge Olsson's film productions. Lundén is undressed, revealing 'sexy' (and for the occasion, unpractical) underwear, as is Mitchell who reveals his toned muscles. As they start to embrace, we get a glimpse of Lundén's breasts, but all of a sudden, they start talking shop for several minutes of screen time still laying on top of each other, and they, in fact, never reassume the intended intercourse. The only other Olsson films where bare breasts can be seen and sex is implied in an exploitative way are in the two slasher/stalker films that the entertainment violence factory produced, *Blood Tracks* (1985) and *Forgotten Wells* (1990), and this in a subgenre where unmotivated nakedness was an inherent convention needed to close the sale (see, for example, Nowell 2011).

This semi-prudent attitude makes Olsson's films stand out in comparison to the production of sexploitation in Sweden in the 1970s and 1980s as well as the common sight of natural nakedness in Nordic mainstream cinema during the same period (see, for example, Ekeroth 2011, where 72 per cent of the just over 200 reviewed Swedish 'exploitation films' can be characterized as sexploitation). Nevertheless, Olsson's approach compares well to the contemporary international low-budget action films, exemplified by films such as *Commando* (1985), *No Retreat, No Surrender* (1986) and *Nico: Above the Law* (1988), where the genre very seldom included sexploitative elements, and in the event that a sex scene had been inserted into the screenplay, they were usually awkward and quickly executed in order for the male heroes to continue to the next action set piece. However, instead of suggesting a more moderate or balanced approach to depictions of sexuality, the marginalization of sexual elements meant that when sexploitative elements did occur, they were just as exploitative as in 'authentic' sexploitation, but arguably so in an even more negative sense. That is, it becomes hard to interpret these elements as subversive, feminist or performative in ways that 'cult' genres such as Nazisploitation and 'cult films' like *The Rocky Horror Picture Show* (1975) sometimes would allow (Mathijs and Sexton 2011: 115) and as some of the key sexploitation films have been interpreted retrospectively.

Camilla Lundén returns in a lead role for the third Carradine vehicle, *Animal Protector*, an action film with considerably higher production value than the other two films, provided by the fact that Charles Aspéria, once more, acted as executive producer. *Animal Protector* is something unique as an eco-critical film where US scientists perform horrifying experiments on animals in order to produce chemical weapons. These experiments take place on a secluded island called Devil's Rock, and the military team is led by the ruthlessly mean Colonel Whitlock, played by David Carradine.

Lundén, in turn, leads an animal activist group called Animal Protector that consists of only female members, in fact played by the same actors as the all-female action team in *Fatal Secret*, plus an additional three female infiltrators. Swedish exploitation enthusiast Daniel Ekeroth describes them deprecatingly as 'foxy '80s-style ladies' (Ekeroth 2011: 22), but they are much more active than this passive description. These animal protectors infiltrate the island and go full-force on the American military at the same time as a CIA agent (Hellquist) sneaks onto the island. This escalates into a full-scale war with never-ending shootouts and fistfights in slow motion and people burning to a crisp as everything around them explodes. The film also includes a protracted torture scene where none other than Mats Helge Olsson performs the torture. In the midst of this mayhem, the female eco-team does not hold back their punches in order to liberate the animals. The film ends with a spectacular five-minute fight scene where Carradine takes on two men before he is finally defeated and killed, thus taking home his pay check.

As with the inclusion of (seemingly progressive) gender politics, the eco-critical theme is included in these films primarily as a MacGuffin, a plot device with little or no narrative motivation. However, the mere existence of these themes demonstrates two things about the entertainment violence factory's production philosophy. First that these elements, somehow, were considered as commercial selling points directed at young international audiences attracted to video violence. While female heroes had become more prominent with television shows like *Charlie's Angels* (1976–81), and environmental conservation had featured in major Hollywood films like *The Mosquito Coast* (1985) and *Gorillas in the Mist* (1988), they do not strike us as particularly obvious selling points for the target consumers of the entertainment violence that these films were peddling. The inclusion of these themes would come off as a bit paradoxical, were it not for the fact that they would eventually become of paramount importance for Nordic and Western societies, namely third-wave feminism and the more hard-core/straight edge animal rights/environmental movements, which made considerable impact in the early 1990s (See Stacy, Howie, and Munford 2007; Potter 2011).

Conclusion

The ability to detect and decipher emerging societal values, along with the use of a combination of emerging and arguably already expired popular culture codes with low production values, is an auteur trademark of Mats Helge Olsson and his entertainment violence factory. Olsson was clearly aware of the fact that they were making exploitation for young audiences, exploiting concretely the negative associations of the term 'entertainment violence', used as a repellent for 'serious' Nordic filmmakers and Swedish society, but likewise considered an attractive element for VHS audiences around the world. The quality of the films produced in the entertainment violence factory is undoubtedly lower in comparison with American counterparts like *A Force of One* (1979), *The Octagon* (1980) and *The Terminator* (1984), but not in comparison with other internationally disguised productions like the Italian *Luca il contrabbandiere* (*The Smuggler*, 1980) and the British *The Ibiza Connection* (1984). To put it bluntly, Mats Helge Olsson produced 'junk films' that were meant to be consumed internationally and without much reflection, and which 'then would be better off forgotten', as the Swedish governmental investigation into the VCR harshly stated on films available on the new video market (Videogramutredningen 1981: 177).

Then again, Mats Helge Olsson and the entertainment violence factory managed to maintain regular film production for nearly ten years, producing films that reached countries, geographical areas, and international audiences that mainstream and/or culturally valuable Nordic film production could only dream of reaching. However, the Swedish and Nordic elements were, paradoxically, both minimized and enhanced at the same time. The lengthy efforts to conceal the Swedish origin of the films with dubbing into English, by internationalizing the actors' and film crews' names, and turning the exteriors around Lidköping into international settings stand in stark contrast to the fact that many of the films decidedly take place in the Nordic countries, for example in *The Ninja Mission* and *The Hired Gun*, where parts of the stories are played out in Sweden, Finland and Denmark, respectively. The local 'Nordic' flavour is thus never really abandoned but instead exploited for global exploitation audiences, where for instance a film like *The Ninja Mission*, with its Nordic/Soviet snowy set pieces, distinguished itself on the Southeast-Asian cinema circuit and home video market.

Never being part of either the mainstream or the Swedish Film Institute's endorsement of 'valuable films', Mats Helge Olsson's self-chosen outsider status is comparable to that of British direct-to-video film producer pair Cliff Twemlow and David Kent-Watson during the 1980s. Neither of them has had any real critical interest in their work, and neither of them made films in the more extreme exploitation field, associated with the Nordic video violence moral panic in 1980–1 and the British video nasties panic of 1982–3, respectively. British film scholars Andy Willis and C. P. Lee argue that 'the rediscovery of the Twemlow and Kent-Watson films demands a rethinking of the history of British exploitation cinema in the 1980s and early 1990s' (Willis and Lee 2009: 70–1). In the same vein, we would like to argue that Mats Helge Olsson's efforts had their specific Nordic challenges, as his is a story that defies a state-sanctioned system guarded by canonization, censorship and funding issues. Although Olsson actually made genre films in a quite traditional sense, these films were still considered as unlawful intrusions into the well-protected Swedish Welfare society. Hence, these films were doubly ousted, in the past by censorship and, in the present, by their exclusion from Swedish/Nordic film history.

References

Åhlander, Lars (ed.) (1989), *Svensk Filmografi 7: 1970–1979*, Stockholm: Svenska Filminstitutet.
Åhlander, Lars (ed.) (1997), *Svensk Filmografi 8: 1980–1989*, Stockholm: Svenska Filminstitutet.
Anon. (1977), 'Frozen Star', Review, *Aftonbladet*, 9 March, 9.

Anon. (1984a), 'Ninjafilm spelas in i Lidköping!', *Lidköpings Tidning*, 25 April.
Anon. (1984b), '50 Top-Grossing Films', *Variety*, 316 (7), 9.
Anon. (1985), 'Big Rental Films of 1984', *Variety*, 317 (8), 16, 78, 90.
Anon. (1986), 'Skräp? – Javisst men vill ju se mina filmer', *Veckans stopp*, 6, 6–7, 20.
Andersson, Ingmar (2013), Interviewed in the documentary, *Regissören som försvann: historien om The Ninja Mission*.
Besa [pseudonym] (1984), 'The Ninja Mission', Review, *Variety*, 315 (3), 136.
'Beslut', Konkursansökan (1981), Lidköping: Kronofogdemyndigheten i Lidköpings distrikt, 25 February.
Blomkvist, Mårten (1984), 'The Ninja Mission', Review, *Dagens Nyheter*, 1 July.
'Bokföringsorder' (1980), Mats Helge Olsson's Applications to the F-Fund, The Business Archive of The Swedish Film Institute.
Bordwell, David and Kristin Thompson (2010), *Film History: An Introduction*, New York: McGraw-Hill.
Bujinkan (2007), 'Bo F Munthe', *Bujinkan Dojo Frankfurt am Main*, Available online: http://www.bujinkan-frankfurt.gmxhome.de/E_Bo_Munthe.htm (accessed 6 March 2018).
Burgman, Torsten (2001), *Rysslandsbilden i Sverige: Från Ivan den förskräcklige till Vladimir Putin*, Lund: Historia Media.
Castonguay, Sylvie (2006), '50 Years of the Video Cassette Recorder', *WIPO Magazine*, November, No.6, Available online: http://www.wipo.int/wipo_magazine/en/2006/06/article_0003.html (accessed 19 February 2018).
Ekeroth, Daniel (2011), *Swedish Sensationfilms: A Clandestine History of Sex, Thrillers, and Kicker Cinema*, New York: Bazillion Points Books.
'Film vist i danske biografer i perioded 1976–2011' (2012), Kilde: Danmarks Statistik /10-04-2012 www.medieraadet.dk (Accessed 30 November 2019).
Fröberg, Anders (1977), 'Filmen som bara visades tre gånger', *SE*, No. 12.
Leif, Furhammar (2003), *Filmen i Sverige: En historia och en fortsättning*, Stockholm: Dialogos.
Gillis, Stacy, Gillian Howie, Gillian and Rebecca Munford (eds) (2007), *Third Wave Feminism: A Critical Exploration*, Basingstoke: Palgrave Macmillan.
Grainge, Paul, Mark Jancovich, and Sharon Monteith (2008), *Film Histories: An Introduction and Reader*, Edinburgh: Edinburgh University Press.
Hansson, Inge (1986), 'Svensk nattklubbsvärd i amerikansk thriller', *Scandinavian Film & Video*, No. 6.
Hedling, Olof (2009), 'Possibilities of Stardom in European Cinema Culture', in Tytti Solia (ed.), *Stellar Encounters: Stardom in Popular European Cinema*, John Libbey: Eastleigh, pp. 256–66.
Henricson, Björn (1980), 'Letter to Mats Helge Olsson', 3 March, Mats Helge Olsson's Application to the F-Fund for "Somewhere, Sometimes", The Business Archive of The Swedish Film Institute.

Kasprzyk, Jurek (2013), Interviewed in the Documentary, *Regissören som försvann: historien om The Ninja Mission* (2013).
'Kosmokatten' (2005), 'VTC (Video Tape Center)', Filmsamling.se. Available online: http://www.filmsamling.se/forum/viewtopic.php?f=10&t=167 (Accessed 21 February 2018).
Lundberg, Börje (1987), 'Mats Helge Olsson in Action', *Expressen*'s supplement *Ljud & Bild*, 8 November, 12–15.
Lunde, Arne (2016), 'The Story of a Bad Girl!: *Summer with Monika*, Sexploitation and the Selling of Erotic Bergman in America', in Elisabet Björklund and Mariah Larsson (eds), *Swedish Cinema and the Sexual Revolution: Critical Essays*, Jefferson, NC: McFarland, pp. 11–20.
Lönroth, Lars (1980), 'Sverige åt svenskarna', Review, *Aftonbladet*, 2 August.
Mathijs, Ernest and Jamie Sexton (2011), *Cult Cinema: An Introduction*, Malden, MA and Oxford: Wiley-Blackwell.
Mats Helge Olsson's Applications to the F-Fund (1978–1980), The Business Archive of The Swedish Film Institute.
Meiland, Lilian (1980), 'Sveriges galnaste man gör Sveriges dyraste film', *Vecko-Revyn*, No. 26.
Nowell, Richard (2011), *Blood Money: A History of the First Teen Slasher Film Cycle*, New York: Continuum.
Olsson, Mats Helge (1987), Interviewed for the Swedish Television Series, *Rekordmagazinet*, aired on Swedish Public Television.
Potter, Will (2011), *Green Is the New Red: An Insider's Account of a Social Movement Under Siege*, San Francisco: City Lights Books.
Rekordmagazinet (1987), aired on Swedish Public Television.
Scott, Peter Dale and Jonathan Marshall (1991), *Cocaine Politics: Drugs, Armies, and the CIA in Central America*, Berkeley, CA: University of California Press.
Sörenson, Elisabeth (1984), 'The Ninja Mission', Review, *Svenska Dagbladet*, 1 July.
Statens biografbyrå (1967a), Censorship Card for *The Dirty Dozen*, Stockholm: Riksarkivet, Statens biografbyrås arkiv, 105.906.
Statens biografbyrå (1967b), Censorship Card for *Bonnie and Clyde*, Stockholm: Riksarkivet, Statens biografbyrås arkiv, 106.087.
Statens biografbyrå (1981), Censorship Card for *Enter the Ninja*, Stockholm: Riksarkivet, Statens biografbyrås arkiv, 122.659.
Statens biografbyrå (1982), Censorship Card for *The Wild Geese*, Stockholm: Riksarkivet, Statens biografbyrås arkiv, 123.770.
Statens biografbyrå (1984a), Censorship Card for *The Ninja Mission*, Stockholm: Riksarkivet, Statens biografbyrås arkiv, 124.790.
Statens biografbyrå (1984b), Censorship Card for *Ninja III: The Domination*, Stockholm: Riksarkivet, Statens biografbyrås arkiv, 125.706.

Statens biografbyrå (1985), Censorship Card for *American Ninja*, Stockholm: Riksarkivet, Statens biografbyrås arkiv, 125.783.

Våldsskildringsutredningen (1988), *Video våld: en rapport från Våldsskildringsutredningen. 2, Förslag till åtgärder: betänkande*, SOU 1988:28, Stockholm: Allmänna förlag.

Videogramutredningen (1981), Video: *Videogramutredningens slutbetänkande*, SOU 1981:55, Stockholm: Liber Förlag/Allmänna förlag.

Wasko, Janet (1994), *Hollywood in the Information Age: Beyond the Silver Screen*, New York: Polity Press.

Willis, Andy and C. P. Lee (2009), 'The Lost World of Twemlow and Kent-Watson: Mancunian Exploitation Film in the 1980s and 1990s', *Journal of British Cinema and Television*, 6(1), 58–72.

Windén, Sten (1981), 'Mats Helge Olsson: Mästare i dyra klipp', *Lektyr*, (6), 8–9, 64.

Wyatt, Justin (1994), *High Concept: Movies and Marketing in Hollywood*, Austin: University of Texas Press.

7

The rise of transnational exploitation in the 1990s–2000s

The 1980s saw the consolidation of two distinct exploitation narratives for Nordic cinemas. On the one hand, several productions used localization strategies to produce indigenous versions of genre films (such as Finnish slashers and Icelandic 'cod-westerns'), largely aimed at domestic audiences. Simultaneously, film producers like Renny Harlin and Mats Helge Olsson viewed domestic audiences as a facet of the global marketplace. While they produced internationally oriented genre films by actively reducing any hint of cultural discount, the films were anomalies in the Nordic cultural landscape. This chapter will show how these trajectories change throughout the 1990s and the early 2000s as the emphasis on popular cinema and genre, already emerging in the 1980s, consolidated as a substantial paradigm shaping the domestic film markets. A key part of this picture is an increased internationalization of both domestic film markets and policy, especially as a consequence of a heightened sense of technological, cultural, political and economic globalization. These, as we chronicle, eventually lead to a situation where the global exploitation narrative starts to overtake the emphasis on localized content due to the ways distribution mechanisms and co-production incentives facilitated a closely connected international media environment, characterized by increased technological and formative integration. At the same time, art cinema continues to delve into exploitative themes and content, albeit in ways that bypass critical castigation and explicit censorship. As they also continue to receive financial support from the film institutes and generate critical respect, films like Tomas Alfredsson's socio-realist art house horror *Låt den rätte komma in* (*Let the Right One In*, 2010) set standards for exploitative violence and gore. Thus, we culminate this chapter with an assessment of such art/exploitation films, especially as they continue to establish the parameters in which more commercial genre cinema had to operate.

Nordic exploitation in the 1990s: Film genres in transition

As suggested in Chapter 5, the censorship and financial support regimes of the Nordic countries had led to a situation where the occasional exploitative genre film would be released, but no standardized patterns of production had emerged, at least as part of the Film Foundation-led system. Independent producers were more successful in procuring a consistent line of production, but even here, the careers of Olsson and Mäkinen, for example, fizzled out by the early 1990s, or films like *Arctic Heat* (1985) and *War Dog* (1986) proved to be one-offs. Nordic cinemas struggled financially during the decade as audience figures decreased and publicly available funding for films was cut. For example, in Finland, the 1990s was a period of serious socioeconomic downturn that affected film culture, with domestic box office reaching a low point comparable to the 1970s (see Ahonen et al. 2004: 5-8). In Sweden, the financial situation created a 'shabby repertoire', according to film historian Leif Furhammar, due to a reliance on 'whimsical' co-productions premised on often unrealistic collaborations and insecure financial arrangements. In addition, he points out that violence became an increasingly prominent theme in mainstream police and action films such as *I lagens namn* ('In the Name of the Law', 1986) and *Jägarna* (*The Hunters*, 1996) (Furhammar 2003: 358-60), further normalizing some of the transgressive tendencies of the previous decades. In Norway, the financial landscape for film funding was about to change dramatically, as films like *Orions belte* (*Orion's Belt*, 1985) had proven that Norwegian filmmakers could not only incorporate an 'American' film style but also compete with Hollywood productions at the Norwegian box office (Iversen 2011: 290). And Denmark saw the breakthrough of Lars von Trier and the highly successful film movement Dogme 95 that shook up the confines of this particular small nation film culture in addition to commercially successful thrillers like *Night Watch* (*Nattevagten*, 1994). The precarious role of commercial genre filmmakers continued to be uncertain in this environment.

While the 1990s was a distinctly sparse period for genre and exploitation cinema, films like the Swedish comedic slasher film *Evil Ed* (1997) dared to challenge these confines. A very low-budget independent genre venture that commenced production in 1992, the film was conceptualized as an explicit critique of the extensive film censorship in Sweden. The film's protagonist Ed let go of his job as an editor of art house productions that had traditionally been the bread and butter of the Swedish film scene. Having to move with the markets shifting towards a more competition-based economy, he now takes a job at a film production company where his job consists of cutting together explicit splatter scenes from the Loose Limbs slasher series. Ed's daily life is inundated with extreme violence that provides the *raison d'être* of these schlocky films, and he soon starts to lose his ability to tell reality from fiction.

Taking aim at the media panic over video violence, *Evil Ed* provides an ironic critique of the norms of the 1980s and the 1990s by effectively producing a film that absolutely exceeds these standards. The explicit use of self-reflexive humour and over-the-top acting both fits the horror genre and provides the film with an ironic relationship with the moral panic still prevailing in contemporary Sweden. The film makes its cultural affiliations clear as the Swedish producers of the Loose Limbs series are portrayed as money hungry exploitative capitalists while Ed's nightmares and hallucinations come from a range of mainstream American fare such as *Gremlins* (1984). At the same time, the combination of excessive gore and slapstick humour adheres to cult comedies like *Braindead* (1992). The targeted politics of these homages, combined with the excessiveness of the gory violence, which clearly exceeds domestic taste culture norms, curiously also aligns with a narrative that seemingly confirms the arguments that video violence leads to societal harm. Simultaneously, it would be counterproductive to view *Evil Ed* as anything but an affectionate splatter film that aims to capitalize on its potential cult reputation as a transgressive contribution to Swedish cinema. By critiquing domestic censorship, the institutional reliance on art films, the marginalization of genre films, as well as the excesses of the media panics, *Evil Ed* provides a comic take on the power of film to generate unintended reactions in the audience, working as a balancing act between explicitly violent genre homage and exploitation of domestic moral codes.

Produced on the tiny budget of 250,000 SEK, *Evil Ed* received its premiere at Stockholm's International Film Festival in 1995 but did not get Swedish theatrical distribution until 1997. While it has since generated a cult following, the majority of its impact has been with fans with whom its homages and exploitation elements connect best. While some of the exploitation productions of the 1980s showcase awareness of the importance of fan cultivation, both the localized and global variations of this era lack the sort of self-reflexive plays with genre conventions that would later emerge as significant features of the exploitation cinema of the 2000s, both in terms of their marketing and production context. *Evil Ed*, in many ways, paves the way for these later successes. While its thematic target – its critique of Swedish censorship – was, largely, a localized exploitation topic, its narrative and thematic form takes a much more pronounced transnational angle, suggesting that the increased integration of domestic production and fan cultures into international exploitation markets was gaining prominence. For one, its Swedish language promotional poster announces these ambitions in no uncertain terms: 'A new Swedish film – and hey, everyone talks in English!' Combined with its genre references and visual style, this complex position between the local/global dynamics of Nordic exploitation enables *Evil Ed*'s metanarratives to encapsulate the contested role of film violence and exploitative genre cinema in the 1990s. Yet, ironically, when it was finally released in 1997, debates over these areas had moved on to a much more permissive state where the film would pass uncut with a 15 certificate.

The certificate is significant as a splatter film of this nature – despite how subversive or critical it aims to be – would have faced significant problems in 1995 when it was first screened at festivals, and especially when it first went

Figure 7.1 The original VHS artwork for *Evil Ed* (1995), showcasing its novelty in Sweden, but with a sticker proclaiming: 'Approved by the censors – without cuts!' Courtesy of Scanbox.

into production in 1992. An interview with Anders Jacobsson, the director, and Göran Lundström, the producer, on TV4, Sweden's largest commercial channel in the 1990s, aired in connection with the 1997 premiere, highlights the extent to which this problem was still very relevant. The studio anchors express disgust after seeing a clip from the film and question the filmmakers' motives: 'Do you become insane after seeing these films?' they exclaim. This suggestion is supported by the third guest, Reidar Jönsson, an autocratic film commissioner at the Swedish Film Institute, and probably best known internationally as the Oscar nominated screenplay writer for *Mitt liv som hund* (*My Life as a Dog*, 1985). Jönsson claims that *Evil Ed* is incomparable to other films since it is 'more or less brain dead concerning its storytelling'. The studio anchors and Jönsson judge the film's moral compass negatively to forcefully endorse the perception that film violence is harmful. When the filmmakers point out that they want to refute this prejudice, they have to do so from a defensive position: 'We wanted to be slightly obstinate and shock a little as these films are not normally made in Sweden. It has been quite fun to go around the system and just do it, although everyone is against this type of genre in Sweden.' The segment then concludes with the anchors posing the question: 'Is there a market for this in Sweden?', to which Jönsson replies by blaming the film's supposed commercial origins: 'The more the education level drops in Sweden, which it does, the greater the market will be for these types of films, because it has to do with how society becomes stupidified. You should think about this, you are part of a very large system that is just based on fooling people' (TV4 1997).

Schaefer (1999), Shiel (2003) and other critics have suggested that exploitation cinema often relies precisely on this type of negative press to generate publicity. Yet, if this sort of publicity fails to manifest in full, these films would face reputational and commercial uncertainty. The domestic reception of *Evil Ed* highlights precisely this point to show how the lack of large-scale critical panic can prove surprisingly problematic as by 1997 the film was no longer perceived to be particularly shocking or transgressive. The film critic Johan Croneman, for example, suggests the film has a lot of ambition but is lacking in execution. He recognizes the intentions of the directors but argues that 'the satire never bites as the story lacks originality' (Croneman 1997). This narrative was repeated in many of the reviews where the discussion would start from its roots as a Swedish B horror film, moving to highlight its uniqueness and the considerable passion of its producers (Andersson 1997). Here, the film's use of references to horror and splatter were met largely positively as a novel perspective to distinguish it from most domestic films. But for these critics, *Evil Ed*'s gore and referential nods are done with no purpose outside of trying to shock or to be different. While such nods highlight its genre inspirations, 'they do not matter when the movie has such a lazy story, slow pace and occasionally amateurish drama. The mixture of horror film, tribute and parody of the same genre also makes it neither scary nor very funny' (Andersson 1997).

While such perspectives contain plenty of positivity amongst the negativity, one could suggest that such conciliatory arguments are even more problematic than outright dismissals as they in many ways completely neuter any of the aggressive or potentially dangerous connotations exploitation films consciously mobilize to stand out in their often-crowded markets. Perceived as an amateurish production, the film was commended for its ability to meet these low standards and demonstrate a measure of professional ability and skill, but its ambitions and scope were considered insufficient to fully attain the qualities required for cult success. As an exploitation film of the 1990s, a considerable part of its relevance comes from its status as a curiosity and a confirmation of the cultural–political rules that still prevailed at the time. But perhaps most significantly, at least for us, is the ways its critical reception establishes a tenacious tendency amongst Nordic film critics to discount exploitative content by understanding them as commercial ploys to attain a notorious reputation (a notion that especially comes into play in the 2000s). At stake here are substantial questions about the ways exploitative films play up even relatively meagre bits of notoriety (see Kääpä, 2012, for evaluation of *Moonlight Sonata*'s original domestic theatrical poster, which featured full topless nudity, since edited out of its DVD cover released in the 2000s) and the ways the restrictions prevailing in the Nordic film infrastructure facilitated conditions for these forms of exploitation to emerge.

Going excessive: Nazi zombies from Norwegian mountains

Zoom twelve years later to 2009. Reanimated Nazis rip a man through the glass window of a secluded cabin in the mountains of Northern Norway. As the man desperately struggles to break free, his head is torn apart by the Nazis as his friends scream in disgust. Soon after, one of the doomed vacationers tries to throw a Molotov cocktail to ward off the aggressors. Instead of igniting the zombies, it clumsily lands on the wall of the cabin, setting it on fire. The combination of gore and slapstick in *Død snø* (*Dead Snow*, 2009) is reminiscent of *Evil Ed* and several international examples of the genre popularized by the splatter films of the 1970s and 1980s. Yet, while *Evil Ed* and many of the standard setting films of the past were crude and occasionally amateurish in production values and applications of film style, the massacre is now orchestrated with high-quality production values as well as the kind of professional acting that befits a much more expensive production than those from the past. Chapter 8 will address the political implications of *Dead Snow*'s Nazi antagonists in detail but for now the generic framework of this splatter film is useful to illustrate the transition from early 1990s exploitation productions to the 2000s. Modelled after Sam Raimi's *The Evil Dead* (1981), the film combines comedy with splatter in innovative ways, often drawing on quirky humour and dynamic aesthetics in much more proficient ways than would have been possible in the past. Displaying extensive genre knowledge and distinct Norwegian cultural references, the film continues the line of localized genre production that can be traced back to the Icelandic Viking trilogy of the 1980s and early 1990s, but now this comes with a much more professionalized sheen that can readily compete with imported productions on a similar level of technical proficiency.

While *Evil Ed* did not manage to make an impact at the Swedish domestic box office, *Dead Snow* was a huge success. In Norway, it was seen by over 100,000 spectators and was met with a considerably more positive critical reaction than many of its genre brethren, even as the critical reception expressed concern over its role in domestic film culture. The critics frequently commended the film for its professional standards, even as some were more critical precisely of the implications of such standards, inquiring why anyone familiar with American zombie cinema would want to see this domestic variation – a film with little to distinguish it from its genre predecessors (Eirik 2009). While the persistent, if expected, comparisons to *Dead Snow*'s genre context, much like with *Evil Ed*, was largely seen as an ongoing problem, now the problem was not so much about meeting these professional standards but doing so in a manner that suggests, in a distinctly non-sensationalist and lacklustre way, that 'there is not much to be ashamed about here' (Eirik 2009). While comments such as this could be seen as positive indications for an independently produced genre film from a film culture where such ventures continued to be rare, for a potential exploitation film, aiming to fully capitalize on notoriety and transgressive standards, such lukewarm endorsements could be fatal. Other reviewers even suggested that the size of the budget – and hence its professional standards – has had a negative effect on the final product, making it slow and lacking in novelty (Selås 2008), and thus not meeting expectations of its exploitative content.

There are substantial repercussions here for linking Nordic genre productions with international exploitation standards as considering a film like *Dead Snow* in the framework of exploitation cinema requires not only extending this framework substantially but also viewing it in relation to domestic standards of deviance and difference – all qualities that could be exploited for PR and commercial gain. However, not only did this cabin-based splatter not result in any moral outrage, *Dead Snow* was perceived to be 'too' professional in being able to operate on the level of international genre standards. These were, of course, the aspiration for similar productions in the 1970s and 1980s, but by 2009, such needs had largely disappeared. The levelling of professional standards generated especially by easy access to the latest digital technology meant that professional film production was no longer an exclusive prospect. Here, 'exclusive' comes with its own double standards, where we are no longer talking about the ability to put together massive budgets or even gain the favour of artistically oriented film institutes, but to have the 'guts' to go out and take a risk that could potentially destroy the artistic reputation of a filmmaker or, even worse, imprison them. Now, kickstarting a production was no longer the challenge – instead, ensuring attention in a cluttered media environment would be the dominant capital that these producers would seek.

The combination of a range of registers – substantial budgets, genre content, professional standards, popular success as well as a critical response that places a film like *Dead Snow* alongside established genre expectations – indicates the key transformations between these two examples. If *Evil Ed* was a true anomaly in mid-1990s film culture, by 2009, these types of gory genre products had established a consolidated presence in all of the Nordic markets. The use of special effects and references to mainstream genre film had ceased to be something extraordinary and were largely mentioned in passing in the reviews of *Dead Snow*. If *Evil Ed* was an embodiment of the changing taste cultures for localized exploitation, *Dead Snow* not only meets all the requirements of localized exploitation by being made in Norwegian and by contextualizing an established genre in a domestic cultural and environmental context, but it also has much more in common with what we identified as global exploitation patterns. This is confirmed by the fact that domestic critics persistently placed it into the context of a much more expansive international genre marketplace, and the film was a considerable success internationally, even receiving a theatrical release in the United States in dubbed form. In many ways, the localized and global exploitation narratives had now coalesced as part of a wider integration of global film markets, one where content can flow easily over borders and reach a wide variety of potential consumers.

The 1990s to the 2010s: Film cultures in transition

What led to these changed circumstances in Nordic film cultures? This and the next two chapters address some of the fundamental changes in both the parameters of Nordic film policy and the transformations in production cultures to interrogate the ways that previously exploitative forms of production were increasingly institutionalized as part of these film cultures. We outline some of these developments with a focus on the interactive dynamics of film policy and content as they provide a complex picture of the diverse modes that exploitation took during this era. Another aspect to note concerns the rhetoric of professionalism as the role of producers and directors who grew up on commercial and genre film production during the 1970s and the 1980s transformed from fans to professional film producers able to take advantage of some of these new policy directions and technological innovations. While there has always been talent with substantial personal investment in genre production, the infrastructure and the policy framework required to facilitate the production and distribution of such films had been traditionally lacking. Thus, to understand the role played by exploitative films, the construction and maintenance of film production infrastructure including economic and educational policy both of which have played especially significant roles in the professionalization of genre production, need to be considered.

As Swedish film scholar Olof Hedling has suggested, the 1990s and 2000s saw the film industry evolve into a part of the 'real economy' due to the integration of regional developments, labour practices, transnational finance and talent (Hedling 2015: 70–5; see also Gustafsson and Kääpä 2015). While many of the productions we cover in this chapter are independently financed, the increasing integration of transgressive film production into wider cultural–economic planning consolidated around a range of factors – production, promotion, distribution, exhibition, censorship, reception – in much more pointed ways to the 1980s, for example.

The turn of the decade brought many challenges to Nordic film cultures. These include the wide adoption of the 50/50 film financing model developed by Denmark in the early 1990s, and then by Norway in 2001, as a pragmatic strategy to support popular domestic cinema. The model provides 50 per cent of the total funds for a production if the other 50 per cent is secured via private capital (Bondebjerg 1997: 21; Iversen 2011: 294). Such incentives increased the financial viability of productions that deviated from the conventional art paradigm still dominating these film cultures as private investment was invariably attracted to films that could produce a clear return on investment. At the same time, a range of producers (see Kääpä 2015) undertook professional qualification studies such as MBAs in higher education settings, and ultimately influenced the ways the business side of film production was perceived in circles of cultural authority. Alongside these above-the-line developments, as the fan site *Nordic Fantasy Info* (2014), for example, suggests, was an increased emphasis on infrastructural skills and talent, which 'need to be built locally, and their presence in Nordic productions contribute to the education of and inspiration for Nordic EFX engineers, designers and artists'. Combined with the transformations in the directions of policy on the film institute level, these developments challenged the perception of genre film as a risky economic and creative practice.

While the production of genres such as horror was still considered problematic due to lingering perceptions of cultural worthiness and the lack of technical know-how in the early years of the 2000s, a more audience-oriented cinema did start to emerge, one that was capable of capitalizing on international trends. This was particularly noticeable in Norway where a cycle of violent slasher films broke through in the early 2000s. The slasher cycle was kicked off by Pål Øie's *Villmark* (*Dark Woods*, 2003), a film about a group of would-be reality TV stars venturing to a secluded cabin in the mountains where they are killed off one by one by a mysterious stalker. The release of the film generated considerable publicity for its novelty as a professionally produced indigenous slasher. While far from conventional exploitation cinema, the cultural–political mechanics accompanying *Villmark*'s release continues the localized exploitation pattern by transplanting the slasher genre into an indigenously Norwegian context, filled with both 'dense' cultural references and marked as 'other' by its use of the Norwegian language. Indeed, its clear debt to the slasher genre did not prohibit it from standing out in Norway as the film garnered Amanda nominations for Best Film and Best Actor of the year for Kristoffer Joner – reflecting some of the critical accolades that *Moonlight Sonata* had accumulated fifteen years earlier in

Finland. Yet, whereas this did not lead to sustained genre production in 1980s Finland, *Villmark* was seen by over 150,000 spectators and resulted in a cycle of similar slasher films, such as the *Fritt Vilt* (*Cold Prey*, 2006–10) franchise and the sequel *Villmark: Asylum* (*Dark Woods 2*, 2015). As with the genre's Italian or American counterparts, the success of these films eventually led to an increase of similar films, which would alternatively include hard-core violence such as *Rovdyr* (*Manhunt*, 2008) or opt for more mainstreamed thrills like in *Snarveien* (*Detour*, 2009).

The sustainability of this cycle (which continues to date as a distinct novelty in the Nordic confines) can thus be attributed to a range of state support mechanisms including the introduction of the 50/50 funding scheme as well as tax incentives that allowed for production costs of a film to be written off. Similar methods had led to an increase in the production of comparatively expensive genre actioners in the 1980s, including *Orion's Belt*. Interest in these productions had tapered off by the early 1990s as the tax laws were transformed and productions costs of films could no longer be written off. The direct correlation between the obliteration of these incentives and the culmination of genre cycle of the 1980s testifies to the fact that Norway is, of course, a small film culture where top-down policy initiatives can directly shape the direction that the film culture eventually takes. The creation of the Norwegian Film Fund in 2001, combining several previously distinct institutes – The Norwegian Film Institute Production, The Audiovisual Production Fund and Norwegian Film Ltd – ensured that domestic film policy was moderated into a more streamlined and diverse set of protocols. While art film remained a priority, the 50/50 model ensured a much more robust infrastructure for genre production (Iversen 2011: 293–7).

At the same time, the film industries of the other Nordic countries started to increase their genre quotas with, for example, Finnish producer Tero Kaukomaa spearheading the Finnish–Chinese co-production *Jadesoturi* (*Jade Warrior*, 2006), a martial arts epic mixing Finnish traditional narratives with Kung Fu (see Kääpä 2010: 270–8). In Denmark, large-scale productions like the fantasy adventure *De fortabte sjæles ø* (*The Island of Lost Souls*, 2007) and *Ved verdens ende* (*At World's End*, 2009) were released, whereas Icelandic producer Julian Kemp directed the slasher film *Reykjavik Whale Watching Massacre* (2009). In Sweden, the Swedish Film Institute funded its first and so far only slasher film, *Strandvaskaren* (*Drowning Ghost*, 2004).

A more 'conventional' exploitative attempt was made by Martin Munthe, who directed *Camp Slaughter* (2004), a low-budget film set 'somewhere in rural

Scandinavia' but where the Swedish actors speak in broken English to meet the intentions of its producers to sell it on the 'American home video market' (Gustafsson 2015: 193). The film is strongly inspired by *The Texas Chainsaw Massacre* (1974) and it is, like its inspiration, extremely violent but the gore is created and cut in an amateurish way that borders on comedy. Consequently, *Camp Slaughter* was loathed by Swedish reviewers who ironically wondered if the Swedish Film Institute could not issue a certificate of work prohibition for the film's director (Bråstedt 2004), a statement that was immediately used in advertisements for the film.

While it is difficult to pinpoint the exact reasons for the emergence of a consolidated line of exploitative genre production in the Nordic countries on the whole, the Norwegian cycle will have acted as a significant indicator of the commercial potential of such films and functioned as an incentive for the other four countries to start investing in genre production. At the same time, areas such as digital technology allowed access to high-quality film production for individuals who previously found themselves excluded due to the prohibitive cost of production arrangements and expertise. While transnational remakes of international genre films have been covered by, for example, Iain Robert Smith's analysis (2014) of productions like *Dünyayı Kurtaran Adam* ('Turkish Star Wars', 1982), Nordic genre variations differ from many of these other international patterns. While Turkish genre emulations, for example, were often attempts to use the templates of popular Hollywood cinema in contexts where the legalities of remaking or adapting films was not a major concern, our examples are much more concerned with taking genre elements and localizing them to fit the cultural–political context of each respective film culture. This would take place by using elements that contributed to a minimization of cultural discount: self-conscious use of genre formulas, the casting of international stars, English as the dominant language, careful placement of explicit content and marketing campaigns that made excessive use of all these registers.

To illustrate how these developed in the first decade of the 2000s we focus on two Nordic slasher films produced ten years apart, the Danish *Flænset: Jalosiens Instinkter* ('Shredded', 2000) and the Icelandic *Reykjavik Whale Watching Massacre*. These two films encapsulate many of the arguments around the institutional positioning of genre/exploitation films. Both films are explicit in their exploitation roots as they feature plentiful gore and a distinct disregard for political correctness. In comparison to a film like *Dead Snow*, they are overtly serious in their approach (despite both leaving room to be read as very dark comedies). Whereas *Dead Snow* revelled in its explosive gore and bad taste villains (and comes much closer to a comedic film like *Braindead* as a consequence), the thrills of *Flænset* and *Reykjavik Whale Watching Massacre* are much more grounded in locating genre conventions in domestic contexts, but in distinctly different ways, arguably dictated by the ten years of institutional and creative development between them.

While a key tendency in Nordic film cultures revolves around the coalescence of localized perspectives on well-worn genre formulas, *Flænset* provides a novel perspective in that it refuses to highlight localized or ethno-symbolic elements, both which were elemental to *Dead Snow*'s success. According to an interview with director Heini Grünbaum, the film was conceptualized and written in English and aimed at an international market. However, when Scandinavian distribution company Scanbox Entertainment offered 1 million DDK for the project, it came with the condition that it had to include a bankable actor to play the leading role, and that it had to be made in Danish. In addition, Lars von Trier's Zentropa provided all the production facilities in exchange for 50 per cent of the film (Horror Unrated 2014). Grünbaum then managed to contract, probably through Henrik Danstrup, the producer of Nicolas Winding Refn's *Pusher* Trilogy (1996-2005), Danish actor Thomas Bo Larsen, known for his roles in films like *Pusher* and *Festen* (*The Celebration*, 1998).

Veering close to both American slashers and serial killer productions, *Flænset* was marketed as an 'Erotic Splatter Thriller' – in similar fashion as Bo Arne Vibenius' films of the 1970s. The film chronicles the breakdown of Jan (Thomas Bo Larsen) who, upon witnessing his wife cheating on him, goes on an extremely aggressive killing spree. The film was particularly unusual in a Danish, as well as a Nordic, context as it mimics the *Friday the 13th* franchise in its use of garden tools as weapons, such as fork hoes for gory slaughter, and the unadulterated rage that Jan unleashes on his victims. The 'erotic' part consists of a graphic sex scene in the beginning of the film, featuring the unfaithful wife, but, at the same time, the film includes several scenes where sex and violence are interlinked. Particularly problematic is a scene, following Jan forcing a half-conscious female hitchhiker to repeatedly stab his wife, where Jan rapes the female hitchhiker, who starts to enjoy this violation. According to the director's commentary track on the DVD, Grünbaum constructed this scene as a homage to the highly problematic rape scene in Sam Peckinpah's *Straw Dogs* (1971), whom he cites as his 'teacher'. He declares the scene to be a 'provocation' in typical exploitation fashion, but then contradicts his statements when he points out, without irony, that the scenes in *Flænset* and *Straw Dogs* are equally 'beautiful' (*Flænset*, 'Audio Commentary with Director', 2000).

It is perhaps no wonder then that when the Danish Film Institute was approached for a grant of 200,000 DDK for marketing support, the filmmakers were turned down, or as Grünbaum interpreted it, 'I guess they were just laughing their asses off – we got nothing from them!' Moreover, Grünbaum claims that Scanbox hated it too 'and they could not see how in the hell they could ever make any money out of it' (Horror Unrated 2014). Accordingly, *Flænset* was shown once in the Cinematheque in Copenhagen and it did get a festival screening at Swedish Fantastic Film Festival in Lund in 2000. Nevertheless, the film was released directly to VHS and DVD, despite featuring contemporary and future stars such as Thomas Bo Larsen and Lars Mikkelsen. In addition, the film received universally negative reviews, according to its producer Isak Thorsen (Gustafsson 2019).

In contrast to this culturally (and eventually economically) homeless production, the Icelandic *Reykjavik Whale Watching Massacre* fulfils most of our categories for global exploitation. It is a slasher set on a fishing trawler off the coast of Reykjavik, produced in English with an international cast headlined

Figure 7.2 The original DVD cover artwork for *Flænset: Jalosiens Instinkter* ('Shredded', 2000). Courtesy of Scanbox.

by Gunnar Hansen, the legendary Leatherface of *The Texas Chainsaw Massacre*. The film plays off its Icelandic setting by using kill techniques derived from the environment including the freezing water and harpoons. At the same time, it ensures that these are seen as distinctly exotic money shots, as part of the paraphernalia that qualifies this production as an Icelandic variation of the slasher film. Yet, crucially, even as it seems to localize slasher standards to Iceland, this is an inherently inverted 'touristic' gaze on Iceland with the main fodder for the disenfranchised local 'hillbillies' – in this case, a family of laid-off fishermen – consisting of a group of international tourists, speaking English in a melange of accents, and thus providing a clear justification for this all important designator of its global aspirations.

Reykjavik Whale Watching Massacre was made with funding support from The Icelandic Film Centre, in addition to its independent financing, including a co-production agreement with Finland's very successful popular film production company Solar Films. Produced on a budget of 4,000,000 ISK, the film's release was preceded with considerable publicity focusing on its novelty as an indigenous Icelandic slasher. The director of the film, Julius Kemp, was interviewed in the English language *Reykjavik Grapevine* to discuss his motivations for making the film. Here, he emphasized his affinity for the genre, naming *The Texas Chainsaw Massacre* as his all-time favourite film, and discussing the ways the film's financing was structured: 'It really came as a surprise when the Icelandic Film Centre, as well as the other Scandinavian patrons, didn't have anything against our slasher flick. The co-producers also saw potential in distribution, which is the main thing in all this: potential. The moneybags proved to be pro-splatter, eventually' (Kristinsson 2009).

The fact that such a film was able to be made in Iceland in 2009 is impressive as Iceland had only produced twenty-seven films throughout the 1980s due to the limited production circumstances and audience potential. This situation started to shift in the 1990s when key foreign production and distribution funds such as Eurimages and the Nordic Film and Television Fund emerged as vital players to cultivate the regional markets. Yet, exploitative films have been distinctly lacking in Iceland with the Viking Trilogy as the only real candidate for such a qualifier. Unsurprisingly, the focus had been on producing comedies and heritage films as these met the resource circumstances of this small national cinema well. As Birgit Thor Moller (2005: 310–17) has suggested, the situation did not transform in the 1990s as genre films remained conspicuous by their absence.

Yet, as with the other Nordic countries, the increasing interest and policy emphasis on popular cinema changed the landscape and facilitated productions such as *Reykjavik Whale Watching Massacre*. Solar Films and Kemp's The Icelandic Film Company had collaborated on the Finnish fantasy film *Dark Floors* (2008) and it seems *Reykjavik Whale Watching Massacre* would have been a future step in genre-based collaboration between the companies. Similarly, all the pre-publicity for the film, in one way or another, focused on the production's novelty. For example, in the Icelandic *Morgunbladid* newspaper, a full-page article on Gunnar Hansen explained his genre history and the different role he plays in this film in comparison to his legendary role as Leatherface. The article explained his Icelandic roots to make a naturalized connection between the star and the genre origins of the film (Anon. 2009b).

At the same time, all of these elements were used in the marketing of the film that adopted a dynamic black and red colour scheme harkening back to the graphics of Saul Bass, with a tagline exclaiming 'Hunting humans in the cold Icelandic waters'. The film was released internationally as *Harpoon: Reykjavik Whale Watching Massacre* with the posters using a wide variety of visual gags featuring harpoons penetrating human bodies. Only the Icelandic poster differed substantially from these as it featured a metallic blood-soaked background highlighted by local star Helgi Bjornsson snarling through a peephole with the words, 'Finally an Icelandic thriller' displayed prominently. At the same time, the writer of the film emphasized its distance from the conventional profile of an Icelandic film:

> We are not making this film for the Icelandic tourism board or to pump up the egos of the Icelandic public. And we are not trying to do what the rest of the Icelandic film industry is doing, which is to make respectable films which they can then go and show abroad and show our country in a good light. Our film is like the bad brother, who is always shut out the back and turns up to spoil the party. (Sigursson in Foster 2012)

This commentary accompanying the release of the film consciously plays up its transnational proximity and distance dynamics in much more explicit ways than those of, for example, *Moonlight Sonata* or *Flænset*. Yet, instead of framing it as a peculiar novelty, the film is presented as an outsider production, but one that is very much anticipated and welcomed. While media coverage addressing the film's novelty may have been optimistic about its contribution to Icelandic film culture, domestic critics were much more negative in their assessment of the film's contributions with *Dagbladur* suggesting the film fails to contribute anything new to the genre. Many of the critics identified all the usual genre tropes and suggested that the basic idea and production qualities, such as the cinematography and editing, work well. But for at least one particular critic (Anon. 2009c), the story is a huge let down as the film as a whole makes no real original contribution to advancing either the genre or Icelandic film culture. The 1 ½ star evaluation captures the problematic position of the film domestically where the critics fail to perceive it as neither a competent genre production like the Norwegian slashers, nor in any shocked or outraged terms as something that transgresses the contemporary norms. That is, as a film that should be censored or banned – two key terms with very lucrative reputational and economic capital. Similarly, *Morgenbladid* used it to illustrate a downward turn in Icelandic cinema, berating the film for its lack of professional quality and suggesting it was a bland attempt at genre film (Anon. 2009d).

Interestingly, it was not its genre or exploitative content that caused problems with the critics. Instead, it was the failure of the film to do anything substantially innovative with this template. The failure here comes from an inability to be either too shocking or too lo-fi to provide any potentially challenging or different material into the domestic cinematic infrastructure. Significantly, such perspectives would emerge as a key critical tendency in the reception of Nordic exploitation cinema of the 2000s. Whereas the negative tone of the critiques in the 1980s had largely focused on dismissing the technical qualities of the localized exploitation films, now the production standards increasingly met those of similarly low-budget international exploitation. However, the positive sheen to be gained from a low-quality guerrilla production or from an emphasis on transgressive violence had dissipated with an influx of similar content arriving into domestic markets with the abolishment of censorship as well as much easier access to diverse content on platforms like YouTube. In the wake of these transformations in the viewing practices of genre audiences, the attempts to produce transgressive exploitation films often struggled to make an impact as they were neither sufficiently innovative to appeal to domestic viewers, nor transgressive enough to generate notoriety with cult audiences.

Whereas some of the Nordic global exploitation examples appeared sufficiently convincing to ascertain a modicum of international success (mostly *Arctic Heat* and *The Ninja Mission*), the majority of the slasher productions of the 2000s were unable to gain much traction. While *Flænset* received a minimal release in some European markets on DVD, a substantial part of *Reykjavik*

Whale Watching Massacre's reputation was generated by the wide release it received internationally at festivals and on DVD. While it was sold as an Icelandic variation on the genre, presumably to allow it to carve out a niche in a saturated marketplace, most of the international critical comments were unenthusiastic about its potential, with *Variety*, for example, calling the film 'An Icelandic knockoff of *The Texas Chainsaw Massacre* aboard a fishing vessel' (Van Hoeij 2010). Among more fan-based audiences, 'Tex Massacre' from the internet site *Bloody Disgusting* captures the proximity and distance balancing well as he suggested that

> It excites me as a genre fan to see a country not known for producing horror films, to mine its cultural zeitgeist and transform that into a personal film. I think in many ways, Kemp and Sigurdsson did that. It's just a shame that lapses in logic and far too great a dependence on stock-issue cliché's litter their otherwise interesting production. The film looks great, providing some stark images and genuine moments of suspense; some of the performances are good, the rest are, if nothing else, inhibited by the simplicity of the script. ('Tex Massacre', 2010)

Thus, even as *Reykjavik Whale Watching Massacre*'s international distribution reinforced the perception of the film as a particularly productive case of global exploitation that sees it exploit both cultural affiliations and technical know-how, critics' comments simultaneously showcase a peculiar sense of dissatisfaction with how the filmmakers used these cultural registers. One way to consider the cultural positioning of the film would be to explore it alongside David Andrews's view of cult films as a 'supergenre' that is both adversarial and complementary to dominant practices, that is, cult cinema 'as a set of illegitimate and dominated cultural positions' (Andrews 2013: 89). The liminality inherent in the proximity and distance politics and critical reception of a film like *Reykjavik Whale Watching Massacre* suggests that the films we discuss do not function particularly well as cult films. Though we have seen certain films including *Hunters of the Night* and *The Ninja Mission* build precisely such a reputation retrospectively in the Nordic countries, a cult reputation is often something that builds over years through audience engagement. It is very rarely something that can be manufactured, especially as a reward for the ways the producers of *Flænset* and *Reykjavik Whale Watching Massacre* explicitly targeted such registers to generate notoriety and, thus, commercial gain.

The fact that such reputations have largely failed to manifest for either the Norwegian slasher cycle or even for *Reykjavik Whale Watching Massacre* is not only a matter of temporal distance. Largely, the issues here connect to the standardization of genre practices and the fact that violent content or emulation of genre formulas had become increasingly conventional in the global cinematic landscape. As Iversen (2016: 332–40) has suggested, Norwegian genre films were by the 2000s perceived as standard mainstream production. While many of the themes of the films are easily categorizable as normative exploitation, they are also part of popular film culture and lacking in the sort of enthusiastic marginal subcultural identity markers that made, for example, some of the films of the 1980s stand out. Thus, the only means to generate attention is to capitalize on their domestic context through the cultural and economic benefits offered by a finely balanced proximity and distance politics. As they take place in landscapes and contexts defined by cultural specificity, identified already in their titles (Reykjavik, Snow), they appear as 'international' variations of established genres. This allows them to lay claim to a rhetoric of authenticity that is of paramount importance for exploitation films. In comparison to the umpteenth sequel or a reboot of a slasher franchise, these elements all contribute to the potential viability of domestic genre cinema.

If localized exploitation of the 1980s had to be characterized as a largely failed attempt to tap into a clear gap in the market – that of domestic genre films, currently populated by American imports – the resurgent genre film of the 2000s was not content with this marginal position. Instead, they were much more focused on producing truly competitive texts able to connect with audiences both domestically and internationally. These films were often intended as popular cinema far removed from the marginal pleasures of traditional forms of international exploitation, even as they were also, arguably, designed to attract attention because of their unique position in the domestic context.

The early 2000s can thus be considered from two particular angles. On the one hand, the institutes had started to provide funds for genre films, but for the most part, these were of the more 'respectable' kind – thus we saw an increase in war films as well as general thriller productions. Secondly, there was a slow build-up of key individuals, sharing both interest in exploitative genre material and technical know-how of production methodologies, now working on productions that would have been considered transgressive in the past. While the film institutes would still not fully acknowledge more explicitly exploitative content with targeted funding (most of the genre funding was allocated to marketing or through schemes like the 50/50 incentives), these years saw the emergence of a more positive infrastructural approach to genre where popular genre films, especially previously shunned forms of action and horror, were viewed much more favourably as having potential to carve out new directions for the film industry, even as they continued to be simultaneously castigated for not fitting with all the appropriate contemporary norms for publicly financed cinema. These developments established the foundations for a situation where more localized exploitation forms transform into a more enthusiastically global one unconcerned with meeting domestic film policy prerogatives or normative moral or taste norms, either as these policy frameworks and norms had shifted or as technological progress was able to generate circumstances where by-passing these restrictions, for example, through digital technology, was increasingly convenient.

Artistic exploitation

While all these developments were taking place in more explicitly commercial genre production, more artistic forms of horror like the Swedish *Let the Right One In* continued to challenge normative taste perceptions. Art films from directors like Ingmar Bergman to Lars von Trier had, of course, used transgressive imagery and themes, but often received very different treatment from both financiers and censors than many of the films discussed in this book. As a consequence of this legacy of artistic and philosophical horror, *Let the Right One In* is in many ways the quintessential Nordic exploitation film as it combines the austere bleakness of Nordic social realism with an artistic quirkiness often associated with internationally successful Nordic cinema, but now integrated with heavy doses of spectacular horror imagery, which would have struggled to find room in the restrictive 1980s, for example. By balancing between the registers of downbeat social realism and extravagant genre content, it manages to exploit two essential realms of the Nordic film policy and industry environment of the 2000s. Here, it plays up a sense of critical prestige through a set of narrative and visual signifiers associated with Nordic social realism, particularly the bleak urban landscapes of suburban Sweden, including the decrepit bars and brutalist concrete that dominates the landscape. Simultaneously, it makes full use of quirkiness and expertise in high-value digital production technology as the 'love story' between two marginalized outcasts, Eli, the vampire, and Oscar, her soon-to-be protector, adopts conventional thematic material from 'respectable' socio-realistic depictions but transforms them through a supernatural genre twist. To complement the bleak suburban landscapes, the film features excessive genre material, such as Eli's protector burning his face with acid in trying to escape the authorities, resulting in a visually potent suicide scene with extensive make-up and gore effects. It also features an impressively spectacular set piece featuring a local alcoholic self-immolating in bed that would have certainly made all the marketing materials of a 1980s exploitation film. As both instances are captured through considerable visual and narrative panache, they merge into a respectable whole that combines art, violence, gore, bleakness and politics.

Such a combination of excessive transgressiveness and cultural respectability has been a part of exploitation cinema from the beginning, but here it is processed through a very specific Nordic lens that fits with the film politics of the era. The interplay between the conventions of social realism and horror again plays off the registers of proximity and distance. The social bleakness – a theme that would largely connote proximity for most domestic spectators – contrasts with the vampire gore and violence. But all of this takes place through deliberate and often distanced framing that harkens back to a more self-consciously artistic cinematic style than the viscera and splatter of the horror film. For example, a scene where Eli dispatches the bullies harassing Oscar at the local swimming pool captures violence perpetrated on children in a way that is simultaneously hugely exploitative – the spectator is confronted with a child's disembodied head and other body parts – and artistic, as the massacre is witnessed from underwater where the off-key framing leaves these elements as incidental to the protagonist's struggles. These tactics have since become something of a hallmark of Nordic art genre hybrids, and they play a huge role in the exploitation film culture that was simultaneously produced alongside such respectable art films. Indeed, without the prevalence of explicit gore in a film like *Let the Right One In*, would the gore scenes of a *Dead Snow* be as acceptable or as 'normalized' as they were to some of the critics?

Perhaps the most appropriate way to justify the inclusion of this distinctly non-traditional 'exploitation film' in this study is by focusing on how its marketing framed these contrasts. The trailer for *Let the Right One In* plays its different registers in explicit ways, as it establishes the socio-realist tone by featuring scenes of Oscar being bullied in in the drab confines of the film's suburban school, but soon transitions to genre material. These include many of the slaughter scenes from the film, including the hospital set-piece, and culminating with a bloodied hand crawling along a doorframe while the title cards play over snowflakes floating against darkness. The Swedish poster similarly features a silhouette of a human-like form pressed against steamed glass with the lower half taken over by an image of one of the victims hanging from a tree. On many of the international posters, the image is superimposed with award recognitions, which provides an intriguing contrast between genre material and the prestige evocations of art cinema. By aspiring to be both art and genre at the same time, the strategies leverage the co-existence of these cultural–political registers and allow the film to communicate with both domestic and international audiences in ways that provides something different but also appropriately and comfortably familiar. As experimentation and art have traditionally met the taste and moral thresholds of domestic film policies relying on public accountability, they have provided a safe venue for introducing more explicit or transgressive content to these particular social and cine-historical contexts – a factor that *Let the Right One In* both affirms and exploits.

The production of prominent cult art films has, thus, facilitated a film culture mindful of international standards while these films introduce challenging representational conventions that would have, at least in the previous decades, run afoul of censorship norms. Whereas the localized exploitation films targeted domestic consumers by producing approximations of international genre productions, and global exploitation used a range of techniques to explicitly scandalize the domestic context and use this media attention to build an international reputation, all complemented by textual features that make the films easily accessible for audiences on a global scale, a film like *Let the Right One In* does not fall easily into these categories. Instead, its main relevance for us is on the ways it influences the larger cultural environment around genre and exploitative content. By institutionalizing explicit genre thematics as well as gore and violence, it invariably contributes to a cultural change in which those elements that previously distinguished exploitation films from the mainstream also transform in status, arguably both legitimizing and negating some of the potential of exploitation to act as a transgressive cultural form as well as a lucrative platform for film business.

Conclusion

The politics of proximity and distance continue to play a substantial role in the 1990s and 2000s as producers of genre cinema would exploit cultural expectations by utilizing directives (such as the increased emphasis on commercial aspects of film culture) to facilitate their productions with tools to compete against imported productions. Many of these films balance between conformity with norms (using heritage or other ethno-symbolic content; abiding with dominant cultural policies) and transgression (pushing limits on violence; integrating previously problematic genre forms into domestic film culture). But at the same time, a lot of the traditional attitudes about quality cinema continued to prevail. This led to a complex situation where genre productions would now qualify for public funding but could not be perceived to be too close to their (especially American) genre brethren. That is, they should not be too enthusiastically global – especially if they were perceived to represent the values of Global Hollywood. Thus, proximity to domestic cultures would often work as a unique selling point for these productions, and would, subsequently, be used as a marketing gimmick internationally. However, as some of the critical reception showcases, cultural norms transform over time, and productions that used to be able to capitalize on their uniqueness found it increasingly difficult to be truly surprising or sufficiently different in a media ecosystem characterized by streaming services and the proliferation of digital tools allowing access to near-professional standards.

Thus, exploitation does not, as we have suggested, only function as a form of cultural production that transgresses moral or cultural attitudes but operates as a complex industrial and cultural politics that may be more revealing about prevailing cultural standards than about specific film texts. This transformation, then, is ultimately about two developments: (1) the attitudes of cultural authorities and (2) the technical capabilities of producers to work with these formulas successfully. These developments, in turn, could only take place as sufficient infrastructure had emerged to support localized genre variations that were now being taken seriously by all sections of the these countries' film industries. Thus, we can consider many of these early 2000s ventures as a form of capacity-building designed to consolidate the industries of these countries. While most of these early films did not get full theatrical releases and instead circulated on home video or as online material, they gave these directors industry exposure that allowed them to consolidate professional careers outside of occasional work as music video directors or in other odd jobs in and outside the industry. The considerable success of Norwegian slashers, both in terms of meeting audience demand but also consolidating a cycle of genre production, is significant in paving the way for a more enthusiastically exploitative form of Nordic film culture. While Norwegian genre filmmakers were at the forefront of these developments regionally, the success of an indigenous genre cycle would have generated ripples in the other national contexts too and led to policy transformations. Of course, it is difficult to project a clear progression from a film like *Flænset* to *Dark Woods* or *Reykjavik Whale Watching Massacre*, and from there to bigger productions like *Dead Snow* and *Iron Sky* (2012) – as these productions would have been in development for several years, and a film entering production at a certain point would not necessarily indicate much about the context in which it was conceptualized – there are clear patterns to decipher. Accordingly, the trajectory from the mid- to late 1990s (a period best characterized as one of distinct drought for Nordic genre content), to the early 2000s (one characterized by experimentation with popular genre and the induction of competitive professional standards), and to the 2010s (when a much more enthusiastically self-aware and professionalized exploitation culture emerges) shows how transnational strategies come to dominate the genre markets.

Thus, the following two chapters will outline how a more self-aware form of global exploitation cinema emerges in the 2000s, one that is enthusiastically based on intertextual references and much more explicit exploitation themes, such as rape–revenge and Nazisploitation films. These Nordic variations on 'established' exploitation cinema genres can be seen as a consequence of the mainstreaming of film genres in the 2000s, precisely as took place with Norway's slasher cycle and the institutionalization of genre into film policy across the Nordic countries. As many of the 'extremes' of the films of the early 2000s were already disappointingly obvious for Nordic critics and audiences, the 2010s would see a concentrated turn to a much more excessive misogynist brand of exploitation film. The trajectories echo some of David Church's arguments about the ways the American horror film recalibrated itself in the early 2000s following the mainstream success of the teen-focused slasher cycle initiated by *Scream* (1996). Church argues that the prominence gained by directors such as Eli Roth, Rob Zombie, James Wan and Alexandre Aja ('the splat pack') and genre variations like torture porn were largely a backlash against this perceived 'feminization' of the genre in the late 1990s. This implies that some of the more progressive gender politics of many a slasher film were upended in favour of more excessive and regressive material, which Church explains to be a consequence of the genre becoming more accessible to wider audiences including both teen and female viewers. Here, 'femininity has long been culturally coded as more physically/emotionally "open" than masculinity, so it should be no surprise that a perceived opening up of "masculine" genres to other viewers would carry patriarchally reviled connotations of vulnerability, weakness and ignorance' (Church 2015: 201–2).

Despite the many problematic connotations of labelling exploitation in gendered terms, the arguments do make sense in relation to the enthusiastic courting of subcultural and regressive tendencies in genre cinema in the United States and elsewhere. While technology and market integration facilitated more commercial productions, this also led to a backlash with a distinct lo-fi, anti-feminized bent that most problematically conducts its politics with a supposedly subversive wink that plays up the retrosploitation credentials of these films. Although Church mentions the Norwegian film *Hora* (*The Whore*, 2009) as one of these examples, we can see the build-up of similar trajectories from the early accessible Norwegian slasher films to the much more aggressive *Reykjavik Whale Watching Massacre*, and back to *Flænset* as a pro/regression that led to the reinvigoration of such 'authentically' exploitative productions in 2010s. *Flænset* not only stands out as a bizarre combination of the localized/globalized and transgressive exploitation approaches but also manages to exist as an anomaly in an international genre context (as well as in a Nordic context) with its mix of gory violence and graphic sex scenes. *Flænset* thus became, unlike the comedic approach of *Evil Ed*, an early example of the politicized dissociation of cult cinema from the 'neutered' mainstream horror cinema dominated by contemporary films like the Norwegian slashers. The macho approach with 'masculine overtones', as discussed by Church (2015: 201–4), is also evident in *Flænset* as most of the poorly written dialogue is about 'stiff cocks', 'limp cocks', the literal castration of cocks and male fantasies about rape and violence, all under the thin guise of jealousy.

The changing standards for popular horror imply another important perspective on this supposed neutering of the aggressive pleasures of the genre. Church (2015: 202) positions this as a challenge for American genre cinema arising largely from remakes of Asian films that took an enthusiastically psychological approach to shock tactics. For him, this cycle of remakes led to a resurgence of much more aggressive and problematic gore pictures relishing their bad taste valourization of patriarchal values and extreme content. Such arguments echo the perspectives of Cook (1976) and McRobbie and Gerber (2000: 12–25), for example, who have suggested that subcultures have 'masculine overtones', leading to other critics like Hollows (2003: 43–7) to argue that cult cinema's disassociation from the neutered commercial content of the mainstream has pervaded cult fandom: mainstream cinema is imagined as feminized mass culture whereas cult films are seen as part of a heroic, masculinized subculture. If in the United States, the rise of psychological horror inspired by Japanese horror films in particular was one crucial aspect that led to the politically problematic aggressively masculinist and misogynist productions of the later years, then it is worth asking if similar patterns can be identified in the Nordic context too. Accordingly, as we will show in the next chapters, similar patterns occur throughout the 2000s in Nordic film as not only do the 'feminized slashers' arguably occupy room from 'real horror' but, in the context of publicly subsidized film culture, art films – the space still considered sacrosanct from censorship impositions – often take the place of more explicitly exploitative product in integrating transgressive ideas into these film cultures. Thus, the next two chapters focus on explaining more of this context by, respectively, focusing on how Nazisploitation took on an unexpected role in commercial Nordic film production, and in the re-emergence and continued co-existence of a more aggressive (and regressive) brand of misogynist patriarchal exploitation cinema.

References

Ahonen, Kimmo, Juha Rosenqvist, Janne Rosenqvist and Päivi Valotie (eds.) (2003), *Taju kankaalle. Uutta suomalaista elokuvaa paikantamassa*. Turku: Kirja-Aurora.
Andersson, Jan-Olov (1997), 'Evil Ed', Review, *Aftonbladet*, 4 May.
Andrews, David (2013), *Theorizing Art Cinemas: Foreign, Cult, Avant-Garde and Beyond*, Austin: University of Texas Press.
Anon. (2009a), 'Interview with Julian Kemp', *Reykjavik Grapewine*, 7 August.
Anon. (2009b), 'Reykjavik Whale Watching Massacre', Review, *Morgunbladid*, 13 August.
Anon. (2009c), 'Reykjavik Whale Watching Massacre', Review, *Dagbladur*, 8 August.
Anon. (2009d), 'Gengisvisitala islenska gamanmynda', *Morgunbladid*, 20 September.
Bondebjerg, Ib (1997), 'Dansk Film 1972–1997: Æstetisk fornyelse og internationalisering', in Ib Bondebjerg, Jesper Andersen and Peter Schepelern (eds), *Dansk film 1972–1997*, Copenhagen: Munksgaard-Rosinante, pp. 10–27.
Bråstedt, Mats (2004), 'Camp Slaughter', Review, *Expressen*, 16 January.
Church, David (2015), *Grindhouse Nostalgia*, Edinburgh: Edinburgh University Press.
Cook, Pam (1976), 'Exploitation Films and Feminism', *Screen*, 17.2, 122–7.
Croneman, Johan (1997), 'Evil Ed', Review, *Dagens Nyheter*, 4 May.
Eirik, Alver (2009), 'Død snø', Review, *Dagbladet*, 8 January.

Flænset, 'Audio Commentary with Director' (2000), DVD, Copenhagen: Scanbox Entertainment.

Foster, Simon (2012), 'Reykjavik Whale Watching Massacre: Sjon Sigursson', SBS, 15 May, available at: https://www.sbs.com.au/movies/article/2012/05/15/reykjavik-w hale-watching-massacre-sj-n-sigurdsson (Accessed 2 July 2019).

Furhammar, Leif (2003), *Filmen i Sverige: En historia i tio kapitel och en fortsättning*, Stockholm: Dialogos and Swedish Film Institute.

Gustafsson, Tommy (2015), 'Slasher in the Snow: The Rise of the Low-Budget Nordic Horror Film', in Tommy Gustafsson and Pietari Kääpä (2015), *Nordic Genre Film: Small Nation Film Culture in the Global Marketplace*, Edinburgh: Edinburgh University Press, pp. 189–202.

Gustafsson, Tommy (2019), Email Interview with Isak Thorsen, 10 May.

Gustafsson, Tommy and Pietari Kääpä (2015), *Nordic Genre Film: Small Nation Film Culture in the Global Marketplace*, Edinburgh: Edinburgh University Press.

Hedling, Olof (2015), 'Cinema in the Welfare State: Notes on Public Support, Regional Film Funds and Swedish Film Policy', in HjortMette and Ursula Lindqvist (eds), *A Companion to Nordic Cinema*, Basingstoke: Palgrave, pp. 60–77.

Hollows, Joanne (2003), 'The Masculinity of Cult', in Mark Jancovich, Antonio Lázaro Reboll, Julian Stringer and Andy Willis (eds), *Defining Cult Movies: The Cultural Politics of Oppositional Taste*, Manchester: Manchester University Press, pp. 43–7.

Horror Unrated (2014), 'Horror-Unrated Retrospekt #7: Flænset! Et interview med den danske instruktør Heini Grünbaum', *Sørensen Exploitation Cinema Proudly Presents*, http://sorensencinema.blogspot.com/2014/07/horror-unrated-retrospekt-7-flnset-et .html, 11 July (Accessed 20 June 2019).

Iversen, Gunnar (2011), *Norsk filmhistorie: Spillefilmen 1911-2011*, Oslo: Universitetsforlaget.

Iversen, Gunnar (2016), 'Between Art and Genre – An Introduction to New Nordic Horror Cinema', in Mette Hjort and Ursula Lindqvist (eds),*The Blackwell Companion to Nordic Cinema*, Oxford: Wiley-Blackwell, pp. 332–50.

Kristinsson, Sigurður Kjartan (2009), 'Slash, Kill, Blood, Guts, Love, Awesome', *The Reykjavik Grapevine*, 3 September.

Kääpä, Pietari (2010), *The National and Beyond*, Oxford: Peter Lang.

Kääpä, Pietari (ed.) (2012), *Directory of World Cinema*, Finland, Bristol: Intellect..

Kääpä, Pietari (2015), 'A Culture of Reciprocity: The Politics of Cultural Exchange in Contemporary Nordic Cinema', in Tommy Gustafsson and Pietari Kääpä, *Nordic Genre Film: Small Nation Film Culture in the Global Marketplace*, Edinburgh: Edinburgh University Press, pp. 244–61.

'Tex Massacre' [pseudonym] (2010), 'Reykjavik Whale Watching Massacre', available at: https://web.archive.org/web/20091025123025/http://www.bloody-disgusting.com/ review/1891 (Accessed 2 July 2019).

McRobbie, Angela and Garber, Jenny (2000)[1978], 'Girls and Subcultures', in Angela McRobbie (ed.), *Feminism and Youth Culture*, Basingstoke: Palgrave Macmillan Press, pp. 12–25.

Møller, Birgir Thor (2005), 'In and Out of Reykjavik', in Andrew Nestingen and T. Elkington (eds),*Transnational Cinema in a Global North : Nordic Cinema in Transition*, Detroit: Wayne State University Press, pp. 307–40.

Nordic Fantasy Info (2014), 'Splatter Matter', available at: https://nordicfantasy.wordpress.com/2014/06/29/splatter-matter/(Accessed 2 July 2019).

Schaefer, Eric (1999), *'Bold!, Daring!, Shocking! True!'*: *A History of Exploitation Films, 1919–1959*, Durham and London: Duke University Press.

Selås, Jon (2009), 'Tarmsleng I villmarken', Review, *Verdens Gang*, 7 January.

Shiel, Mark (2003), 'Why Call Them Trash Movies?', *Scope*, https://www.nottingham.ac.uk/scope/documents/2003/may-2003/shiel.pdf (Accessed 4 July 2019).

TV4 (1997), 'Interview with Anders Jacobsson and Göran Lundström', *Nyhets morgon*, 3 May.

Van Hoeij, Boyd (2010), 'Reykjavik Whale Watching Massacre', Review, Variety, 25 February.

8

Nordic Nazisploitation in the digital media environment of the 2000s

On 17 January 2019, the Facebook page for the *Iron Sky* franchise posted a set of pictures depicting a glitzy showbiz event at Tennispalatsi, Finland's largest venue for cinematic grandeur. The images showcase hundreds of people queuing at night to take part in the *Iron Sky Night*, including the premiere of *Iron Sky 2: The Coming Race* (2019). The crowd included celebrities from Finnish media to international cult icons such as Udo Kier, all entertaining a packed audience in front of a massive screen. Such depictions are typical tactics for screenings of major blockbusters, but a clue that something was slightly off here comes from the recurring images of people in Nazi costumes, displaying not so much far-right anger, but sheer camp pleasure at dressing up as Adolf Hitler. Some wear a full SS leather coat as they smile and pose, while others sport gas masks. Some are content with only leather caps, but others don full SS uniforms, smiling while their corporate passes prominently display the word Veikkaus ('lottery' – standing in for the key sponsor of the event the National Lottery of Finland), providing an intriguing contrast with the historical connotations of the uniforms.

What can this bizarre combination of Hollywood-style industry premieres, celebrity events, promotional displays and a range of potentially offensive references to perhaps the darkest period in world history tell us about Nordic exploitation culture? The *Iron Sky* franchise is renowned for two things: (1) its narrative is based on the outlandish idea of Nazis, having fled to the moon in 1945, colonizing contemporary America; (2) it was the first crowdfunded film to be produced on a large budget (7.5 million EUR, a substantial sum for any Nordic production, though only about $500,000 were from crowdfunding). These two areas, however, only tell a part of the story. The key to understanding *Iron Sky*'s complex cultural history comes from its association with fan communities. These associations were fostered by both the franchise's thematic mining of cult iconography and narratives and courting of the fan community generated by the

Figure 8.1 An image from the premiere of *Iron Sky: The Coming Race* (2019), posted on the #IronSky Facebook page, depicting fans dressed up in Nazi paraphernalia. Courtesy of Heikki Sulander / Facebook.

Star Wreck franchise. *Star Wreck* and *Iron Sky* share the same creative team, led by director Timo Vuorensola and producer Samuli Torssonen, with *Star Wreck* consisting of homemade short films spanning from 1992 to 2000. The franchise also led to a feature-length production *Star Wreck: In the Pirkinning* (2005), which is, according to some sources, the most popular film made in Finland in terms of the number of spectators reached as it was not only released for free online but shown on national broadcast television to an audience exceeding one million households. The *Star Wreck* franchise had allowed Vuorensola and Torssonen to consolidate a firm connection with a fan base that could be used for promotional and crowdsourcing activities for their *Iron Sky* venture. These connections were used by the producers to generate a substantial myth around the *Iron Sky* franchise, which included fan sites, teaser trailers, comics, sneak peaks and eventually a crowdfunding platform that allowed *Iron Sky* to claim a position as the first major production to use digital crowdfunding platforms successfully. Crowdsourcing activities, and, especially, the buzz generated by the success of these activities, were instrumental in carving a wider audience market for this small nation product, which makes perfect sense to complement what was, at the time of its release, the most expensive Finnish film to date. The allocation of production support by the FFI to the amount of 800,000 EUR, the largest sum available for domestic productions at the time, was essential in order to source the more significant international venture capital. Here, the reputational (and real) capital from crowdfunding and from the Finnish Film Institute acted in symbiosis to distinguish the production in the global marketplace, allowing it to secure venture capital from Germany and Australia, which made up most of its expansive budget.

The production history of *Iron Sky* provides an example of the challenges and advantages of working in a small nation film culture while tapping into the global mainstream. By drawing on these different registers, as chronicled in Kääpä (2019: 151–9), the production of *Iron Sky* mobilized several resources – a pre-existing loyal audience base, controversial thematic material, flirtations with mainstream popular culture, genre comparisons – but used them in distinctly 'disruptive' ways that promised both technological innovation and popular commercial attractions in a self-referential genre package. *Iron Sky*'s novelty value made it a considerable success both domestically (with over 150,000 tickets sold) and internationally where it generated enough return on investment to justify the production of a sequel. Yet, one area often forgotten in this melange of references and franchising success is the role of exploitative content, specifically the use of the Nazi trope as a popular culture reference point. At stake here are fundamental questions over cultural affiliations and appropriation of history for entertainment. The collision between self-aware contemporary pop culture and the comedic use of the Nazis positions *Iron Sky* as not only a case of popular cinema exploiting historical tragedies but also where it is the fans who are the key stakeholders of cultural and political meaning in integrating this controversial theme into the confines of small nation film culture. The significance of their role concerns their participation not only in the actual production of the films through crowdsourcing activities but also in extending the franchise into cosplay and social media activity. It is these fan activities that provide the key focus for this chapter.

The Nazi on film

Before we zero in on these fan practices and their role in Nordic exploitation film culture, it is necessary to briefly establish the context for the exploitative uses of the Nazi in Nordic cinema. The Nazi has functioned as a pervasive trope in global film culture, taking on the role of an ultimate villain in a wide variety of films, from subversive genre films like *Inglourious Basterds* (2009) to more prestige productions such as *Der Untergang* (*Downfall*, 2004). The Nazi continues to be used as a foe or a more generalized symbol for evil in cinema, particularly in historical films. They are frequently featured in Nordic films from Denmark and Norway, in particular, as these countries were occupied by Nazi forces during the Second World War, resulting in large-scale historical films about the domestic resistance in, respectively, *Flammen & Citronen* (*The Flame and the Citroen*, 2008) and *Max Manus* (*Max Manus: Man of War*, 2008). At the same time, the iconography of the Nazis has pervaded popular culture to such a large extent that historical veracity has all but lost most of its meaning. One only has to consider Steven Spielberg's use of Nazi villains, oscillating between the black and white horrors of *Schindler's List* (1993) to quippy references to comical villains ('I hate those guys,' as stated by Indiana Jones) in *Indiana Jones and the Last Crusade* (1989). Comic stereotypes of Nazis have become increasingly commonplace since at least Mel Brooks' *The Producers* (1967) whereby a safe distance is maintained with the absolute horror of the Holocaust, though historians have been uncomfortable with these depictions including well-meaning films like *Schindler's List* that evade the unrepresentability of the event through spectacle – see various chapters in Loshitzky (1997). Ultimately, the gamut of cinematic Nazis runs from historical veracity to popular culture appropriations.

Outside of these 'respected' uses of Nazi characters and symbolism, a much seedier capitalization on the Nazis has become increasingly prevalent in global film culture. While Nazism and sexuality had been paralleled in respected films from Roberto Rosselini's *Roma città aperta* (*Rome Open City*, 1945) to Sidney Lumet's *The Pawnbroker* (1964), the Nazisploitation genre exploded with *Ilsa: She-Wolf of the SS* (1975). This Canadian production featured a female concentration camp supervisor who would abuse her role and powers to both initiate sex and torture inmates to death. The *Ilsa* franchise resulted in three sequels where the attraction was on sadomasochistic torture scenes (often featuring the frequently naked Ilsa) rather than showcases of hard-core sex or any normative sense of titillation. The huge success of the *Ilsa* franchise led to a whole cycle of Nazi torture films (the 'sadiconazista' genre), often produced in Italy with titles such as *Gestapo's Last Orgy* (1977). While these productions have subsequently been evaluated from a range of perspectives, including more obviously critical feminist views (see Mailender 2011: 175–95), the political focus on genocide and on the Holocaust cannot be ignored. These films, very obviously, play on respectable films like *Il portiere di notte* (*The Night Porter*, 1974) or even *Cabaret* (1972). However, the fact that the focus moves away from psychological exploration, or explicit existential critique of the conflicted role of art, into a scene where *Ilsa* tries to prove females can sustain more pain by having her (naked) minions whip a male and a female to death to see which gender survives longest, testifies to the aspirations of these films as cultural commentary.

The Nazis are used in these films as part of a purely exploitative imaginary, equating them with sexual extremes and the most elemental of vulgarities. As ethically problematic as these depictions are, they are part of the process of transforming historical Nazism into an empty signifier to be used for a wide variety of cinematic purposes. Thus, it is not surprising to find that Nazisploitation has frequently been incorporated into academic literature as the extreme content of these films opens up to interrogation through multiple critical frameworks, as witnessed especially in the edited collection on Nazisploitation by Magilow, Bridges and Lugt (2011) (see also Buttenworth and Abbenhuis 2010). Some of these studies have focused on Nazisploitation films to highlight the extremes of misogyny and sexual depravity (Richardson 2011: 38–55) while others focus on exposing ideological tendencies and preoccupations in historical memory studies (Fiddler and Banwell 2019: 141–54). Some consider them as cultural historical documents that indicate changing mores and standards of decency where the Nazi trope functions as a persistent cinematic trope malleable for a variety of cinematic contexts (Stiglegger 2011: 238–58), while some interpret these disassociated representations of fascism as embodying some of the complex contours between low and high culture (Betz 2013: 495–513).

In addition to the sadiconazista genre, another persistent variation of the cinematic Nazi includes a recent surge in films combining Nazi antagonists and zombies. Films such as *Shock Waves* (1977) and Jean Rollin's *Le lac des morts vivants* (*Zombie Lake*, 1981) feature the reanimated corpses of Nazi soldiers attacking unsuspecting victims as they capitalize on the popularity of the post-*Night of the Living Dead* zombie film, but also avoid any of the explicit political commentary of Romero's hugely influential film. *Shock Waves* provides only incidental references to historical realities and the Nazi theme largely appears as a means to distinguish the lumbering monsters from other similar genre stalwarts and to provide Peter Cushing with a suitably gloomy monologue about experimentations gone wrong in the creation of his Totenkorpf (Death Corps). Rollin's film attempts to situate its monsters in a historical context as its narrative focuses on French villagers who massacred a group of Nazi soldiers during the Second World War, but any allusions to a serious exploration of traumatic histories are dispelled by the Nazi zombies who awaken to terrorize a group of skinny-dipping volleyball players. Here, the connections to historical National Socialism are arguably even flimsier than in the sadoconazista genre as the historical context becomes a generic background reference point – Nazism operates here as a form of shallow history-less postmodernist simulacra, as American philosopher Fredric Jameson (1991) might put it.

Moving closer to the present day – and the adoption of these conventions into Nordic cinema – we have seen productions like the British *Outpost* (2008) reanimate the genre in the wake of the popularity of zombie narratives in international film and television, leading to the production of two, ever-cheapening, sequels. Furthermore, the equation of Second World War settings, Nazi experiments, genre clichés and exploitation strategies have become transmedia stalwarts in video games such as the *Wolfenstein* franchise (1981–2017), in contemporary blockbusters like Marvel's *Captain America* (2011) or the JJ Abrams produced *Overlord* (2018), and even the Swedish short film and YouTube hit *Kung Fury* (2015). Through such modes of incorporation, Nazi thematics and iconography have been institutionalized as part of mainstream film culture (Kozma 2011: 55–72) where the Nazis are transformed into simulacra, as images of history lacking any real depth. As part of these representational tendencies, the image of the Nazis is so far removed from the realities of National Socialism as to become something practically and, especially, perversely attractive, at least in a commercial sense. This history of cinematic Nazisploitation positions the Nazi simulacra as exploitative not so much based on explicit or transgressive content, but more by divesting the Nazis of historicity and repackaging them as entertainment or spectacle without historical depth. Through such mechanisms, these media texts literally exploit history and repurpose it for the particular conditions of their production environments. While these particular tropes have already, then, been frequently used in, for example, Hollywood cinema and European exploitation, their role in the Nordic policy and production context requires further elaboration.

Nordic Nazisploitation: *Dead Snow*

Iron Sky is not the only recent Nordic production to feature Nazis as the 'main attraction' as Tommy Wirkola's Nazi zombie franchise *Død snø* (*Dead Snow*,

2009–2014) can testify. Starting off as a part of the contemporaneously popular cycle of Norwegian slashers, as analysed in Chapter 7, the film provides an update on the Nazi zombie subgenre through its narrative of a group of filmmakers getting slaughtered in the Northern Norwegian mountains by reanimated Nazi soldiers. While its immediate inspiration clearly consists of films like *Shock Waves*, *Dead Snow* uses a range of references to Norwegian cinema and culture to indigenize this content as most of the humour comes from playing with historical references to the Nazi occupation or from slapstick moments derived from the environmental conditions of a snow-bound Northern Norway.

The result has been analysed from a multitude of perspectives as a reflection of the Nazi occupation of Norway during Second World War, that is, as an evocation of unfinished war time business (Moseng and Vibeto 2011: 30–41) or as a depiction of the shame of collaboration where past sins buried in the snowy mountains come back to haunt the present day (Jüngerkes and Wienand 2011: 238–58). While *Dead Snow* continues a long history of Nazi representations in Norwegian cinema (mainly in the context of historical war films), its contextualization with the zombie genre provides a particular indigenous twist that allows the film to capitalize on its uniqueness in both the domestic and international markets. These strategies play with registers of proximity and distance as the close correlation with domestic political and cultural history as well as intimate knowledge of international genre conventions was vital for *Dead Snow* as it was produced independently of state support and had to consequently carve out a market niche to maximize its return on investment. Rhetorically positioning it as both popular cinema ('slasher film with Nazi zombies') and distinct variations of that cinema ('*Norwegian* slasher film with Nazi zombies') has thus been essential for both its domestic and international success.

Intriguingly, potential controversies over the Nazi theme were a concern for the filmmakers: 'In the first one we were worried, especially in the north. We have family who were heavily involved in the war up there. But there has been nothing in Norway, no reactions at all to it, which was surprising. We never heard anything negative – at least not to our face' (Wirkola in Buckley 2014). This attempt to consider the historical context is intriguing as the lack of critical reaction to filmmakers capitalizing on the Nazi occupation, especially in a humorous entertaining way, suggests that the inclusion of Nazis as characters in an irreverent genre film was not seen as a historical political problem by individuals who may still hold those historical connections and memories. With historical distance and popular cultural appropriation, the Nazis seem to have become a generalized villain trope that is often distinct from the actuality of historical context. By disassociating them from historical reality, they become pop culture standards – something we saw with, for example, the humorous glamourization of Nazi props at the premiere of *Iron Sky 2: The Coming Race* in 2019.

Such modes of appropriation are hugely problematic, but they – or more appropriately, their lack of historical context – also reveal many crucial aspects concerning the state of Nordic film culture. *Dead Snow* was a considerable success at the domestic box office with over 100,000 tickets sold, yet its general critical reception was much more mixed and can serve to highlight some of the contradictions between historical verisimilitude and exploitative commercialism. A key concern for the Norwegian critics was not the politicized potential of the Nazis of *Dead Snow* but instead the ways it taps into American genre vernacular. In a positive review highlighting its unique role in Norwegian film culture, the film was seen as 'a pure genre film made with exuberant enthusiasm' (Selås 2009). For others, this relationship was precisely the cause of its problems as some would identify it as the first zombie film from Norway but argued that such categorizations were not sufficient to distinguish it from the competition: 'If you are either a gore fan or have never seen a zombie movie and are unfamiliar with the last 30 years of splatter horror you should see this instead of its many mediocre American relatives. *Dead Snow* is not worse than most of them' (Alver 2009). For critics, the ways that global genre formulas were adapted to the Norwegian context emerged as the main point of concern, as the introduction of specifically Hollywood conventions into the annals of Norwegian cinema was met with a measure of scepticism, echoing the reception of genre films throughout the preceding decades. The Nazi theme received no real attention as a political point, but if it was mentioned, it was overwhelmingly perceived only as a generic trope, and certainly not as a tangible ethical point of concern.

Wirkola's comments reflect these approaches when discussing the choice for the monsters of the film. To him, Nazi zombies are 'double evil' as the connotations of the zombie as an undead monster, and Nazis as the worst of humankind, combine to provide a cinematic evocation of an approximation of 'evil', as shallow monsters with no particular cultural depth (Tommy Wirkola in Buckley 2014). In comparison to the arguably more serious uses of the trope in films like *Shock Waves* or *Zombie Lake*, *Dead Snow* captures a much more tongue-in-cheek approach to its villains. While the former two films do not exactly aspire to historical verisimilitude or a serious treatise of fascist ideologies, *Dead Snow* has more in common with horror comedies than the earlier variations of the subgenre. This is most explicit in the style adopted by the film. Gone are most allusions to generating dread or tension as gore and slapstick violence instead fill their place. While the tone is clearly inspired by *The Evil Dead* franchise – a point of reference that becomes even more obvious in the sequel – the ways the film frames Nazism is not that much different from how these imaginaries have operated in the excessively trashy productions of the sadiconazista cycle. While *Dead Snow* is much more obviously comedic, its contribution to the international cycle of Nazisploitation films participates in the normalization of the Nazi figure into something almost mythical, like vampires or werewolves, creatures from lore and fantasy, designed to emphasize the genre credibility of this Norwegian production. While Jüngerkes and Wienand (2011: 240) have suggested that 'from the perspective of film history, the zombies of *Dead Snow* offer nothing original', we could argue that this lack of history is precisely the point here, as witnessed in the critical reception of the film. By tapping into these proliferating cultural imaginaries, *Dead Snow* uses Nazisploitation as cultural capital designed to connect it with international genre cinema. While this is far removed from any sense of Nazi or right-wing ideology, it is perhaps doubly problematic precisely because of this distance.

Figure 8.2 Screen grab from *Død snø* (*Dead Snow* 2009), featuring its Nazi zombie antagonists pursuing hapless teens down a Norwegian mountain. Courtesy of Miho Film.

If the politically problematic content of the first *Dead Snow* did not feed into its reception, such considerations were even less conspicuous in the production of *Død snø 2* (*Dead Snow 2: Red vs Dead*, 2014). Whereas *Dead Snow* featured incidental comedic Nazi characters, this slapstick perspective dominates the sequel even down to its 'gamified' subtitle. The story continues directly from *Dead Snow* as the last survivor Martin is chased by the lead Nazi Herzog through Northern Norway. In a long list of references to *Evil Dead 2: Dead by Dawn* (1987), *Braindead* (1992) and other horror comedies, Herzog's arm is attached to Martin who struggles to control it but discovers that it can reanimate the dead. He uses his new powers to awaken a group of Russian POWs who take on the Nazis in an extended battle that is replete with references from football hooliganism to *Braveheart* (1995). The rest of the film takes a much broader comedic turn as the cast of characters now involves American zombie hunters who run an internet platform, the Zombie Squad, as well as cameo roles featuring domestic stars such as Kristoffer Joner as a decomposing victim. Herzog also gets more animated as he now strategically commands a Nazi platoon in order to finish a massacre he was ordered to carry out during the Second World War.

The bizarre combination of historical allusions and the film's enthusiastically irreverent lack of historicity is especially prominent with the ultimate concession to commercial franchise building, the jokey pre- and post-credits scene. These consist of short scenes where one of the victims has necrophiliac sex with another zombie, followed by a scene where Herzog's disembodied head comes back to life, in a scene that can only be a reference to *Re-Animator* (1985). These sorts of allusions to postmodernist pop culture and the use of explicit franchising machinations are far from the sadiconazista exploitation cinema of the 1970s, as well as more prestigious productions like *The Night Porter*. While the *Dead Snow* films certainly contain references to historical atrocities and the Nazis are still depicted as monsters, they contribute to a revisionist politics where 'these themes of Nazi symbolism and iconography persist because they are continuously "remediated" for new audiences' (Jüngerkes and Wienand 2011: 215). With these remediations, a safe distance is constructed from the horrors of real history. By referencing pop culture texts from the *Indiana Jones* franchise to computer games like *Wolfenstein*, the *Dead Snow* franchise expands to cult fans and allows the films to secure festival screenings and commercial releases in markets where Nordic films typically struggle. Thus, it is not surprising that while the first production was shunned from receiving production support from the Norwegian Film Institute (NFI), *Dead Snow 2: Red vs Dead* was awarded funds by the NFI for its promotional campaign in 2015.

Instead of working with targeting exploitative or underground registers, the *Dead Snow* films take on a culturally specific strategy that operates as part of a reinvigorated Nordic approach to popular genre film aimed at carving a niche in the international genre markets. Here, elements associated with exploitation cinema, including excessive gore and comic Nazis, allow them to stand out from more serious fare like *Max Manus* and *Kampen om tungtvannet* (*The Heavy Water War*, 2015) featuring Nazis as antagonists. Yet, Nordicness distinguishes the *Dead Snow* franchise from the sadiconazista genre as well as the more generic (and culturally indistinguishable) Nazi zombie DTV product, exemplifying our suggestion that Nordic exploitation tends to attain more specific relevance and spaces of attention when it manages these balancing strategies between proximity and distance carefully.

Comic Nazis: *Iron Sky*

If *Dead Snow* used Nazi simulacra to target both domestic and international audiences well versed with the splatter and zombie film, the *Iron Sky* franchise is much more connected with the Nazis envisioned in blockbuster cinema. The specifics of its production history have been covered elsewhere (Kääpä 2015: 244–59) but the transmedia imagery identified above consolidates the proximity and distance strategies that would appeal to domestic funders and international audiences, especially with the all-important fanboy demographic. As explained earlier, *Star Wreck*'s success was certainly instrumental in *Iron Sky*'s attempts to attract investors and cultivate an ongoing customer base. The quirkiness of the pitch relied exclusively on Nazis (but on the moon!) instead of the nominal narrative of the film, which focuses on an American astronaut's attempt to rehabilitate to society after being captured by said Nazis. The narrative of the film played a minuscule part in the promotion, as, for example, the teaser from 2008 featured spec footage consisting of sprawling shots of the moonbase and a pigeon landing and defecating on an iron eagle (capped off by the tagline: 'In 1945, the Nazis fled to the Moon. In 2012 they are coming back'). While the use of science fiction and cult film tropes generated a fertile basis for a 'fanchise' (as the producers would later term their fan service properties), Nazi iconography was explicitly used to cultivate a cult reputation essential for distinguishing

Figure 8.3 The US release artwork for *Dead Snow: Red vs. Dead* (2014), highlighting the genre references of the film as well as its commercialization of Nazi iconography. Courtesy of Well Go USA Entertainment.

the production from other similar science fiction genre fare featuring alien invasions and exploding buildings as well as to internationalize a production from a distinctly small national film culture.

As with the other Nazisploitation films, the film makes no promise of 'bold, daring, shocking, true' content (to quote the title of Schaefer's groundbreaking work), nor of specific themes that would cause moral panic or media scandals. Instead, the reliance is distinctly on quirkiness, a theme we have already established as a particularly Nordic commercial internationalization strategy. Accordingly, the narrative of the film sees Sarah

Palin take over the US presidency, profiting from a chaotic culture obsessed with social media and celebrities, where the outlandishness of the Nazis does not appear jarring, or even particularly interesting. The often-broad political satire and mobilization of genre tropes from *Independence Day* (1996) to *The Matrix* (1999) makes this anything but a typical exploitation film as it more closely resembles films like *Men In Black* (1997) and *Mars Attacks!* (1996) than those from the B-movie exploitation production company Asylum Pictures, for example. Key parts of the publicity efforts of the franchise focused on connecting with the more respectable registers of the aforementioned Hollywood studio productions as this, being the most expensive film ever made in Finland, was not meant to be sleazy niche exploitation, but true blockbuster cinema. The use of historical realities – Nazism – as humorous commercial signifiers is a key part of this, and indicates that, at least during the several decades it took to develop the franchise, Nazis were not seen as a potentially politically problematic point.

Iron Sky is in a peculiar position as it fits both the parameters of national cinema in terms of its infrastructure and production history, but it is also designed with a very global orientation in mind. Here, the use of Nazi iconography brings with it a credible international theme (the film is noteworthy for not including any particularly Finnish content), but this theme is divorced from the reality of the Nazis as a historical force responsible for unaccountable travesties and horrors. As the film emphasizes visual spectacle of spacefaring Zeppelins and stormtroopers bumbling about a Swastika-shaped moon station, the Nazis of *Iron Sky* are best seen as pop culture Nazis, more at home in the world of Indiana Jones than the homicidal ideologues of the fascistic German far right. Coupled with the satirical tone of the film as well as its expressive visual effects, *Iron Sky* situates its references in a liminal cultural space where connecting it to a lineage of exploitation cinema has much more to do with allusions to mainstream pop culture and visual spectacle without historical depth than anything to do with Finland's problematic historical connections with the Nazis during the Second World War. Yet, as societal discourse evolved into the contemporary 'age of hate' in the 2010s, the Nazi theme would emerge as a key flashpoint in social media discourse around the franchise – a discourse that was essential to establishing its credentials in the first place. It is to these social media discussions we now turn as they illustrate some of the complexities of commercial audience management practices clashing with the real-life historical context of the rise of fascist ideologies.

Figure 8.4 Screen grab from *Iron Sky* (2012), featuring its high concept blockbuster spectacle and Nazi iconography. Courtesy of Blindspot Pictures Oy.

Carving space for neo-Nazisploitation

Although fans provided the initial kickstart for this budding franchise, social media provided the vessel for generating both financial and social capital necessary for sustaining it (see Kääpä 2015: 245–9). Here, the fan sourcing and crowdfunding efforts were integral to generating its international profile and, arguably, in securing the requisite funding for its 7.5 million EUR budget. The ability to generate a convincing package testifying of the venture's commercial viability to its potential investors ensured that fans and the prosumer ethos were an essential part of this production mode from its inception. At the same time, scholars of fan practices and cultures (Jenkins 2013; Hills 2002) remind us that these communities often seek to assert ownership over popular culture franchises. Such practices especially apply to franchises like *Iron Sky* where fan service and a collaborative ethos are part of the business model. Significantly, these practices have not only contributed to its success but also led to an arguable democratization of views on its content that wrests control away from the production team and resulted in a diversity of interpretations of its cultural and political implications. These comments are important for us as they emphasize the ways exploitation content is invariably premised on meeting audience demands, even if these demands sometimes operate in distinctly unpredictable ways.

The online presence of *Iron Sky* on social media platforms like Facebook and Twitter was established in the early days of these platforms (though the *Iron Sky The Movie* page identifies its start date as 1945, as it would). Here, the discussions from 2008 onwards up to the release of the first film in 2012 often exhibited confusion over the film's intentions as fans and commentators derided the project for what they considered its superficially silly premise. Some suggested the project glorifies and celebrates Nazis in its extravagant visual spectacle and adherence to contemporary blockbuster narrative trajectories while others saw the film as more closely aligned with the mockbuster genre, indicating the diversity of reading strategies the film facilitated. To summarize these reactions, some approached the film as a campy mockbuster, whereas others perceived it as a Nazisploitation film. At the same time, other commentators found these extremes frustrating and identified the film as, precisely, critical of these tendencies:

> Who let all the douches in here? It's science fiction and satire. It's supposed to be campy. It's supposed to make folks laugh. Sorry that it is not like every other pre-processed pre-packaged [sic] Hollywood piece of drek out there. The fact that this is a science fiction feature film from Nor-fucking-way, means it deserves some huge props.... They're not glorifying the Nazis for fuck's sake. They're the hapless villains in this film. The Nazis are the primary butt of the film's jokes. ('Malcolm Shein')

Such interpretations of the film highlight its multiple textual applications as well as the ways the producers' tactics of emphasizing multiple registers – from the exploitative Nazi simulacra to commercial genre conventions – works in the film's favour by allowing it to appeal to a variety of audiences. The reference to 'Nor-fucking-way' is also an illustrative example of the exchangeability between the Nordic countries, indicating that the film was perceived, in part, as something unique but also culturally locatable, even while audiences were not excessively concerned with its particularly cultural or industrial origins. Simultaneously, the producers did not forget that controversy generates publicity as they made a splash at Comic Con 2012 in San Francisco accompanied by a Babe Army of over a dozen young women semi-clad in 'fräulein' costumes and *Iron Sky* armbands. These sorts of frivolous publicity tactics do not veer far from the gimmickry of revered exploitation auteurs such as William Castle, but, simultaneously, they indicate that the producers were unconcerned with any authentic historical connotations of Nazi or far-right ideologies. Even after the security at Cannes 2012 shut down the Babe Army parade, these events were used on the franchise's social media accounts to drum up further publicity. It is clear that the connotations of the Holocaust or of other historical atrocities were never fully considered, or if they were, a safe historical veneer seems to have been established between them and the film. These notions were frequently reflected in fan discourse:

> You must remember that this is a movie. It is supposed to be enjoyable to watch. There is really no reason to be irritated by it. I remember what it was really like in the 1940's [sic]. This movie does not really explain all of the atrocities that the Nazi's committed. Maybe I feel this way because I haven't seen the movie yet. When I see it, I hope to have a better idea about what it was all about. ('Chas Palleschi')

The identification of this as a 'movie', while acknowledging the complex play of signifiers present in the film, continues a more rational assessment of the film beyond the political applications to which it was subjected by some users. At the same time, the fact that the film generates discussion even amongst those who have not seen it indicates the franchise's position as an open text enabling a diversity of readings and applications. This sort of openness provides it with the necessary cult and popular appeal even as the film makes use of the particularities of the Nordic film financing policy and opportunities to accumulate international capital by managing the more extreme responses fans may have had in relation to its themes.

While there are various modes of fan appropriation present in these early discussions, dialogue between fans and producers on Iron Sky the Film continued to operate very much in web 2.0 mode (see Gauntlett, for more on distinctions between web 2.0 and 3.0) with occasional posts by the moderators and limited interaction. This allowed the moderators to ensure that every reference to Nazism would be consistently framed in a humorous or genre referential manner, even when this concerns hawking Nazi uniforms or gas masks through the franchise shop. In comparison, the @Ironsky franchise page works along a much more pronounced 3.0 principle with the discussion focusing on interaction and a personal touch to discussion management. Accordingly, social media moderators engage in discussion with the fans and, in addition, the page uses a first name basis for the relevant creatives behind the project (Timo, Petri, etc.) to emphasize a personalized approach to fan management and audience cultivation. Simultaneously, the moderators focus attention on the emergent ways that exploitation film strategies must adapt to the demands of the network/information society of the twenty-first century. While many of the same old tactics apply here – identifying and amplifying aspects of audience preferences to cater directly to them and using a range of registers from both commercial and cult reference bases – an expectation of reciprocal content creation (something prioritized by the franchise from its inception) continues to emphasize the centrality of long-term fan cultivation, even as it provides obvious commercial and artistic opportunities for the creatives behind the project. Through such strategies, the notion of the long tail (Anderson 2009), of cultivating a variety of niche audiences to sustain a long-term and committed audience base, takes on additional connotations for *Iron Sky* as it aspired to consolidate itself as a hybrid franchise with a loyal cult fan base (cultivated especially via transmedia narratives in comic book and game form). It provides a striking challenge to Hjort and Petrie's suggestion that small nation films tend to be shot on location, with lower budgets, and drawing on national literary and topographical tropes (Hjort and Petrie 2007: 78–9). Instead, *Iron Sky* testifies to some of the advantages of using these infrastructures and cultural constellations to produce films that are based on highly flexible and creative work patterns, ones that challenge and, in many ways, exploit precisely these infrastructures.

Social media and *Dead Snow*

As explicit and in-tune management of a diversity of demographics had become essential for the *Iron Sky* franchise, the *Dead Snow* franchise attempted to use similar social media strategies for enticing fans. While nowhere near the scale of the *Iron Sky* franchise's fan service attempts, *Dead Snow*'s producers maintained a presence on Facebook and YouTube. These pages were used to post commentary on festival successes and independent screenings as well as other publicity opportunities. Similar political dynamics as *Iron Sky* were at play here, using humorous perspectives on pop culture Nazis: for example, the tagline of the first film – 'Ein, Zwei, Die!' – held a considerable presence in these materials as did the second's 'Heil Five'. Alternatively, it was referred to as the 'sequel you did Nazi coming'. Buoyed by the success of *Iron Sky* with crowdfunding, an Indiegogo fundraiser with a goal of 100,000 EUR was established for *Dead Snow 2* with the tagline: 'you could very well end up getting your girlfriend a birthday greeting from a bunch of Nazi zombies.' Despite these elaborate plans, on 7 January 2015 the campaign announced that it was refunding all fan donations.

The managers of the crowd campaign revealed that they had found the task overwhelming and had to cancel a substantial part of the promised events and bonuses (Indiegogo 2014).

The *Dead Snow* Facebook page was fully active only during 2015, the year of the release of *Dead Snow 2*, and has not had any significant updates since then. This brief focus on its social media profile, as well as the general failure in its management, shows that the project was focused on fans in a very different way from the *Iron Sky* franchise. Both sought to capitalize on the cult reputation of Nazi pop culture, but fan service is a two-way street, much more so than in previous examples of exploitation cinema covered in this study. While the large majority of Nordic exploitation productions had not used fan communities to any substantial extent, digital network cultures necessitate a clearer correlation between producers and audiences, especially when dealing with these meta-exploitative productions with distinctly identifiable fan demographics. Thus, the failure of the *Dead Snow* campaign demonstrates that these exploitation producers were not fully conversant with the requirements and obligations of this new stage in audience development. The focus, as the producers of *Dead Snow* were quick to state, was on carrying out the production, so insufficient attention was paid to these adjacent areas. While the use of tongue-in-cheek approaches to Nazi culture travelled over from *Iron Sky*, the *Dead Snow* pages reveal the limitations of designing clever campaigns aimed at cultivating cult loyalty – the investment in social media management must be sustainable in its human resources as well as in its approach to creativity.

Balancing ideologies

Returning to *Iron Sky*, the significance of audience engagement emerges as a key metric to measure success, especially in comparison to *Dead Snow*'s mismanaged campaign. In comparison to this failure, *Iron Sky*'s fan management dynamics can be illustrated, for example through the activities conducted at the franchise's merchandise store The Reich Stuff, which emphasizes the need to directly respond to fan demand, but also balance aspects of exploitation culture with political concerns. The store is accompanied by glamorous visual design and allows the purchase of model figures of the Moon Troopers (effectively SS stormtroopers but with space masks) and accessories such as t-shirts with colourful illustrations reminiscent of propaganda posters from the 1930s and the 1940s.

These activities outline a novel development for Nordic media culture, namely an understanding of how franchising is an essential part of the film industry's operations to generate audience interest, but also its potential as a means to generate auxiliary markets. While strategies such as novelizations and other merchandise have been a rarity in Nordic film culture (Markus Selin's path-breaking efforts with *Arctic Heat* in 1985 stand tall as a key example of such activities), this level of integrating an auxiliary commercial sensibility to *Iron Sky*'s franchising efforts provides an additional angle on its exploitative connotations. The comic book aesthetics pervading much of the franchise's promotional efforts are yet another example of distanciation devices separating it from real history (as evidenced by the publication of the prequel to the film in comic book format), but this pop culture appropriation goes even further in fan discussion. For example, some fans would clamour for costumes of the Reich villains and express dissatisfaction that they were not available. Fan service was instead conducted at conventions attended by the Moon Troopers, but once more, these appearances were rarely considered politically problematic by fans (in comparison to reactions at major exhibitions like Cannes or Comic Con) as the Facebook posts for these appearances generated only one comment out of nineteen to suggest that these promotional techniques were 'tasteless' (#IronSky).

Following the financial and measured critical success of the first film, the production crew focused on establishing the seeds for a franchise that would expand beyond the Nazi gimmickry of the first film. The sequel *Iron Sky: The Coming Race* shifted the scope of the franchise by focusing on The Vril, a race of lizard people. The gallery of villains featured 'celebrities' from the pope to Margaret Thatcher, from Steve Jobs to Palin and, finally, Hitler riding a dinosaur at the centre of hollow Earth. The expansion of the villain gallery is a typical strategy for any budding franchise, but the ideological and political connotations of the villains as well as the use of comic performers like Tom Green and the Dudesons indicates a continuing irreverence to depicting the historical veracity of the real-life figures the film features. Of course, historical veracity has never been the intention of the producers of the franchise, but the wide scope of references from the Nazis to a manipulative Mark Zuckerberg, from right-wing ideologists like Thatcher to the Apple cult and Steve Jobs, showcases the mechanics established by the first film's representation of the Nazis in a clearly subversive and parodic, yet also sufficiently commercially exploitative, frame.

As we saw with some of the comments on the potentially exploitative connotations of the first film, fans continued to view the potential political flashpoints of the franchise as playful simulacra. Irreverence, a productive way to describe the relationship between audiences and exploitation film culture, is at work in comments such as, 'Can there be anything cooler than Nazis who ride dinosaurs?' ('Jere Stenius'), or 'It's like candy for children on cocaine' ('Malcolm Fritzche'). Clearly, the fascistic connotations of the Nazis had little bearing on these discussions. At the same time, the franchise merchandising expanded outside of only catering to fanboys with products like the Iron Sky Overkill Energy Drink, accompanied by the tagline 'Taste the Blitzkrieg'. The ability of the franchise to monetize every aspect of the production, already present in the crowdfunding campaign, was used to generate a sense of intimate contact with fans allowing them to buy the costumes for the stormtroopers for 2,200 EUR at an auction or including amongst the crowdfunding perks a chance to be eaten by a dinosaur on film.

This sense of intimacy and connectedness is a vital part of any fan service activity, but simultaneously, the franchise's close connections with film financing and distribution infrastructure in its native Finland enabled it to be more than a fan phenomenon catering for a niche connoisseur. For example, 'The Iron Sky Evening' on 10 January 2015 on the domestic YLE 2 channel included the premiere of the director's cut of the first film as well as a broadcast of the making of documentary for the film with the tagline 'Moon Nazis take over YLE'. Thus, the franchise was clearly operating on registers that designate its hybrid role as a genre exploitationer and a novel part of national film culture precisely due to its positioning as daring but commercial national cinema and, specifically, as a film with exploitation connotations that meet international standards. Here, Nazi iconography was perceived as a sufficiently harmless means to distinguish the film from, predominantly, much of the contemporary domestic film productions, but also from similar imported blockbusters relying on computer-generated graphics (CGI) spectacle, now with the enthusiastic stamp of domestic technological and professional know-how qualifying it as an entirely different type of blockbuster.

Ideology strikes back

Throughout the early years of the *Iron Sky* franchise, political connotations were relegated to some of the more extreme margins of the franchise's Facebook page. Occasional comments took the discussion back to real-world politics, such as one case focusing on problems with being able to purchase or wear the franchise shirts in Australia where Nazi iconography is effectively banned from unhistorical displays in public. But for the most part, the discussions focused on the narrative qualities of the first film with some of the fans expressing discontent with its silliness, whereas others found precisely these qualities appealing. At the same time, the series was hit with a lawsuit by one of the VFX animators on the project challenging its intellectual property ownership, and while the case was ultimately decided in favour of Kaukomaa and Vuorensola, attending to the issue contributed to other ongoing problems with financing and finishing the VFX on *Iron Sky: The Coming Race*. This led to a substantial delay to the film's schedule, which, as ever with the always-on expectations of networked media, resulted in a fan backlash. Whereas discussion had been largely positive when the film was still intended for release in 2017, this transformed from anticipatory rhetoric to much more critical trollish behaviour with some, especially, questioning the integrity of the producers. The lawsuit was eventually dismissed by Finnish courts, but as the date of the release had to be pushed back by more than a year, the fan outrage piled on.

These frustrations also filtered into political discussions. As Trump's presidency was taking hold in 2017, the political discussion around the franchise intensified, especially as much of the first film had focused on the then-outlandish prospect of a Palin presidency. The equation of the Nazis with conservative US politics had been the focus in some of the earlier social media discussion, but as the second film effectively targeted all the hallmarks of American conservatism, problems in partisan political debate escalated. A critical focus on the Republican leadership was only one angle in the film as other controversies erupted with a gun toting villainous Jesus featuring heavily in the early promotional materials resulting in some fans unfriending the page as a consequence. Other notable instances included actor Kari Ketonen playing a dancing Putin, which received a high level of attention on Russian television news. Several comments elaborated on the film's politics with some suggesting that '*Iron Sky* has a political and social agenda to attack and satirize the conservative right and all of their institutions, so you're either on board with that, or you move along' ('Steve Boutchyard'). Similarly, a post about equal marriage by the page moderators was met with divisive opinions as several commentators reacted negatively to what they perceived to be a liberal agenda while others supported the moderators: 'Revelation: the makers of this movie are not Nazis or right wingers' ('Jari Kääpä'). This was the approach taken by several commentators with some suggesting: 'Love people complaining about it being political as if they completely missed the obvious subtext of the first one' ('James Costello'). At the same time, some explicitly addressed the Nazi side of the story: 'I expect fans of *Iron Sky* to be able to laugh with Nazis' ('Jorg Willemens'). All of these instances work to highlight the complex cultural politics of exploitation cinema where diverse audiences place individual texts in a range of registers. Here, some are outraged by these attacks on established values and more, whereas others explicitly take much pleasure in precisely this outrage.

While most of the official posts were based on humorous perspectives ('Let's make Iron Sky The Coming Race the date movie of the century, since nothing says "Ich Liebe Dich" like Adolf riding on a T-Rex, right?' #IronSky 2017), political developments soon intervened. With Trump's inauguration and events like the Charlottesville demonstrations, humorous caricatures of Nazis have undoubtedly lost some of their entertainment appeal. These events led to an intensification of fan debate on the franchise's Facebook page. Some of the users started to explicitly reference the political and ideological implications of the presidential politics of Palin in the first film with comments such as 'Sorry, the Gropenfuhrer just beat you to it at today's presidential inauguration' ('Emanuele Gelsi'). Predictably, the debate focused on some commentators positioning the 'non-moon-based-Nazis marching on the street' ('Kit Grant') as a problem for the film even as others would compare the fictional Nazis to the anti-fascists ('Barter Kowalik'). The fictional text was thus appropriated for a wide range of politicized perspectives, testifying to exploitative content acting as a locus point for diverse political agendas. Some even took these approaches to an extreme end by suggesting 'People who are not US citizens should not comment on other countries. Worry about your own countries' ('Scott Thompson'). In response to some of these comments, the page moderators released a trailer featuring a Donald Trump caricature that, in an immature Trumpian manner, gets upset when he finds out that he did not make the cut for *Iron Sky 2*, which includes fellow 'crazy' colleagues such as Margaret Thatcher, Vladimir Putin and Adolf Hitler. The trailer ends with a banner that reads, 'Guaranteed Trump Free Product'.

The franchise's use of Nazi iconography thus resonated with a wide variety of political perspectives, instigating considerable moral outrage as well as general enthusiasm over these transgressive qualities. They even led to major newspapers like *The Guardian* to comment on the franchise through an explicitly politicized framework: 'That there exists a movie where Nazis make a lunge at power in 2018 is creepy enough. But its determined preposterousness gels all too well with the utter senselessness of the resurgence of Nazism in America' (Bramesco 2018). Thus, what may have started with popular culture Nazis in a harmless and explicitly commercial genre spoof had now become incorporated into much more pervasive and grounded political discourses. Such attention is vital for exploitation cinema as it provides these films with purpose and free publicity, which, obviously, works in favour of a franchise like *Iron Sky*. At the same time, the implications and consequences of a building moral panic and implicit censorship have increased in the contemporary volatile atmosphere where social media echo chambers sharply distinguish opinions and politics are conducted on platforms where, for example, accusations of being a snowflake can be bandied about by both sides of the political spectrum. In such a media environment, controversy can take on distinctly negative shades as it influences the commercial imperatives of a franchise, especially one as reliant on catering to both wide audiences and specialist interests as *Iron Sky*.

Conclusion: The fanchise

Iron Sky dealt with Nazi themes in such an unusually carefree way that German audiences had not considered this as a mainstream 'local' film. But when the Nazi theme is pushed to the back, as a sort of scenery of evil, it may turn into a problematic flirtation with a difficult topic. 'Hitler' is now only one joke amongst 'Apple cultists' and Sarah Palin. Humour has a problem if it is conducted on an extreme theme, as one has to be very skilled as well as rude enough, or otherwise it falls flat. Nazis and Apple are real things, but they have certain differences. (Kinnunen 2019)

In discussing *Iron Sky 2: The Coming Race*'s premiere, Finnish film critic and influential cultural commentator Kalle Kinnunen summarizes the problematic connotations of *Iron Sky*'s simulacra Nazis. The fact that *Iron Sky* was shot in Germany with local actors and a substantial domestic financial component indicates that its political slant was not considered problematic in a country where displays of Nazi insignia in public space are strictly prohibited. Similarly, while these associations generated some discussion in their Nordic production contexts, any politicized use of Nazi ideology had been clearly diluted by decades of commercial production capitalizing on National Socialist iconography transformed into pop culture simulacra. While most of *Iron*

Sky's success with crowdsourcing was used as a factor justifying its domestic cultural subsidies, the film's thematic focus was conducted in a framework most obviously associated with at best explicitly commercial genre cinema, or, more problematically, with a range of thematic content associated with the B-movie or even some of the most notorious extremes of exploitation cinema. These references are very much part of the business model for both *Dead Snow* and *Iron Sky*, which may be Nordic in their historical connotations (*Dead Snow* and occupation; *Iron Sky* and Finnish collaboration), but ultimately work as meta-productions emphasizing the Nazi as an empty caricature, as a depthless signifier of imported pop culture instead of a real historical referent. Yet, the idea of featuring Nazis as protagonists in an irreverent comedy was not met with any real sense of controversy as the focus, instead, was on a disassociated sense of popular culture where the franchise content, specifically to do with the commercialized use of Nazi iconography, was not read as politically sensitive material but more as part of self-aware popular culture.

The complex role of Nazi iconography in these films operates at a liminal distance from both mainstream and exploitation cinema. They are both transgressive and commercial, adapting to both in ways that do not commit wholesale to either of these registers but, instead, traverse a fine balance between them. If in the 1980s and the 1990s copying genre formulas consolidated exploitation as a reflection of the marginal cultural status of such 'shamelessly' commercial productions, the 2000s and participatory digital culture fundamentally transformed these circumstances to a situation where commercialism and internationalism were now seen as innovative disruptions. Chapter 9 will focus on these transformations in more detail, especially as the argument that *Dead Snow* and *Iron Sky* do not, in fact, offer much to distinguish themselves thematically from exploitation films like *Moonlight Sonata* or *The Ninja Mission* holds a certain truth about it.

While online platforms were essential in cultivating the fanbase of these franchises and allowing them to reach much wider audiences than those available domestically, simulacra Nazis, as we have suggested, were essential in capturing sufficient wide-scale media attention and fan devotion to both franchises. Yet, these connotations, as simultaneously transgressive and mainstream fodder (effectively the kind of material on which fanboy franchises thrive), would prove problematic as the political circumstances transformed. Nazi signifiers took on different connotations as the activities of right-wing fascists making use of the very Nazi symbols emphasized in both the marketing and fan service activities of both franchises hit global headlines, and eugenics and racial profiling rhetoric became reintegrated into social and political discussion. If Nazis had been part of popular entertainment culture, now voracious questions about the veracity and moral connotations of a careless approach to historicity started to appear.

Yet, at the same time, dissatisfaction at what fans perceived to be mismanagement of crowdsourcing and fan service activities escalated this sort of critique. The *Iron Sky* platform, in particular, provides an intriguing flashpoint for an updated view of the speed and intensity of exploitation culture in the digital age. Here, we see how material previously considered transgressive is mobilized to establish commercial franchises and simultaneously cater for audiences that would have been niche demographics, but which now connote long-tail consumer reserves. Still, this exploitation crowd is fickle with a short attention span, which in the past had not been a major concern for exploitation producers seeking to make a quick buck. Nevertheless, with the unusual combination of self-reflexive criticism of popular culture and high stakes production value, the *Iron Sky* franchise, in particular, testifies to the challenges faced by the business models of contemporary exploitation producers.

Both franchises have nevertheless survived to fight another day. *Dead Snow 2* was hugely successful internationally and received financial support from the NFI. The *Iron Sky* franchise is currently part of an expansive strategy called The Iron Sky Universe, partially owned by shareholders and fans, including a third instalment *Iron Sky: The Ark*, filmed completely in China and financed by Chinese capital. Other plans include a television show in development and enhancing the merchandising 'universe' of the franchise. This is part of 'The Fanchise' strategy aimed at sustaining fan participation in all aspects of the production, from elaborate modes of narrative input to enhancing their role in promotional efforts, while also capitalizing on this very same financial and creative input. Such developments indicate that the franchise is largely divorced from more conventional definitions of exploitation film operating on the basis of cheap production costs and loud publicity. While sharing some of these principles, in the *Iron Sky* franchise, the intense level of capital investment and co-production incentives play out at a huge scale that have the potential to establish new directions for Nordic film cultures.

To emphasize these aspirations, the *Iron Sky* Facebook page updated on 27 November 2018 by announcing the VIP premiere of *The Coming Race*. Accompanying the announcement was a short film featuring crudely animated caricatures of Vuorensola and Kaukomaa explaining the availability of tickets to the premiere. The animations use impressions of the soon-to-be world premiere outside Tennispalatsi, the premium theatre complex in Helsinki, and feature an intricately animated CGI dinosaur stomping on the red carpet. The connotations of such material establish a tone far from a marginal underground film. Instead, they signify the extent to which the producers, at the very least, considered the franchise's significance to be about commercial appeal and substantial financial gains in both Finland and internationally. Further compounding this impression, the video is clearly aimed at international markets as it is in English and uses visual language more akin to *South Park* (1997–) than the traditional aesthetics of lo-fi exploitation cinema. While these incentives are very obviously a part of ensuring the franchise operates well beyond its national confines, they also lead to an identity crisis where it is challenging to consider the film as a 'Finnish production' due to its international cast and thematic range – a notion that still featured heavily in much of its domestic promotional material. Accordingly, by the time of announcement of the third instalment, *Iron Sky: The Ark*, to be set exclusively in China, the series had ventured far from its roots as a Nordic Nazisploitation picture.

While these expansive strategies continue to sustain the franchise, there is, inevitably, a dark underlining to these practices. While strategies to monetize Nazis provides a unique slant on exploitation in the sense that historical horrors, in comparison to the truly transgressive qualities of the sadiconazista genre, have taken on almost mainstream commercial qualities, it is necessary to return back to concerns over the rootlessness of the reference scale of *Iron Sky: The Coming Race*, something that many critics vocalized upon the domestic release of the film in February 2019. The opening weekend in Finland delivered disastrous news for the producers as the film only managed to attract 15,040 customers, a substantial decrease from the first film's 76,027 tickets sold during its opening weekend in 2012. Although the main hope rests on its financial performance at the international markets, the film was not accepted to screen at Berlinale 2019 either. This is significant as the first film made a huge splash at this festival, leading it to generate 474,623 ticket sales at the German box office, eventually selling 934,361 tickets in the EU (Lumiere 2019). While the sequel has received a theatrical release in the UK, this turned out to be a crowdfunded screening series through Our Screen, a company providing services to enable fans to organize their own cult film screenings. At the time of writing, only a screening at London's Piccadilly Square Vue cinema has been confirmed with 103 tickets sold. The rest of the ten screenings remain unconfirmed. This may be better than the theatrical distribution fiasco for the first film, where the production company had sold rights for a full-scale theatrical release, but the distribution company backed out and only did screenings for one day. Yet, for a film with a budget of 18.5 million EUR, small-scale fan screenings must not be entirely satisfactory. Although they are, intriguingly, more appropriate for the exploitation roots of the franchise, they do not quite mesh with the transformations of this franchise into a 'fanchise'.

The travails encountered by the sequel emphasize the fragility of Nordic exploitation, especially as the early success of the franchise was based on playing with expectations and registers in a way that never sided with political affiliations or conventional notions of cultural taste. Yet, as we saw with the underperformance of the much-hyped Tarantino–Rodriguez collaboration *Grindhouse* (2007), using exploitation as a mainstream strategy is precarious as disruptions to the lifecycle of film cultures can be productive and monetizable, but they can also end up as too jarring or too externalized to work productively alongside the rules of the game. Although this uncertainty and expedient capitalization on passing trends provides a precise encapsulation of the modus operandi of traditional exploitation film, the ongoing disruptive fluctuations of the digital media environment – the very essence, which makes it viable for budding filmmakers like Vuorensola – makes it frustratingly traditional and unyielding as those experienced by a Visa Mäkinen pushing the boundaries of early 1980s Finnish film culture or of a Mats Helge Olsson capitalizing on video technology and the cultivation of audience knowledge about genre films. If we can gather anything from these successes and failures, it has to be the notion that boundaries between exploiting exploitative and respectable registers (especially when pitching this combination to the mainstream) continues to be a seismic fracture point defining Nordsploitation.

References

Alver Eirik (2009), 'Blodpudding pa vidda', *Dagbladet*, 9 January 2009.
Anderson, Chris (2009), *The Long Tail*, New York: Hachette Books.
Betz, Mark (2013), 'High and Low and in Between', *Screen*, 54 (4), 495–513.
Bramesco, Charles (2018), 'Moon Nazis and Sex in Space', *The Guardian*, 3 January 2018.
Buckley, Heather (2014), 'Tommy Wirkola Talks Dead Snow 2', available at: https://www.dreadcentral.com/news/73625/exclusive-tommy-wirkola-talks-dead-snow-2-red-vs-dead/ (Accessed 3 July 2019).

Buttsworth, Sara and Maartje Abbenhuis (eds) (2010), *Monsters in the Mirror: Representations of Nazism in Post-War Popular Culture*, Westport: Greenwood Publishing Group.

Fiddler, Michael and Stacy Banwell (2019), 'Forget All Your Taboos: Transgressive Memory and Nazisploitation', *Studies in European Cinema*, 16 (2), 141–54.

Gauntlett, David (2013), 'Foreword', in Simon Lindgren, *New Noise: A Cultural Sociology of Digital Disruption*, New York: Peter Lang.

Jenkins, Henry (2013), *Textual Poachers: Television Fans and Participatory Culture*, New York: SAGE.

Hills, Matt (2002), *Fan Cultures*, New York: Routledge.

Indiegogo (2014), 'Dead Snow 2', available at: https://www.indiegogo.com/projects/dead-snow-red-vs-dead-aka-dead-snow-2#/ (Accessed 3 July 2019).

Jameson, Fredric (1991), *Postmodernism: Or, the Cultural Logic of Late Capitalism*, Durham: Duke University Press.

Jüngerkes, Sven and Christine Wienand (2011), 'A Past That Refuses to Die: Nazi Zombie Film and the Legacy of Occupation', in Daniel H. Magilow, Elizabeth Bridges and Kristin T. Vander Lugt (eds), *Nazisploitation: The Nazi Image in Lowbrow Cinema and Culture*, New York: Bloomsbury, pp. 238–58.

Kääpä, Pietari (2015), 'A Culture of Reciprocity – Producing Genre Film in the Nordic Region', in Tommy Gustafsson and Pietari Kääpä (eds), *Nordic Genre Film*, Edinburgh: Edinburgh University Press, pp. 244–59.

Kääpä, Pietari (2019), 'From Nordic Gloom to Nordic Cool: Genre as an Industrial Strategy', in Ciara Barrett and Silvia Dibeltulo (eds), *Genres in Transition*, London: Routledge, pp. 151–64.

Kinnunen, Kalle (2019), 'Iron Sky: The Coming Race – tupla vai kuitti?', *Suomen kuvalehti*, 14 January 2019, available at: https://suomenkuvalehti.fi/kuvien-takaa/iron-sky-the-coming-race-tupla-vai-kuitti/ (Accessed 3 July 2019).

Kozma, Alicia (2011), 'Ilsa and Elsa: Nazisploitation, Mainstream Film, and Cinematic Transference', in Daniel H. Magilow, Elizabeth Bridges and Kristin T. Vander Lugt (eds), *Nazisploitation: The Nazi Image in Low-brow Cinema and Culture*, New York: Bloomsbury, pp. 55–72.

Loshitzky, Yosefa (ed.) (1997), *Spielberg's Holocaust: Critical Perspectives on Schindler's List*, Bloomington: Indiana University Press.

Lumiere (2019), 'Iron Sky', http://lumiere.obs.coe.int/web/search/index.php (Accessed 24 June 2019).

Magilow, Daniel H. Elizabeth Bridges and Kristin T. Vander Lugt (eds) (2011), *Nazisploitation: The Nazi Image in Low-brow Cinema and Culture*, New York: Bloomsbury

Mailender, Elissa (2011), 'Meshes of Power: The Concentration Camp as Pulp or Art House in Liliana Cavani's The Night Porter', in Daniel H. Magilow, Elizabeth Bridges and Kristin T. Vander Lugt (eds), *Nazisploitation: The Nazi Image in Low-Brow Cinema and Culture*, New York: Bloomsbury, pp. 175–95.

Moseng, Jo Sondre and Håvard Vibeto (2011) 'Hunting High and Low: Notes on Nazi Zombies, Francophiles and National Cinemas'", *Film International*, 9 (2), 30–41.

Richardson, Michael (2011), 'Sexual Deviance and the Naked Body in Cinematic Representations of Nazis', in Daniel H. Magilow, Elizabeth Bridges, and Kristin T. Vander Lugt (eds), *Nazisploitation: The Nazi Image in Low-Brow Cinema and Culture*, New York: Bloomsbury, pp. 38–55.

Selås, Jon (2009), 'Tarmsleng I Villmarken', Review, *Verdens Gang*, 7 January 2009.

Stiglegger, Marcus (2011), 'Origins, Histories, and Genealogies: Cinema Beyond Good and Evil? Nazi Exploitation in the Cinema of the 1970s and Its Heritage', in Daniel H. Magilow, Elizabeth Bridges and Kristin T. Vander Lugt (eds), *Nazisploitation: The Nazi Image in Low-brow Cinema and Culture*, New York: Bloomsbury, pp. 21–37.

9

Kung Fu cops and killer bunnies

Proximity and distance strategies in Nordic exploitation film, 2010–19

Captured in a striking pastiche of vibrant colours and digitally composited CGI landscapes, a caricature of a 1980s yuppie yells into his massive top-of-the-line Nokia phone as he walks down a beachfront in an idiosyncratic Miami landscape. Suddenly, he is shot in the head by an unseen assailant who reveals himself to be Adolf Hitler. The furious Nazi leader appears, in full uniform, in what must be for him an unfamiliar landscape as he starts to shoot up a whole police department, improbably, through the phone receiver. The attack is stopped by a cop in a leather jacket and red bandanna – he is Kung Fury, the greatest cop in the world. Fury was once simultaneously hit by lightning and bitten by a cobra, which made him ascertain the powers of the Chosen One. It turns out that Hitler also masters Kung Fu powers, as he was the world's greatest martial artist in the 1940s, going by the title of Kung Führer. The two martial arts masters are set on a collision course, combining ninjas, dinosaurs, time travel and synth pop, set against a backdrop littered with references to 1980s action films and Nordic myths (including a trip back in time to meet Thor).

This outlandish cocktail of film references is *Kung Fury*, a 2015 short film directed by the Swede David Sandberg, who moved from directing music videos and commercials to producing his dream project through Kickstarter funding. The production of the short film was launched on the basis of a short trailer which showcased the scope of the film and its referential palette. After the trailer went viral on YouTube, the Kickstarter goal was set at 200,000 USD. The final production received over 600,000 USD in fan donations, which allowed the project to commence production. It also received official backing from the Swedish Film Institute to the tune of 1.8 million SEK, indicating another instance of fan culture consolidating into legitimate film culture, much as was

Figure 9.1 Screen grab from the trailer for *Kung Fury* (2015), emphasizing its retrosploitation aesthetics and featuring Hitler as Kung Fuhrer in yet another simulacrum Nazi pastiche. Courtesy of Laser Unicorns.

the case with *Iron Sky* (2012). The production was released free online, but after close to thirty-three million hits on YouTube, it has been picked up by Netflix, Apple and other large streaming conglomerates, leading to Sandberg signing a production deal on a full-length feature film starring Arnold Schwarzenegger and Michael Fassbender.

The production and distribution history of *Kung Fury* provides a dynamic case of capitalizing on new technological innovations and shifts in film politics. Much like *Iron Sky*, *Kung Fury* was an attempt to engage new technological forms and distribution platforms with genre production functioning as the ideal referent base to initially entice fan audiences and use them to broaden out to more mainstream production and distribution environments. Helen Ahlsson, Film Commissioner at the Swedish Film Institute, summarizes these dynamics well:

> Not only did the film prove that a thirty minute film can become a smash hit on YouTube, it also showed that festivals do take on broad action comedies, as long as they are cleverly written and artistically challenging; finally it demonstrated that the old fashion distribution windows don't always make sense. (Nordic Film and Television Fund 2015)

Yet, while technological and infrastructural transformations, certainly, provide one level of significance here, the changing dynamics of cultural proximity and distance are just as, if not more, significant. These dynamics rely on distance from the domestic norms, largely accumulated on the basis of *Kung Fury*'s extensive international genre references. In addition, it distances itself from these very same international genre norms by drawing on its small nation film culture context by highlighting the fact that these are not large budget Hollywood creations, but independent productions that rely on the myth of creative authorship conducted with limited resources. Simultaneously, a sense of proximity emerges in the way *Kung Fury* selectively affiliates its reference base with these very same domestic and international norms. The short film would have made less impact, arguably, if it had only been based on digital prowess showcasing an ability to mimic Hollywood cinema. But by combining references from as far afield as Sylvester Stallone's *Cobra* (1986) to Nordic mythological figures, the production was able to capitalize on these dynamics in a way that caters to an irreverent sense of cultural relevance that is the lifeblood of fan and cult cinema production. By acting simultaneously as a distinctly Swedish film and as a self-referential transnational genre production, *Kung Fury* managed to break through infrastructural challenges and perceptions over appropriate 'national cinema' in a small national context.

While *Kung Fury* was able to disrupt established patterns coordinating the limits of the possible in these small film industries, its range of references seeks to underline the notion that most of the contemporary 'digi-exploitation' has never been about an engagement with truly marginalized or subcultural values. *Kung Fury* is not alone in projecting a Nordic sense of digital exploitation premised on the emergence of a networked twenty-first century media culture. A similar case worth noting is the Swedish no budget short horror film *Lights Out* (2013), directed and produced by David F Sandberg, published on Vimeo and YouTube, where it has been viewed eleven and thirteen million times, respectively, thus attracting Hollywood attention. Sandberg has since then directed a feature length version of *Lights Out* (2016), followed by *Annabelle: Creation* (2017) and *Shazam!* (2019). Clearly then, new forms of production and distribution technology have allowed Nordic producers to consolidate international connections and cultivate new audiences outside domestic markets. These productions continue the pattern of fanboy franchises like *Iron Sky*, which balance commercial and niche audiences in ways not too different from previous exploitation cycles where their reference basis is, crucially, far removed from any sense of cultural discount, of appearing too culturally specific to appeal to international audiences. As we will see in this chapter, such a dynamic is precisely the basis for our conceptualization of Nordic exploitation, one where the lines between the appropriate and the impermissible may not be delineated based on ethical or artistic norms, but between distinctions of commercial credibility and international genre references.

Contemporary patterns

Kung Fury provides an important intervention in this study as it consolidates the proximity and distance framework as a viable illustration of the uniqueness of Nordic exploitation cinema. Effectively, for us these productions – and we use the term pointedly to emphasize the careful commercial positioning of these films – exist in a unique cultural–historical setting where they can be simultaneously transgressive and commercial. Building on some of the questions evoked by *Kung Fury*, this chapter will focus on three other case studies to highlight emerging patterns in the Nordic exploitation environment. The first of these is the Finnish–Spanish co-production venture *It Came from the Desert* (2017), an adaptation of the 1989 cult classic video game. Cultural proximity is a key strategy for the film that relies on a similar set of references as *Kung Fury* – comprised largely of American pop culture including frequent and explicit tongue-in-cheek evocations of 1950s monster films repurposed as media content that flows across borders with no indication of cultural discount. Yet, while the genre fluency of many of these productions erases any challenging boundaries, the producers invariably refocus attention on their national origins to indicate their difference from the long line of cheap B-movie productions by the likes of Asylum Pictures. Here, *It Came from the Desert* provides an intriguing case study as it evokes classic exploitation (especially the type of drive-in films that are frequently used as signifiers of exploitation cinema in contemporary films), but it is also a particularly productive example of the contemporary proximity and distance strategies that characterize the ways Nordic exploitation positions itself as a part of this cultural heritage.

Simultaneously, it would be myopic to insist that Nordic exploitation film culture concerns only flashy 'new media' digital productions. To emphasize that the gritty subversive independent exploitation scene of the William Castles and the Wes Cravens survives in the Nordic cultural climate, we focus on Norwegian film director Reinert Kiil, who continues to enjoy a substantial degree of notoriety for the rape–revenge shocker *Hora* (*The Whore*, 2009), arguably one of only a handful of 'real' exploitation films made in the Nordic context. As we outline, the film aspires to something much more than exploitation in a conventional,

Figure 9.2 Screen grab from *It Came from the Desert* (2018). A homage to animated informational films, referencing both the original 'duck-and-cover' products and their use in the films of Joe Dante et al. Courtesy of OY Bufo AB.

crude sense of the word. Its role as a revisionist version of the notorious rape–revenge cycle is one thing, but the fact that the film it most pays homage to – not so much on a textual level but as a cultural industrial product – is Tarantino and Rodriguez's *Grindhouse* (2007), positions it concretely in our proximity and distance register, as a film that capitalizes on perceptions of the shock value of integrating exploitation content into the Nordic context. At the same time, it taps into the resurgent global popularity of the retrosploitation genre form (see Church 2015: 119–75) and exploits the familiarity of international audiences with these conventions by having these forms adopted by a Nordic producer, which, thus, provides the film with a marketing angle that distinguishes the production from similar competition both domestically and internationally.

The chapter concludes with an exploration of *Bunny the Killer Thing* (2015), an independent production from Finland, that very self-consciously positions itself as a cult movie. In comparison to the digital expansionism of *Kung Fury* and *Iron Sky*, *Bunny the Killer Thing* uses minimal resources and a lo-fi aesthetic to consciously cultivate an international reputation. While the film itself does contain a considerable amount of excessive material – including an emphasis on rape and genitalia – the marketing of the film is particularly important here. By using rhetorical tactics and explicit connections to international genre productions, the producers of the film provide a powerful reminder of what is at stake in exploitation cinema. More than any attempt to challenge conventional ethical or political norms, exploitation is, and arguably, always has been, about commerce and opportunistic positioning of cinematic products.

Policy incentives: The Nordic genre support programmes

Before exploring these films in detail, it is worth briefly considering some of the infrastructural movements that facilitated the increased production of films that self-consciously use or explicitly capitalize on exploitation conventions. While straight-up exploitation productions have become more frequent in the contemporary context largely due to the affordability of new technologies and distribution opportunities, policy and strategic interventions like The Nordic Genre Boost (NGB) and Nordic Genre Invasion (NGI) have played a substantial part in these developments. Nordic Genre Invasion was established in 2013 by Finnish producers Mikko Aromaa and Tero Kaukomaa and financed in part by Krea Nord, an organization designated to support cultural co-operation between the Nordic countries. NGI's aim was to consolidate a shared marketing platform for Nordic genre films at Cannes Film Festival and other international festivals. This strategy encapsulates many of the balancing acts discussed in this book whereby genre film references act as key forms of cultural capital designed to sell these productions predominantly to international audiences. The venture situates genre as a significant creative angle embraced by Nordic film producers so that genre production emerges as a commercial and popular initiative that operates as an essential part of the brand appeal of the Nordic film industry.

NGI collaborated with Nordic Film and Television Fund's The Nordic Genre Boost in 2015 to produce and promote genre films and prestige productions like the Oscar-nominated *Gräns* (*Border*, 2018). While this film received the organization's largest total funding subsidies of the past five years or so, having acquired financial support for all aspects of its life cycle, including development, production, distribution and its marketing strategies, *Border*'s heady mix of complex aesthetic and narrative content and genre dynamics make it much more of an art house production akin to *Let the Right One In* and, thus, does not feature in this study. Perhaps the most explicit exploitation production to receive funding through these mechanisms is Lars von Trier's *The House that Jack Built* (2018), which received over 3.5 million NOK in production support. We will address von Trier's film in more depth in the conclusion of this book as the reception of the film serves to highlight how high culture aspirations and unabashed integration of low cultural capital intertwine in Nordic exploitation.

While these productions straddle the line between exploitation and art, several NGI productions that received considerable financial support are much less ambiguous in their aspirations. For example, *Bloodsuckers* (2020), a film focusing on giant mosquitoes preying on unfortunate tourists in Lapland, received 200,000 NOK for its strategic development. Such perspectives are not very surprising considering the mandate of the organization that aims to promote internationalization strategies, consisting of localized exploitation productions mixing domestic cultural references with transnational exploitation formats. The rationale for these financial support decisions follows in the wake of several successful genre productions breaking out internationally and generating a perception of a thriving Nordic genre cinema 'scene' (see Kääpä 2019: 151–8). Prominent productions such as *Big Game* (2015), *Iron Sky*, *Kung Fury* and *Død Snø* (*Dead Snow*, 2009) are noteworthy for mimicking blockbuster marquee headliners of the 1980s and the 1990s while referencing other cultural registers such as the general popularity of Nordic Noir where genre, of course, plays a huge role. Because of the success of not only straight-up genre work, but also the contemporaneously popular retrosploitation approach, it is not surprising to see these organizations support productions with distinct exploitation roots such as *It Came from the Desert*.

Directed by the Finn Marko Mäkilaakso, the approach of *It Came from the Desert* shares much with the likes of Asylum Pictures (already explicit in its 'mockbuster' title), but since it features an executive producer credit for Tero Kaukomaa and production support from the Finnish Film Institute, there is more at play here than only cashing in on a quick franchise association. The proximity and distance strategies of its production history explain its complex cultural position. Proximity, in this case, consists of genre familiarity. Loosely based on the classic creature feature *Them* (1954), the production is full of jokey references to film history, as well as special thanks to the likes of Joe Dante and Lloyd Kaufman. Such references would seem to distance it from any immediately identifiable Nordic cultural proximity, and the film is an international collaboration combining private capital from Spain and Finland as it was shot in both locations. At the same time, it received funds from the Finnish Film Institute (20,000 EUR for development; 150,000 EUR for production), as well as regional funds from Länsisuomen elokuvakomissio and other means of support from Helsinki's Aalto University. These production roots clash visibly with the narrative of the film focusing on marauding giant ants attacking American teens partying in the desert.

While this distanced set of cultural references may seem incompatible in theory, *It Came from the Desert* aligns with key dynamics in global exploitation film culture. In interviews with director Mäkilaakso (Clout communications 2019), he frequently discusses how both the monster films of the 1950s and the American genre filmmaking throughout the 1980s influenced his work. The latter comes through explicitly with the film's repeated references to a fictional franchise titled *The Eradicator* (a clear reference to a range of Schwarzenegger/Stallone productions of the 1980s). Yet, it is also significant that Mäkilaakso takes the discussion back to its production roots:

> I give all the respect in the world to the Finnish Film Foundation who bravely supported and gave financing to the movie. Trust me; it's a really brave thing to do in Finland! So maybe after this movie the Finns will see that I am not giving up and I'm still making these genre movies which I LOVE from the bottom of my heart! (Clout communications 2019)

Crucially, the significantly friendlier approach from and towards the Nordic Film Institutes evinced by both *It Came from the Desert* and *Kung Fury* operates in clear contrast to what scholars like Mathjis and Sexton (2011: 70–5) identify as normative strategies in European exploitation film production. That is, the tendency to rely on public subsidies while at the same time critiquing these very same infrastructures in order to generate antagonistic or anti-establishment perspectives, despite all of the already accumulated capital, financial or otherwise. The change in attitudes on behalf of the exploitation creatives testifies to a transformed policy environment where genre productions are now perceived in much more favourable terms. Such developments suggest an intriguing reversal of (and potential challenge to) some of the earlier dynamics of exclusion on which exploitation directors thrived.

These perspectives were reflected in much of the reception of *It Came from the Desert*, which often noted its shortcomings but found merit in its aspirations to produce something unique in a small nation film context. While the film did not do particularly well on its theatrical release at Finnish cinemas, reviewers acknowledged its attempts at creating something new in Finnish film culture:

> This is a dynamic and positive film, one that gets most of its merit from its background, but not so much its content. The uniqueness of the film is its country of origin, its upbeat and friendly attitude to film production and its punk attitude to what kinds of films should be made. (Kauraoja 2018)

These types of reviews are significant in highlighting some of the shifting attitudes towards exploitative content. Positive appreciation of the film's 'friendly attitude' and general enthusiasm for their maverick production operations fits well with a newly found critical appreciation of previously shunned 'auteurs' like Tommy Wiseau and Ray Rudy Moore, evidenced by some of the recent humorous biopics devoted to their gung-ho artistic practices. By embodying a nostalgic attitude to cinematic schlock and an overtly optimistic approach to no-holds-barred innovative low-budget film production, films such as *It Came from the Desert* align with patterns in transnational exploitation film culture where enthusiasm and reverential knowledge of historical trends is of paramount importance. Simultaneously, by setting these films in a context not previously associated with these sorts of production shenanigans – Finland – the filmmakers' irreverent approach becomes revered as 'punk attitude', despite the fact that the final film does not deter that much from other similar mockbusters like the *Sharknado* (2013–18) franchise.

The reception of *It Came from the Desert* by international critics echoed the largely positive views of the Finnish critics, especially in blogs and fan sites devoted to genre film. These sites are relevant considering the targeting mechanisms of the film's content and marketing cater heavily to fan audiences (while leaving room for some breakout potential a' la *Iron Sky*). At the same time, it is admittedly difficult to find any large media outlets even acknowledging *It Came from the Desert*'s existence, a notion that emphasizes the necessary sense of moderation we need to take in claiming anything about the general popularity of these films. Out of these fan sites, several commented on the film's ability to function as efficient entertainment. Instead of being an in-jokey referential nod to fanboy audiences, for some, it was '[S]martly scripted, extremely funny and very creepy, with terrific special effects' (Therkelsen 2018). For this blogger, its ability to provide value for money for its audience demographic (very unlikely to in any sense consist of a wide general audience but instead of a very close-knit and invariably niche group) was a real asset: 'It knows its audience, it plays to its strengths, and it entertains through and through' (Attack from Planet B 2018). For some, *It Came from the Desert*'s strengths came from its ability to work with a clear genre context: 'You can't ask for much more from a creature feature, and *It Came from the Desert* knows its audience and its strengths well' (The Craggus 2018). At the same time, its positive qualities emerge from its ability to provide a clever reworking of genre standards: 'Keeping up with the current post-modern trends, *It Came from the Desert* provides a nostalgic vibe that remains respectful to its computer game roots' (Cinemacy 2017). For these particular fan critics, *It Came from the Desert* did not function as cheap exploitation of retro- or nostalgia-culture. Instead, it was perceived to be an authentically clever play on genre norms and their role in contemporary mainstream film culture.

It Came from the Desert received a solid level of distribution internationally, with theatrical distribution in both Finland and Spain and DVD releases in several international territories. Whether this success was due to its ability to play around cultural discount in creative ways by using a cultural palette exclusively referential of American films or by selectively highlighting its small nation cinema roots, these strategies inevitably pose questions on the use of public funds to support productions with no claim to traditional artistic credibility. Or, for that matter, advancing national cultural interests (at least ones that fall readily into categories acceptable by the relevant cultural institutions). By erasing all suggestions of national specificity and thereby circumventing any indications of cultural discount, such films are indicative of a highly cognizant approach to navigating global exploitation cinema. While co-productions, in particular, have frequently been associated with a sense of cultural homelessness that has led to pervasive critiques of such placeless strategies (Hjort 2000: 103–18), for us, the lack of contextualization in a film like *It Came from the Desert* is, precisely, the point. By actively erasing any marker of Finnishness or Spanishness from the production, from language to visual signifiers, whereby both registers now aim to resemble an unidentifiable American desert location, the politics of dislocation seem to wrench *It Came from the Desert* away from being a particularly relevant case of Nordic exploitation. Yet, this argument is counterproductive as the Nordic roots of the production emerge as the fundamental raison d'existence of *It Came from the Desert*, especially if we consider the comments of its director and its complex production history. The dynamics of proximity and distance are at full play in the digitalized production culture and global distribution networks. Here, the producers of the film, alongside both domestic and international critics, enthusiastically work above the level of national film cultural affiliations, even as they simultaneously exploit the infrastructural role that national film cultural institutions continue to play. At the same time, the producers continue to distance themselves from these very same institutions to appear sufficiently transgressive.

From *Iron Sky* to *Dead Snow*, from *Kung Fury* to *It Came from the Desert*, these are primarily fan productions but ones that have distinct professional aspirations. Not only do all the respective filmmakers discuss their inspirations and allegiances in explicit depth, but the films would literally fall flat without their extensive bank of references. Although the heavy level of intertextuality is certainly a key attraction, fans do not only exploit existing properties but also tend to poach them for their own purposes as Jenkins (2013: 8–41) has famously noted. They repackage the existing texts to fit into alternative or emerging modes of cultural production, as we have seen with many of these films using social media and other digital platforms. Yet, the way these productions combine fan service with official funding streams suggests that they are best considered as productions exploiting different registers of cultural value. For one, the use of new technologies that reorient production workflows and designations of professional and cultural authority allows the films to exploit the cultural circuits on which they travel, from festivals to fan websites, where they are frequently identified as indigenous productions and, thus, as idiosyncratic contributions to established modes of global exploitation production. Therefore, these productions consciously position themselves as appealing to a wide range of diverse registers, all of which can be exploited to carve lucrative niches for previously problematic types of film content. Although many of their key selling points link with 'traditionally exploitative' film content (i.e. films with low culture aspirations or morally transgressive themes), they are not perceived as such by national film institutions. In comparison to the previous decades when such 'shameless' commercialism would have been actively shunned, commercial potential now functions as a desirable quality in these small nation film cultures enmeshed in global markets, and thus generates largely beneficial forms of cultural capital for all concerned. Consequently, it is not exactly surprising to note that exploitation is now an integrated part of the Nordic film industry, albeit in ways that highlight transformations in the transgressive constitution of film content.

Going lo-fi

If *Kung Fury* and *It Came from the Desert* show how innovations in digital media production and distribution provide new challenges and opportunities for Nordic producers, a much more orthodox exploitation culture continues to operate in the institutional margins. Although this book has largely avoided amateur film production, exploitation has invariably been associated with fan entrepreneurs trying their luck at a particular contemporaneously popular trend. This has led to business people (instead of explicitly artistic creatives) like Visa Mäkinen and Mats Helge Olsson producing facsimiles of contemporary popular international genre forms albeit often hampered by their limited production means. Yet, these limitations often work in favour of the producers as the crudeness and unabashed DIY-attitude has, at least in retrospective, sustained interest in their work.

Although Sandberg and Mäkilaakso capitalize on genre know-how and digital production infrastructure, other contemporary Nordic peers go for a much more lo-fi approach that harkens back less to the spectacular genre entertainment of American cinema in the 1950s or the 1980s, but to the independent exploitation films of the 1970s. Norwegian independent filmmaker Reinert Kiil has enthusiastically embraced an attitude to excess and schlock that characterized some of the most notorious work of filmmakers like Meir Zarchi to produce what amounts to, arguably, one of the most excessively self-aware Nordic exploitation films – *The Whore*. Kiil is a relevant case study as he is in an unusual position to have produced 'indie' films with small but increasing budgets and also secured theatrical releases for all of his films. Yet, it is worth emphasising that the label of indie filmmaker evokes a different response in the Nordic context to those in the US markets. Here, the aura of a producer working independently does not gesture to the kind of 'credibility' generated by the Tarantino and Rodriquez' of the mini-major system in Hollywood. Instead, independence in the Nordic context is much more about the margins of a media environment defined by the film institute infrastructure that governs the Nordic film industries. Here, being indie means working outside of the support infrastructure that facilitates budgets for even the most inexpensive of productions and ensures a level of distribution in theatres and broadcast channels. Missing out on this support equates to a truly marginal position for film producers meaning that one has to either finance the theatrical screenings themselves or try to seek distribution support, as happened in the case of *Død Snø 2* (*Dead Snow 2: Red vs. Dead*, 2014). In any case, a commercial theatrical release establishes a considerable threshold between amateur production capable of generating sufficient return on investment through streaming services and those seeking the types of returns that only a cinematic release can generate.

The Whore is an intriguing disruption in Nordic film history, being an excessively gory rape–revenge pastiche that does not even attempt to abide with conventional taste or censorship norms. The film was financed privately by Kiil through a compendium of different sources. Most of it came from sponsorships sold on the basis of the film's commercial potential that aimed to capitalize on its proposed notoriety and, arguably, the prominence of *Grindhouse*'s release in the preceding years. As the costs were a minimal 240,000 NOK, mostly spent on transportation and food, the film did not require a significant level of investment to complete production, and according to Kiil, he would never have been able to find private investors for the film due to its unprecedented role as a Norwegian exploitation film. When viewing the first cut, many of the sponsors were appalled at some of the explicit content, and Kiil had to go back to blur out all images featuring logos or slogans, as well as pay the sponsors back the funds they invested in the film (Kääpä 2018).

One fundamental problem, according to Kiil, was the fact that the film was 'the first hard and rough exploitation film made in Norway' and thus it fell into an unconventional cultural space (Kääpä 2018). For us, the film is emblematic of the proximity and distance strategies of Nordic exploitation. It adheres to genre formulas, particularly many of the rape–revenge films produced in the wake of *I Spit on Your Grave* (1978). However, this is done in a very self-conscious way that distances it from the low culture aspirations of many of these antecedent productions. The first is the retro style adopted for the marketing of the film with digital gimmickry highlighting the poster's close emulation of the marketing style of many of the post-*Grindhouse* cycle of retrosploitation films like *Machete* (2010) and *Hobo with a Shotgun* (2011) (though interestingly *The Whore*'s poster preceded these two productions). The back cover screams (in Norwegian) that this is the first ever grindhouse film to come out of Norway, whereas a quote from *Filmrage* in English outlines 'Reineert Kiil's *Hora*, a Norwegian rape–revenge movie and *Grindhouse* tribute, may very well be the surprise of the year, and one of the best low-budget films to come out of Scandinavia in a long time'. These tactics see the proximity and distance devices at work where the film is both part of global exploitation cinema at the same time as it is enthusiastically 'authentically' Norwegian. In addition, the stylistic choices adopted for the film directly emulate the retrosploitation strategies established by *Grindhouse*. The action is repeatedly interrupted by cigarette burns and black and white footage that disrupts some of the more extreme scenes and, crucially, other basic narrative moments. These were included after Kiil watched Tarantino's film and saw, according to him, a different way to approach the genre. Accordingly, the production was 'filmed digital, but we tried to make it more like a real film' (Kääpä 2018).

Although one could interpret these moments as distanciation devices designed to flip the narrative gaze onto the spectator, they are more productively understood as instances where a clear debt is paid to global exploitation

Figure 9.3 Screen grab from *Hora* (*The Whore*, 2009), featuring its retrosploitation aesthetics and homages in full play. Courtesy of Kiil Produksjon.

production, while adherence to the dynamics of localized exploitation are used to ground these efforts. In many of the interviews around the film, Kiil was certain to politicize the production as something distinct from anything done in Norwegian film. For him, this was 'a timeless art-house exploitation film and first of its kind in Scandinavia where the audience is confronted with violence and torture' (Kääpä 2018). By emphasizing the uncomfortable associations and notoriety of torture porn, he seems to have aimed to generate a complex love/hate relationship with the viewers, much in the same way as companies like Troma had mobilized 'badness' as a qualifier of their productions. Appropriately, Troma is referenced by Kiil in discussing *The Whore*, which is in his words 'trash with a 80s B-movie vibe' (Kääpä 2018). This alignment with other exploitation companies sets the film up as a transgressive, potentially dangerous product where these areas are used to drum up controversy, and thus generate publicity.

Accordingly, positioning the film as a global–local retrosploitation production – simulacra without the depth – suggests that instead of something truly transgressive, the tactics adopted by Kiil are more explicitly commercial strategies. It is important to note that *Grindhouse* was not intended as a marginal small-scale production, but aspired to wide-scale success, as evident in its cost (53 million USD), its 83 per cent score on *Rotten Tomatoes*, as well as the way it was promoted through its name directors. Yet, it would be difficult for *The Whore* to achieve similar commercial and critical prestige due to its context. Consequently, its violent assaults use much more explicit imagery that would never have made it to commercial theatres in the United States, including a bloodied rectum during the prolonged rape scene and visceral close-ups of dismembered male organs after Vibeke takes her revenge on her assailants. In comparison, the jokey CGI graphics of *Planet Terror* (2007) pale next to the grimness of *The Whore*, and even the deliberate schlockiness of *Death Proof* (2007) is undermined by its top-gear production standards and the casting of household names like Kurt Russell. For *The Whore*, the casting of porn star Vibeke (she was the only choice for a role requiring this level of nudity according to Kiil) and the lo-fi aesthetics arguably provide the production with a certain level of credibility lacking in its large-scale predecessor. At the same time, adhering so close to the 'innovative' standards set by pastiche exploitation ensures the film lands in an uncomfortable liminal space where its self-reflexive gimmickry withholds its exploitative potential, whereas the often explicitly misogynistic content – whether intentional or not – makes it anything but a respected art film in the vein of, say, the French *Baise-Moi* (*Rape Me*, 2000). While the two share many similarities in thematic and aesthetic terms, *The Whore* lacks any real critique of misogynist attitudes or the ambivalence of *Baise-Moi* that sparked complex debates on its gender politics.

Again, brief comparisons between the promotional campaigns of *The Whore* and *Baise-Moi* highlight this difference. The marketing for *Baise-Moi* uses a typical strategy reflecting its high culture positioning, with quotations by respected critics and the inclusion of several laurel leaf award identifiers, set against a generally ambiguous background reflecting the visual style of the film. With *The Whore*, the posters and the trailer use only references to exploitation cinema, emphasizing the blood and gore promise inherent to the film. At the same time, the graphics are, as explained, similar to the promotional campaign for *Grindhouse*, resulting in a tactic that in some ways tries to increase its transgressive cultural standards, but which simultaneously reveals its commercialist aspirations. Exploitation marketing has invariably focused on shocking content that exceeds cultural and political norms, but as we have outlined, *Grindhouse* was never positioned as low culture but instead as a potential commercial success befitting the reputations of both its production house Dimension/Miramax and its two directors. Ironically, the replication of these ambiguous strategies evident in the repositioning of a Norwegian exploitation film like *The Whore*, at least to some extent, undermines the underground standards to which it seemingly aspires.

The attempt at positioning Nordic exploitation cinema in international flows of genre content brings us concretely back to the proximity and distance dynamics that characterize Nordic exploitation cinema. Here, many of the cultural complications of a small film culture necessitate standardization of production along global norms, yet the lack of official state financial support for production and distribution necessitates playing up their cultural distinctions. Cultural discount does not accurately describe the processes taking place here. Instead, *The Whore* is situated as an exception in both cases – it is simultaneously exploitative transgressiveness and popular globalized commercialism, even as it positions itself outside of the domestic norms, including distinctions of 'sensible' taste. This makes it a key example of proximity and distance whereby Nordic exploitation is best characterized by its complex liminality between aspiring to castigation for its transgressions and generating popular attention because of these transgressions. Through this, even films that are consciously classified as exploitation take on diverse cultural and political meanings that emerge as a result of the particular industrial and cultural infrastructure of the Nordic small nation context.

The Whore generated most attention in international markets as it received DVD distribution on several genre labels and garnered attention on Kiil as director. He, in turn, has been open about the film's conscious market positioning: '*The Whore* was my film school where I made a home invasion film we have seen a 100 times' (Kääpä 2018). Nevertheless, Kiil adds that the Norwegian context contributes a new twist on the genre. These connections were further accentuated in the follow-up mockumentary *Inside the Whore* (2012). The film chronicles the disastrous production of an exploitation picture where the director, played by Kiil, goes off the rails and starts harassing the cast and crew. The targets are much more obviously Norwegian as after the opening credits (which consists of the credits overlaid on a dancing naked woman), a censorship board assembles to view, presumably, the first film in an auditorium. Unsurprisingly, the participants dismiss the film as utter nonsense, unbefitting the art that they are in the business of supporting. By ridiculing what it sees as the petty egomania of state authorities, the film seems to evoke a similar politics of auteurist enfant terrible of art cinema – from Lars von Trier to Jean-Luc Godard – to cultivate an image of Kiil as a rebel, a transgressive and dangerous auteur. The sequel can be considered more as a paratext to the original film instead of an independent film as it is only seventy-eight minutes long and has received a minimal release. Understanding it as a paratext contributes to the original film's complex cultural positioning as these elements in many ways challenge its hardened, dirty exploitation credentials. It now takes on an aura of self-aware resistance to cultural norms much as the expensive production standards and critical prestige of *Grindhouse* ensured that it would never be mistaken for a real hard-core exploitation film. Instead, strategies such as this highlight a fluency with cultural influences that is much more indicative of the heavily, and increasingly, global constitution of Nordic exploitation cinema and the aspirations of its directors. Thus, the ambiguous and deliberate positioning of *The Whore* makes it a complex example of precisely the type of proximity and distance strategies outlined earlier.

At the same time, it is interesting to note that the Norwegian critics seem to have been intimately aware of these complex positionings. Several commentators understood the film as a clear play on exploitation norms (Norum 2008) and, as much as was the case with *Dead Snow*'s use of genre forms and excessive violence, they showcase awareness of these strategies not as something potentially shocking or transgressive, but as explicit attention seeking based on commercial prerogatives. They are understood as precisely what they are – commercial ploys to break out of the constraints of these small national film industries by adopting gung-ho marginality as effectively a promotional angle. Consequently, what they are not is the type of material that would cause a moral panic or lead to the type of notoriety that saw films like *The Last House on the Left* (1972), *Thriller – en grym film* (*They Call Her One Eye*, 1974) and *I Spit on Your Grave* generate (largely desirable) outraged headlines in the past.

Flirting with the mainstream

The majority of Kiil's career continues this self-aware capitalization on a performative outsider mentality. Since *Inside the Whore*, Kiil has produced two more mainstream low-budget horror films, *Huset* (*The House*, 2016) and *Juleblod* (*Christmas Blood*, 2017). The first of these features Nazi protagonists who hide out in a haunted farmhouse during the Second World War; the latter is a slasher film set during Christmas. While neither would qualify under normative designations of exploitation cinema, their production histories are useful as a means to evaluate the complex production politics with which these proximity and distance filmmakers engage. Kiil did not secure any institutional funding for either film but did find alternative sources of finance in addition to the sponsorship packages that provide lifelines for these independent productions. For example, the Film Camp in the northern Nordkapp region of Norway provided support for *The House* as the crew were filming in the region, which allowed the organization to display local creative capacity by encouraging the production to hire local services and talent. Similar strategies based on networking and the use of emerging regional funding were mobilized for the production of *Christmas Blood* as Kiil sourced money from local tourist companies that focus on showcasing the region. In addition, he used funding from Film Camp as productions of this level could be promoted on the basis of emphasizing talent capacity building in locations where the media industry is still in nascent development. According to him, 'this was not only aimed at promoting the Nordkapp region but putting the place on the map to emphasize that it is possible to make a film there' (Kääpä 2018).

These mechanisms for capacity building provide an intriguing twist on the perceived lack of societal worth in exploitation film production. The backers had no issue with the explicit content of the films as their main priority was to focus on securing return on investment. In this case, this was to do with showcasing professional production capabilities instead of emphasizing financial returns. Thus, many of the sponsors came from unexpected areas like hair products or makeup services, where local service providers would be able to display their talent. Ultimately, most of the money gained from these activities was used to cover areas like heating and food as the total amount of support was low and Kiil did not pre-sell the rights to the films. While innovative means of financing independent productions certainly manifest here, the precarious working conditions of independent Nordic directors is again highlighted by these mechanisms, thus bridging the practices of filmmakers in the 2000s with the previous decades where directors like Mäkinen and Olsson would make use of tax incentives and gaps in the market to keep producing films at relatively low costs.

Christmas Blood and *The House* prove to be particularly relevant for understanding Nordic exploitation as a balance between transgressive material and mainstream attractions. For Kiil, '*The House* is an art-house film, but *Christmas Blood* is more slapstick and exploitation mainstream that has a sales mark' (Kääpä 2018). These descriptions consciously use diverse registers to place these films on a cultural spectrum where *The House* is positioned as a nod to more orthodox Norwegian film culture, but, in contrast, *Christmas Blood* is intended as a much more openly commercial genre product. These aspirations are reflected in the production of the film as it was shot on over thirty locations with forty actors and was complimented by a much more proactive distribution strategy with festival and theatrical distribution (Nordisk Film Kino 2017).

The balancing act between explicitly commercial aspirations (*Christmas Blood*, for Kiil, has a 'sales target') and transgressive standards is easy to identify in the film's content as much of it is more conventional than *The Whore* films but also more obviously exploitative than *The House* (which emphasizes mood and suggestion more than explicit gore). Simultaneously, the film's conventional slasher narrative, focusing on a group of young women stalked by a killer in a Santa Claus suit in a north Norwegian town, only appears exploitative in a Nordic context where such genre production continues to be rare. Here, the idea of an independent Norwegian slasher, financed partially with regional funds, appears transgressive, but after a cycle of increasingly similar productions, including many of the Norwegian slashers of the early 2000s, it is worth asking if this assertion holds up.

As we saw with *The Whore*, the proximity and distance strategies mobilized by the film are reflected in the domestic critical reception. Here, the balancing act between outright transgression and awareness of the commercial potential of this very transgressiveness pervades the critiques. Similarly, far from the rough and dirty comparison points for *The Whore*, Kiil compares *Christmas Blood* to *Home Alone* (1990) and argues that this is a Norwegian film from another universe – 'exciting with a lot of blood but also characters you can identify with' (Anon. 2017a). Such permissively transgressive but conventionally entertaining descriptions indicate again how those proximity and distance cultural signifiers characterize a Norwegian exploitation film aspiring to be both globally notorious, but only so because it is steeped in local roots.

While critics had been able to navigate the transgressions of *The Whore* to identify many of its excesses as conscious uses of genre conventions, *The House* and *Christmas Blood* were from the outset considered in more explicitly mainstreamed ways. *The House*, for example, generated some generally positive reviews where Kiil was commended for turning to classic genre production after exploitation films (Hedenstad 2017). Simultaneously, the film was previewed on the Norwegian TV2 channel in a special showing clips from the film and featuring an interview with Kiil. This was complemented by an interview with popular film website *Film Front* (2017), where instead of positioning Kiil as an exploitation maverick, he discusses his inspirations including Michael Bay, Stanley Kubrick, James Cameron and Quentin Tarantino, providing a referential frame far removed from filmmakers like Meir Zarchi, the notorious filmmaker responsible for *I Spit on Your Grave*. By positioning the film alongside mainstream Hollywood entertainment as well as part of the domestic media infrastructure, the politics of these discussions operate much more consciously along conventional taste cultures than the nominal label of exploitation cinema.

The reception of *Christmas Blood* highlights a similar sense of awareness of the film's commercial aspirations which generally ignores any attempt to position it as a potentially dangerous piece of transgressive cinema. In *Cinema*, it is identified as 'a good old-fashioned film' with Kiil in particular congratulated for managing to stand out as a genre filmmaker in the Norwegian film scene (Anon. 2017b). But *Aftenposten*, on the other hand, suggests the outcome is a depressing film due to weaknesses arising from its low budget (Anon. 2017c). Others found the film similarly lacking: for them, 'it is easy to like Reinert Kiil's efforts to be the first exploitation filmmaker' in the country, but for this critic, whereas the film touches on many genre highpoints, it also lacks a real script and narrative approach, as well as being generally misogynistic in tone (Vestmo 2017). At the same time, some suggested that the slasher roots of the film would limit its commercial potential (Koren 2017). While slashers like *Villmark* (*Dark Woods*, 2003) had connected with general audiences, the novelty of these approaches had waned in the last ten years, at least for these critics. Responding to transformations in censorship laws and the general relaxation over violent content in games and other media, it is not entirely surprising to see Kiil include explicit hard-core material in *The Whore* and fountains of gore in *Christmas Blood*. While these do provide moments of transgressiveness, the scope of these cultural shifts means that exploitation, as a label and a marketing tool, no longer guarantees notoriety or commercial success.

Some of these developments establish a parallel to the situation in Denmark and Sweden in the beginning of the 1970s, where the decriminalization of porn had led to an overproduction of soft-core and hard-core sexploitation, thus prompting filmmakers like Jørgen Hallum and Bo Arne Vibenius to challenge other taboos by combining sex and Christianity and sex and violence as the novelty of sex and pornography had worn off. Seen from this perspective, Kiil was arguably not just late, as the Norwegian film censorship was abolished in 2004, but out of synch when it came to exploitative and provocative films. While films like *Dværgen* (*The Sinful Dwarf*, 1973) and *They Call Her One Eye* were commercial exploitations that broke both moral and legal laws, *The Whore* turned out to be more of a fan production in awe of retrosploitation auteurs like Rodriguez and Tarantino. As a consequence, *Christmas Blood* did not stand out from the Norwegian slasher cycle in any pronounced way.

Most problematically for these balancing strategies, *Christmas Blood* was only viewed by 4,370 spectators in domestic cinemas, which meant that the film failed to qualify for the Norwegian Film Institute's post-release support. This policy provides 100 per cent of ticket sales back to producers of films who attract more than 35,000 spectators domestically (in marked contrast to policy incentives such as Sweden's F-Fund in the late 1970s, which was based on sustaining the industry by subsidizing the losses suffered by producers). Furthermore, the film was produced as a 'credit film' whereby many of the key labourers would only be paid if the film was successful enough at the box office to return on its investment. While controversial, these policies and labour practices are integral to increasing private capital support in the domestic film industry, especially for productions like *Christmas Blood* that have aspirations and potential to break out to commercial success due to their genre roots.

For Kiil, the risks are acceptable as, according to him, everyone involved in the production would have been aware of these concerns (Kääpä 2018). Yet, industry consultants such as Sverre Pedersen argue that these arrangements can be exploitative in their own right, even if they are fully transparent and not an industry secret, whereas others, such as Marianne Kleven from Norwegian Film Development, suggest that such practices are a systematic problem in an underfunded sector (Anon. 2017d). Yet, according to both, film professionals are not to blame here as there are several precedents that have become considerable successes and such strategies are often the only way to get a film like *Christmas Blood* made in the first place. Thus, Kiil's practices are endemic of a systematic problem in the Nordic film sector where independent filmmakers have to struggle to get their productions off the ground. Despite policy incentives to promote popular genre production and new technologies allowing exploitation film producers to engage in progressive flirtations with commercial success, it is clear that the more orthodox variant of Nordic exploitation (in comparison to high concept productions like *Iron Sky* and *Kung Fury*) continues to struggle in the margins.

Killer bunnies on the loose

If some of these patterns indicate a pessimistic reversal of fortunes for exploitation producers, the Finnish independent production *Bunny the Killer Thing* provides a more optimistic coda that wraps up many of the proximity and distance politics outlined throughout the chapter. Produced entirely independently of institutional support, the film, a loose narrative combining partying teens, English gangsters, chemical experiments and a rampaging man-in-suit bunny, combines fan enthusiasm with extreme content.

Compared with most other productions covered in this chapter, save for *The Whore*, there is no clear textual attempt made here to appeal to general audiences. To illustrate, the film's prologue starts with an English writer arriving at a secluded cabin with his girlfriend. They are immediately attacked by a local gang who shoot her head off in extreme close-up. A mad scientist injects potion into the writer's neck and turns him into the eponymous Bunny Thing who goes on a rampage to rape and kill a gang of city youth who arrive into the region for a party. The tone is established immediately during the animated opening credits where Bunny literally shoots his load all over the credits. Clearly, the producers had invested most of their energy into shock value as the film goes for as extreme content as possible. In addition to a range of misogynist and racist jokes throughout, the real 'attraction' is the eponymous Bunny. Only communicating by screaming 'pussy', Bunny rapes the orifices of his victims (and even an eye socket) while attacks are preceded by it swinging its elongated penis in circular motion (or the 'helicopter move' in juvenile vernacular). The film does its best to capitalize on its exploitation premise, including excessive and frequent nudity, the casting of Finnish porn star Henry Saari, several dismemberments of male organs, and the utterly nonsensical storyline featuring three British mercenaries who have kidnapped a Swedish pop star so she can be turned into another bunny monster.

Figure 9.4 Screen grab from *Bunny the Killer Thing* (2015), featuring its explicit and excessive plays on genre imagery drawn from *Evil Dead II: Dead by Dawn* (1987) and others. Courtesy of Black Lion Pictures.

Implicit to all the films discussed in this chapter is an understanding of exploitation cinema as a truly transnational genre and a vibrant commercial opportunity. *Bunny the Killer Thing* does not deter from this as although the narrative consciously taps into the lowest forms of culture (while also referencing art productions like Walerian Borowczyk's films), the intention seems not to have been to produce an inaccessible bargain-basement exploitation film. Instead, the producers outline its reference basis as follows:

> *Bunny the Killer Thing* is a hilarious full-length horror-comedy, made in the genres of splatter and camp films. The film makes fun of 'cabin in the woods' -type films. The film's creature design is made to honor the 80's 'Man in a monster suit' -films. The film has been made with international cast, for international audience [sic]! The film's main language is English. (bunnythekillerthing.com 2015)

The description explains the many idiosyncrasies of the film, including the plotline featuring the British mercenaries who seem to have very literally been included to exploit international audience potential. Although camp and splatter are referenced, the description is largely focused on popular genre references, indicating that, on one level, the film aspired towards more commercial production standards. Furthermore, its distribution strategies reflected many of these ambitions. Far from the typical release for independent cult films, *Bunny the Killer Thing* was distributed in domestic theatres via the dominant theatrical distribution company Finnkino at thirty-three screens nationwide, which is a substantial range for a small exploitation film. At the same time, its marketing was aimed at an audience aware of its genre roots and its aspirations to a distinctly bad taste cult status, best exemplified by its tagline: 'It's after your pussy'. Yet, despite the wide distribution strategy, the film did not receive support from The Finnish Film Foundation (though interestingly, *It Came from the Desert* received 150,000 EUR and *Iron Sky 2* 1 million EUR in the same funding cycle) and only 2,177 paying customers bought tickets. More problematically, the film was consciously aimed at international markets, yet these release strategies were supported by an Indiegogo campaign that failed to take off as it only received 359 EUR of its 9,900 EUR goal. This failure can be attributed to unclear crowdfunding logic as the campaign brief suggested the film had already secured a domestic theatrical release and the funds were to be used for the international campaign, yet the outline includes comments about covering the crew's expenses. As we saw with *Dead Snow*'s failed campaign, crowdfunding is a precise business requiring careful management, and in this case, fan support of the kind essential to success on *Iron Sky*'s scale did not materialize.

While the domestic release and fan campaigns faltered, *Bunny the Killer Thing* was much more successful on the international festival circuit as it won awards at, for example, the San Paulo Cinefantasy and Fright Night Theatre festivals. It also received several positive reviews on fan sites such as *Shattered Ravings* and *Legless Corpse*, indicating that it was connecting with its intended audiences at least on a basic level, whereas more established sites like *Joblo.com* and *Dread Central* used terms like 'Horribly offensive' and 'NSFW' to describe it. Such phrases are unequivocally positive for *Bunny the Killer Thing* as they can generate notoriety and controversy, especially amongst internet fan communities specializing in cult and exploitation. In an additional bonus, the trailer was banned by YouTube, which will have undoubtedly only increased interest in the film. As a consequence, the film has received DVD and Bluray releases internationally with specialist labels such as the Canadian Raven Banner and Artsploitation, including a three-disc limited edition release on the latter label featuring stylized cover art which censored Bunny's 'thing' with a carrot – all playing up its irreverent exploitation connotations.

Crucially, as with the other proximity and distance exploitationers, the director of the film Joonas Makkonen ensured that interviews touched on both the film's exploitation potential and its novelty in the Finnish context. He also used a similar tactic as Kiil, Olsson and several other Nordic directors before him in directly addressing the lack of infrastructural support for domestic genre

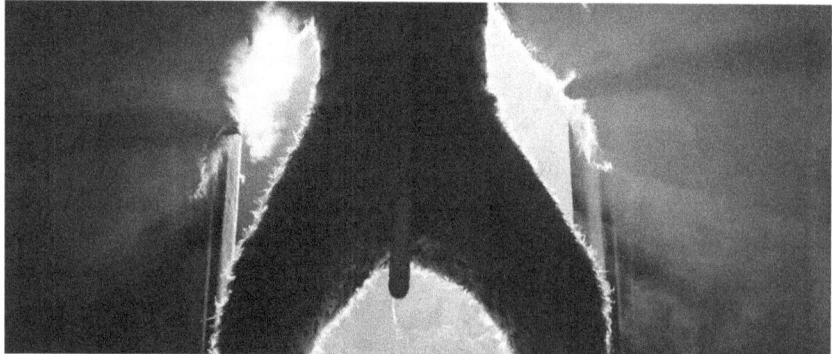

Figure 9.5 Screen grab from *Bunny the Killer Thing* (2015). The juvenile comedic emphasis on the eponymous man-in-suit monster's private parts which displays both its explicit attempts to shock and the base level of its humour. Courtesy of Black Lion Pictures.

productions, ingraining the film in an oppositional politics critically engaged with a short-sighted, hypocritical establishment:

> They [the FFI] make comedies, drama-comedies, romantic comedies. There should be more Finnish genre films. I do know though that the main problem in Finland is the country's film foundation, which is a control-freak organization without the will to support strong genre films. I hope the change is happening now in the organization because Finland does have so much potential to become a good genre film country. Genre films would be more international as well. The Film Foundation is sometimes so odd, it's like they don't care about the business side of filmmaking, nor the artistic side of it. (Makkonen in Luhtala 2015)

The cultural and political positioning of the film not only as a counter-hegemonic product, but simultaneously as a potentially accessible genre film indicates that the producers were aware of the necessity of appealing to these diverse registers. And while they seem to have succeeded by securing a wide release in Finnish cinemas, other parts of the critical reception reveal a more complex understanding of its cultural role. Domestic reviews invariably discuss its origins as an independent genre production that continues to be a rarity in Finland. Some relate it to the career of Peter Jackson by positioning the film as an example of domestic responses to bad taste culture, which may provide a platform to expand into 'serious' production later (Rissanen 2015). Such commentary, of course, indicates another instance of critical alignment of exploitation as explicit and self-aware commercialism. Yet, the need for exploitation films to generate notoriety is challenged by many of these reviews that suggest that the film does not go far enough in its splatter and over-the-top qualities. As we saw with the Norwegian critics and *The Whore*, these films tend to be understood as explicit commercial ploys, where their shock value is seen as a deliberate strategic provocation, and not as something truly challenging or transgressive of contemporary norms. At the same time, some of the critical interpretations of *Bunny the Killer Thing* did attempt to view it through a counter-cultural perspective, suggesting it needs to be considered as a powerful critique of Finnish nation branding, here presented as a backwards, xenophobic and misogynist country (Eljaala 2015). Similarly, YLE (2015), the national broadcaster, commented on its international success in positive terms, suggesting that the limited spectator figures were to be expected, and the real interest in the film lies abroad, such as in the United States and Spain where the film's genre content and 'rally-English' (referencing the very broken English often spoken by Finland's well-known motorsports figures) would work much more efficiently.

Domestically, then, the film generated a complex response, from dismissal to acknowledgment of its commercial potential. Yet, what it did not evoke, at all, was a sense of moral panic or revulsion. While it did achieve a level of success through its international distribution, some of the responses echo the domestic reception's ambivalence. Fan sites such as *Addicted to Horror* (2016) suggested the film fails on a basic level to engage the connoisseur spectator: 'I really don't have much to say about this other than that I really didn't like this. It's not funny, it's not scary, and thus it's not entertaining'. Similarly, another fan site, Loser City, evaluated its shock potential: 'it wants you to be angry at it, to be infuriated at the scandalous places it goes. But really, it's not too dissimilar from hearing a small child quietly say "fuck"' (LoserCityBoss 2015). Clearly, then, in an over-inundated marketplace, especially one where streaming platforms provide gore fans endless flows of explicit content, simply being explicit is not sufficient to generate attention. It is also noteworthy that several Amazon reviews express confusion and disappointment over the film's content as they state that about 40 per cent of it is in Finnish with the rest in heavily accented English.

The results are thus clearly mixed despite some of the positive press its international strategies had generated. But appropriately, the aspects that were commended – the awards at genre festivals, positive indications of extreme content, its role as a Finnish splatter exploitation film, indications of a sustained cult – do connote a level of reputational success that enabled a small Finnish amateur production to generate attention. This in its own right implies the cultural and commercial worth that exploitation strategies continue to hold as potential career pathways for producers who have both been initiated to the field through likeminded films and who struggle to gain the cultural and industry capital necessary to break through the institutional infrastructural barriers.

Conclusion

As a culmination to this chapter on contemporary patterns in Nordic exploitation film cultures, *Bunny the Killer Thing* emphasizes the potential implications of a general mainstreaming of exploitation cinema. As we have suggested, exploitation films, at least in the Nordic countries, are more often about commerce than breaking ethical standards. They lead to cycles and production trends that can institutionalize transgressive content. Yet, such strategies can be problematic when form becomes formulaic as, then, it loses any transgressive potential to which it may have aspired. This is especially clear with many of the case studies explored where we have identified patterns of production using exploitative thematic material to distinguish a film in the domestic markets, but also simultaneously mobilizing national cultural signifiers to distinguish the very same products internationally. These productions – as diverse as the large-scale spoofery of *Kung Fury* to gritty independent films like *The Whore*; from *It Came from the Desert*'s digital gimmickry to *Bunny the Killer Thing*'s sexual violence – all showcase clear differences in tone and cultural–political circumstances not only to one another but also in relation to previous decades of Nordic exploitation film.

Yet, two areas bind these contemporary Nordic productions and distinguish them from previous eras: a heightened sense of awareness of genre conventions and explicit attempts to blur (and capitalize on) the distinction between producers and fans. Exploitation in the Nordic context is no longer about marginality or subverting conventions but about capitalizing on a compendium of registers. These adhere to certain aspects of more orthodox understandings of exploitation as the films themselves contain all the required content for exploitation films – including exploding heads and limbs, copious nudity, bad acting, technological problems – but the ways these films approach them, especially the last two, are especially revealing. For example, in *The Whore* or *Kung Fury*, the limitations of the format do not appear due to budget constraints but instead as stylistic gimmicks connecting the productions to their producers' experiences of first viewing similar content on VHS, or even to recontextualized memories of theatrical projections as happens with appropriations of pastiche films like *Grindhouse*. Shoddy quality, such as unprofessional acting or low-quality effects, is part of the package that makes these productions seem 'global'. And although these developments are indeed prevalent on a transnational level, they are nonetheless identifiably Nordic. Instead of challenging dominant norms, these films are, for us, exploitative as they make use of a range of developments in Nordic genre film production, from a conscious interplay between professional and fan activities to capitalizing on indie credibility. Crucially, all of this takes place as they adhere to the institutional logic of the Nordic film industry, by either using new policy developments or positioning themselves as antagonistic to their cultural and political norms. In this, they are not unique as such as, for example, the institutionalization of the professional fan is a key idiom of contemporary transnational popular or cult production – one only needs to consider Tarantino's work here. Where these Nordic films are significantly different is in showcasing an apt awareness of institutional infrastructures that facilitate production, where both the presence and the absence of support for genre production can be used rhetorically to position these films as commercially viable, yet thematically transgressive products that have the potential to appeal to both cult and wider audiences.

References

Anon. (2017a), 'Juleblod', Review, *Framtida*, 31 October.
Anon. (2017b), 'Juleblod', Review, *Cinema*, 2 November.
Anon. (2017c), 'Juleblod', Review, *Aftenposten*, 1 November.
Anon. (2017d), 'Juleblod ble slaktet or floppet pa kino', *Dagbladet*, 5 December. Available at: www.dagbladet.no%2Fkultur%2Fjuleblod-ble-slaktet-og-floppet-pa-kino-dermed-far-ikke-filmarbeiderne-betalt (Accessed 3 July 2019).
Artsploitation (2018), 'Bunny the Killer Thing', Review, available at: http://www.artsploitationfilms.com/film/bunny-the-killer-thing/?fbclid=IwAR27SeXAH0fLjUBne8DKGE4xvscr6VvmrY54VibGrkxdjEv86fWojb80df (Accessed 4 July 2019).
Attack from Planet B (2018), 'It Came from the Desert', Review, available at: https://www.attackfromplanetb.com/2018/10/an-interview-with-director-marko-makilaakso-it-came-from-the-desert/?fbclid=IwAR3sfxpAOo4-2FJHMSiIkR0_NsrscRBV6W5 5mh2iXMLex6eNa4yXGay93Q0 (Accessed 4 July 2019).
Bunny The Killer Thing (2015), available at www.bunnythekillerthing.com (Accessed 10 July 2019).
Church, David (2015), *Grindhouse Nostalgia*, Edinburgh: Edinburgh University Press.
Cinemacy (2017), 'It Came from the Desert', Review, available at: http://cinemacy.com/came-desert-review/ (Accessed 4 July 2019).
Clout Communications (2019), 'An Exclusive Interview with Marko Makilaakso', available at: http://cloutcom.co.uk/marko-makilaakso-interview/ (Accessed 10 July 2019).
Eljaala, Ellen (2015), 'Bunny the Killer Thing ja sen syvempi merkitys', *Voima*, available at: https://voima.fi/artikkeli/2015/bunny-the-killer-thing-ja-sen-syvempi-merkitys/ (Accessed 4 July 2019).
Film Front (2017), 'Intervju mit Huset-regissor Reineer Kiil', *Film Front*, 11 April 2017.
Hedenstad, Marte (2017), 'Juleblod', Review, *NRK Radio*, 3 November 2017.
Hjort, Mette (2000), 'Thematizing the Nation', in Mette Hjort and Scott MacKenzie (eds), *Cinema and Nation*, London: BFI, pp. 103–18.
Hjort, Mette and Duncan Petrie (eds.) (2007), *The Cinema of Small Nations*, Edinburgh: Edinburgh University Press.
Jenkins, Henry (2013), *Textual Poachers: Television Fans and Participatory Culture*, New York: Routledge.

Kauraoja, Valtteri (2018), 'It Came from the Desert', Review, *Film-o-holic*, 7 September 2018.

Kääpä, Pietari (2018),'Skype interview with Reineert Kiil', 20 July 2018.

Kääpä, Pietari (2019), 'From Nordic Gloom to Nordic Cool', in Silvia Dibeltulo and Ciara Barrett (eds), *Rethinking Genre in Contemporary Cinema*, Basingstoke: Palgrave, pp. 151–74.

Koren, Alexander (2017), 'Juleblod', Review, *Kinomagasinet*, 8 November.

LoserCity Boss [pseudonym] (2015), 'Bunny the Killer Thing', Review, *Loser City*, available at: http://loser-city.com/features/bunny-the-killer-thing-review (Accessed 3 July 2019).

Luhtala, Jouko (2015), 'Jänis joka tappaa, Film-O-Holic', available at: http://www.film-o-holic.com/haastattelut/joonas-makkonen-bunny-the-killer-thing/ (Accessed 3 July 2019).

Mathijs, Ernest and Jamie Sexton (2011), *Cult Cinema: An Introduction*, Malden, MA: Wiley-Blackwell.

Nilsson, Kim (2019), 'The House that Jack Built', Review, *Kommunalarbetaren*, 15 March.

Nordisk Film Kino (2017), 'Juleblod', promotional, available at: https://www.nfkino.no/oslo/kommer/article1303166.ece (Accessed 3 July 2019).

Nordisk Film og TV Fund (2015), 'Kung Fury YouTube Fury', available at: http://www.nordiskfilmogtvfond.com/news/stories/kung-fury-youtube-fury (Accessed 3 July 2019).

Norum, Fredrik (2008), 'Hora from Finnmark', *NRK*, 5 December.

Rissanen, Juho (2015), 'Bunny the Killer Thing kertoo himokkaasta tappajajäniksestä', *Iltalehti*, 7 November 2015.

Vestmo, Birger (2017), 'Juleblod, Skreggelid kjedelig skrekkfilm', Review, *NRK*, 2 November.

The Craggus (2018), 'It Came from the Desert', Review, available at: https://thecraggus.com/2018/06/24/it-came-from-the-desert-2018-review/?fbclid=IwAR00wtQBuxs7wNG5pFpAZbw:PPvhjEJOIqaSGDVq7CWtGViWMgcOnhxr5xo (Accessed 3 July 2019).

Therkelsen, Michael (2018), 'It Came from the Desert DVD Release', The Horror Society, available at: https://www.horrorsociety.com/2018/05/31/marko-makilaaksos-it-came-from-the-desert-crawls-to-us-dvd-on-june-5th/?fbclid=IwAR2LnLdau8us3-l9K9s3SY5BdG0f_0kGqTYVQJ2ParEKTVfmJZpq_DHhJGg (Accessed 3 July 2019).

YLE (2015), 'Kauhukomedian ralli-englanti huvittaa ulkomailla', 11 November.

10

Conclusion

Beyond the art house

The Nordic exploitation scene has emerged as a thriving space for innovating with new technologies and transgressive forms of content. Underlying all these developments are fundamental transformations in film policy and the willingness of directors and producers to explore emerging modes of audience management and engagement. Certainly, there is a lot of exciting activity taking place in these film cultures that in some ways mimic transnational trends, and in many others, display the uniqueness of the context. Yet, some areas seem to stay the same. One is the prevalence of a cultural political focus on the art film. Despite the new markets that many of these films use to generate sufficient return on their (often private) investment, most of the infrastructure continues to be dominated by the traditional film funding system governed by the Film Institutes and other cultural organizations subsidizing domestic film production. While these institutes no longer shun genre productions, a substantial part of their operations continues to be devoted to artistic or experimental cinema, instigating circumstances where even relatively non-sensationalist genre cinema can take on exploitative connotations due to their explicitly commercial approach. Consequently, Nordsploitation is a transnational phenomenon that operates at the point of contact between global cultural patterns and more localized cultural political strategies.

To reinforce the sense that Nordic exploitation cinema is distinct from the global 'norms' of transnational exploitation film culture, we finish this book with a brief exploration of the career of Lars von Trier, the enfant terrible of Nordic film. Producing films in English with international casts and settings since the early 1980s, von Trier is no stranger to exploitation cinema. Showcasing a dynamic ability to merge genre conventions, such as the musical and social realist drama in *Dancer in the Dark* (2000), or science fiction and psychological study with *Melancholia* (2011), von Trier's films have often been both recognized and critiqued for their sexual content and depictions of women as martyrs. Some have even read his works as containing sufficient ambiguity to allow them to be interpreted as embodying liberal or feminist values (see Badley 2010: 70–100; Bainbridge 2007: 44–57 for more on these debates). Whatever the case, von Trier's career in the 2010s has taken this flippant attitude to societal norms and political correctness in new directions with, for example, the sexually explicit content of *Nymphomaniac* (2013) or his remarks in Cannes regarding Hitler and the Nazis in 2011 that made him a persona non grata at the festival for over five years. It would not be difficult to argue that in both the content of his films and in his management of his public persona, von Trier is an exploitation auteur extraordinaire.

Yet, the significant controversy that surrounded the release of his latest film *The House that Jack Built* (2018) highlights the complexity of such claims in both a transnational and a Nordic context. Aiming to study the banality of evil, von Trier set out to make a provocative serial killer film that dissects the genre and reinterprets interconnections between violence and art. Focusing on the eponymous Jack (played by Matt Dillon), the film chronicles a two decade murder spree. With images constructed in meticulous detail that sometimes resemble Renaissance paintings, the film continues von Trier's distanced obsession with the bizarre attractions of the American way of life. Gender dynamics are another theme frequently linked to von Trier's films and here they come under often darkly comical observation as the film's overarching voiceover conversation between Verge (Bruno Ganz) and Jack satirizes his obsession with killing women, who are frequently depicted as lacking logic or as just 'simply' stupid. Whether this is self-irony at play, as von Trier has been frequently critiqued for the abuse women receive in and on the set of his films, or a continuation of a thematic obsession characterizing his work, is up to debate. Unsurprisingly, critics were quick to read the narrative as a self-reflective piece on the role and responsibility of the artist, especially in the wake of von Trier's ban from the Cannes festival, almost as a confessional of an artist whose career has been dedicated to exploitation of various kinds. Yet, some were adamant that the film revels in the violence and misogyny it ostensibly critiques, operating almost as a celebratory winking pastiche of von Trier's previous transgressions (Tallerico 2018).

While controversy must have surely been the goal here, the film's violence emerged as the focal point of controversy as reports of over a hundred walkouts at the premiere screening fuelled the debate surrounding *The House that Jack*

Built. Its US release was similarly controversial as the Motion Picture Association of America (MPAA) refused to certify the film with an R rating required for mainstream cinema releases. While *Nymphomaniac* had been released as NC-17, effectively a label indicating an unrated cut of an often-significant artistic film or of a deliberate challenge to censorship norms as with Paul Verhoeven's *Showgirls* (1995), the distributor for *The House that Jack Built* insisted an R-rated cut be produced. Whether this was due to the star power of the cast or the general popularity of the serial killer genre is again another discussion, but the MPAA cut up to four minutes of material from the film for its general release. The uncut version was released for a single day of screenings, thus allowing the film to generate the type (and hype) of notoriety desired. It is worth noting that these sorts of publicity outcries were increasingly rare in the 2010s as cable and streaming television shows like *Hannibal* (2013–15) and *The Walking Dead* (2010–) had, by now, far surpassed the cinematic medium in the amounts of gore and violence they would display on a weekly basis. The idea of a new 'genre' film supposedly too hard and excessive to be released cinematically paired with festival prestige as well as stars like Dillon and Uma Thurman must have been a tantalizing way to generate attention to a 150 minute pseudo-philosophical rumination on the notion of evil.

Yet, the violence of the film does require more attention as it is often deliberately shocking in its attempt to push the boundaries of screen representation. The two most notorious scenes were heavily cut for the US release. The first of these features a massacre of a family where Jack practices his shooting skills on two young children, all observed in considerable detail via the lens of his rifle. He positions the now dead children in mannered poses with the camera lingering on their dismembered bodies and exposed craniums while he forces their mother to feed them cake. In another scene to follow, Jack conducts a taxidermic operation on one of the children, drawing his face into a cruel grimace resembling a particularly disturbing mannequin. The second controversial scene features the 'only love' Jack had, a woman he refuses to call by her name Jacqueline, identifying her only as Simple. In one of the most excessive scenes in Nordic cinema, he ties her to a radiator after canvassing her breasts with surgical incision marks and then proceeds to cut one of her breasts off. The lingering anticipation of such extreme violence can only be seen to foreground the lurid and the demeaning as entertainment values.

This sort of extreme sexualized violence had been strictly banned in the Nordic countries in the previous decades. A comparison with the notorious video nasty

Maniac (1980) is appropriate here, as not only does the film resemble *The House that Jack Built* in its storyline but it also features some of the most extreme violence of a very violent decade in film production. *Maniac* was particularly well known for its detailed gore effects by make-up mastermind Tom Savini, with one scene in particular featuring the artist Savini himself as the victim of a particularly graphic head explosion scene. The film claimed to be a serious dissection of a diseased mind, stuck in the kind of deplorable dystopia captured by Martin Scorsese's *Taxi Driver* (1976). But instead of a semi-relatable Robert de Niro, Joe Spinell's overweight maternally obsessed mutilation of female victims was much less critically respected. *Maniac* was either heavily cut or totally banned during the 1980s in all of the Nordic countries with most censors viewing it as one of the most extreme examples of the plague of video violence. To build on these artistic–political reverberations, *The House that Jack Built* came under fire for a scene where the young Jack cuts off a duckling's leg and then watches it desperately waddle in circles in the water. Animal violence was another frequent point of discontent with video nasties, with Ruggerio Deodato's *Cannibal Holocaust* (1980) especially deservedly encountering problems with censors and audiences. Jack's acts of violence are achieved with digital effects with PETA providing its usual 'no animals were harmed' disclaimer at the end, and the film even received a commendation from the organization for how it links this sort of violence with later psychopathic behaviour. Yet, these associations must not have been unfamiliar for von Trier who relishes the extremes to which he can go, while he (seemingly) uses these extremes as a critical point he aims to make about the role of art in society.

If the hard excesses of *Maniac* pale in comparison with the supposed artistry of von Trier's film, it is intriguing to ask if standards for extreme or unethical behaviour had changed in the four intervening decades, or if the fluidity of censorship norms is to do with the critical prestige of a Zito versus a von Trier. Here, *The House that Jack Built* is ultimately revealing in the ways it operates in the wider political economy of the Nordic film industry. The production was comparatively expensive as it came in at over 8 million EUR, which is the type of budget we have only seen with prestigious heritage productions or effects-heavy films like *Iron Sky*. In a strange way, *The House that Jack Built* meets both standards as its shock value is heavily based on gore effects and genre thrills. At the same time, it is very much a prestige production with high-quality production values and the intellectual reputation of its director. The fact that the production received support exceeding millions of euros from organizations like the Danish and Swedish Film Institutes, respectively, as well as the Nordic Film and Television Fund, tells us a lot about the role of the revered male auteur in Nordic film culture. Even with a film that is 'playfully misogynist' (and hence nothing but fully misogynist) receiving such enthusiastic support from cultural institutions details two things: (1) the much critiqued 'old boys club' mentality is not dissipating despite the role of new executives and more balanced socio-cultural paradigms such as the Swedish Film Institute's Gender Equality Report, and (2) exploitative excess continues to be agreeable if it is done in a framework acceptable by the parameters set by the Film Institutes.

The House that Jack Built is, on one hand, the ultimate example of the merger of genre and art film within a Nordic context. Here, exploitation functions as art and art functions as exploitation in similar ways to what we saw already when Nordic film companies used exploitative tactics during the early 1900s to lure audiences to the cinema. On the other hand, von Trier's gorifications end up remarkably detached as they are now 'art' in a way that is comparable to the provocations of Kiil's *The Whore*, ones which were arguably undermined by its deference to the pastiche exploitation of *Grindhouse*, the difference being, of course, the humongous difference in the budgets. Or as a Swedish reviewer writes:

> Danish director Lars von Trier wants to upset the public with his violent film where Matt Dillon's ice-cold title character thinks that murder of women and children can be beautiful art. The bitter aftertaste could have been mitigated if the film had some kind of message. Despite the strong scenes, the most disturbing thing is the lengthy conversations about a male-sprained ego that is mostly pure waffle. Zzzz. (Nilsson 2019)

These critical perspectives testify to an urgent need to separate artistic claims from critical realities. While 'auteurs' may now have more freedom for self-expression, especially related to violence, critical aversion to their works persists, but now accentuated by an even more pervasive sense of seeing any transgressions as deliberate provocations, designed as publicity stunts. At the same time, the myth of the male auteur continues to provide these productions with a free get-out-of-jail card that not only allows him to gain substantial production funding but also wide theatrical releases. While these may be largely accentuated by the star casts of von Trier's productions, we must also remember that these tactics were used by exploitation auteurs like Olsson in the 1980s without the large-scale cultural and infrastructural support that is provided here. In some ways, the ability of von Trier to attain such strong infrastructural support testifies to the idea that significant aspects of the Nordic film infrastructure remain as archaic as in the past. While self-aware exploitation films have certainly pushed boundaries and transgressed cinematic norms, sometimes with innovative results using the latest advances in digital technology, sometimes with a return to more normative exploitation content, albeit on very diverse cultural registers, the film cultures of these countries continue to be bound by established norms and conventions.

If anything, the films covered in this book highlight the necessity of uncovering alternative histories that challenge the dominance of Film Institutions and the prevalence of revered film artists. From von Trier to Alfredsson, these directors use the same standards and even many of the excessive touches as marginalized exploitation directors, yet they are able to sustain careers and reputations that continue to facilitate their careers. While there are fundamental differences, of course, in, for example, von Trier and Olsson's technical abilities and cultural reference points, the role of exploitation practices and influences is much more concerned with the gate-keeping practices restricting entry into 'respectable' film culture. If the same standards of violence and other illicit content are treated differently based on the status of a director or the aspirations of a film, then these practices highlight the invariable subjectivity of the concept of exploitation. Such developments go in other directions too as we have seen with the introduction of innovative digital media content using nostalgia and retro-attractions to make Nordic film competitive. Here, one of the strengths of focusing on exploitation is its ability to uncover incentives and cycles, which facilitate change, but such modes are invariably reliant on wider patterns in film policy and cultural taste, and, as such, prone to both expedient expiry dates and subsequent regressions to conservative norms.

References

Badley, Linda (2010), *Lars von Trier*, Chicago: University of Illinois Press.
Bainbridge, Caroline (2007), *The Cinema of Lars von Trier*, New York: Wallflower Press.
Nilsson, Kim (2019), 'The House that Jack Built', Review, *Kommunalarbetaren*, 15 March.
Tallerico, Brian (2018), 'The House that Jack Built', Review, rogerebert.com, available at: https://www.rogerebert.com/reviews/the-house-that-jack-built-2018 (Accessed 3 July 2019).

Index

7 km/tim (1972)   61
50/50   26, 182–3, 191
491 (1964)   45–6, 65, 78

Aalto University   237
AB Svenska Biografteatern   32, 39, 50
Abrams, JJ   206
Acuarela Video   147
Afgrunden (*The Abyss*, 1910)   1, 34–6, 39
Agentti 000 ja kuoleman kurvit (*Agent 000 and the Curves of Death*, 1983)   125, 127
Ahlsson, Helen   232
Aja, Alexander   196
Alanen, Asko   119
Albatros Video   147
Alfie (2004)   4
Allied Artists   8
Alpha Pictures   147, 149
Amazon   256
American Academy of Paediatrics   75
American International Pictures (AIP)   8, 48, 66
American Ninja (1985)   152
Anderson, Eva   165
Andersson, Ingmar   163
Andrews, David   190
The Angry Red Planet (1959)   48, 55
Animal Protector (1988)   147, 162–3, 166
Anita–ur en tonårsflickas dagbok (*Anita–Swedish Nymphet*, 1974)   63
Ann och Eve–de erotiska (*Ann and Eve*, 1970)   56
Annabelle: The Creation (2017)   233
Apple   149
Arena Home Video   147
Aromaa, Mikko   236
Aros Video   147
Artsploitation.com   254
Aspéria, Charles   149–50, 152, 156, 166
Asylum Pictures   213, 234, 237
A-Team, The (1983–7)   164

Atlas Video   147
Attentatet (1980)   143–4
Audiovisual Production Fund, The   183
Aufklärungsfilme   23, 40–1, 50
Avatar Film Corporation Limited   147

Babettes gæstebud (*Babette's Feast*, 1987)   114
Baise-moi (*Rape Me* 2000)   245
Balsam, Martin   67
Bang, Poul   48
Baretta (1975–8)   76
Barker, Martin   17
Barry, Christopher   9
Bass, Saul   188
BAV Film AB   62
Bay, Michael   249
Bazin, André   77
Bellis, Andreas   68–9
Ben-Yehuda, Nachman   92
Berg-Ejvind och hans hustru (*The Outlaw and His Wife*, 1918)   1
Bergendahl, Pelle   81
Bergman, Ingmar   61, 78, 161, 192
Berlinale   110, 226
Bernard, Mark   15
Besökarna (*The Visitors*, 1988)   19, 107–8, 116, 120–3, 136
Bieniuszewicz, Hanna   151–3, 155
Big Game (2015)   237
Bille, Torben   60–1
Björkstrand, Gustav   96
Bjørne jagt i Rusland (1908)   33
Bjornsson, Helgi   188
Black Lion Pictures   252, 254
Blake, Linnie   9, 25
Bland vildar och vilda djur (*Among Savages and Wild Animals*, 1920)   42
Blandt Syd-Amerikas Urskovsindianere (1922)   42
Blödaren (*Bleeder*, 1983)   22
Blom, August   34, 36

Blood Tracks (1985)   2–8, 11, 13, 147, 165
Bloodsport (1988)   97–8
Bloodsuckers (2020)   237
Bloody Disgusting   190
Bonanza (1959–73)   47, 143
Bonnie and Clyde (1967)   49, 90, 153
Boogeyman, The (1980)   83, 94
Boorman, John   109
Borowczyk, Walerian   253
Boutchyard, Steve   221
Brain Waves (1982)   149
Braindead (1992)   175, 185, 210
Braveheart (1995)   210
Breaking Point (1975)   68–71
Bridges, Elizabeth   205
British Board of Film Classification   95
Broberg, Curt   151
Bron/Broen (*The Bridge*, 2011–18)   164
Brooks, Mel   204
Brown, Christopher   92
Bruzelius, Madeleine   158
Bullitt (1968)   90
Bunny the Killer Thing (2015)   48, 235, 251–7
Burns, Marilyn   93
Burton, Richard   162
Buttgereit, Jörg   9

Cabaret (1972)   90, 205
Cameron, James   249
Camp Slaughter (2004)   183–4
Cannes Film Festival   66, 71, 236
Cannibal Holocaust (1980)   92, 264
Cannon Films   152
Cannon Video   147
Canon (1971–6)   76
Captain America (2011)   206
Carlsson, Anders   32
Carlström, Björn   130
Carpenter, John   119
Carradine, David   147, 162–3, 166
Castle, William   215
CB Films Video   147
Centennial (1978–9)   47
Charlie's Angels (1976–81)   167
Church, David   136, 196–7
CIC Victor Video   147
Claydon, Bernard   145

Clover, Carol J   93
Cobra (1986)   233
Cod Western   114
Cohen, Stanley   79
Collins, Guy   149–50, 156
Comic Con   215, 219
Commando (1985)   165
Conan the Barbarian (1982)   113
Cook, Pam   197
Craven, Wes   234
Croneman, Johan   177
Cushing, Peter   205

Dalquist, Ulf   89
Dancer in the Dark (2000)   261
Danstrup, Henrik   185
Dante, Joe   235, 237
Dark Fantasy   99
De fortabte sjæles ø (*The Island of Lost Souls*, 2007)   183
De Palma, Brian   122
Death Proof (2007)   245
Death Trap (1977)   83
Den hvide slavehandel (*The White Slave Trade*, 1910)   35–9
Den hvide slavehandels sidste offer (1910)   36
Den hvide slavinde (1907)   36
Deodato, Ruggero   92, 264
Der Untergang (*Downfall*, 2004)   204
Det händer i natt (1956)   45
Devonsville Terror, The (1983)   149
DG Film   135
Diedrich, Ellen   37
Die Hard (1988)   97
Die Hard 2 (1990)   134
Die Zombiejäger (2005)   22
Dillon, Matt   262–3
Dimension Films   245
The Dirty Dozen (1967)   49, 153
Disney Co   147
Distribuidora Internacional de Filmes   147
Divine   61
Død snø (*Dead Snow*, 2009)   27, 178–80, 184–5, 193, 196, 206–11, 217–18, 224, 237, 240
Død snø 2 (*Dead Snow 2: Red vs Dead*, 2014)   210–12, 217–18, 225, 242

Dogme   95, 174
Dracula (1931)   76
Dread Central   254
Dudesons, The   219
Dünyayı Kurtaran Adam ('Turkish Star Wars', 1982)   184
Dværgen (*The Sinful Dwarf*, 1973)   59–62, 71–2
Dworkin, Andrea   92

Eagle Island (1986)   147, 159–61
Earle, Timothy   161
Eastwood, Clint   113
Easy Action   3–4, 6
Easy Rider (1969)   49
Ekeroth, Daniel   166
Elit-Film AB   71
Elthammar, Olle   92
Elwin, Göran   82–3, 85, 87
Emigrant (1910)   39
Emigranten (1910)   39
Engberg, Marguerite   35
Englene (1973)   59, 71
Enter the Ninja (1981)   152
Eriga Video distribusjon   147
Eriksson, Erik   81
Erlandsson, 'Big Bengt'   142–3
Esselte CIC Video   147
Etter Rubicon (*After Rubicon*, 1987)   129
Eurimages   187
Europa Film   67, 71, 143–4
European Fantastic Film Festivals Federation   99
Evil Dead, The (1981)   96, 179, 209
Evil Dead, The: Dead by Dawn (1987)   210, 252
Evil Ed (1997)   174–7, 179–80, 197
Excalibur (1981)   113
Exorcist, The (1973)   59
Exponerad (*Exposed*, 1971)   63, 71
Exterminator, The (1980)   97
Exterminator 2, The (1984)   117

Facebook   100, 201–2, 214, 217–20, 222, 225
Falsche Scham (1926)   41–2
Fantastisk Film Festival in Lund   99
Fassbender, Michael   232

Fatal Secret (1988)   147, 162–6
Fellini, Federico   58
Ferdinand, der Pussyschreck (1977)   71
Festen (*The Celebration*, 1998)   185
F-Fund   142–4, 251
Film Camp   247–8
Film Front   249
Filmkrönikan (1956–2008)   85
Filmrage   243
Finnish Board of Film Classification, The (VET)   96, 98
Finnish Film Archive, The   119
Finnish Film Foundation, The   107, 116–17, 238, 253
Finnish Public Television (YLE)   96, 220, 255
Finnkino   253
Firefox (1982)   160
First Blood (1982)   108, 131
Flænset: Jalosiens Instinkter ('Shredded', 2000)   184–6, 188–90, 196–7
Flammen og Citronen (*The Flame and the Citroen*, 2008)   204
Force of One, A (1979)   167
Forgotten Wells (1990)   165
Foster, Jodie   94
Fotorama   36
Från cell till människa (1936)   41
Frankenstein (1931)   76
Freddy Krueger   2
Fremer, Björn   122
Friday the 13th (1980)   13, 19, 97, 116, 185
Fritt Vilt (*Cold Prey*, 2006)   183
Frozen Star, The (1977)   55
Fuller, Eduardo (a.k.a. Vidal Raski)   59–60
Funny People (1976)   143
Furhammar, Leif   174
Furyô anego den: Inoshika Ochô (*Sex and Fury*, 1973)   63

Ganz, Bruno   262
Gåten Ragnarok (*Ragnarok: The Viking Apocalypse*, 2013)   48
Gender Equality Report   265
Gestapo's Last Orgy (1977)   204
Ghostbusters (1984)   147
Ghostbusters II (1989)   147

Giulietta degli spiriti (*Juliet of the Spirits*, 1965) 58
Glädjekällan (*Spring of Joy*, 1993) 164
Globus, Yoram 152
Godard, Jean-Luc 246
Gojira (*Godzilla*, 1954) 48
Golan, Menahem 152
Gone with the Wind (1939) 93
Goode, Erich 92
Gore Hound 99
Gore, Tipper 75
Gorillas in the Mist (1988) 167
Göta Elf-katastrofen (1908) 31–4
Gräns (*Border*, 2018) 236
Green, Tom 219
Gremlins (1984) 175
Grindhouse (2007) 15–16, 227, 235, 243–6, 257, 265
Grünbaum, Heini 185–6
Gudlaugsson, Hrafn 107
Guðmundsson, Ágúst 109
Guldbagge 111, 164
Guld til præriens skrappe drenge (*Gold for the Tough Guys of the Prairie*, 1971) 55
Gulliver's Travels (1939) 149

Hallner, Ann 38
Halloween (1978) 19, 93, 116
Hallum, Jørgen 59, 250
Hannibal (2013–15) 263
Happy Days (1974–84) 89
Harding, Jeff 4
Harlin, Renny 25, 96, 101, 108, 123, 131–2, 134, 173
Haste, Hans 48
Heavy Metal Horror 3–4
Hedling, Olof 181
Heja Sverige! (1979) 143–5
Hellas Cosmos Video 147
Heller-Nicholas, Alexandra 63
Hellquist, Anders Roland 164–6
Hem Films Scandinavia 135
High Chaparral 142–3
Highlander II (1991) 149
Highlight Video 147
Hill, Walter 117
Hired Gun, The (1989) 147, 161–2, 168

HIT of Poland 147, 163
Hitchcock, Alfred 162
Hitler, Adolf 201, 219, 222–3, 231–2, 262
Hjertén, Hanserik 66
Hjort, Mette 11–12, 106, 217
Hobo with a Shotgun (2011) 243
Hoffman, Dustin 160
Höjdestrand, Erik 82, 87
Hollows, Joanne 197
Holocaust 204, 215
Home Alone (1990) 249
Hon dansade en sommar (*One Summer of Happiness*, 1951) 56, 161
Hooper, Toby 117
Hopf, Heinz 68
Hora (*The Whore*, 2009) 27, 64, 197, 234, 242, 244–7, 249–50, 252, 255, 257, 265
House (1985) 120
House on Sorority Row, The (1983) 3
House that Jack Built, The (2018) 27, 236, 262–5
Howco International Pictures 8
Hrafninn flýgur (*When the Raven Flies*, 1984) 19, 21, 109–15, 119–22
Hübenbecher, Daniel 130
Hur Marie träffade Fredrik, åsnan Rebus, kängurun Ploj och (1969) 61–2
Huset (*The House*, 2016) 247
Hviti Vikingurinn (*The White Viking*, 1991) 114–15
Hydra (2003) 22

Ibiza Connection, The (1984) 167
Icelandic Film Centre 111, 187
Icelandic Film Company, The 188
Icelandic Film Foundation 108
I död mans spår (1975) 55, 141–2
I lagens namn (1986) 174
Il Consigliore (Counselor at Crime, 1973) 67
Il portiere di notte (*The Night Porter*, 1974) 205, 210
Ilsa: She-Wolf of the SS (1975) 204–5
In Borneo–The Land of the Head-Hunters (1920) 42
Independence Day (1996) 213
Indiana Jones and the Last Crusade (1989) 204

Indiegogo   217, 253
Inglorious Bastards, The (1978)   149
Inglourious Basterds (2009)   204
Inside the Whore (2012)   246–7
Invasion of the Animal People (1962)   47
Investment Group, The   149
Invisible Man, The (1933)   76
I racconti di Canterbury (*Canterbury Tales*, 1972)   58
Iron Sky (2012)   27, 196, 201–3, 206, 211–18, 220, 223–5, 232–3, 235, 237, 239–40, 251, 264
Iron Sky: The Coming Race (2019)   201–2, 218–26, 253–4
Í skugga hrafnsins (*In the Shadow of the Raven*, 1988)   114
I Spit on Your Grave (1978)   64, 72, 89, 243, 247, 249
It Came from the Desert (2017)   27, 48, 234–5, 237–41, 253, 257
Ivarson, Inge   57–8
Iversen, Gunnar   114, 130, 191

Jäätävä polte (*Arctic Heat* aka *Born American*, 1985)   19–21, 96, 108, 131–8, 142, 160, 174, 189, 219
Jackson, Michael   3
Jackson, Peter   255
Jacob, Matthew   150
Jacobsson, Anders   177
Jadesoturi (*Jade Warrior*, 2006)   183
Jägarna (*The Hunters*, 1996)   174
Jag är nyfiken–blå (*I Am Curious–Blue*, 1968)   68
Jag är nyfiken–gul (*I am Curious–Yellow*, 1967)   11, 68
Jameson, Fredric   206
Jancovich, Mark   14
Janus Films   78
Jengi (*The Gang*, 1963)   46, 49
Jenkins, Henry   241
Jern, Christer   160
Joblo.com   254
Jobs, Steve   219
Joner, Kristoffer   182, 210
Jönsson, Reidar   177
Juleblod (*Christmas Blood*, 2017)   247–51

Jüngerkes, Sven   209
Jungfrukällan (*The Virgin Spring*, 1960)   49, 64

Kääpä, Jari   221
Kääpä, Pietari   203
Kaikenlaisia karkulaisia (*Fugitives of All Kinds*, 1981)   125
Kampen om tungtvannet (*The Heavy Water War*, 2015)   211
Kartoffelwesterns   55
Kasprzyk, Jurek   151
Kaufman, Lloyd   237
Kaukomaa, Tero   183, 221, 225, 236–7
Keller, Clara   61
Kemp, Julian   183, 187, 190
Kendrick, James   16–17
Kent-Watson, David   168
Ketonen, Kari   221
Kickstarter   231
Kier, Udo   201
Kiil, Reinert   22, 234, 242–51, 254, 265
Kiil Produksjon   244
Kill Bill Vol.1 (2003)   64, 94, 162
Kill Bill Vol.2 (2004)   64, 94, 162
Kinnunen, Kalle   223
KISS Meets the Phantom of the Park (1978)   4
Kleven, Marianne   251
Kojak (1973–8)   76
Kolberger, Krzysztof   151–3
Körkarlen (*The Phantom Chariot*, 1920)   1
Kosmorama   36
Kosugi, Shô   152
Krea Nord   236
Kristen demokratisk samling   78
Kubrick, Stanley   249
Kumonosu-jō (*Throne of Blood*, 1957)   113
Kung Fu (1972–5)   162
Kung Fury (2015)   27, 206, 231–5, 237–8, 240–1, 251, 257
Kurosawa, Akira   113
Kuutamosonaatti (*Moonlight Sonata*, 1988)   19, 107–8, 116–23, 136, 178, 182, 188, 224

Lagercrantz, Olof   49
Land og synir (*Land and sons*, 1980)   108
Larsen, Thomas Bo   185–6
Larsen, Viggo   32
Larsson, Mariah   70
Laser Unicorns   232
Last House on the Left, The (1972)   49, 64, 247
Låt den rätte komma in (*Let the Right One In*, 2010)   173, 192–4, 236
Le lac des morts vivants (*Zombie Lake*, 1981)   205, 208
Lee, C. P.   141, 168
Leone, Sergio   65
Lights Out (2013)   233
Lights Out (2016)   233
Likainen puolitusina (*The Dirty Half Dozen*, 1982)   125
Lindberg, Christina   62–4, 66, 68
Lindfors, Rolf   39
Lingonberry Western   25, 55, 141–3
Lommel, Ulli   149
Loshitzky, Yosefa   204
Løvejagten (*The Lion Hunt*, 1907)   32–4
Luca il contrabbandiere (*The Smuggler*, 1980)   167
Lumirae, Pertti   119
Lundén, Camilla   164–6
Lundgren, Roger   150
Lundsten, Ralph   68
Lundström, Göran   177

McDonagh, Marshall   65
Machete (2010)   243
MacKinnon, Catharine   92
McLuhan, Marshall   79
McRobbie, Angela   197
Mad Bunch, The (1989)   56, 147, 162–5
Made in Sweden (1971)   63
Madsen, Gerda   61
Magic Video   147
Magilow, Daniel T.   205
Magnum, P.I. (1980–8)   47
Magnusson, Charles   31–2, 34, 39
Mäkilaakso, Marko   237–8, 242
Mäkinen, Visa   25, 108, 123–7, 129, 174, 227, 241, 248
Makkonen, Joonas   254

Malo Video   147
Man From Button Willow, The (1965)   149
Maniac (1980)   98, 264
Män som hatar kvinnor (*The Girl with the Dragon Tattoo*, 2009)   164
Marathon Man, The (1976)   160
Mars Attacks! (1996)   213
Maskula, Tapani   119, 125
Mathijs, Ernest   5–6, 8, 12, 14, 145
Matrix, The (1999)   213
Mattsson, Arne   56, 161
Max Manus (*Max Manus: Man of War*, 2008)   204, 211
Med prins Wilhelm på afrikanska jaktstigar (*On Safari in Africa with Prince Wilhelm*, 1922)   42, 44
Media Home Entertainment   147
Medusa Video   147
Melancholia (2011)   262
Melchior, Ib   48
Men in Black (1997)   213
Mendik, Xavier   5–6, 14
Miami Vice (1984–90)   47
Miho Film   209
Mikkelsen, Lars   186
Miramax   245
Missing in Action (1984)   108, 132–3
Missing in Action Distribution   147
Mitäs me sankarit (1981)   124
Mitt liv som hund (*My Life as a Dog*, 1985)   177
Moderata samlingspartiet   94
Mohr, Gerald   55
Moller, Birgit Thor   187
Mondo Cane (1962)   44
Monty Python and the Holy Grail (1975) 143–4
Moore, Ray Rudy   239
Moore, Roger   162
Morricone, Ennio   113
Mosquito Coast, The (1985)   167
Motion Picture Association of America   263
Mottram, Ron   35
Ms .45 (1981)   64
Mummy, The (1932)   76
Munthe, Bo F   151–2
Munthe, Martin   183
Mutilator, The (1984)   3

National PTA   75
National Viewers' and Listeners' Association   92
National Vigilance Association, The (NVA)   38
Nattevagten (*Night Watch*, 1994)   174
Nea Kinisi Video   147
Neale, Steve   129
Nekromantik (1987)   9, 25
New German Cinema   9
New Line Cinema   2, 147, 156
New Line Home Video   147
Nico: Above the Law (1988)   165
Nielsen, Asta   39
Nightmare on Elm Street, A (1984)   2–4, 107, 116, 118
Nightmare on Elm Street 4, A (1988)   134
Nilsson, Anders   150–1, 161
Ninja III: The Domination (1984)   152
Ninja Mission, The (1984)   2, 7, 19, 25, 132, 146–59, 161–2, 168, 189–90, 224
Nixon, Richard   164
Noll tolerans (1999)   151
Nordic Fantasy Info   182
Nordic Film and Television Fund, The   187, 236, 265
Nordic Genre Boost, The   236
Nordic Genre Invasion   236
Nordisk Film Kompagni   23, 33, 35–6, 50, 106
No Retreat, No Surrender (1986)   165
Norris, Chuck   20, 131–2, 164
Norris, Mike   20, 132, 134–5
Norsk Film A/S   78
Norwegian Film Development   251
Norwegian Film Fund, The   183
Norwegian Film Institute, The   183, 211, 251
Norwegian Film Ltd.   183
Novio   147
NS Video   147
Nymphomaniac (2013)   262–3

Octagon, The (1980)   167
Öholm, Siewert   76
Øie, Pål   182
Oi juku-mikä Lauantai (1980)   124
Oliver, Laurence   160
Olsen, Lauritz   37

Olsen, Ole   32–3, 36
Olsson, Mats Helge   3–4, 6–7, 20, 22, 25, 56, 65, 101, 123, 130, 132, 138, 141–68, 173, 227, 241
Orions Belte (*Orion's Belt*, 1985)   129–30, 160, 174, 183
O'Rourke, Tom   160
Osbourne, Ozzy   4
Oscarsson, Per   143–4
Öström , Eva   165
Outpost, The (2008)   206
Overlord (2018)   206

Paersch, Henrik   134
Palin, Sarah   213, 219, 221–3
Pan-Canadian Film Distributors   147
Parents Music Resource Center (PMRC)   75
Pasanen, Spede   106, 123
Pasolini, Pier Paolo   49, 58
Pawnbroker, The (1964)   204
Peckinpah, Sam   154, 185
Pedersen, Sverre   251
Per un Pugno Di Dollari (*A Fistful of Dollars*, 1964)   65–6, 109
Persona (1966)   61
Petrie, Duncan   11–12, 106
Piela, Mikko   119
Pink, Sidney W   48
Pink Flamingos (1972)   61
Pi pi pil. . . pilleri (*The P . . . p . . . pill*, 1982)   125
Planet Terror (2007)   245
Poliziottesco   126–7
Poltergeist (1982)   116, 120
Poole, Nicolas   59
Positions danoises (1977)   71
Præriens skrappe drenge (*Tough Guys of the Prairie*, 1970)   55
Predator (1987)   117
Prince   4
Prince, Stephen   17
Producers, The (1967)   204
Producers Corporation, The   149
Profore Movie Productions   149
Prom Night (1981)   13
Prom Night II: Hello Mary Lou (1987)   97
Prostitutka (1926)   41
Psycho (1960)   119

Purple Rain (1984)   4
Pusher (1996)   185
Putin, Vladimir   221–2

Raimi, Sam   179
Rambo III (1988)   97
Rambo: First Blood Part II (1985)   108, 133
Råstam, Hans   151
Raven Banner   254
RCA/Columbia-Hoyts Home Video   147
R.C.V.2001 Video   147
Reagan, Roland   76, 164
Re-Animator (1985)   210
Red Dawn (1984)   160
Refn, Nicolas Winding   185
Regissören som försvann: historien om The Ninja Mission (2013)   156
Rekordmagazinet (1985–91)   158
Reptilicus (1961)   46–8
Resurrection of Michael Myers Part 2, The (1989)   22
Revenge of the Ninja (1983)   127, 152
Reykjavik Whale Watching Massacre (2009)   183–5
Rhinoceros   99
Robocop (1987)   97, 107
Roche, David   8
Rockford Files, The (1974–80)   76
Rocktober Blood (1984)   4
Rocky Horror Picture Show, The (1975)   166
Rocky IV (1985)   160
Rodriquez, Robert   227, 235, 250
Rollin, Jean   205
Roma città aperta (*Rome Open City*, 1945)   204
Romero, George   205
Roth, Eli   16, 196
Rötmånad (*What Are You Doing after the Orgy*, 1970)   63
Rotten Tomatoes   244
Rovdyr (*Manhunt*, 2008)   183
Russell, Kurt   245
Russian Terminator (a.k.a. *Russian Ninja*, 1990)   147, 161
Rymdinvasion i Lappland (1959)   46–8

Saari, Henry   252
Saekyong Video   147
Sällskapsresan (1980)   4
Samsung   149
Sandberg, David T.   231–3, 242
Sanders, Anita   58
Saturday Night Fever (1977)   124
Savini, Tom   98, 264
Scanbox Entertainment   176, 185–6
Schaefer, Eric   8, 15, 23, 35–6, 40–1, 43, 46, 50, 177
Schildt, Jurgen   67
Schiller, Hans   110, 122
Schindler's List (1993)   204
Schwarzenegger, Arnold   164, 232, 238
Sconce, Jeffery   10
Scorched Heat (1987)   122
Scorsese, Martin   264
Scream (1996)   196
Sedergren, Jari   97
Selin, Markus   131–2, 134, 219
Sensuela (1973)   18, 46, 127
Sexton, Jamie   8, 12, 75, 145, 238
Sharknado (2013–18)   239
Shazam! (2019)   233
Shiel, Mark   14, 177
Shipka, Danny   10
Shock Waves (1977)   205, 207–8
Showgirls (1995)   263
Silence of the Lambs (1991)   94
Silverhawk (1987)   161
Sima, Jonas   67
Simmons, Gene   4
Siponen, Frank   125
Sjöman, Vilgot   78
Skorpionens tegn (*Agent 69 in the Sign of Scorpio*, 1977)   61
Skräcken har 1000 ögon (*Fear Has 1000 Eyes*, 1973)   57–9, 70
Skyttens tegn (*Agent 69 Jensen in the Sign of Sagittarius*, 1978)   61
Smart Egg Picture   4, 149
Smith, Anthony   111
Smith, Iain Robert   184
Smutiga fingrar (1973)   56–8
Snarveien (*Detour*, 2009)   183
Snuff (1976)   92
Sobolev, Vladimir   133

Soinio, Olli   118–19
Solar Films   134, 187–8
Soldier Blue (1970)   113
Sommaren med Monika (*Summer with Monika* a.k.a. *Monika, the Story of a Bad Girl*, 1953)   161
Son of the Sheik, The (1926)   93
Sony   147, 149
Sorvali, Kari   118
South Park (1997)   226
Southern Comfort (1981)   117
Space Truckers (1996)   149
Spaghetti Western   55, 65, 111, 113
Spielberg, Steven   204
Spies Like Us (1985)   4
Spinell, Joe   264
Spökligan (1987)   147
Spring för livet (*Run for Your Life*, 1997)   164
Stagman, Bo   4
Stallone, Sylvester   132, 233, 238
Star Wreck: In the Pirkinning (2005)   202, 211
Statens filmproduksjonsutvalg   130
Stevenson, Jack   59, 69
Stole, Mink   61
Strandvaskaren (*The Drowning Ghost*, 2004)   183
Straw Dogs (1971)   93, 185–6
Studio S (1975–84)   80–8, 91, 93–4, 97
Succéfilm AB   147
Svensk Filmindustri (SF)   23, 32, 44, 50, 106
Svensson, Peter A.   150
Sverige åt svenskarna (1980)   4, 25, 143–6, 149, 151, 157
Swedish Action Film Force   149
Swedish Board of Film Censorship   5, 47, 65–7, 69, 78, 95, 153, 159
Swedish Film Institute, The   61–2, 99, 120, 138, 142, 144–5, 147, 177, 183–4, 231–2
Swedish Film Review Council   56, 65
Swedish Public Television (SVT)   81, 113

Tapper, Susie   155
Tarantino, Quentin   15–16, 64, 227, 235, 242, 249–50
Taste of Hell, A (1973)   83, 93, 149
Taxi Driver (1976)   264
Tennispalatsi   201, 226
Terminator, The (1984)   107, 167
Terror (1978)   83
Texas Chainsaw Massacre, The (1974)   81, 83–5, 87, 91, 93–5, 117, 119, 184, 187, 190
Thatcher, Margaret   76, 219, 222
Thelma & Louise (1991)   164
Them (1954)   237
Thorsen, Isak   59, 71–2, 186
Thriller–en grym film (*They Call Her One Eye*, 1974)   20, 24, 61–8, 71–2, 105–7, 247, 250
Thurman, Uma   64, 94, 263
Thyrén, Peo   4
Toiviainen, Sakari   127
Tolkien, J. R. R.   113
To mistenkeliga personer (1950)   45
Tool Box Murders (1978)   83
Top Tape   147
Törnudd, Klaus   133
Torssonen, Samuli   202
Touch of Evil (1955)   47
Tourist Trap (1979)   83
Trädgårdsmästaren (*The Broken Springrose*, 1912)   32
Transworld Video   147
Trick or Treat (1986)   4
Trier, Lars von   27, 174, 192, 246, 261–2, 264–6
Trolljegeren (*Trollhunter*, 2010)   48
Troma Pictures   244
Trump, Donald   222
Tulio, Teuvo   18, 46
Tuuli, Markku   125
Tvingad att leva (1980)   143–4
Twemlow, Cliff   168
Twitter   214
Tybjerg, Casper   36
Tystnaden (*The Silence*, 1963)   78

Unenge, Dag   150–1, 158
Universal   11, 147
Ur kärlekens språk (*Language of Love*, 1969)   57, 71
US Supreme Court   147–8

Útlaginn (*Outlaw: the Saga of Gisli*, 1981) 109
Uuno Turhapuro (*Numbskull Emptybrook*, 1973) 106

Valkoinen peura (*The White Reindeer*, 1954) 20–1
van Damme, Jean-Claude 98, 164
Vapaaduunari Ville-Kalle (*Freelancer Ville-Kalle*, 1984) 126
Vargtimmen (*Hour of the Wolf*, 1968) 20, 61
VDM Video 147
Ved verdens ende (*At World's End*, 2009) 183
Verhoeven, Paul 263
Vibenius, Bo Arne 61–72, 185, 250
Vic Video Brazil 147, 163
Video for Pleasure Distribution 147
video nasties 24, 75, 79, 81, 89, 100, 168, 264
Video Rondo 147
Video Tape Center (VTC) 149
Videolaki valmisteilla (1985) 96
Viking Film 112
Villmark (*Dark Woods*, 2003) 182–3, 250
Villmark: Asylum (*Dark Woods 2*, 2015) 183
Virgin Home Video 147
Vista Home Video 2–3, 147
Vogel, Virgil W 47
Vorhees, Jason 113
VPS Video 147
Vuorensola, Timo 202, 221, 225, 227

W.A.S.P. 76
Walking Dead, The (2010) 263
Wan, James 196

War Dog (1986) 130, 174
Warner Music 4
Welles, Orson 47
Whitehouse, Mary 92
Wickman, Torgny 57
Wienand, Christine 209
Wikström, Jan-Erik 80, 87–8
Wild Bunch, The (1969) 49
Wild Geese, The (1978) 162
Wild West Story (1964) 55
Willis, Andy 141, 168
Winkler, Henry 89
Wirkola, Tommy 206, 208
Wiseau, Tommy 239
Wolfenstein (1981–2017) 206, 210
Women against Pornography (WAP) 92
Women against Violence against Women (WAVAW) 92
Woo, John 98
Wredlund, Bertil 39
Wyatt, Justin 155

Yojimbo (1954) 109
Yön saalistajat (*Hunters of the Night*, 1984) 126–9, 136–7, 190
Young German Cinema 9
Young Indiana Jones (1992–6) 150
YouTube 22, 189, 206, 217, 231–3, 254

Zarchi, Meir 242, 249
Zardos (1973) 109
Zentropa 185
Zito, Joe 264
Zodiac Film Group 149
Zombie, Rob 16, 196
Zombie Flesh Eaters (*Zombie 2*, 1980) 89, 149
Zuckerberg, Mark 219

www.ingramcontent.com/pod-product-compliance
Lightning Source LLC
Chambersburg PA
CBHW072128290426
44111CB00012B/1827